The Unruly Ocean

This book introduces non-specialist readers to the history of how human societies have sought to control, use and exploit our oceans, seas and shorelines over time in different geographical and cultural contexts.

The Unruly Ocean examines the development of the modern international legal regime – the law of the sea, maritime law, marine environmental and pollution law, fisheries regulation, and underwater cultural heritage law – and considers how effective these laws have been in addressing the many challenges facing marine and coastal environments ranging from piracy and war to oil spills and the extraction of marine resources. It concludes by discussing the socio-ecological crises facing the world's oceans, seas and shorelines, and explores current ideas for reimagining a legal regime that restores the health of our oceanic realm and offers a more holistic, transboundary, rights-based approach to ocean governance.

This book will be of value to law and non-law undergraduate and postgraduate students, as well as research scholars and other educated audiences interested in a legal history of the world's oceans, seas and shorelines.

Dr Erika Techera is Professor of Law at The University of Western Australia. She researches on international and comparative environmental law, particularly oceans. She is a co-editor of the *Routledge Handbook of International Environmental Law*, 2021, and co-author of *International Law of Sharks*, 2017.

Dr Joy McCann is an environmental historian affiliated with the University of Tasmania. Her research focuses on oceans, ice, islands and coastlines of the southern hemisphere, and her publications include *Wild Sea: A History of the Southern Ocean*, 2019.

Oceans, Seas and Shorelines: Cultural, Environmental, and Natural Histories
Edited by Viv Westbrook and Mark Nicholls

Images of oceans discoloured with pollutants, seas cluttered with plastics, and shorelines strewn with distressed marine life, entangled in nets, covered in oil, diseased and dying, as a direct result of human activity are becoming all too familiar. As we become more aware of the destruction of nature, through repeated media alerts, the risk is that we become desensitised. There is an urgent need to find different ways of approaching these environments in crisis so that new strategies for change can emerge.

This series approaches oceans, seas and shorelines in terms of the contributions that these natural environments have made to the evolution of human civilisations. It also draws attention to the impact that human civilisations throughout the world have had on these environments.

Several volumes currently in process are the work of teams of academics, often researching together for the first time, from institutions across the world to forge studies of the natural and cultural environmental history of oceans, seas and shorelines from within their disciplinary areas.

Teams of international scholars are invited to contribute proposals for co-authored books or edited volumes of essays that address the series' aims from within their own disciplines. The books must be written in an accessible style that scholars, students and general readers can engage with.

The Unruly Ocean
Law and Justice in the World's Oceans, Seas and Shorelines
Erika Techera and Joy McCann

The Unruly Ocean

Law and Justice in the World's Oceans, Seas and Shorelines

Erika Techera and Joy McCann

Routledge
Taylor & Francis Group
NEW YORK AND LONDON

First published 2025
by Routledge
605 Third Avenue, New York, NY 10158

and by Routledge
4 Park Square, Milton Park, Abingdon, Oxon OX14 4RN

Routledge is an imprint of the Taylor & Francis Group, an informa business

British Library Cataloguing-in-Publication Data
A catalogue record for this book is available from the British Library

Library of Congress Cataloging-in-Publication Data
Names: Techera, Erika J., author. | McCann, Joy, 1954– author.
Title: The unruly ocean : law and justice in the world's oceans, seas, and shorelines / Erika Techera and Joy McCann.
Description: Abingdon, Oxon [UK] ; New York, NY : Routledge, 2025. | Series: Oceans, seas and shorelines: cultural, environmental, and natural histories | Includes bibliographical references and index.
Identifiers: LCCN 2024027308 (print) | LCCN 2024027309 (ebook) | ISBN 9780367437183 (hardback) | ISBN 9781032881638 (paperback) | ISBN 9781003005261 (ebook)
Subjects: LCSH: Maritime law. | Law of the sea. | Shorelines—Law and legislation. | Marine pollution—Law and legislation.
Classification: LCC K1150 .T43 2025 (print) | LCC K1150 (ebook) | DDC 341.4/5—dc23/eng/20240826
LC record available at https://lccn.loc.gov/2024027308
LC ebook record available at https://lccn.loc.gov/2024027309

ISBN: 978-0-367-43718-3 (hbk)
ISBN: 978-1-032-88163-8 (pbk)
ISBN: 978-1-003-00526-1 (ebk)

DOI: 10.4324/9781003005261

Typeset in Times New Roman
by Apex CoVantage, LLC

Contents

List of figures vii
List of international agreements, treaties and conventions viii
List of acronyms xii
Foreword xv

Introduction 1

PART I
The ocean as territory 15

1 Undercurrents: legal approaches and maritime concepts 17

2 Fluid boundaries: shoreline borders and maritime zones 40

3 Disorder at Sea: piracy, war and illegality 60

PART II
The ocean as resource 81

4 An 'inexhaustible' bounty: fishing and farming of marine life 83

5 Seafaring: ships and shipping in law 115

6 Disrupting the flow: construction and extraction in the deep ocean 144

PART III
The ocean as ecosystem 167

7 The fragile ocean: protecting species and ecosystems 169

8 Ocean space: protecting marine areas and regions 193

PART IV
The ocean as repository 219

9 Waste: discharge, dumping and debris at sea 221

10 Shipwrecks to sea shanties: safeguarding maritime cultural heritage 245

11 Ways of knowing: ocean knowledge, research and data 268

PART V
The ocean as future 299

12 Anthropocene ocean: turning the tide of ocean governance 301

Index *322*

Figures

0.1 Map accompanying second edition (1937) of IHO publication *Limits of Oceans and Seas*, Special Publication 23. 5
1.1 Title page from Hugo Grotius, *Mare Liberum sive de jure quod Batavis competit ad Indicana commercia dissertatio.* 24
2.1 Totora reed fishing boats on the beach at Huanchaco, Peru. 45
2.2 Image depicting the limits and spaces under the sovereignty or jurisdiction of the coastal State. 49
3.1 Map showing German submarine operations around the British Isles during World War I. 69
4.1 Types of fishing and equipment used around the world. 86
5.1 Engraving of Phoenician sailors and merchants who were renowned for their achievements in maritime navigation and trade in the Mediterranean region. 117
5.2 The Plimsoll mark on the side of a ship. 120
6.1 Landing the shore end of the Atlantic cable. Painting by Robert Charles Dugley, 1866 [oil on canvas]. 145
7.1 A woman wearing a 'Chanticleer' hat made of bird feathers, circa 1912. 172
8.1 Whaling on Danes Island, Arctic Ocean. Painting by Abraham Speeck, artist (Dutch), 1634. 195
8.2 An emperor penguin (*Aptenodytes forsteri*) chick with parent and an unrelated chick on sea ice in the Ross Sea, Antarctica. 198
9.1 Oil spill response volunteers cleaning up on a beach in Spain, 2004. 225
10.1 Engraving of French pirate, François l'Olonnais (nicknamed 'Flail of the Spaniards'), who was active in the Caribbean during the 1660s. 249
10.2 Submerged remains of Emperor Claudius' nymphaeum, in the underwater Archaeological Park of Baiae. 254
11.1 Engraving of scientists and crew on board *HMS Challenger* in 1872–76 examining marine specimens dragged up by the *Challenger*'s nets. 273
11.2 Members of the Unmanned Underwater Vehicle detachment, Commander, Task Group (CTG) 56.1, guide a UUV as it is lowered into the water. 284

International agreements, treaties and conventions

Agreed Measures for the Conservation of Antarctic Fauna and Flora (1964)
Agreement for the Implementation of the Provisions of the UN Convention on the Law of the Sea of 10 December 1982 Relating to the Conservation and Management of Straddling Fish Stocks and Highly Migratory Fish Stocks (1995) (Fish Stocks Agreement)
Agreement on Cooperation on Marine Oil Pollution, Preparedness and Response in the Arctic (2013)
Agreement on Port State Measures to Prevent, Deter and Eliminate Illegal, Unreported and Unregulated Fishing (2009) (Port State Measures Agreement)
Agreement on the Conservation of Cetaceans of The Black Sea, Mediterranean Sea and Contiguous Atlantic Area (1996) (ACCOBAMS)
Agreement Under the United Nations Convention on the Law of the Sea on the Conservation and Sustainable Use of Marine Biological Diversity of Areas beyond National Jurisdiction (2023) (High Seas Treaty or BBNJ Agreement)
Antarctic Treaty (1959) (ATS)
Athens Charter for the Restoration of Historic Monuments (1931)
C029 – Forced Labour Convention (1930)
Convention for Cooperation in the Protection and Development of the Marine and Coastal Environment of the West and Central African Region (1981) (Abidjan Convention)
Convention for the Protection and Development of the Marine Environment in the Wider Caribbean Region (1983) (Cartagena Convention)
Convention for the Conservation of Antarctic Seals (1972)
Convention for the Prevention of Marine Pollution by Dumping from Ships and Aircraft (1972) (Oslo Convention)
Convention for the Prohibition of Fishing with Long Driftnets in the South Pacific (1989) (Wellington Convention)
Convention on the Prohibition of the Development, Production, Stockpiling and Use of Chemical Weapons and on Their Destruction (1993) (Chemical Weapons Convention)

Convention for the Protection, Management and Development of the Marine and Coastal Environment of the Eastern African Region (1985) (Nairobi Convention).
Convention on the Protection of the Black Sea against Pollution (1992) (Bucharest Convention)
Convention for the Protection of the Marine Environment and the Coastal Region of the Mediterranean (1995) (Barcelona Convention)
Convention on the Protection of the Marine Environment of the Baltic Sea Area (1992) (Helsinki Convention/HELCOM)
Convention for the Protection of the Marine Environment of the Caspian Sea (2003) (Tehran Convention)
Convention for the Protection of the Marine Environment of the North-East Atlantic (1992) (OSPAR Convention)
Convention for the Protection of the Natural Resources and Environment of the South Pacific Region (1986) (Noumea Convention)
Convention for the Protection of the World Cultural and Natural Heritage (1972) (World Heritage Convention)
Convention for the Safeguarding of Intangible Cultural Heritage (2003) (CSICH)
Convention for the Suppression of the Traffic in Persons and of the Exploitation of the Prostitution of Others (1949)
Convention on Biological Diversity (1992) (CBD)
Convention on Fishing and Conservation of the Living Resources of the High Seas (1958) (Geneva Convention on Fishing and Conservation of the Living Resources of the High Seas)
Convention on International Trade in Endangered Species of Wild Fauna and Flora (1973) (CITES)
Convention on Limitation of Liability for Maritime Claims (1976)
Convention on the Conservation of Antarctic Marine Living Resources (1980) (CCAMLR)
Convention on the Conservation of Migratory Species of Wild Animals (1979) (CMS)
Convention on the Continental Shelf (1958) (Geneva Convention on the Continental Shelf)
Convention on the High Seas (1958) (Geneva Convention on the High Seas)
Convention on the International Regulations for Preventing Collisions at Sea (1972)
Convention on the Prevention of Marine Pollution by Dumping of Wastes and Other Matter (1972) (London Convention)
Convention on the Protection and Promotion of the Diversity of Cultural Expressions
Convention on the Protection of the Underwater Cultural Heritage
Convention on the Territorial Sea and the Contiguous Zone (1958) (Geneva Convention on the Territorial Sea and Contiguous Zone)

Convention on Wetlands of International Importance Especially as Waterfowl Habitat (1971) (Ramsar Convention).
Declaration concerning the Laws of Naval War (1909) (London Declaration)
Declaration of the United Nations Conference on the Human Environment (1972) (Stockholm Declaration)
Declaration of Principles Governing the Seabed and the Ocean Floor, and the Subsoil Thereof, beyond the Limits of National Jurisdiction (1970)
Geneva Convention for the Amelioration of the Condition of the Wounded, Sick, and Shipwrecked Members of Armed Forces at Sea (1949)
Hague Convention on the Protection of Cultural Property in the Event of Armed Conflicts (1954)
ILO Convention No 169 Concerning Indigenous and Tribal Peoples in Independent Countries, (1989) (ILO 169)
International Agreement for the Suppression of 'White Slave Traffic' (1904)
International Charter for the Conservation and Restoration of Monuments and Sites (1964) (The Venice Charter)
International Convention for the Control and Management of Ships' Ballast Water and Sediments (2004) (Ballast Water Convention)
International Convention for the Prevention of Pollution by Ships (1973 as modified by the Protocol of 1978) (MARPOL 73/78)
International Convention for the Prevention of Pollution of the Sea by Oil (1954) (OILPOL)
International Convention for the Protection of Birds that Are Useful for Agriculture (1902)
International Convention for the Regulation of Whaling (1946) (ICRW)
International Convention for the Safety of Life at Sea (1974) (SOLAS)
International Convention for the Suppression of Traffic in Women and Children (1921)
International Convention on Civil Liability for Oil Pollution Damage (1969)
International Convention on Maritime Search and Rescue (1979) (SAR Convention)
International Convention on Oil Pollution Preparedness, Response and Cooperation (1990)
International Convention on Salvage (1989)
International Convention on the Control of Harmful Anti-fouling Systems on Ships (2001).
International Convention Relating to Intervention on the High Seas in Cases of Oil Pollution Casualties (1969)
Nagoya Protocol on Access to Genetic Resources and the Fair and Equitable Sharing of Benefits Arising from Their Utilization (2010) (Nagoya Protocol)
Paris Agreement (2015)
Polar Bear Agreement (1973)

Protocol against the Smuggling of Migrants by Land, Sea and Air (2000)
Protocol on Environmental Protection to the Antarctic Treaty (1991)
Protocol to Prevent, Suppress and Punish Trafficking in Persons, Especially Women and Children (2000)
Protocol to the Convention on the Prevention of Marine Pollution by Dumping of Wastes and Other Matter, 1972, (1996) (London Protocol)
Protocol to Prevent, Suppress and Punish Trafficking in Persons, Especially Women and Children (2000)
Rio Declaration on Environment and Development (1992) (Rio Declaration)
Treaty for the Protection of Artistic and Scientific Institutions and Historical Monuments
United Nations Convention against Transnational Organized Crime (2000)
United Nations Convention on the Law of the Sea, (adopted 10 December 1982, entered into force 16 November 1994) 1833 UNTS 3.
UNESCO Convention on the Means of Prohibiting and Preventing the Illicit Import, Export and Transfer of Ownership of Cultural Property (1970) (UNESCO Convention)
UNIDROIT Convention on Stolen or Illegally Exported Cultural Objects (1995) (UNIDROIT Convention)
United Nations Framework Convention on Climate Change (1992) (UNFCCC)
Universal Declaration of Human Rights (1948) (UDR)
World Charter for Nature (1983)

Acronyms

AIS	Automatic Identification System
ASEAN	Association of Southeast Asian Nations
ASMA	Antarctic Specially Managed Area
ASPA	Antarctic Specially Protected Area
ATS	Antarctic Treaty System
AUV	autonomous underwater vehicles
BBNJ	Biodiversity Beyond National Jurisdiction
BCE	before the common era
BIOMASS	Biological Investigations of Marine Antarctic Systems and Stocks
CBD	Convention on Biological Diversity
CCAMLR	Convention on the Conservation of Antarctic Marine Living Resources
CE	Common era
CFCs	chlorofluorocarbons
CITES	Convention on International Trade in Endangered Species of Wild Fauna and Flora
CMM	conservation management measure
CMS	Convention on the Conservation of Migratory Species of Wild Animals
COLREGs	*Convention on the International Regulations for Preventing Collisions at Sea*
CPUCH	Convention on the Protection of the Underwater Cultural Heritage
CRAMRA	Convention on the Regulation of Antarctic Mineral Resources Activities
CSIRO	Commonwealth Scientific and Industrial Research Organisation (Australia)
DNA	Deoxyribonucleic acid
DOALOS	UN Division of Ocean Affairs and the Law of the Sea Office
EBM	ecosystem-based management

EBSA	ecologically and biologically significant area
EEZ	Exclusive Economic Zone
FAD	fish aggregating device
EU	European Union
FAO	Food and Agriculture Organization
GATT	General Agreement on Tariffs and Trade
GESAMP	Joint Group of Experts on the Scientific Aspects of Marine Environmental Protection
GFCM	General Fishery Commission for the Mediterranean
GHG	greenhouse gas
GOOS	Global Ocean Observing System
ICCAT	International Convention for the Conservation of Atlantic Tunas
ICES	International Council for the Exploration of the Sea
ICOMOS	International Council on Monuments and Sites
ICRW	International Convention for the Regulation of Whaling
ICZM	integrated coastal zone management
IFREMER	French Research Institute for Exploitation of the Sea
IHO	International Hydrographic Organization
ILO	International Labour Organization
IMO	International Maritime Organization
INTERPOL	International Criminal Police Organization
IOTC	Indian Ocean Tuna Commission
ISA	International Seabed Authority
IUCN	International Union for Conservation of Nature
IUU	illegal, unreported and unregulated fishing
LMMA	Locally Managed Marine Area
MARPOL	International Convention for the Prevention of Pollution from Ships
MDGs	Millennium Development Goals
MEPSEAS	Marine Environment Protection of the South-East Asian Seas
MGR	marine genetic resources
MPA	marine protected area
MSP	marine spatial planning
NATO	North Atlantic Treaty Organization
NDC	Nationally Determined Contribution (climate change)
NEAFC	North East Atlantic Fisheries Commission
NGO	non-governmental organisation
OILPOL	International Convention for the Prevention of Pollution of the Sea by Oil
OSPAR	Convention for the Protection of the Marine Environment of the North-East Atlantic
OUV	Outstanding Universal Value (World Heritage Convention)

PA	Paris Agreement
PAM	protected area management
PSSA	Particularly Sensitive Seas Area
RFBs	Regional Fisheries Bodies
RFMO	regional fishery management organisation
RSCAPs	Regional Seas Conventions and Action Plans
RSP	Regional Seas Programme (UNEP)
ROV	remotely operated vehicle
SAR	*International Convention on Maritime Search and Rescue*
SCAR	Scientific Committee (Antarctic Treaty System)
SDG	Sustainable Development Goals
SEAFO	Southeast Atlantic Fishery Organization
SIOFA	South Indian Ocean Fisheries Agreement
SOLAS	Safety of Life at Sea Convention
SPAW	Specially Protected Areas and Wildlife
SPRFMO	South Pacific Regional Fishery Management Organisation
SWIOFC	South Western Indian Ocean Fisheries Commission
TBGRI	Tropical Botanic Gardens and Research Institute (India)
TWAIL	Third World Approaches to International Law
UK	United Kingdom
UN	United Nations
UNCED	United Nations Conference on Environment and Development (1992)
UNCLOS	United Nations Convention on the Law of the Sea
UNEA	United Nations Environment Assembly
UNEP	United Nations Environment Programme
UNESCO	United Nations Educational, Scientific and Cultural Organization
UNESCO-IOC	Intergovernmental Oceanographic Commission of the UN Educational, Scientific and Cultural Organization
UNFCCC	United Nations Framework Convention on Climate Change
UNGA	United Nations General Assembly
UNIDROIT	International Institute for the Unification of Private Law
USD	US Dollars
US	United States
VMS	Vessel Monitoring Systems
WHC	World Heritage Convention
WHOI	Woods Hole Oceanographic Institute (US)
WoRMS	World Register of Marine Species
WTO	World Trade Organization
WWF	World Wide Fund for Nature (formerly World Wildlife Fund)

Foreword

Law is one of the most important tools that humans possess to regulate how we use, exploit and share our ocean environments and prevent, mitigate or control the associated environmental impacts. In developing an international legal regime for oceans, seas and shorelines, lawmakers have created a complex system of ocean governance enshrined in the law of the sea, maritime law, marine environmental law and marine pollution law, fisheries regulation, and underwater cultural heritage law. In the process, however, this system has severed water from land, living organisms from marine habitats, seabeds from shorelines and surfaces from water columns. In addition, law is frequently backward looking and reactionary, responding to problems slowly and long after they have become apparent. The exponential growth in human uses and destructive impacts on the marine environment highlight the fact that our current laws, whilst impressively broad and nuanced, are failing to address the major challenges facing the marine environment today.

This book introduces non-specialist readers to the laws that govern the world's oceans, seas and shorelines. It explores how these laws have been created over time, in different geographical and cultural contexts, to regulate human behaviour and maintain productivity. It discusses how the doctrine of freedom of the seas and the binary separation of land and sea have fundamentally shaped modern laws governing oceans, seas and shorelines, and considers emerging legal approaches that offer compelling solutions to the multiple climate, pollution, overharvesting and biodiversity crises affecting the health and integrity of our planetary ocean.

Introduction

How inappropriate to call this planet Earth when it is quite clearly Ocean.
Arthur C Clarke

Overview

Law is essentially a system of rules developed over time by a society to define the rights, obligations and responsibilities of its members. These rules or laws are never static. Indeed, all laws evolve as the social or political conditions of the dominant culture change. The legal regime that exists for the world's oceans, seas and shorelines today has been shaped over many centuries and is rooted in western cultural beliefs and practices. However, the multiple challenges that now face the ocean environment call into question the efficacy of this legal regime. Conflicts over ocean spaces and resources continue, and many societies are unwilling or unable to prevent the damage being wrought on the marine environment. Moreover, scientific studies indicate that planetary boundaries may soon be breached, and this will result in irreversible damage as climate and ecological tipping points are reached.[1]

In the following chapters we trace the development of legal regimes relating to oceans, seas and shorelines in different places and eras, including aspects of both western law and traditional or customary law. The history of these laws offers a valuable lens through which to examine changing (and sometimes unchanging) beliefs, values and ideas about the marine environment across time periods, cultures and contexts. These developments remain relevant and influential today, although their fitness for purpose is increasingly under challenge. Whilst specific domestic laws are not explored in any depth, we aim to identify common origins and threads across different politico-legal contexts. Ultimately, we draw on multi-disciplinary perspectives and scholarship in law and history to address the problem of why this complex, multi-layered regime of treaties and laws is failing to avert the multiple crises affecting the world's oceans, seas and shorelines, and we propose ways that a new ocean imaginary might enable lawmakers to rise to the challenge.

DOI: 10.4324/9781003005261-1

Oceans, seas and shorelines in human history

Oceans dominate planet Earth. From space, Earth appears bluish in colour, with almost three-quarters of its surface covered by water. Indeed, in terms of volume, the world ocean contains 97% of all our water, with the remaining 3% frozen in glaciers and ice sheets or present as fresh water. Some seas are directly connected with oceans and others enclosed or semi-enclosed, yet all contain saltwater. For most of human history, people have lived along shorelines – the place where land and saltwater meet at the edges of the world's oceans and seas. Anatomically modern *Homo sapiens* are thought to have evolved in Africa some 300,000 years ago during a period of major climate change,[2] while the discovery of ancient clambakes suggests that early humans were exploiting marine resources for food such as mussels and abalone from around 165,000 years ago.[3] The importance of marine resources in human evolution remains the subject of ongoing debate, but one recent study analysing genetic, paleoclimate and archaeological data found that one branch of modern humans probably migrated to the southwestern coast of Africa around 130,000 to 110,000 years ago and thrived on shellfish and other marine species.[4] Some researchers have even speculated that the systematic harvesting of such nutrient-rich marine species may have played a crucial role in the development of large-brained, technologically advanced early humans in southern Africa.[5] As coastal settlements emerged, these early humans would also have foraged along the shoreline for building materials and treasures, just as later generations have done. One of the oldest surviving pieces of early human jewellery, for example, was made of marine snail shells and is estimated to be around 142,000 years old.[6]

Ocean cosmologies

Traditional and Indigenous coastal and island communities relied not only on the sea's living and non-living resources. They also developed intimate knowledge of its features, established relationships with other groups living on nearby coasts and islands, and fostered distinctive marine cultural identities. Inevitably, societies with a long history of knowledge and use of the marine environment also developed a sense of ownership or custodianship of its waters and resources.[7] One group of early humans, for example, left Africa around 72,000 years ago and travelled east, inhabiting the mega continent known as Sahul – a prehistoric continent including Australia and New Guinea – around 50,000 years ago.[8] Around 5,000 years ago, master seafarers voyaged east beyond the Solomon Islands and settled the widely scattered island groups of the Pacific Ocean. According to the Tongan/Fijian anthropologist and writer Epeli Hau'ofa, Pacific islanders regarded the ocean as 'seas of islands', where land was a small element within the physical and spiritual territory that extended into the depths of the sea and up to the heavens.

Many other cultures around the world associate the beginning of the world with the ocean.[9] In Egyptian cosmology (known from Pyramid Texts composed from circa 3,000 BCE), Atum – the god of gods – emerged from a primordial sea called Nun (or Nu), which surrounded the land of the ancient Egyptians, and those with divine status were required to cross the Nun in order to reach the afterlife in the land of the dead. The Vedic religion of ancient Indian cosmology (circa 1750 BCE) explained the origin of the 'western ocean' through stories of Varuna, the Hindu god of oceans. Ancient Greeks (circa 700 BCE) believed that the ocean encircled the land in a boundless river known as Oceanus, the son of Uranus (Heaven) and Gaea (Earth), who gave birth to a pantheon of powerful deities. Beyond Oceanus lay the land of Cimmerii, the entrance to the underworld.[10] The *Kojiki*, the oldest Japanese sacred text compiled by imperial scholars in 712 CE, tells of the creation of primordial heavens and seas when the land floated like oil on the ocean waters.[11]

Greek and Roman mythology held that the rocks known as the Pillars of Hercules, which stand at the end of the Strait of Gibraltar between the Mediterranean Sea and the Atlantic Ocean, marked the limits of the known world. The Indigenous peoples of the Caribbean, the *Taíno*, believe that the birth of the ocean, and living resources within it, was one of the first acts of creation.[12] Genesis, the first book of the *Bible* (circa 1,400 BCE), narrates the primaeval history of the world involving a great Flood, and early Christian cosmology represented the sea as a terrifying place, a 'great abyss' containing debris from the biblical Flood haunted by the souls of the damned. The image of a ship came to symbolise the Christian church navigating the stormy seas as it ferried its cargo of human souls to the safety of the shore. This imagery of the ocean as chaotic and hostile remained influential in Christian cosmology until well into the 19th century.

From the 15th century, human perceptions of the ocean underwent a dramatic transformation as European mariners learnt to harness the knowledge of ocean winds and currents, enabling them to venture beyond local coastlines and seas to forge longer sailing routes between the Earth's continents. By the 18th century, literary accounts of long-distance voyaging and the increasing popularity of seaside recreation were shaping western perceptions of the ocean. The Industrial Revolution was also making its mark as steamships replaced wind-powered vessels, bringing the vast oceanic realm within reach, and rendering its limitless bounty ripe for exploitation. As Rozwadowski has written: 'As a space outside society, the ocean was available to be defined by its utility for humans'.[13]

The influence of these early ocean imaginaries can still be seen in modern societies including in their laws and legal institutions. In a few contemporary cultures – predominantly those comprising Indigenous and traditional peoples – more holistic legal approaches are evident. Yet in the vast majority of ocean governance arrangements, land and sea, marine environment and species, water and ice, oceans and atmosphere are each subject to separate laws and institutions rather than as interconnected elements within Earth's planetary system.

Mapping the world ocean

As will be seen throughout this book, early human societies developed customary rules around access to shorelines and marine areas and traditional practices associated with harvesting, navigation, use and sharing of resources. When the envoys of European empires voyaged into the Pacific region in the 16th century, they used European law as a powerful tool of colonisation, often displacing local laws and governance with a legal system developed in a very different geopolitical and cultural context.[14] New understandings of the nature and global reach of the world ocean emerged with these long-distance voyages of exploration and empire-building, drawing on geographical and maritime knowledge gleaned from ancient texts. In the Indian Ocean, mariners had already succeeded in mastering the seasonal monsoons to propel their vessels between the coasts of Asia and Africa, not only enabling the exchange of exotic items between the continents but also facilitating the spread of global religions such as Buddhism, Hinduism and Islam.

By then the Indian Ocean region was at the centre of a vast maritime trade network extending from the Persian Gulf and Red Sea to the South China Sea. Meanwhile, European ships were also venturing into the Atlantic Ocean and around the coast of Africa, lured by the promise of lucrative new markets in the Indian Ocean. The voyages of Vasco da Gama around the Cape of Good Hope in 1498, for example, encouraged the development of Portuguese trading networks in the Indian Ocean and – ultimately – in the Atlantic and Pacific Oceans. The four transatlantic voyages of the Genoese navigator Christopher Columbus, between 1492 and 1504, marked a new era of maritime exchange – including the movement of ideas, people and diseases – between the 'Old World' of Africa, Asia and Europe and the 'New World' of the Americas.[15] The so-called European 'Age of Discovery' in the mid-15th to mid-16th centuries inspired the production of some of the earliest maps of the world. The earliest known printed map from 1470 showed the three continents of Asia, Europe and Africa surrounded by an ocean river. Renaissance cartographers also drew from classical legends and reports from mariners to illustrate their maps with marine creatures and mythical sea monsters filling blank spaces, to convey the mysteries and dangers of ocean travel.[16] By the 17th century, world maps were depicting the beginnings of a world ocean with interconnected basins and seas.[17] These maps facilitated claims of sovereignty over land and inshore coastal waters, while the voyages introduced European maritime rules and trading customs to new places and peoples.

The introduction of steamships and the expansion of long-distance voyaging in the 19th century increased the need for greater navigational safety and standardised ocean maps. In 1921, major maritime nations agreed to form the International Hydrographic Organization (IHO), and States set about defining the boundaries between the major ocean basins and seas drawing on existing nautical charts and the accumulated wisdom of ocean navigation. The process of imposing precise boundaries on the world ocean, however, would prove contentious. When the IHO published its first edition of *Limits of Oceans and Seas* in 1928, it described the boundaries of the Pacific, Atlantic, Indian, Arctic and Southern oceans; the seas within them including the Baltic, Mediterranean, and South China and Eastern Archipelagic seas; and many smaller separate seas, gulfs and straits. Nevertheless, differences emerged between the States over the third edition published in 1953. The IHO attempted to resolve the disputed boundaries in a draft fourth edition in 2002 but failed to achieve a consensus and the 1953 edition showing the boundaries of 148 oceans and seas remains as the official reference for international nautical maps and charts.[18]

Controlling the maritime environment

With increasing geographical knowledge and maritime trade also came increased competition amongst European powers pursuing new sources of wealth and control over maritime trade routes. This competition soon became a contest for

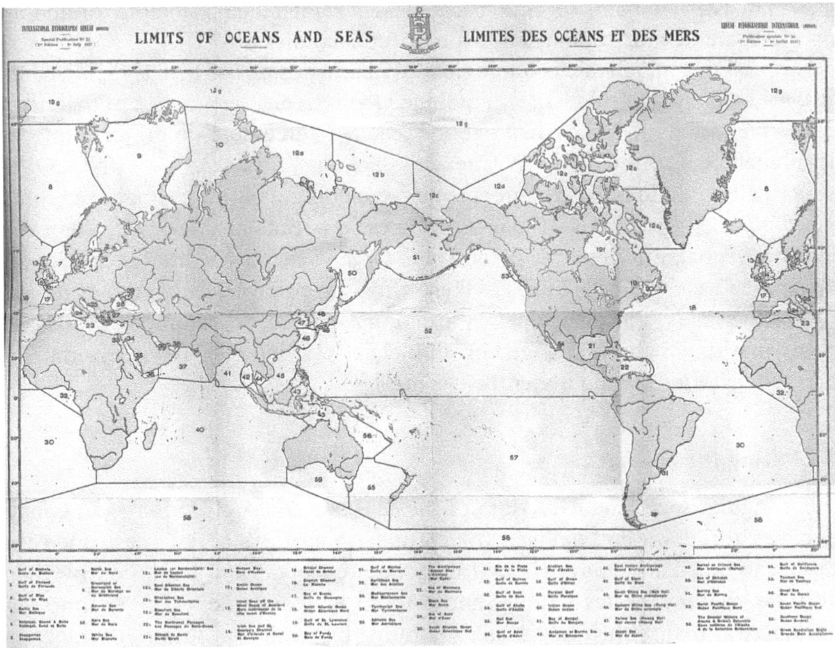

Figure 0.1 Map accompanying second edition (1937) of IHO publication *Limits of Oceans and Seas*, Special Publication 23. (US National Oceanic and Atmospheric Administration, Central Library Historical Collections.)

control of the ocean itself. As Sir Walter Raleigh, the English explorer and privateer, observed in an essay written in circa 1615:

> He who commands the sea, commands the trade routes of the world.
> He who commands the trade routes, commands the trade.
> He who commands the trade, commands the riches of the world, and hence the world itself.[19]

As conflicts mounted over the rights of States to navigate, claim and exploit the maritime environment, the question of who controls ocean space would become a matter of debate amongst the leading jurists of European maritime powers. Hugo Grotius, the Dutch jurist and scholar, in a pamphlet known as *Mare Liberum* (*The Freedom of the Seas*) published in 1609, argued that the seas were free for all to use, that navigation and fishing were the primary uses of the ocean, and that the ocean's resources were inexhaustible. In 1703 Cornelius van Bynkershoek published his treatise *De dominio maris dissertation*, proposing a 3-nautical-mile territorial sea, with sovereignty to the adjacent coastal State, that represented the distance a cannon shot could be fired from shore to effectively protect it. The 'cannon-shot rule' became an accepted legal principle for delimiting maritime territory amongst most maritime nations.

Surprisingly, given the technological advances during the 19th and 20th centuries, the cannon-shot rule largely continued to underpin the practice of delimiting territorial seas until 1982 when nations reached agreement on uniform international maritime zones in *the UN Convention on the Law of the Sea* (UNCLOS).[20] Nevertheless, diplomatic disagreements have continued to arise between States regarding the legal status of maritime zones in oceans and seas with high economic potential, most notably in the South China Sea, the Mediterranean Sea and the Arctic Ocean.[21] The legacies of these efforts to control oceanic routes remain. The Netherlands, Portugal, Spain, Britain and France, for example, all became strong maritime nations engaged in conflicts at sea, and even today external and remote territories remain under their control.[22]

Exploiting the ocean

These legal principles of freedom of the seas and the right of States to control their territorial waters, devised by European maritime nations, assumed that the ocean and its resources could only be controlled and exploited by those with the knowledge, technology and military power to do so. Over time they facilitated a major shift in human relationships with the ocean environment, from the subsistence use of marine resources to intensive commercial exploitation, with implications for how European laws evolved to regulate and manage the scale of the exploitation. The most significant shifts occurred from the 18th century when Europe's maritime powers, spurred by the growth of long-distance maritime trade and the freedom to exploit the high seas, ventured far from their own heavily fished seas in pursuit of the apparently limitless marine resources of the Pacific, Indian, Atlantic and Southern Oceans. By the 19th century, few parts of the world's oceans and seas were spared the relentless depletion of local marine resources to meet the demand in western markets for fur, oils and fish.[23]

In the same period, the world's oceans and seas were attracting scientific interest. This curiosity in the physical characteristics of the marine environment ranged from the study of tides, geomagnetism, meteorology and bathymetry to investigations of the deep ocean and the mysterious creatures that inhabited it. Nations offered financial incentives to promote scientific research to support the expansion of their global maritime empires, including the development of standardised marine charts, tide tables and sailing directions. By the late 19th century, scientific investigations of the deep ocean – most notably the *HMS Challenger* expedition in 1872–76[24] – were transforming understanding of the deep ocean and, in the process, science became an important tool in the quest of western maritime powers to control the surfaces and depths of the world's oceans, seas and shorelines. By 1910, no less than 26 marine laboratories had been established across northern Europe and North America and, in most cases, these combined fisheries research with their biological studies. This centrality of science remains today, evidenced by the declaration of the UN Decade of Ocean Science for Sustainable Development (2021–2030), with the enigmatic by-line of 'the science we need for the ocean we want'.[25]

Sea fishing has always been central to the subsistence of local peoples and to the economy of traditional coastal and island communities. Some species, such as Atlantic cod (*Gadus morhua*) found in the cold depths of the North Atlantic, were an important commodity in maritime trade from as early as the Viking era around the 8th to 11th century CE. With the rise of larger-scale commercial fishing in the 19th century, however, local fish populations plummeted, and sea fishing fleets moved on to new grounds – a pattern that would be repeated in oceans and seas around the world.[26] In this way, the exploitation of marine resources went hand in hand with territorial ambitions of maritime nations as they sought to extend their power over lucrative fishing grounds. New harvesting strategies and techniques developed in the late 19th century also enabled commercial fishers to increase their catches, while innovations in processing led to an expansion in the number of species that could be harvested and the distances that they could be exported. In 1883, the renowned scientist Thomas Huxley declared that sea fisheries were inexhaustible, an idea that continued to underpin the expansion of ocean exploitation well into the 20th century.[27] With the formation of the International Council for the Exploration of the Seas (ICES) in 1902, the aims of fisheries science and the fishing industry converged, setting the scene for the rapid escalation of industrial fishing, particularly after World War II.[28] Nevertheless, there is a strong history of fisheries regulations, in almost all parts of the world, largely focused on maintaining the industry. From early Roman laws in the Mediterranean to customary laws in Pacific Island States, they followed remarkably similar patterns and have continued to evolve over several millennia.

The commercial whaling industry is an important historical example of a fishing sector, its regulation and the use of law over time, and ultimately the shift in attitudes to conservation of these species that we see today. Amongst the earliest whale hunters were the Indigenous Inuit peoples of the Arctic region and the Basques of the Bay of Biscay in Europe.[29] European whalers began harvesting in the Atlantic and Pacific Oceans in the early 18th century and, by the 19th century, steam-powered vessels and harpoon cannons allowed large numbers of whales to be hunted commercially across greater ocean areas including the polar regions.[30] By the 1930s, the rapid decline in whale numbers became evident, leading to restrictions on the operation of factory fleets followed by the first international regulatory agreement on whaling. After World War II, the United Nations established the International Whaling Commission, in 1945. Two years later, the *International Convention for the Regulation of Whaling* came into force 'to provide for the proper conservation of whale stocks and thus make possible the orderly development of the whaling industry'.[31] By the 1970s, the combination of declining markets for whale products, and the rise of the modern environmental movement and public anti-whaling sentiment, sounded the death knell for the commercial whaling industry, and in 1982 the International Whaling Commission declared an international moratorium on all commercial whaling.[32] Nevertheless, some nations continue to carry out whaling, as non-parties to the Convention or, more controversially, for scientific research purposes, a claim that led Australia to bring proceedings in the International Court of Justice against Japan alleging that Japan's programme of killing whales in the Southern Ocean each year did not constitute legitimate research. Australia succeeded in the litigation in 2014, but this led to Japan withdrawing from the Convention in 2019, and it is now no longer a member State bound by the Convention provisions. Although public opinion clearly favours conservation of whales over fishing them – demonstrated by the continual growth of the whale-watching industry – as late as 2018 some nations were suggesting that whaling could be reintroduced.[33]

Western perceptions of the world's oceans have undergone significant changes in response to new scientific insights and the development of advanced submarine technologies, shifting geopolitical relationships and increasing competition for ocean resources. Simultaneously, cultural relationships with the marine environment have changed in many developed nations, and traditional approaches have attracted renewed interest with the emergence of newly independent nations and increasing recognition of Indigenous peoples and their values. In some instances, customary laws and cultural practices were acknowledged when colonial rule ended,[34] while others are only now being recognised and reflected in the development of ocean laws and regulatory frameworks, albeit frequently falling short of ownership rights.[35] In the Pacific region, for example, governments are now harnessing Indigenous knowledge of the marine environment and ancestral voyaging knowledge to help local communities to manage their resources and prepare for the future impacts of climate change and biodiversity loss.[36]

Surveying the legal landscape

About a quarter of the world's population is estimated to live in low-elevation coastal zones, putting ever-increasing pressures on fragile shorelines and coastal ecosystems. These pressures are being brought into sharp focus as nations pursue ambitious blue economy agenda that depends in part on growing wealth from the ocean. The biodiversity extinction crisis, for example, has devastated terrestrial species, but scientists also warn of the cumulative impacts on marine species as a result of habitat destruction, overexploitation, land-based development and pollution. Climate change is also causing significant problems in marine and coastal areas, raising concerns about its impacts including ocean warming and acidification, sea level rise and the repercussions of extreme weather events. Although coastal marine species such as mangroves and seagrasses have been shown to help in mitigating these impacts, including as carbon sinks for CO_2 and reducing wave energy, they are frequently removed to make way for residential and commercial infrastructure.

Law tends to develop slowly and evolve over time in response to particular challenges. It has not always succeeded in halting negative human impacts on oceans and coasts, but that does not necessarily diminish its importance or effectiveness in reducing damaging and harmful effects. Foundational legal principles, concepts and approaches continue to underpin laws for oceans, seas and shorelines. The law of the sea has resolved disagreements over maritime jurisdictions and boundaries, and confirmed the freedom of the seas as well as other areas of law including maritime piracy. This history, and its influence on fundamental principles, are explored in Chapters 1 and 2, while the legal responses to conflicts between peoples and nations, in terms of both warfare and piracy, are examined in Chapter 3. Maritime law (Chapter 5) and marine pollution law (Chapter 9) have successfully prevented and reduced impacts from incidental and deliberate disposal of waste at sea. The regulation of fishing has a long history that has evolved into a specialised area of law (Chapter 4), while conservation laws focused on specific species and oceanic spaces (Chapters 7 and 8) have largely failed to halt the legacies of marine exploitation fostered by State competition for resources and the legal principle of 'freedom of the seas'. Nevertheless, cultural heritage law (Chapter 10) reflects a concerted international effort to protect and preserve human-made objects and sites and their associated cultural values, while other laws seek to facilitate expansion of human knowledge about the oceanic environment (Chapter 11). Recent socio-legal developments based on the concept of ocean rights and justice, and the reconceptualisation of the oceanic realm as an integral part of the planetary system (Chapter 12), offer a glimmer of hope for the future of the Anthropocene ocean.

Notes

1 The concept of planetary boundaries includes nine interrelated processes that regulate the stability and resilience of Earth systems and '[c]rossing boundaries increases the risk of generating large-scale abrupt or irreversible environmental changes'. Ocean acidification is one of the nine boundaries, as are freshwater change, biosphere integrity and climate change: "Planetary Boundaries," *Stockholm Resilience Centre*, accessed January 31, 2024, www.stockholmresilience.org/research/planetary-boundaries.html.
2 "Homo Sapiens," *Smithsonian Institution National Museum of Natural History*, accessed January 3, 2024, https://humanorigins.si.edu/evidence/human-fossils/species/homo-sapiens.
3 Ann Gibbons, "Coastal Artifacts Suggest Early Beginnings for Modern Behaviour," *Science* 318, no. 5849 (October 19, 2007): 377.
4 Eva K. F. Chan et al., "Human Origins in a Southern African Palaeo-Wetland and First Migrations," *Nature* 575 (October 28, 2019): 185–89. John R. Gillis, *The Human Shore: Seacoasts in Human History* (Chicago: University of Chicago Press, 2012), 19, 22–25.
5 K. Kyriacou, D. M. Blackhurst, J. E. Parkington, and A. D. Marais, "Marine and Terrestrial Foods as a Source of Brain-Selective Nutrients for Early Modern Humans in the Southwestern Cape, South Africa," *Journal of Human Evolution* 97 (August 2016): 86–96.
6 Sarah Cascone, "Archaeologists Just Discovered the World's Oldest Jewelry: This Set of 150,000-Year-Old Snail-Shell Beads in Morocco," *Artnet* (November 19, 2021), https://news.artnet.com/art-world/worlds-oldest-jewelry-morocco-2037635. Our knowledge of how these early human societies perceived and used the marine environment is continually evolving, although long-term changes in sea levels have submerged or destroyed many archaeological sites. See for example Geoff Bailey and Hayley C. Cawthra, "The Significance of Sea-Level Change and Ancient Submerged Landscapes in Human Dispersal and Development: A Geoarchaeological Perspective," *Oceanologia* 65, no. 1 (January–March 2023): 50–70, https://doi.org/10.1016/j.oceano.2021.10.002. Gillis, *The Human Shore*, 24.
7 Gillis, *The Human Shore*, 25. Gillis suggests that '[f]or most of our existence . . . land and sea constituted a single ecotone'.
8 Genomic studies indicate that Australia's Indigenous peoples are direct descendants of the first people to leave Africa up to 75,000 years ago, and have the oldest living cultures on Earth. See Anna-Sapfo Malaspinas et al., "A Genomic History of Aboriginal Australia," *Nature* 538 (September 21, 2016): 207–14. Morten Rasmussen et al., "An Aboriginal Australian Genome Reveals Separate Human Dispersals into Asia," *Science* 334, no. 6052 (September 22, 2011): 94–98, www.science.org/doi/10.1126/science.1211177. "Australia's First Peoples," *The Australian Institute of Aboriginal and Torres Strait Islander Studies (AIATSIS)*, accessed January 18, 2024, https://aiatsis.gov.au/explore/australias-first-peoples. David Nield, "Scientists Reveal How Humans First Populated the Megacontinent of Sahul," *Science Alert* (February 14, 2023), www.sciencealert.com/scientists-reveal-how-humans-first-populated-the-ancient-megacontinent-of-sahul.
9 Eric Paul Roorda, ed., *The Ocean Reader: History, Culture, Politics* (Durham: Duke University Press, 2020), 5.
10 Hesiod, "Aphrodite Born from Sea Spray," in *The Ocean Reader*, ed. Roorda, 10–12; The Editors of Encyclopaedia Britannica, "Oceanus," *Encyclopedia Britannica* (May 12, 2010), accessed September 16, 2022, www.britannica.com/topic/Oceanus.
11 Ō no Yasumaro, "Izanagi and Izanami, Japanese Sea Gods," in *The Ocean Reader*, ed. Roorda, 13.

12 Samuel M. Wilson, *The Indigenous People of the Caribbean* (Gainesville, FL: University Press of Florida, 1999).
13 Helen M. Rozwadowski, *Vast Expanses: A History of the Oceans* (London: Reaktion Books Ltd, 2018), 151.
14 Ibid.
15 Roger F. Buschmann, *Oceans in World History* (New York: McGraw Hill, 2007).
16 Irus Braverman and Elizabeth R. Johnson, *Blue Legalities: The Life and Law of the Sea* (Durham: Duke University Press, 2020), 5.
17 Rozwadowski, *Vast Expanses*, 79–86.
18 The IHO drafted a fourth edition in 2002, but IHO Member States were unable to agree on aspects of it. See International Hydrographic Organization (IHO), *Limits of Oceans and Seas* (Special Publication No. 23) (Monte-Carlo: IHO, 1953), accessed March 1, 2024, https://epic.awi.de/id/eprint/29772/1/IHO1953a.pdf and International Hydrographic Organization (IHO), *Limits of Oceans and Seas* (Online Draft 4th Edition, 2002), accessed March 1, 2024, https://legacy.iho.int/mtg_docs/com_wg/S-23WG/S-23WG_Misc/Draft_2002/Draft_2002.htm.
19 Walter Raleigh, *Judicious and Select Essayes and Observations by That Renowned and Learned Knight, Sir Walter Raleigh* (London: Printed by T.W. for Humphrey Moseley, 1650), 20.
20 As will be seen in later chapters, this Convention is the premier global agreement on the law of the sea. For the full text, see "United Nations Convention on the Law of the Sea," *United Nations*, accessed March 1, 2024, www.un.org/depts/los/convention_agreements/texts/unclos/closindx.htm.
21 See "United Nations Conference on the Law of the Sea, Geneva (24 February-27 April 1958)," *United Nations*, accessed March 1, 2024, https://legal.un.org/diplomaticconferences/1958_los/.
22 Although many former colonies later became independent nations in the latter half of the 20th century, a number of external territories still exist: the US, UK, France and Spain all have remaining colonies, and the Netherlands and Australia overseas dependencies. Some of these remain highly controversial, such as the British Indian Ocean Territories (Chagos Islands): Daniel Boffey, "Negotiations on Chagos Islands' Sovereignty Face Legal Challenge," *The Guardian* (January 10, 2023), www.theguardian.com/world/2023/jan/09/negotiations-chagos-islands-sovereignty-legal-challenge-talks-uk-mauritius.
23 Rozwadowski, *Vast Expanses*, 95–96.
24 The voyage covered 68,890 nautical miles and discovered over 4,000 previously unknown marine species. The results were published in the *Report of the Scientific Results of the Exploring Voyage of H.M.S. Challenger during the Years 1873–76*, Challenger Expedition (1872–1876) (Edinburgh: Neill, 1880–1895).
25 "The Ocean Decade," *UN Decade of Ocean Science for Sustainable Development*, accessed December 19, 2023, www.oceandecade.org/.
26 See for example Greenpeace, "The Collapse of Newfoundland Cod," in *The Ocean Reader*, ed. Roorda, 144–47.
27 T. H. Huxley, "Inaugural Address: Fisheries Exhibition, London, 1883," in *The Scientific Memoirs of Thomas Henry Huxley*, supplementary volume, ed. Michael Foster and E. Ray Lankester (London: Macmillan, 1903), 80–89. Also see Jennifer Hubbard, "In the Wake of Politics: The Political and Economic Construction of Fisheries Biology, 1860–1970," *Isis* 105, no. 2 (2014): 366–67.
28 Rozwadowski, *Vast Expanses*, 136–42.
29 See for example Alex Aguilar, "Basque Whaling in the North Atlantic Ocean," in *The Ocean Reader*, ed. Roorda, 123–25.

30 Editors of Encyclopaedia Britannica, "Whale Oil," *Encyclopedia Britannica* (June 2, 2011), accessed October 7, 2022, www.britannica.com/technology/whale-oil.
31 Joy McCann, *Wild Sea: A History of the Southern Ocean* (Chicago: University of Chicago Press, 2019), 161–72; Gordon Elliott Fogg, *A History of Antarctic Science* (Cambridge: Cambridge University Press, 1992), 240, 387. For the full text of the Convention see "IWC Key Documents," *International Whaling Commission*, accessed March 1, 2024, https://iwc.int/commission/convention.
32 James D. Hansom and John E. Gordon, *Antarctic Environments and Resources: A Geographical Perspective* (Abingdon: Routledge, 2013, 1998), 205.
33 See for example Marc Mangel, "Whales, Science, and Scientific Whaling in the International Court of Justice," *Proceedings of the National Academy of Science, USA* 113, no. 51 (December 20, 2016): 14523–27, https://doi.org/10.1073%2Fpnas.1604988113. Michael J. Moore, *We Are All Whalers: The Plight of Whales and Our Responsibility* (Chicago: University of Chicago Press, 2021).
34 For example, customary law has been recognised in multiple constitutions and in specific statutes, as set out in: Katrina Cuskelly, *Customs and Constitutions: State Recognition of Customary Law around the World* (Bangkok: IUCN, 2011), accessed March 1, 2024, https://portals.iucn.org/library/efiles/documents/2011-101.pdf.
35 In Fiji, for example, the legal status of traditional fishing rights (*qoliqoli* rights) has never been restored. Yet in Samoa, the traditional village council (*fono*) has the power to pass enforceable fisheries by-laws under the *Village Fono Act* (1990), and in Vanuatu the *Environment Management and Conservation Act* (2002) provides for custom landowner-led Community Conservation Areas, which can include marine areas.
36 "Indigenous Knowledge in the Pacific Islands and the UN Ocean Decade," *UNESCO Intergovernmental Oceanographic Commission*, accessed March 1, 2024, https://oceandecade.org/news/indigenous-knowledge-in-the-pacific-islands-and-the-un-ocean-decade.

Bibliography

Aguilar, Alex. "Basque Whaling in the North Atlantic Ocean." In *The Ocean Reader*, edited by Eric Paul Roorda, 123–25. Durham: Duke University Press, 2020.
Australian Institute of Aboriginal and Torres Strait Islander Studies (AIATSIS). "Australia's First Peoples." Accessed January 18, 2024. https://aiatsis.gov.au/explore/australias-first-peoples, updated October 11, 2022.
Bailey, Geoff, and Hayley C. Cawthra. "The Significance of Sea-Level Change and Ancient Submerged Landscapes in Human Dispersal and Development: A Geoarchaeological Perspective." *Oceanologia* 65, no. 1 (January–March 2023): 50–70.
Boffey, Daniel. "Negotiations on Chagos Islands' Sovereignty Face Legal Challenge." *The Guardian* (January 10, 2023). www.theguardian.com/world/2023/jan/09/negotiations-chagos-islands-sovereignty-legal-challenge-talks-uk-mauritius.
Braverman, Irus, and Elizabeth R. Johnson. *Blue Legalities: The Life and Law of the Sea*. Durham: Duke University Press, 2020.
Buschmann, Roger F. *Oceans in World History*. New York: McGraw Hill, 2007.
Cascone, Sarah. "Archaeologists Just Discovered the World's Oldest Jewelry: This Set of 150,000-Year-Old Snail-Shell Beads in Morocco." *Artnet* (November 19, 2021). https://news.artnet.com/art-world/worlds-oldest-jewelry-morocco-2037635.
Challenger Expedition (1872–1876). *Report of the Scientific Results of the Exploring Voyage of H.M.S. Challenger during the Years 1873–76*. Edinburgh: Neill, 1880–1895.
Chan, Eva K. F. et al. "Human Origins in a Southern African Palaeo-Wetland and First Migrations." *Nature* 575 (October 28, 2019): 185–89.

Cuskelly, Katrina. *Customs and Constitutions: State Recognition of Customary Law Around the World*. Bangkok: IUCN, 2011. Accessed March 1, 2024. https://portals.iucn.org/library/efiles/documents/2011-101.pdf.

Editors of the Encyclopedia Britannica. "Oceanus." *Encyclopedia Britannica* (May 12, 2010). Accessed September 16, 2022. www.britannica.com/topic/Oceanus.

Editors of the Encyclopedia Britannica. "Whale Oil." *Encyclopedia Britannica* (June 2, 2011). Accessed October 7, 2022. www.britannica.com/technology/whale-oil.

Fogg, Gordon Elliott. *A History of Antarctic Science*. Cambridge: Cambridge University Press, 1992.

Gibbons, Ann. "Coastal Artifacts Suggest Early Beginnings for Modern Behaviour." *Science* 318, no. 5849 (October 19, 2007): 377.

Gillis, John R. *The Human Shore: Seacoasts in Human History*. Chicago: University of Chicago Press, 2012.

Greenpeace. "The Collapse of Newfoundland Cod." In *The Ocean Reader*, edited by Eric Paul Roorda, 144–47. Durham: Duke University Press, 2020.

Hansom, James D., and John E. Gordon, *Antarctic Environments and Resources: A Geographical Perspective*. Abingdon: Routledge, 1998.

Hesiod. "Aphrodite Born from Sea Spray." In *The Ocean Reader*, edited by Eric Paul Roorda, 10–12. Durham: Duke University Press, 2020.

Hubbard, Jennifer. "In the Wake of Politics: The Political and Economic Construction of Fisheries Biology, 1860–1970." *Isis* 105, no. 2 (2014): 366–67.

Huxley, T. H. "Inaugural Address: Fisheries Exhibition, London, 1883." In *The Scientific Memoirs of Thomas Henry Huxley*, supplementary volume, edited by Michael Foster and E. Ray Lankester, 80–89. London: Macmillan, 1903.

International Hydrographic Organization (IHO). *Limits of Oceans and Seas*. Monte-Carlo: IHO, 1953. Accessed March 1, 2024. https://epic.awi.de/id/eprint/29772/1/IHO1953a.pdf.

International Hydrographic Organization (IHO). *Limits of Oceans and Seas*. Online Draft 4th Edition, 2002. Accessed March 1, 2024. https://legacy.iho.int/mtg_docs/com_wg/S-23WG/S-23WG_Misc/Draft_2002/Draft_2002.htm.

International Whaling Commission. "IWC Key Documents." Accessed March 1, 2024. https://iwc.int/commission/convention.

Kyriacou, K., D. M. Blackhurst, J. E. Parkington, and A. D. Marais. "Marine and Terrestrial Foods as a Source of Brain-Selective Nutrients for Early Modern Humans in the Southwestern Cape, South Africa." *Journal of Human Evolution* 97 (August 2016): 86–96.

Lovelock, James E. "Hands Up for the Gaia Hypothesis." *Nature* 344, no. 6262 (March 8, 1990): 102.

Malaspinas, Anna-Sapfo et al. "A Genomic History of Aboriginal Australia." *Nature* 538 (September 21, 2016): 207–14.

Mangel, Marc. "Whales, Science, and Scientific Whaling in the International Court of Justice." *Proceedings of the National Academy of Science, USA* 113, no. 51 (December 20, 2016): 14523–27. Accessed March 1, 2024. https://doi.org/10.1073%2Fpnas.1604988113.

McCann, Joy. *Wild Sea: A History of the Southern Ocean*. Chicago: University of Chicago Press, 2019.

Moore, Michael J. *We Are All Whalers: The Plight of Whales and Our Responsibility*. Chicago: University of Chicago Press, 2021.

Nield, David. "Scientists Reveal How Humans First Populated the Megacontinent of Sahul." *Science Alert* (February 14, 2023). www.sciencealert.com/scientists-reveal-how-humans-first-populated-the-ancient-megacontinent-of-sahul.

Ō no Yasumaro. "Izanagi and Izanami, Japanese Sea Gods." In *The Ocean Reader*, edited by Eric Paul Roorda, 13. Durham: Duke University Press, 2020.
Raleigh, Walter. *Judicious and Select Essayes and Observations by That Renowned and Learned Knight, Sir Walter Raleigh*. London: Printed by T.W. for Humphrey Moseley, 1650.
Rasmussen, Morten et al. "An Aboriginal Australian Genome Reveals Separate Human Dispersals into Asia." *Science* 334, no. 6052 (September 22, 2011): 94–98. www.science.org/doi/10.1126/science.1211177.
Roorda, Eric Paul, ed. *The Ocean Reader: History, Culture, Politics*. Durham: Duke University Press, 2020.
Rozwadowski, Helen M. *Vast Expanses: A History of the Oceans*. London: Reaktion Books Ltd, 2018.
Smithsonian Institution National Museum of Natural History. "Homo Sapiens." Accessed January 3, 2024. https://humanorigins.si.edu/evidence/human-fossils/species/homo-sapiens.
Stockholm Resilience Centre. "Planetary Boundaries." Accessed January 31, 2024. www.stockholmresilience.org/research/planetary-boundaries.html.
UN Decade of Ocean Science for Sustainable Development. "The Ocean Decade." Accessed December 19, 2023. www.oceandecade.org/.
UNESCO Intergovernmental Oceanographic Commission. "Indigenous Knowledge in the Pacific Islands and the UN Ocean Decade." Accessed March 1, 2024. https://oceandecade.org/news/indigenous-knowledge-in-the-pacific-islands-and-the-un-ocean-decade.
United Nations. "United Nations Conference on the Law of the Sea." Accessed March 1, 2024. https://legal.un.org/diplomaticconferences/1958_los/.
United Nations. "United Nations Convention on the Law of the Sea." Accessed March 1, 2024. www.un.org/depts/los/convention_agreements/texts/unclos/closindx.htm.
Wilson, Samuel M. *The Indigenous People of the Caribbean*. Gainesville, FL: University Press of Florida, 1999.

Part I

The ocean as territory

1 Undercurrents

Legal approaches and maritime concepts

By the law of nature these things are common to mankind, the air, running water, the sea and consequently the shores of the sea.

Laws of Justinian, 535 AD.

Overview

Modern humans (*Homo sapiens*) have long exploited the world's oceans, seas and shorelines[1] for food and tools.[2] Across time and in different societies, humans have drawn on their knowledge and beliefs about the marine environment to regulate its use, introducing laws to control human behaviour and ensure that the ocean can continue to provide for human needs.[3] Traditional knowledge, and the more recent evolution of western natural sciences, reflect these different forms of knowledge and beliefs about marine and coastal environments, the living species and ecosystems within them, and the non-living resources and processes relating to them, as well as the extent of human impacts, including over-harvesting, extinctions, pollution events and climate change.

In order to understand the laws that have been created to govern human uses of oceans, seas and shorelines, it is vital to appreciate the different worldviews and cultural practices that underpin them. Understanding these is important because they form the foundation of laws in the various legal systems of the world today. Research has shown that Indigenous and traditional peoples, many in island communities, created marine tenure systems and were aware of the risk of over-exploitation and degradation.[4] Drawing on traditional knowledge of the marine environment, they adopted early customary practices, rules and laws in response to scarcity, to avoid conflict over access and resources, and for sacred and cultural reasons (also a feature of religious laws).[5] In western societies, however, the myth of the ocean's inexhaustible resources and ability to absorb the effects of human activities came to dominate western civil and common law systems.[6] It was these nations that exercised their maritime power from the 16th century and began to build empires and colonies. In doing so traditional

DOI: 10.4324/9781003005261-3

governance approaches and customary laws were suppressed, and western common and civil law systems imposed. For many former colonies, it was not until the second half of the 20th century that they gained independence and could restore their traditional legal systems. For some nations, too much damage had been done and they could not be resurrected. In other places customary governance institutions and law were reinstated, although they usually existed alongside the colonial structures and laws.

Laws and practices relating to oceans – navigation and fishing rights, territorial claims, maritime shipping practices, and rules relating to conflicts at sea – developed over many centuries. The 20th century saw many of these customary arrangements codified into written international maritime and law of the sea conventions. With the creation of the United Nations in 1945, and the rise of the environmental movement in the 1960s onwards, multiple international environmental treaties were adopted. These instruments set global standards, including State obligations and international cooperation requirements and benefits. Newly independent nations signed and ratified these treaties alongside their more developed and industrialised neighbours. As the treaties included State commitments that all signatory nations were obliged to implement, the introduction of new law or revision of existing legislation became necessary. In this way, the adoption of international treaties had the effect of homogenising domestic marine environmental, shipping, and pollution laws as well as laws for maritime zones and dispute settlement.[7] Thus, although pure common, civil, religious or customary law systems exist today, they are frequently in legally pluralist or mixed law contexts. Nevertheless, given the failure (or at least the limited success) of contemporary, conventional approaches to secure the health of the ocean environment, there is growing global interest in the renaissance of customary law and traditional knowledge, and the worldviews that underpin it.[8]

In this chapter we explore two key concepts that have dominated laws governing oceans, seas and shorelines. First, the binary separation of land and sea which, although not universal, pervades laws across the globe. Worldviews about land and water may differ – including perspectives on the potential divide between them – yet a binary approach eclipses others in the legal treatment of the marine and coastal environment. Second, the continued dominance of the concept of 'freedom of the seas', first developed in Europe in the 17th century, has led to the prevailing extractive, utilitarian approach to oceans that we see today, focusing on marine and coastal species and areas as resources for human exploitation. Both of these approaches have shaped western and international lawmaking for oceans, seas and shorelines. This chapter also explores the paradigm shifts that occurred with the rise of the environmental movement, and some of the more recent approaches to lawmaking that have responded to human impacts on the marine environment.

Legal systems of the world

Although the laws in various countries differ, there are five principal legal systems in the world:

Common law arose out of customs and practices that over time developed into a body of laws. Common law systems are distinguishable from civil law as both written (legislation and judicial decisions (judgments) are sources of law. Common law countries include the UK, the US, Canada and Australia.

Civil law systems also derive from customs as well as Roman Law. A key feature is the codification of law. Civil law countries are predominantly found in mainland Europe.

Religious law systems are based on sacred texts and faith-based traditions. They include Sharia, Halakha and Canon law, the most widespread of which is Islamic Law. Many Middle Eastern countries have religious law as their foundation, as well as States such as the Maldives.

Customary law systems are based on traditional customs and practices and are often unwritten. Customary law is found in Africa and the South Pacific, although rarely is a contemporary law based solely on custom.

Mixed or legally pluralist systems combine one or more of the aforementioned, often as a result of post-colonialism. Nations such as the Philippines, for example, include common, civil, customary and religious laws.

Fundamental underpinnings

The land-sea divide

Marine and coastal ecosystems are intimately connected, with some animals living in one of these environments and others, including seabirds, crustaceans, amphibians and reptiles, moving freely between the two. Some species and ecosystems are also dependent or rely upon environmental associations and oceanographic processes that cross the shoreline. Laws, however, are created by people to control human behaviour, to regulate human activities and to resolve disputes, invariably adopting an anthropocentric approach to the land-water interface that ignores or erases the fluid and dynamic nature of oceans, seas and shorelines. For thousands of years humans used the coastal strip to migrate, finding food on land and in the shallows, and living close to the shoreline. This has led to human communities, throughout history, creating different ways of perceiving and relating

Levels and scales of law

International law includes Treaties, Conventions and multilateral agreements, adopted collectively by States by consensus. Modern international law evolved around 400 years ago, although its origins are thousands of years old. Contemporary international law has predominantly been agreed upon through United Nations processes since its creation in 1945. Treaties and Conventions are legally binding on States that are parties to them. Declarations are international soft or informal law and are not legally binding. Other sources of international law include customary international law (not to be confused with domestic customary law), which are the rules that develop from the general practice of States and accepted by States as law, general principles of law recognised by nations, and decisions of international courts (such as the International Court of Justice) and the teachings of highly qualified scholars.

Domestic or national law is adopted by governments in individual States and includes legislation, Acts and Statutes as well as case law. The different systems of law are set out in the textbox.

Sub-national, local or provincial law is developed and adopted by local governments or other governance bodies and can take the form of regulations, decrees and by-laws as well as unwritten customary laws.

to the marine environment according to their geographical locations, cultures and traditional practices. Many traditional communities continue to practice their belief systems and live lifestyles based on non-western worldviews, at least in part. These relationships are shaped by distinctive cultural, ecological and historical knowledge and customary practices passed down through generations. Many do not distinguish between land and sea in their construction of territory, nor do they consider its economic or material value as separate from its cultural and spiritual significance. The Atlantic coastline of north-eastern Canada, for example, is the traditional territory of the Mi'kmaq, Innu, Wolastoqiyik, Peskotomuhkati, Nunatsiavut, Southern Inuit of NunatukKavut and the ancestral homelands of the Mi'kmaq and Beothuk peoples, each of whom have a unique relationship with their traditional ocean territory to which they are spiritually and culturally connected.[9] These customs, practices and beliefs shape customary laws. For Australia's Meriam peoples of Murray Island, traditional law bestows rights to territory as well as the responsibility to care for and receive its gifts to be shared with others. As Nonie Sharp explains, the Meriam are a 'sea people' and the sites and tracks created by their ancestors are inseparable from Meriam identity, a concept shared by other coastal Aboriginal and Torres Strait Islander peoples: 'This, an inalienable system, contrasts with the dominant European perspective in which the individual alone owns this object'.[10] Indigenous relationships embody many different principles and values, but their different forms of traditional knowledge tend to share similar principles including 'responsibility, respect, reciprocity and connectivity to each other and the environment'.[11] In the South Pacific, for example, this stewardship underpinned customary governance arrangements whereby village land included near-shore waters out to the nearest reef and sometimes beyond.[12]

As communities grew, they established complex village governance structures or medieval feudal systems based on military or hereditary hierarchies. The concept of the nation State is a relatively modern political phenomenon, commonly thought to have emerged with the rise of the system of States known as the Westphalian system in reference to the Peace of Westphalia, signed in 1648, which ended the Thirty Years' War.[13] A key principle of international law is that each State has sovereignty over its own territory and domestic affairs, and that each State is equal under international law. Today, all of the places with permanent human habitations are located within nation States, each with their own legal systems and legislation. Where customary legal systems have persisted, survived colonisation and/or where they have been restored, Indigenous worldviews are sometimes captured in law. For example, in Vanuatu, 'land' is defined in legislation as including the submerged seabed highlighting a worldview that does not separate land and water: 'any estate, any interest in or benefit to land, all things growing on land, houses, buildings, improvements and all other things on land, land beneath water, the seabed extending to the seaside of any offshore reef but no further and the subsoil thereof'.[14] Yet this is a rare example.

Common or civil law systems dominate in States with European origins and, although these differ, there are some common elements. One legal concept in common is that people (and artificial entities such as corporations) can own terrestrial land and, subject to planning, development and environmental laws, they may do what they wish with it. In contrast, the marine environment is in public ownership, and governments own, control and manage both the waters and the submerged lands seaward of the shoreline. Here there is a clear divide between land and water: real property, in private hands, ends where the land meets the sea. This means that laws, and the owners and decision makers are very different in the two domains. As a result, marine species may cross these boundaries but how they may be impacted by humans, and how human activities are regulated, differs markedly.

The separation of land from tidal waters is particularly relevant to laws relating to the shoreline which falls between the high water mark and the low water mark (see Chapter 2). Based on the aforementioned rules, the shoreline is public land, controlled and managed by governments. Here it is not property ownership laws that are relevant, but jurisdictional rules[15] relating to responsibilities and obligations.[16] As will be seen in Chapter 2, detailed rules exist in almost all nations to determine the precise points at which land becomes sea, where private ownership ends and public ownership begins. Further rules determine public rights of access and use, and legislation provides permitting systems for other activities. Layered on top of this are the divisions between levels of government that determine the jurisdiction and authority of each. Little account is taken of the challenges this presents for species that cross the land-water interface, or processes that interact across these invisible boundaries. Whilst lawmakers have sought ways to overcome this binary, as discussed later in this chapter, ocean-centred approaches that provide a 'voice' for marine species and the ocean itself remain absent.

Freedom of the seas

The western construction of ocean space as public territory belonging to the State or monarch emerged in a radically different cultural and social context than Indigenous societies, giving rise to the doctrine of freedom of the seas. The origins can be traced back to Roman Law, but the freedom of the seas emerged following later dramatic shifts that took place in England as the Crown gradually erased customary rights to coastal resources and established common-law rights to territorial seas.[17] The idea found fertile ground in the imperial expansionism of the 17th century as European ships ventured across the high seas in search of new markets and trade routes. The Dutch jurist and scholar Hugo Grotius, in a pamphlet known as *Mare Liberum* (*The Freedom of the Seas*) published in 1609, argued that the ocean was so vast that no nation could appropriate it and that it should therefore remain the same as it had been created:

> The sea is common to all . . . because it is so limitless it cannot become a possession of any one, and because it is adapted for the use of all, whether we consider [it] from the point of view of navigation or fisheries.[18]

Grotius noted that, unlike land, people cannot inhabit the ocean or divide it into territories. The idea implicit in Grotius's argument was persuasive – that water and air were nature's gifts and could not be alienated as private property. *Mare Liberum* expounded the idea that a State should have unhindered use of the high seas for navigation and fishing, and that a State's rights and jurisdiction over the ocean should be limited to a specific belt of water extending from the coastlines. The rest of the oceans and seas, in Grotius's words, 'were free to all nations but belonged to none of them'.[19] As competition increased between the Dutch and English over coastal fishing rights and long-distance trade routes, the English jurist John Selden made the case in his 1619 treatise *Mare clausum* ('closed sea') that a State possessed the right to control an adjacent sea, ocean or other navigable body of water as part of its sovereign territory, while recognising the concept of freedom of the seas beyond the State's national waters. His argument was based, in part, on English claims to 'sovereignty at sea dating back to pre-Norman times', and 'the principle that seas beyond the horizon . . . are open to all nations'.

These two competing doctrines, advanced by Dutch and English scholars, became a defining narrative in the history of international law of the sea and is often referred to as the 'battle of books'. However, as geographer Alison Reiser points out, the concept of freedom of the seas that emerged from this period not only reflected the legal doctrines of Grotius and Seddon. It was also shaped by the broader geopolitical context in the form of competition for control over the lucrative North Atlantic herring fisheries. Grotius was aware that the herring trade was central to the economy of the new Dutch Republic, and his doctrine reflected the belief that the migrating shoals of herring were inexhaustible because they represented the divine rhythms of nature. Seddon similarly drew on the idea of natural law, but his doctrine was underpinned by the belief that Great Britain had sovereign rights to the rich herring shoals around its shores.[20]

While *Mare Liberum* represented the first effective argument for freedom of the seas in modern times and became a fundamental principle of the international law of the sea for three centuries, tensions frequently arose between larger maritime powers that favoured the free seas doctrine, and smaller, less powerful States arguing for limitations on navigation and exploitation of the high seas. As explored in Chapter 2, this led to various claims of ownership to territorial seas adjacent to coastal States. The principles established by Grotius were concerned with freedom of the seas in peacetime. However, they raised very different considerations in times of war.[21] The right of a nation to remove enemy goods from a neutral ship – interpreted by the Dutch as 'free ships, free goods' – had been a controversial matter during the 17th and 18th centuries. In signing the 1856 Paris Declaration to end hostilities associated with the Crimean War, the parties accepted that they would seize neither enemy goods on neutral vessels nor neutral goods on enemy vessels.[22] Whilst this did not translate to freedom of the seas, the Declaration did achieve a number of measures that limited State rights on the high seas. The US withheld its formal adherence to the Paris Declaration and continued to pursue its principle of immunity of private property at sea although, when the Civil War erupted in 1861 and again in 1898 during its war against Spain, the US affirmed that it would respect the principles of the Paris Declaration for the duration of the hostilities. In 1904 the US Congress formally adopted the doctrine of immunity of private property on the seas in times of war.[23]

During the hostilities of World War I, Britain, Germany and the US each sought to define the concept of freedom of the seas within the context of their own ambitions for maritime dominance. John Holladay Latané, a scholar of American foreign policy, observed that despite its widespread use there was no common understanding of what freedom of the seas actually meant in times of

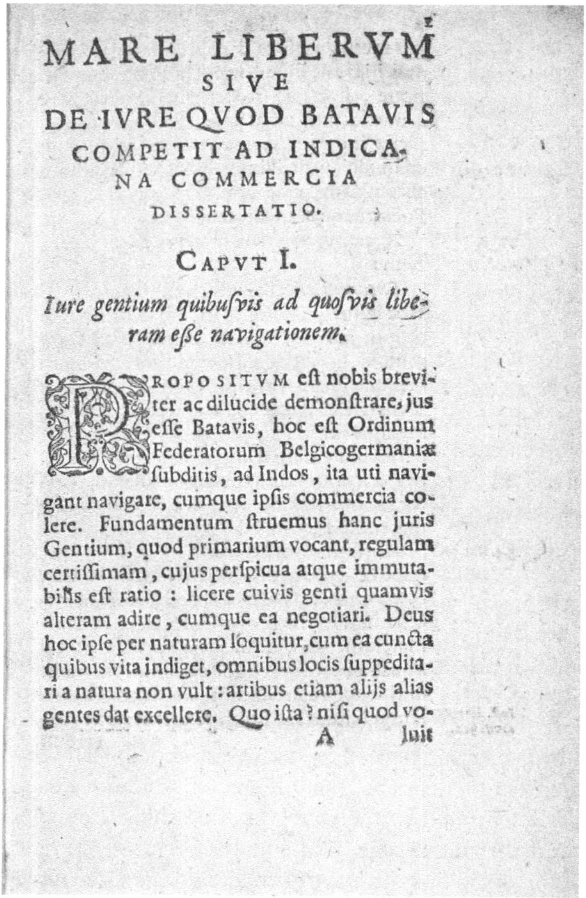

MARE LIBERVM
SIVE
DE IVRE QVOD BATAVIS
COMPETIT AD INDICA-
NA COMMERCIA
DISSERTATIO.

CAPVT I.

Iure gentium quibuſvis ad quoſvis liberam eſſe navigationem.

PROPOSITVM eſt nobis breviter ac dilucide demonſtrare, jus eſſe Batavis, hoc eſt Ordinum Federatorum Belgicogermaniæ ſubditis, ad Indos, ita uti navigant navigare, cumque ipſis commercia colere. Fundamentum ſtruemus hanc juris Gentium, quod primarium vocant, regulam certiſſimam, cujus perſpicua atque immutabilis eſt ratio: licere cuivis genti quamvis alteram adire, cumque ea negotiari. Deus hoc ipſe per naturam loquitur, cum ea cuncta quibus vita indiget, omnibus locis ſuppeditari a natura non vult: artibus etiam alijs alias gentes dat excellere. Quo iſta? niſi quod vo-

A luit

Figure 1.1 Title page from Hugo Grotius, *Mare Liberum sive de jure quod Batavis competit ad Indicana commercia dissertatio.* (Published by Lodewijk Elzevir, 1609; Royal Library of the Netherlands Collection.)

conflict. Writing in 1919, he noted that the term 'seas' in this context meant 'high seas', and that the concept of 'high' – commonly used to describe roads or rivers which are common, open and public – may have reflected both the apparent elevation of the sea surface and the idea of the ocean as a highway. In his analysis, he cited a legal interpretation by the US Supreme Court in 1893:

> It is to be observed also that the term 'high' in one of its significations is used to denote that which is common, open, and public. Thus, every road or way or navigable river which is used freely by the public is a 'high' way. So a large

> body of navigable water other than a river, which is of an extent beyond the measurement of one's unaided vision, and is open and unconfined, and not under the exclusive control of any one nation or people, but is the free highway of adjoining nations or people, must fall under the definition of 'high seas' within the meaning of the statute.[24]

The devastating suffering and destruction wrought by the military conflicts of World War I placed an enormous burden on governments to develop an international approach to the settlement of disputes between States by legal or judicial means. In 1918, US President Woodrow Wilson addressed a joint session of the US Congress to outline his proposals for a post-war peace settlement known as the 'Fourteen Points', the second of which focused on freedom of navigation on the seas outside territorial waters in peace and war, except where the seas were 'closed in whole or in part by international action for the enforcement of international covenants'.[25] The Fourteen Points were subsequently accepted by the Allies and formed the basis for the Covenant of the League of Nations.

In the years after World War II, the expansive imperialism that saw maritime powers dominating the exploitation of the ocean's resources brought them into increasing conflict with coastal States, many of which were demanding greater control over the resources and security of their offshore marine environments. At the same time, many nations were increasingly concerned with the impact of long-distance fishing fleets on coastal fish stocks, and threats to the health of ecosystems and coastal communities posed by pollution from long-distance cargo vessels.[26]

The UN laid the groundwork for codifying international laws relating to the world's oceans and seas at the first Conference on the Law of the Sea held in Geneva in 1956–58. The Conference resulted in agreement on four treaties: the *Convention on the High Seas*, *Convention on the Territorial Sea and Contiguous Zone*, *Convention on the Continental Shelf*, and *Convention on Fishing and Conservation of Living Resources of the High Seas*. When the UN conducted the second Conference on the Law of the Sea in Geneva in 1960, however, it failed to produce any new agreements on oceans and seas. By the time the third United Nations Conference on the Law of the Sea began discussions in 1973 in New York, the UN was aiming to resolve several problems, including claims by various nations to expand their territorial waters. The negotiations were fraught with tensions, disagreement and compromise that would become the hallmark of international law of the sea.[27]

The third conference, involving more than 160 nations, dragged on until 1982 when participants were finally able to reach a consensus on the provisions of the *UN Convention on the Law of the Sea* (UNCLOS).[28] Notwithstanding these difficulties, the new Convention was said to be a 'constitution for the ocean'. It has provided stability and certainty for the international law of the sea and has stood the test of time. UNCLOS articulated the doctrine of freedom of the seas in ways that both cemented and constrained what had prevailed for 300 years. It distinguished specific parts of the world's oceans and seas, settling maritime zones including internal waters, territorial waters, archipelagic waters, contiguous zones, exclusive economic zones (EEZs), and continental shelves, all measured from carefully defined baselines. It embraced the old doctrine of freedom of the seas by specifying that all waters beyond national jurisdiction were 'international waters', free to be used by all nations but belonging to none.[29] This doctrine of 'freedom of the seas' was unpacked to include freedom of navigation, fishing, the laying of submarine cables and pipelines, and the freedom to fly over the high seas. Yet even on the high seas, the Convention established obligations to protect and preserve the marine environment and to protect freedom of scientific research. Significantly, the Convention stated that the seabed under the high seas – the Area – was the common heritage of humankind and established a legal regime for controlling mineral resource exploitation in the deep seabed beyond the jurisdiction of individual States.[30]

Beyond the maritime zones, UNCLOS articulated differing rights and obligations for coastal, flag and port States, including their authority to regulate. Yet, the vastness of the ocean has made surveillance, monitoring and enforcement challenging. One of the contemporary issues faced by nations, and the world, is ensuring effective implementation and compliance with existing laws. Compliance with ocean laws is largely a matter for coastal States, which implement many provisions in international treaties and develop national legislation for their waters. This is particularly the case in relation to environmental matters.[31] Nevertheless, some maritime law instruments place obligations on the flag State (the nation where the ship is registered, for example) and some have also focused on port States (such as the Port State Measures Agreement explored later in this book). In general, international treaties have tended to include only limited reference to monitoring, compliance checking and non-compliance measures.[32] Although UNCLOS includes dispute resolution provisions, sanctions are not included and enforcement is left to nation States with respect to domestic laws. In addition, certain issues have not been addressed in UNCLOS in any detail, most notably developments in maritime security, biodiversity loss and environmental degradation, human rights and labour protections, access to economic resources (including on the seabed and in the water column), and more recent challenges including climate change and new technologies.[33] It has been left to subsequent international laws to provide rules in relation to these areas, yet they invariably do not seek to undermine UNCLOS, and positively reinforce its applicability including the backdrop of the doctrine of freedom of the seas.

Fields of law relevant to oceans, seas and shorelines

Law of the Sea is a body of public international law developed from historical customs (customary international law) and agreements that largely emerged after World War II. Today, it is commonly associated with the

UN Convention on the Law of the Sea (1982). The international law of the sea establishes key maritime zones, governs the geographical jurisdictions of coastal States, and provides principles and rules of access for all States as well as maritime piracy, the conservation and utilisation, protection and preservation of the ocean environment and its natural resources. See Chapters 2 and 3.

Maritime or Admiralty law is the law relating to ships and the commercial business of shipping. International maritime law relates to international waters (i.e., ships sailing in waters outside of State jurisdiction). The United Nations International Maritime Organisation (IMO) is responsible for establishing international maritime laws and standards for member States, with a significant focus on addressing marine pollution from ships, safety of life at sea, and salvage law. See Chapter 5.

Fisheries law relates to the regulation of fishing and management of fish stocks. At the international level it is the Food and Agriculture Organisation (FAO) that has the mandate for food security and provides data on global fish stocks. The FAO supports the Regional Fishery Management Organisations and has developed laws for migratory and straddling stocks, in compliance with international law, and to address illegal fishing. See Chapter 4.

Marine environmental law is focused on conservation of marine species, ecosystems and areas. It is the United Nations Environment Programme (UNEP) that supports the conservation treaties related to marine species, the hazardous waste conventions, and the Regional Seas Programmes (including work on land-based marine pollution) and is leading negotiations for a new marine plastic debris treaty.

Shoreline law is not a field of law as such, and rules relating to ownership at the land-water interface fall under domestic property law. See Chapter 2.

Growing concern for the marine environment

Early awareness

The impact that humans could have on the marine environment, at scales well beyond the local, became increasingly clear in the 18th and 19th centuries. Steller's Sea Cow, for example, was declared to have been hunted to extinction as early as 1768.[34] Yet the belief that marine resources were inexhaustible persisted in the industrialising world, based upon faulty catch calculations and misunderstandings about marine biology and ecology.[35] Arguably, it was not finally dispelled until the early 20th century as the field of fisheries science emerged and accounts by fishers pointed to signs of depletion[36] This was triggered by the decline of whales and the impacts on the whaling industry in the 1940s, followed by the collapse of several fisheries in the 1950s–1970s, while several significant oil spills graphically demonstrated the limits of the ocean's ability to absorb waste.[37] These events drew international attention and heralded the beginning of the environmental movement.

The modern environmental movement emerged in the 1960s as community groups and political parties began to recognise their shared objectives of environmental protection, social justice and grassroots democracy. Public environmental campaigns gained momentum in the 1970s and 1980s with growing public awareness of major environmental catastrophes such as the nuclear accidents at Three Mile Island (1979) and Chernobyl (1986) and the publication of several influential books including *Silent Spring* by US marine biologist Rachel Carson.[38] Carson had published three earlier books about the marine environment,[39] but it was her later book that captured the public's imagination. Garrett Hardin was another author whose work shaped public environmental discourses. In his essay *The Tragedy of the Commons*, he argued that a person tends to use a common resource – such as the oceans – in ways that diminish other people's use of it.[40] He believed that what is owned by no one is cared for by no one, and advocated for making the commons a private possession and adopting regulations to restrict public access to resources. This thinking can be seen, in part, in UNCLOS where large ocean areas which were once high seas were enclosed as EEZs to be controlled, and cared for, by States.

The environmental movement was also instrumental in shaping the legal history of oceans, seas and shorelines. The introduction of international pollution and conservation treaties in the 1970s and 1980s, as well as domestic legislation, for example, focused on protecting threatened species and ensuring that people had access to clean air and water.[41] The first-ever global environmental conference was hosted by the UN in 1972. The Conference on the Human Environment (Stockholm Conference) was a seminal event, albeit still squarely centred around humans. For the first time the environment featured at the core of an international meeting along with poverty and development. There were several key outcomes of the Conference, including the adoption of the Stockholm Declaration (a framework of principles) and a Resolution to establish the UN Environment Programme (UNEP) (a new global institution). The *Stockholm Declaration*, although not legally binding itself, contained 26 principles that have been widely endorsed and remain relevant today.[42] They include concepts such as the right to an environment of quality, and principles that resources must be safeguarded for present and future generations, that the Earth's capacity to produce resources must be maintained, restored or improved and non-renewable resources must not be exhausted. In addition, they confirm that humans have a responsibility to safeguard and wisely manage wildlife and habitats, to prevent discharge of toxic substances, and serious or irreversible damage to the environment. Only one specific reference is made to oceans in recognition of the most pressing issue at that time: 'States shall take all possible steps to prevent pollution of the seas by substances that are liable to create hazards to human health, to harm living resources and marine life' (Principle 7). The principles in the *Stockholm Declaration* were bolstered by their later inclusion in the *Rio Declaration on Environment and Development* (1992) (Rio Declaration), and some have now become enforceable (through codification in other written laws or through practice by recognition as customary international law).

Sustainable development

Safeguarding the environment for future generations and efforts to balance economic development and environmental conservation/protection have proved difficult to achieve. In 1987 the Brundtland Commission published a report *Our Common Future* which, for the first time, referred to the concept of 'sustainable development', defined as development that meets the needs of the present without compromising future generations to meet their own needs. Sustainable development was swiftly popularised as a concept, although it remained ill-defined and many indicators associated with it continued to worsen. It was not until the Rio Declaration (1992) that greater clarity was provided. Emerging from the UN Conference on Environment and Development (UNCED or the Rio Conference), the first global environmental conference since 1972, the Rio Declaration placed less focus on 'humans' and more concern for the environment, albeit in the context of development. Although legal measures were not the only focus at UNCED, they were front and centre with the adoption of multiple instruments including several new treaties (see later in the chapter), the *Rio Declaration* (a non-binding instrument), and *Agenda 21* (an action plan indicating how objectives could be achieved). The *Rio Declaration* reiterated and expanded upon principles in the *Stockholm Declaration*, and it is these principles that lie at the heart of international environmental law today.

By this time many of the former colonies had become independent, and there was concern for the economic development of these nations in the global south. But the environment had also suffered in the intervening 20 years, prompting the inclusion of sustainable development in the Rio Declaration alongside prevention of environmental damage, precaution in the absence of full scientific certainty, polluters to pay for the damage they cause, the need for environmental impact assessments and recognition that common but differentiated responsibilities should be adopted to achieve equity amongst developed and developing countries, in addition to the right to development. Agenda 21 included a whole chapter on oceans, seas and coastal areas in which specific suggestions were made about how to encourage biodiversity conservation including 'surveys of marine biodiversity, inventories of endangered species and critical coastal and marine habitats; establishment and management of protected areas; and support of scientific research and dissemination of its results'.[43]

The third global conference was the World Summit on Sustainable Development (2002), and a similar approach was taken with the adoption of the *Johannesburg Declaration*, which reiterated a commitment to sustainable development with an added focus on the importance of implementation. At the later Rio +20 Conference (2012), the global community adopted the Sustainable Development Goals (SDGs) as part of the *2030 Agenda for Sustainable Development*.[44] The SDGs followed on from the Millennium Development Goals, which had not included any specific marine targets. Relevantly, SDG14 focused explicitly on *Life Below Water* to 'conserve and sustainably use the oceans, seas and marine resources for sustainable development' with targets for marine pollution, fisheries, species and habitat conservation and indeed the implementation of law itself. The agreement of these (non-binding) goals was a valuable addition to international law as they set tangible, quantified targets often with associated dates. Although many have not been achieved, they provide measurable aims and have inspired action by States and a myriad of other actors.

This overview demonstrates the emergence of environmental concerns and growing attention being given to oceans. All of these developments, however, remain constrained by the legacy of laws that focus separately on land and water and doctrines such as the freedom of seas, which continues to undermine efforts to mitigate human activities on and in the ocean. Yet some developments have sought to change the foundational seascape, albeit with limited success to date.

Changing the conceptual seascape

Integrated coastal zone management (often known as ICZM) is one approach that, in part, seeks to overcome the binary divide between land and water. Although no global treaties address this topic, the concept of integrated coastal zone management emerged during the Rio Conference. As noted earlier, the *Rio Declaration* was one outcome of the Conference, but so too was the adoption of *Agenda 21* – a plan of action for sustainable development. Chapter 17 of *Agenda 21* focuses on protection of oceans, seas and coastal areas and includes several references to integrated coastal zone management as a way to dynamically, interactively and sustainably manage marine and coastal areas and guidance for States on ways to address pollution.[45] Although decades old now, *Agenda 21* remains a powerful guiding document incorporating ideas and approaches that are yet to be implemented today. Notably, integrated coastal zone management has not found its way into the wording of any international law instrument and has had limited impact at the national level (with some exceptions).

Planning law has also been applied to the ocean environment in the form of marine spatial planning. This involves spatial and temporal distribution of human activities, such as fishing, shipping routes, tourism, research, traditional uses and conservation areas.[46] Another approach that emerged in the 1970s, and was taken up in the 1980s in States such as Australia, involved creating zoning plans for marine protected areas, including the Great Barrier Reef.[47] It has subsequently attracted growing worldwide attention on greater scales, with nations such as the Cook Islands declaring all waters to be a marine protected area, zoned for different uses to create a framework for sustainable development and conservation.[48]

Ecosystem-based management (often referred to as EBM) is interlinked with ICZM but also can constrain the freedom of the seas and limitations of State maritime jurisdictions. The word ecosystem did not appear in early wildlife and natural resource regulations, and it was not until 1992 when the *Convention on Biological Diversity* (CBD) was adopted that the word became firmly embedded in international law.[49] Ecosystem-based management integrates environmental, social and economic dimensions into resource management decisions to advance conservation and sustainable use of natural resources.[50] Rather than focusing on political-legal boundaries, EBM centres on non-human ecosystems. The concept originated in science and has found its way into several legal instruments in relation to fisheries and conservation. Nevertheless, its uptake remains patchy and genuine ecosystem approaches, which are not compromised by human wants and needs, are rare.

Two further developments are worthy of note. First, the emergence of the concept of 'governance', which has no universally accepted definition but can be conceived of as comprising the institutions and groups (at any level), rules (binding and non-binding laws) and processes involved in decision-making.[51] In essence, it broadens the legal lens by including non-State actors (such as corporations, expert bodies, NGOs, civil society, community and traditional groups) and formal and informal laws, as well as regulatory instruments devised by other bodies (codes of conduct imposed on members of peak bodies, for example). International law is constrained in terms of the actors involved – only States can make and enforce international law – and yet the power of corporations and civil society cannot be underestimated. Many treaty bodies, relevant to oceans, seas and shorelines, permit observers in their proceedings and draw on the expertise of non-governmental organisations such as the International Union for Conservation of Nature (IUCN).[52] Intergovernmental bodies, such as the Arctic Council, have gone further and permitted the involvement of organisations of Indigenous Arctic peoples as permanent participants.[53] Yet international law, given its inherent focus on States, is ill-equipped to provide a forum for multiple stakeholders.

The final way in which some of the limitations of early underpinnings of legal approaches to oceans, seas and shorelines may be overcome is by taking a rights-based approach, through for example a right to a healthy environment and/or by extending rights to the non-human world. Human rights by definition are only extended to *Homo sapiens* and the fundamental human rights contained in the *Universal Declaration of Human Rights* and the two Covenants do not refer to the environment.[54] There were few global developments in this area until 2012

Defining legal approaches

Laws are rules adopted by formal governing authorities (governments and other social institutions) recognised as binding and enforceable. Laws can be written (Acts, statutes, legislation) or drawn from court judgments (case law).

Policy is not law, as it is non-binding and provides the overarching aims an authority is seeking to achieve. Law is one tool that can be used to achieve policy goals.

Regulations often augment the law and themselves may be binding rules or non-binding. The latter can take the form of governmental guidelines or procedures that provide greater detail than the law itself. In some cases, private organisations (such as companies and associations) adopt non-binding codes of conduct and other self-regulatory instruments.

Governance is a broader concept that comprises laws and regulations, as well as governing authorities and other institutions, plus processes for law- and decision-making. It can also include a wider range of actors, beyond governing and public actors, including private industry, non-governmental organisations, civil society groups and experts. Various forms or types of governance have developed including multi-layered governance, collaborative ecosystem governance and, relevantly, oceans governance.

when the Human Rights Council appointed an expert to explore human rights to a healthy environment leading to the recognition of such rights in 2020.[55] Yet, much earlier, the *Stockholm Declaration* had noted that

> [b]oth aspects of [hu]man's environment, the natural and the [hu]man-made, are essential to his [sic] well-being and to the enjoyment of basic human rights the right to life itself' and that people 'have the fundamental right to freedom, equality and adequate conditions of life, in an environment of a quality.[56]

In the intervening years, the right to an environment of quality or a healthy environment has since been enshrined in a number of regional Charters,[57] national constitutions and Bills of Rights.[58] Clearly, a rights-based approach can be applied to other living things, and indeed a right of legal standing to bring proceedings to protect the environment has been legislated in some jurisdictions – notably in nations such as the US and Australia. Yet to date no global instrument, and only very limited national jurisdictions, have recognised the rights of nature. Instead, sentient animals are commonly treated as private property. Notwithstanding this lack of legal recognition, in the past decades some advances have been made with forests, mountains and rivers being given rights in India, New Zealand and Colombia.[59] In addition the draft *Universal Declaration of Ocean Rights*[60] and the draft *Declaration for the Rights of Antarctica*[61] evidence growing interest in rights-based approaches. Therefore, arguably, the progression of marine environmental laws could involve a rights-based approach to provide fairer and more just outcomes for oceans.

Conclusion

The negotiation and ratification of UNCLOS, despite the difficulties of the process, is widely recognised as a considerable achievement. The key aim of UNCLOS was to provide an international legal framework for settling maritime zones, managing competing interests in the use of the world's oceans and seas, and creating certainty and a systematic approach to the law of the sea drawing on centuries of maritime knowledge. Its longevity and continued support speak to its resilience in the face of growing challenges. Nevertheless, it is appropriate to ask the question of whether UNCLOS can be judged as successful. Just as the 'commons' were enclosed on land, so too were large and productive parts of the ocean. The goal was to give States greater management over larger marine areas, in part to resolve disputes about them, but also to incentivise care and control of the ocean environment. Arguably UNCLOS has enabled exploitation close to, and in some cases beyond, sustainable limits.

So is UNCLOS, as a 'constitution for the oceans', equipped for the future? It could be argued that many of its provisions, such as the obligations to protect and preserve the marine environment, have not been effective. On the other hand, it may be unreasonable to expect that a single legal instrument can prevent degradation of oceans, seas and shorelines. Multiple international environmental treaties and maritime law conventions serve to fill some of the gaps with successes in certain areas as the following chapters explore. Yet these laws provide considerable flexibility for nations to interpret the provisions and implement them in ways that suit the domestic context, which can hinder uniformity and the global uptake of best practice. Compliance is also challenging, given the lack of any global body to monitor implementation, and the absence of a framework of measures to address non-compliance. Enforcement involves gathering evidence to prove a breach of the law, and sometimes bringing court proceedings to resolve disputes or sanction offenders. Increasing compliance with the law would assist it to become more effective without the need for costly, and politico-legally unattractive, enforcement efforts.

Frequently legal developments have been reactive rather than proactive, and even collectively gaps remain in the legal landscape. Although some laws have certainly been progressive, there is no assurance that regression cannot occur, particularly in the face of human, food and economic security concerns, which continue to trump the needs of oceans. It is therefore arguable whether genuine protection and preservation of marine species, ecosystems, habitats and processes can be achieved until there is a fundamental shift in philosophical approaches to, and conceptual underpinnings of, laws for oceans, seas and shorelines. The chapters that follow seek to expand on the legal history in relation to a selection of legal sub-fields and topics, before returning to future prospects for oceans, seas and shorelines.

The developments described earlier demonstrate various efforts made to overcome the conceptual land-sea divide, to constrain the doctrine of freedom of the seas and to extend the concept of rights beyond the human realm. However, they are currently limited in their effectiveness and have yet to provide a meaningful form of ocean justice. The concept of justice for oceans has emerged relatively recently with 'blue justice' focusing on fisheries and ensuring blue economy and blue growth initiatives are sustainable and free from crime.[62] Broader conceptions of 'ocean justice', although nascent, seek to expand thinking beyond the ocean as a source of fungible resources, to encompass more ecological, holistic imaginaries.[63] However, despite the promise that such a concept provides, the role that law can play in facilitating ocean justice – at least in the context of the body of law explored in this book – remains opaque.

Notes

1 In this book oceans and seas are considered as saltwater areas. Shorelines means the place where the saltwater meets land and is used synonymously with seashore and coastline. Marine and coastal are words also used to reflect the saltwater environment and the land-water interface.

2 Archaeologists have found some of the earliest evidence of marine harvesting by modern humans on the south coast of South Africa, dating from about 160,000 years ago in a period known as the Middle Stone Age. One site contained marine fish bones and bone spears as well as the remains of fur seals, penguins and marine birds. See for example Rintaro Ono, "Human History of Maritime Exploitation and Adaptation Process to Coastal and Marine Environments: A View from the Case of Wallacea and the Pacific," in *Applied Studies of Coastal and Marine Environments*, ed. Maged Marghany (Croatia: InTech, 2016), accessed March 1, 2024, www.intechopen.com/chapters/49956. See also John R. Gillis, *The Human Shore* (Chicago: University of Chicago Press, 2012), 5.

3 Laws are binding and enforceable rules adopted by formal governing authorities (governments, councils and other social institutions recognised as having official power to govern societies). Laws can be written (Acts, statutes, legislation), drawn from court judgments (case law), or unwritten, depending upon the legal system utilised. Law can be distinguished from policy which is non-binding and provides the overarching aims a governing authority is seeking to achieve. Law is one tool that can be used to achieve policy goals.

4 Alan M. Friedlander, "Marine Conservation Oceania: Past, Present and Future," *Marine Pollution Bulletin* 135 (2018): 139–49.

5 Ibid.

6 See, for example, Callum Roberts, *The Unnatural History of the Sea* (Washington, DC: Island Press, 2007) and Larry A. Nielsen, "The Evolution of Fisheries Management Philosophy," *Marine Fisheries Review* 1226 (1976): 15–23.
7 Although such implementation remains piecemeal, as set out in the chapters that follow.
8 Friedlander, "Marine Conservation Oceania." See also R. E. Johannes, "The Renaissance of Community-Based Marine Resource Management in Oceania," *Annual Review of Ecology and Systematics* 33 (2002): 317–40.
9 MaryJane Proulx, Lydia Ross, Christina Macdonald, Shayla Fitzsimmons, and Michael Smit, "Indigenous Traditional Ecological Knowledge and Ocean Observing: A Review of Successful Partnerships," *Frontiers in Marine Science* 21, no. 8 (2021): 1–17, www.frontiersin.org/articles/10.3389/fmars.2021.703938/full.
10 Nonie Sharp, "Reimagining Sea Space: From Grotius to Mabo," in *Customary Marine Tenure in Australia*, ed. Nicholas Peterson and Bruce Rigsby (Sydney: Sydney University Press, 2019), https://open.sydneyuniversitypress.com.au/9781743323892/cmta-reimagining-sea-space-from-grotius-to-mabo.html#Chapter3.
11 Proulx et al., "Indigenous Traditional Ecological Knowledge," 2.
12 R. E. Johannes, "Traditional Marine Conservation Methods in Oceania and Their Demise," *Annual Review of Ecology and Systematics* 9 (1978): 349–64.
13 See "Peace of Westphalia," *Encyclopaedia Britannica*, accessed March 1, 2024, www.britannica.com/event/Peace-of-Westphalia.
14 *Land Acquisition Act (2006)*, s.1.
15 Jurisdiction means the extent of any law- and decision-making power. A jurisdiction can be a whole nation, province or locally defined area, or a specific set of activities over which power or control is exercised.
16 In many countries, different levels of government control the shoreline than offshore marine areas. In Australia, for example, local governments have jurisdiction between the high and low water marks. State governments control from the low water mark seaward to 3 nautical miles and the Commonwealth government has jurisdiction beyond that.
17 Sharp, "Reimagining Sea Space."
18 Hugo Grotius, *The Freedom of the Seas, or the Right Which Belongs to the Dutch to Take Part in the East Indian Trade. A Dissertation* (translated with a revision of the Latin text of 1633 by Ralph van Deman Magoffin) (Oxford: Oxford University Press, 1916), 28.
19 Ibid.
20 Alison Reiser, "Hugo Grotius, Free Seas, and the Political Biology of Herring," in *Blue Legalities: The Life and Laws of the Sea*, ed. Irus Braverman and Elizabeth R. Johnson (Durham: Duke University Press, 2019), 201–3.
21 John Burgess et al., eds., *Law of the Sea: A Policy Primer* (Medford, MA: The Fletcher School of Law and Diplomacy, Tufts University, 2017), 6.
22 "Declaration Respecting Maritime Law. Paris, 16 April 1856," *International Committee of the Red Cross (ICRC)*, accessed March 1, 2024, https://ihl-databases.icrc.org/en/ihl-treaties/paris-decl-1856.
23 Anonymous, "Limitations on the Doctrine of Governmental Immunity from Suit," *Columbia Law Review* 41, no. 7 (November 1941): 1236–47.
24 John H. Latané, "The Freedom of the Seas," *The Annals of the American Academy of Political and Social Science* 84, no. 1 (January 1919): 161–70.
25 Editors of Encyclopaedia, "Fourteen Points," *Encyclopedia Britannica* (January 1, 2022), accessed March 1, 2024, www.britannica.com/event/Fourteen-Points.

26 "Oceans and the Law of the Sea," *United Nations*, accessed March 1, 2024, www.un.org/en/global-issues/oceans-and-the-law-of-the-sea.
27 In maritime law the doctrine of 'freedom of the seas' refers to the 'high seas', meaning all parts of the oceans and seas of the planet that are not part of a territorial sea or internal waters of a state. The high seas make up half of Earth's surface and cover over two-thirds of the world's ocean.
28 In this book, UNCLOS is used throughout, but in other publications the same Convention is referred to as the Law of the Sea Convention (LOSC). For the full text of UNCLOS, see "United Nations Convention on the Law of the Sea," *United Nations*, accessed March 1, 2024, www.un.org/depts/los/convention_agreements/texts/unclos/closindx.htm.
29 Interestingly, the term 'high seas' remained in use.
30 UNCLOS Part XI.
31 See UNCLOS Articles 30 and 31 in relation to warships, and Article 253 regarding marine scientific research.
32 See UNCLOS Article 204 regarding monitoring the risks or effects of pollution.
33 House of Lords, *The Law of the Sea in the 21st Century* (London: House of Lords, 2022), accessed March 1, 2024, https://committees.parliament.uk/publications/9005/documents/159002/default/, 15–16.
34 Josh Davis, "Steller's Sea Cow: The First Historical Extinction of a Marine Mammal at Human Hands," *Natural History Museum*, accessed March 1, 2024, www.nhm.ac.uk/discover/stellers-sea-cow-first-historical-extinction-of-marine-mammal-at-human-hands.html.
35 Roberts, *The Unnatural History of the Sea*, 163–70.
36 Ibid. See also Nielsen, "The Evolution of Fisheries Management Philosophy."
37 Gregory Ferguson-Cradler, "Fisheries' Collapse and the Making of a Global Event, 1950s–1970s," *Journal of Global History* 13, no. 3 (2018): 399–424, https://doi.org/10.1017/S1740022818000219.
38 Rachel Carson, *Silent Spring* (Boston, MA: Houghton Mifflin, 1962).
39 Rachel Carson, *Under the Sea-Wind* (1941), *The Sea around Us* (1950) and *The Edge of the Sea* (1955), reprinted as Rachel Carson, *The Sea Trilogy* (New York: Library of America, 2021).
40 Garret Hardin, "Tragedy of the Commons," *Science* 162 (1968): 1243–48.
41 These developments are explored in the chapters that follow.
42 For the full text of the Stockholm Declaration see "Report of the United Nations Conference on the Human Environment," *United Nations*, accessed March 1, 2024, https://documents.un.org/doc/undoc/gen/nl7/300/05/pdf/nl730005.pdf.
43 "United Nations Sustainable Development," *Agenda 21*, accessed March 1, 2024, https://sustainabledevelopment.un.org/content/documents/Agenda21.pdf, para. 17.7.
44 "Transforming Our World: The 2030 Agenda for Sustainable Development," *United Nations*, accessed March 1, 2024, https://sdgs.un.org/2030agenda.
45 Agenda 21, para. 17.6, 17.11, 17.15, 17.17 and 17.134.
46 "Marine Spatial Planning," *UNESCO Intergovernmental Oceanographic Commission*, accessed March 1, 2024, www.ioc.unesco.org/en/marine-spatial-planning.
47 C. Ehler., J. Zaucha, and K. Gee, "Maritime/Marine Spatial Planning at the Interface of Research and Practice," in *Maritime Spatial Planning*, ed. J. Zaucha and K. Gee (Cham: Palgrave Macmillan, 2019), https://doi.org/10.1007/978-3-319-98696-8_1.
48 "Marae Moana: The Sacred Ocean," *Conservation International*, accessed March 1, 2024, www.conservation.org/projects/marae-moana-cook-islands-marine-park.
49 An ecosystem can be distinguished from an individual or group of species as it includes all the living things in a specific area and how they interact with the non-living environment. Ecosystem thinking is, therefore, holistic and respects the interconnectedness of all elements of the ocean.

50 "Ecosystem-based Approaches," *United Nations Environment Programmes (UNEP)*, accessed March 1, 2024, www.unep.org/topics/ocean-seas-and-coasts/ecosystem-based-approaches.
51 The concept was referred to in Agenda 21 and subsequent global conferences. In the final report of the Rio +20 Conference on Sustainable Development (2012), it was said that 'effective governance at the local, subnational, national, regional and globals levels [requires] the voices and interests of all is critical for advancing sustainable development', in United Nations General Assembly, *The Future We Want*, UNGA Res A/66/288 (2012), para. 76 and 252.
52 The IUCN has a role in the World Heritage Convention in relation to natural heritage sites, and also under several wildlife treaties.
53 "Arctic Council," accessed March 1, 2024, https://arctic-council.org/.
54 "Human Rights Instruments," *UN Human Rights*, accessed March 1, 2024, www.ohchr.org/en/instruments-listings.
55 "Special Rapporteur on Human Rights and the Environment," *UN Human Rights*, accessed March 1, 2024, www.ohchr.org/en/special-procedures/sr-environment
56 Stockholm Declaration Principle 1.
57 African Charter of Human and Peoples' Rights, the Additional Protocol to the American Convention on Human Rights in the Area of Economic, Social and Cultural Rights, the Arab Charter of Human Rights and the Association of Southeast Asian Nations' Human Rights Declaration.
58 Over 75% of States recognise the right to a healthy environment either through regional human rights treaties, national constitutions or through domestic legislation.
59 See Chapter 7.
60 "Towards a Universal Declaration of Ocean Rights (UDOR)," *Earth Law Centre*, accessed March 1, 2024, www.earthlawcenter.org/ocean-rights.
61 "Declaration for the Rights of Antarctica," *Antarctica Rights*, accessed March 1, 2024, www.antarcticarights.org/.
62 "Blue Justice," accessed March 1, 2024, https://bluejustice.org/.
63 See, for example, "Ocean Justice," accessed March 1, 2024, https://oceanjustice.com.au/.

Bibliography

Anonymous. "Limitations on the Doctrine of Governmental Immunity from Suit." *Columbia Law Review* 41, no. 7 (November 1941): 1236–47.

Antarctica Rights. "Declaration for the Rights of Antarctica." Accessed March 1, 2024, www.antarcticarights.org/.

"Arctic Council." Accessed March 1, 2024. https://arctic-council.org/.

"Blue Justice." Accessed March 1, 2024. https://bluejustice.org/.

Burgess, John et al., eds. *Law of the Sea: A Policy Primer*. Medford, MA: The Fletcher School of Law and Diplomacy, Tufts University, 2017. https://sites.tufts.edu/lawofthesea/files/2017/07/LawoftheSeaPrimer.pdf

Carson, Rachel. *Silent Spring*. Boston, MA: Houghton Mifflin, 1962.

Carson, Rachel. *Under the Sea-Wind* (1941), *The Sea Around Us* (1950), *The Edge of the Sea* (1955). Reprinted as Rachel Carson, *The Sea Trilogy*. New York: Library of America, 2021.

Conservation International. "Marae Moana: The Sacred Ocean." Accessed March 1, 2024. www.conservation.org/projects/marae-moana-cook-islands-marine-park.

Davis, Josh. "Steller's Sea Cow: The First Historical Extinction of a Marine Mammal at Human Hands." *Natural History Museum*. Accessed March 1, 2024. https://www.nhm.ac.uk/discover/stellers-sea-cow-first-historical-extinction-of-marine-mammal-at-human-hands.html.

Earth Law Centre. "Towards a Universal Declaration of Ocean Rights (UDOR)." Accessed March 1, 2024. www.earthlawcenter.org/ocean-rights.

Editors of the Encyclopaedia Britannica. "Fourteen Points." *Encyclopedia Britannica* (January 1, 2022). Accessed March 1, 2024. www.britannica.com/event/Fourteen-Points

Editors of the Encyclopaedia Britannica. "Peace of Westphalia." *Encyclopaedia Britannica*. Accessed March 1, 2024. www.britannica.com/event/Peace-of-Westphalia.

Ehler, C., J. Zaucha, and K. Gee. "Maritime/Marine Spatial Planning at the Interface of Research and Practice." In *Maritime Spatial Planning*, edited by J. Zaucha and K. Gee. Cham: Palgrave Macmillan, 2019. Accessed March 1, 2024. https://doi.org/10.1007/978-3-319-98696-8_1.

Ferguson-Cradler, Gregory. "Fisheries' Collapse and the Making of a Global Event, 1950s–1970s." *Journal of Global History* 13, no. 3 (2018): 399–424. https://doi.org/10.1017/S1740022818000219.

Friedlander, Alan M. "Marine Conservation Oceania: Past, Present and Future." *Marine Pollution Bulletin* 135 (2018): 139–49.

Gillis, John R. *The Human Shore*. Chicago: University of Chicago Press, 2012.

Grotius, Hugo. *The Freedom of the Seas, or the Right Which Belongs to the Dutch to Take Part in the East Indian Trade. A Dissertation*. Translated with a revision of the Latin text of 1633 by Ralph van Deman Magoffin. Oxford: Oxford University Press, 1916.

Hardin, Garret. "Tragedy of the Commons." *Science* 162 (1968): 1243–48.

House of Lords. *The Law of the Sea in the 21st Century*. London: House of Lords, 2022. Accessed March 1, 2024, https://committees.parliament.uk/publications/9005/documents/159002/default/, 15–16.

International Committee of the Red Cross (ICRC). "Declaration Respecting Maritime Law. Paris, 16 April 1856." Accessed March 1, 2024. https://ihl-databases.icrc.org/en/ihl-treaties/paris-decl-1856.

Johannes, R. E. "The Renaissance of Community-Based Marine Resource Management in Oceania." *Annual Review of Ecology and Systematics* 33 (2002): 317–40.

Johannes, R. E. "Traditional Marine Conservation Methods in Oceania and Their Demise." *Annual Review of Ecology and Systematics* 9 (1978): 349–64.

Latané, John H. "The Freedom of the Seas." *The Annals of the American Academy of Political and Social Science* 84, no. 1 (January 1919): 161–70.

Nielsen, Larry A. "The Evolution of Fisheries Management Philosophy." *Marine Fisheries Review* 1226 (1976): 15–23.

"Ocean Justice." Accessed March 1, 2024. https://oceanjustice.com.au/.

Ono, Rintaro. "Human History of Maritime Exploitation and Adaptation Process to Coastal and Marine Environments: A View from the Case of Wallacea and the Pacific." In *Applied Studies of Coastal and Marine Environments*, edited by Maged Marghany. Croatia: InTech, 2016. Accessed March 1, 2024. www.intechopen.com/chapters/49956.

Proulx, MaryJane et al. "Indigenous Traditional Ecological Knowledge and Ocean Observing: A Review of Successful Partnerships." *Frontiers in Marine Science* 21, no. 8 (2021): 1–17. www.frontiersin.org/articles/10.3389/fmars.2021.703938/full.

Reiser, Alison. "Hugo Grotius, Free Seas, and the Political Biology of Herring." In *Blue Legalities: The Life and Laws of the Sea*, edited by Irus Braverman and Elizabeth R. Johnson. Durham: Duke University Press, 2019.

Roberts, Callum. *The Unnatural History of the Sea*. Washington, DC: Island Press, 2007.

Sharp, Nonie. "Reimagining Sea Space: From Grotius to Mabo." In *Customary Marine Tenure in Australia*, edited by Nicholas Peterson and Bruce Rigsby. Sydney: Sydney University Press, 2019. https://open.sydneyuniversitypress.com.au/9781743323892/cmta-reimagining-sea-space-from-grotius-to-mabo.html#Chapter3.

UN Human Rights. "Human Rights Instruments." Accessed March 1, 2024. www.ohchr.org/en/instruments-listings.

UN Human Rights. "Special Rapporteur on Human Rights and the Environment." Accessed March 1, 2024. www.ohchr.org/en/special-procedures/sr-environment
UNESCO Intergovernmental Oceanographic Commission. "Marine Spatial Planning." Accessed March 1, 2024. www.ioc.unesco.org/en/marine-spatial-planning.
United Nations. "Oceans and the Law of the Sea." Accessed March 1, 2024. www.un.org/en/global-issues/oceans-and-the-law-of-the-sea.
United Nations. "Report of the United Nations Conference on the Human Environment." Accessed March 1, 2024. https://documents.un.org/doc/undoc/gen/nl7/300/05/pdf/nl730005.pdf.
United Nations. "Transforming Our World: the 2030 Agenda for Sustainable Development." Accessed March 1, 2024. https://sdgs.un.org/2030agenda.
United Nations. "United Nations Convention on the Law of the Sea." Accessed March 1, 2024. www.un.org/depts/los/convention_agreements/texts/unclos/closindx.htm.
United Nations Environment Programme (UNEP). "Ecosystem-Based Approaches." Accessed March 1, 2024. www.unep.org/topics/ocean-seas-and-coasts/ecosystem-based-approaches.
United Nations General Assembly. *The Future We Want*. UNGA Res A/66/288 (2012).
United Nations Sustainable Development. "Agenda 21." Accessed March 1, 2024, https://sustainabledevelopment.un.org/content/documents/Agenda21.pdf.

2 Fluid boundaries

Shoreline borders and maritime zones

At sea, as on land and in the air, authority has been spatially allocated, within designated boundaries, in order to serve a variety of legal and administrative purposes: to assert rights, to acknowledge responsibilities, and to clarify the scope of designated kinds of official action.

Douglas M Johnston, 1998

Overview

The part of Earth's surface that we know as the world ocean has undergone many changes in deep geological time. Indeed, throughout Earth's history, the planet's crust has been endlessly shaped and reshaped by the forces of plate tectonics, erosion and climate, altering the amount of land that rises above sea level. The modern coastline of mainland Australia, for example, was only formed around 6,000 years ago, at the end of the last Ice Age. Prior to that, much of the world's ocean water was locked away in the form of continental ice and global sea levels were much lower, exposing land that is now underwater.[1] These changes occur at extreme timescales, yet climate change is now causing movements in land along shorelines, and altering sea levels faster than ever before, ensuring that the law relating to ocean boundaries remains highly relevant today.

As human societies and settlements began to form on coastal land, customs and rules invariably emerged, evolving into customary tenure systems with land considered common property and communities having shared rights to its use and enjoyment together with stewardship obligations.[2] Some of the traditional, customary tenure systems have persisted or been restored in recent decades.[3] Under the Roman Empire, however, exclusive use of land became well-accepted and the practice consolidated in subsequent feudal systems and the enclosure of 'commons'.[4] The ability of people to privately own terrestrial land became widespread in western industrialised States from the 19th century.[5] Eventually, these would become real or private property rights,[6] which persist today and permit ownership of land with the control and management of those spaces being in private hands.

DOI: 10.4324/9781003005261-4

Conversely, coastal waters and submerged lands were generally considered in law as public property, belonging to the State and not able to be privately owned in the same way as terrestrial areas.[7] Whilst not universal, many traditional and Indigenous peoples continued to maintain or claim communal tenure rights across the land-water interface.[8] The shoreline thus came to represent a boundary, dividing ocean from land although, in some places, traditional and/or community rights of access came into conflict with those claiming ownership and control.[9]

With the rise of nation States, land was redefined as sovereign territory within national borders, and territorial claims were also made to adjacent marine areas. Coastal or near-shore waters, with their rich marine ecosystems, have long played a key role in human survival. Early human populations relied heavily on the living resources of these areas for sustenance and later for barter and trade. The right to use coastal waters for migration, navigation and transport was also relied upon. As outlined in Chapter 1, the concept of the freedom of the seas underpinned the uses of marine areas and became an established legal principle in western European law from the 17th century. During the 20th century, however, coastal fishing dramatically escalated, with over 90% of the world's fish catches harvested in these waters highlighting their economic value to adjacent coastal States.[10] The extent of State ownership of these waters became increasingly controversial and was not finally settled until the adoption of the *UN Convention on the Law of the Sea* (UNCLOS) in 1982.[11] One of the key objectives of UNCLOS was to divide the world's oceans and seas, not by property rights but by jurisdictional areas known as maritime zones. Property boundaries and jurisdictional zones require legal definitions and delimitation rules. We find these rules in property law and the law of the sea.[12] This chapter explores the legal history of boundary-making, and the rules that have been adopted for coastal and maritime zones at the shoreline and in oceans and seas.

Coasts and shorelines

As explored in Chapter 1, not all worldviews abruptly separate land from water. But in most States in the world, there are clear divisions and differential legal arrangements for land and sea. Land is where we humans live and the shoreline where we engage with the ocean, and so it is appropriate that the law that applies at the coastline is explored first.

State interests

States have keen interests in coastlines as they demarcate the limits of national territory. Coastline boundaries are notoriously difficult to measure – their length varies depending on the method of measurement used and the level of detail represented in maps. The fractal (non-regular) properties of coastlines also present difficulties in delimiting shoreline boundaries, a problem known as the 'coastline paradox'.[13] As a result, the geographical complexity of shorelines has led to conflicts between neighbouring coastal States. These issues have largely been resolved since UNCLOS was adopted, although boundary disputes do still exist.

The Alaskan Panhandle

In 1903, the boundary between Alaska and Canada on the fjord-dense region known as the 'Alaskan Panhandle' became the subject of international arbitration over a dispute between the United Kingdom (then responsible for Canada's borders) and the US. During the 18th and 19th centuries Russian explorers, whalers and traders began colonising this coastal region across the Bering Sea – the traditional territories of the Łingit (Tlingit) and Haida peoples – with its abundant populations of fish and sea otters. In 1825 the Russian and British governments signed the Treaty of Saint Petersburg, defining Russia's territory along the southern coastline and inland to 10 marine leagues (56 kilometres). The mountainous eastern area was not regarded as valuable and remained unbounded. In 1867, as the Canadian colonies moved towards Confederation, Russia sold its Alaskan territory to the US without a clear delineation of the eastern portion. The matter came to a head with the Klondike gold rush in 1897 when the US and Canada disputed how the eastern border, as defined in the 1825 Treaty, should be measured from the coast. The US argued that the coast was defined as the point where the Pacific Ocean waters touched the mainland, while the Canadians considered it to be the western boundary of the channel islands. A joint commission in 1898–99 failed to settle the dispute, but an international tribunal appointed to resolve the boundary issue ruled in favour of the US, prompting Canada to pursue an independent foreign policy.[14]

Private property rights

Within individual nations, it is terrestrial land which individuals, corporations and other groups can own. Ownership rights in relation to land were once more absolute than they are today, with owners able to do what they wished. They are now subject to planning, development and environmental laws, but still landowners can choose to develop, reside or operate businesses, farm or rewild land that they own. The body of law related to terrestrial land ownership is known as real estate, real property or private property law and, as discussed later, does have some limited relevance to oceans, seas and shorelines. Real property in private hands ends where the land meets the sea. In contrast to terrestrial areas, the marine environment is publicly owned, and across the world it is governments that control and manage both the waters and the submerged lands seaward of the shoreline.

However, the precise point at which terrestrial land ends and the ocean begins is not easy to define. The interface between land and ocean is naturally fluid, subject to tidal changes and, increasingly, rising sea levels. Defining the shoreline boundary is, therefore, no easy task. As Rachel Carson noted:

> For no two successive days is the shoreline precisely the same. Not only do the tides advance and retreat in their eternal rhythms, but the level of the sea itself is never at rest. . . . Today a little more land may belong to the sea, tomorrow a little less. Always the edge of the sea remains an elusive and indefinable boundary.[15]

Yet as will be seen throughout this book, lawmakers have constantly defined the indefinable and divided and categorised objects, places and living things, sometimes illogically and in unhelpful ways. In terms of shoreline and real property law, scientific knowledge and data has been utilised to define the boundary, and to provide some additional rules to account for natural, dynamic, tidal processes which can shift and change this boundary.[16]

Under Roman Law in the 6th century CE, the seashore was considered 'common to all [hu]mankind' and 'extends as far as the greatest winter flood runs up'.[17] In medieval English courts the theory of 'public trust doctrine' evolved,[18] and the high water mark was settled as the legal boundary between tidal waters and terrestrial land in the 17th century.[19] Today, land (including submerged land) seaward of the high water mark belongs to the State or Crown and is held in trust for public purposes.[20] The high water mark, of course, is not itself fixed and has been variously defined based on statistical averages depending on tides and phases of the Moon. Detailed rules in each jurisdiction provide for the calculation but, in each case, it is the high water mark that separates tidal waters and terrestrial land.

Beyond cyclical changes, there are other natural coastal processes that can gradually alter the land-water interface. Accretion refers to the gradual deposits of alluvion and sediment through the action of tidal waters which have the effect of imperceptibly increasing the land area. Similarly, if tidal waters retreat (dereliction) more land is exposed above the high water mark. In both cases the property boundary moves seaward and the landowner's area increases. Conversely, where water advances (diluvion), or if tidal waters wash away coastal deposits (erosion), terrestrial land is lost and the property boundary moves landward, reducing the area of land in private ownership.

These legal rules demonstrate how lawmakers have responded to scientific knowledge of oceans, defining boundaries in ways that can be calculated and accounting for natural ocean processes which dynamically alter shorelines. This law remains relevant today because these coastal processes continue as they have always done. Climate change has, however, shone a new light on this field of law, with sea level rise already occurring in some places and extreme weather events resulting in increased coastal erosion. Similarly, weather events can result in depositions of sand and other material along different parts of the shoreline, increasing land areas for some landowners. The same legal rules apply to these impacts of climate change, provided they are natural and gradual. Nevertheless, no compensation is payable for the loss or gain of land in these circumstances. This raises several current concerns: whether landowners have a right to defend property against the sea,[21] and/or whether governments have obligations to intervene to protect coastal property.[22]

Intertidal zones

Seaward of the high water mark, the seabed is regarded as public (Crown) land held by the government, although this public land can usually be sold by the government.[23] Between the high and low water mark are tidal areas which are in public hands, although often managed by State, provincial or local governments. These rules are different between nations and are therefore regulated by domestic law. Exploring seawards, it is the law of the sea – as international law – that provides rules for determining how much of marine territory nations own or control. Under the law of the sea, it is the low water mark that is used as the baseline for calculating the territorial seas.

Sea country rights: the Blue Mud Bay case

The right to control the intertidal zone (the area between the high and low tide mark) has been a controversial matter for coastal Indigenous peoples around the world, particularly those seeking to reinvigorate traditional ownership rights. In 2008, a landmark decision was made by the High Court of Australia in what became known as the Blue Mud Bay case, a large, partly enclosed bay on the eastern coast of Arnhem Land in the Northern Territory. The coastal and marine areas of northern Australia are renowned for their large tidal ranges and abundance of marine life in the intertidal zone. This 'sea country' also contains traditional sacred sites and songlines that have the same cultural importance as those on land. The case, brought by the Yolngu people, confirmed that traditional owners of Aboriginal-owned areas on the Northern Territory coastline have exclusive access rights to the tidal waters overlying their land. In other words, the intertidal zone was legally 'Aboriginal land', regardless of the fact that tidal waters may periodically cover it.[24] Prior to the High Court decision, an interim arrangement was in place, allowing commercial operators and recreational fishers to fish in these areas, but the Court found that a fishing licence granted by the local fisheries authorities did not authorise the holder to enter waters within the boundaries of Aboriginal land which, under local laws, extends to the low water mark.

The right to control the intertidal zone in the Northern Territory has had wider implications for the recognition of traditional laws and customs under common law, providing for Aboriginal people to hunt and gather resources and maintain their cultural traditions.[25]

Figure 2.1 Totora reed fishing boats on the beach at Huanchaco, Peru. (Image courtesy of Roy & Danielle.)

History of ocean boundary-making

Early claims

Coastal communities and coastal States have always laid claim to ownership and/or control of coastal waters, simultaneously maintaining the freedom of the high seas. With increasing geographical knowledge and maritime trade, conflicts mounted over the rights of States to navigate, claim and exploit the maritime environment more broadly, and the question of who controls ocean spaces would become a matter of debate amongst the leading jurists of European maritime powers. During the Roman Empire, the world's oceans and seas were regarded as *res communis* – belonging to everyone – and free to be used but not appropriated. That changed after the fall of the Roman Empire when oceans and seas came to be regarded as *res nullius* – belonging to no one – and subject to claims by maritime powers.

The first recorded ocean boundary in western European history was imposed by Pope Alexander VI in the Treaty of Tordesillas on 7 June 1494. The papal bulls established a line of demarcation between Spanish and Portuguese territories around the globe, extending from the North Pole to the South Pole, granting Spain exclusive navigation rights to those parts of the globe that lay to the west of the line and those parts that lay to the east to Portugal. Nevertheless, with no means of determining longitude and little knowledge of the location of the world's oceans and continents, the precise location of the boundary line proved elusive and territorial disputes occasionally erupted.[26] A new boundary was sanctioned in 1506, enabling the Portuguese empire to claim the coastline of Brazil and ultimately to colonise large areas of the South American continent.[27] Significantly, this history highlighted prevailing attitudes towards the ocean and the lack of regard to the needs of the marine environment. The international agreements were used to provide a basis for claiming territories that were not yet discovered and bestowed legal authority over ocean resources.[28]

Grotius, Selden and van Bynkershoek

It was the Dutch East India Company, formed by the Dutch government in 1602, that commissioned Hugo Grotius, the Dutch jurist and scholar, to defend its right to a Portuguese merchant ship it had seized in the Strait of Singapore. In a pamphlet known as *Mare Liberum* (*The Freedom of the Seas*) published in 1609, Grotius argued that historically the seas were free for all to use and dismissed Portuguese claims to the ocean space noting that, unlike land, people cannot inhabit the ocean or divide it into territories. Significantly, he also asserted that navigation and fishing were the primary uses of the ocean, and that these were inexhaustible. As competition increased between the Dutch and English empires over coastal fishing rights and long-distance trade routes, the English jurist John Selden made the case in his 1619 treatise *Mare clausum* ('closed sea') that a state possessed the right to control an adjacent sea, ocean or other navigable body of water as part of its sovereign territory, while recognising the concept of freedom of the seas beyond the State's national waters. His argument was based, in part, on English claims to 'sovereignty at sea dating back to pre-Norman times', and 'the principle that seas beyond the horizon . . . are open to all nations'.[29]

Europe's maritime powers considered various proposals to define the extent of a state's maritime territory. In 1703 Cornelius van Bynkershoek published his treatise *De dominio maris dissertation*, proposing a 3-nautical-mile territorial sea that represented the distance a cannon shot could be fired from shore to effectively protect it. This 'cannon-shot rule' became an accepted legal principle for delimiting maritime territory amongst most maritime nations, although Scandinavian States initially continued their practice of delimiting a 'continuous belt of neutrality' until that too was replaced by the cannon-shot rule.[30] It was not until the 20th century that nations began extending their jurisdiction over the oceans, some to 12 nautical miles and others to 200 nautical miles.[31] Nevertheless, and surprisingly given that technological advances in ships and weaponry during the 19th and 20th centuries increased the range of military defence of territorial waters, the cannon-shot rule largely continued to underpin the practice of delimiting territorial seas until the reformation of the international law of the sea and the settling of maritime zones under the UNCLOS.

Leading up to UNCLOS

Significant tensions did not arise until the 20th century.[32] At that time, some States sought greater rights in relation to living and non-living resources, and others raised concerns about pollution and conservation of fisheries. The League of Nations hosted a conference in 1930 but no agreements were made. In 1945, the US President, Harry S Truman, issued two executive orders known as the Truman Proclamations, setting off what Martin Glassner called 'the great sea rush of the 20th century'.[33] The first Truman Proclamation declared that the US would regulate fisheries along its coasts, although the zones would remain part of the high seas with no restrictions on navigation. The second proclamation claimed that the non-living resources on the continental shelf belonged to the US.[34] Elsewhere, some States extended their territorial seas to 12 nautical miles, and Latin American countries claimed 200 nautical mile sea territories through legislation recognising the *zona maritima*, patrimonial sea or extended territorial sea.[35] These competing claims were not ultimately settled for some decades.

By the 1950s, only a few maritime boundary agreements existed, and most human activities on the world's oceans and seas were governed using longstanding arrangements designed to facilitate the movement of ships rather than to grant coastal States jurisdiction over the marine environment adjacent to their shores. With the dramatic growth and diversification in uses of the world's oceans – facilitated by the emergence of new technologies – a more precise delimitation of maritime zones became an urgent priority. In response to attempts by various coastal States to expand control over marine areas adjacent to coastlines, the international community requested that the newly established United Nations International Law Commission consider codifying the existing laws relating to oceans. The Commission prepared four draft conventions, and these were discussed and adopted at the first Conference on the Law of the Sea by the 86 participating nations.[36] The four conventions, commonly known as the *1958*

Geneva Conventions, created legal regimes governing territorial seas and contiguous zones, the continental shelf, the high seas, and fishing and conservation of the living resources of the high seas.[37] Collectively, the four Conventions represented a significant step in international ocean law, although they were unable to find agreement on the maximum breadth of the territorial sea. These treaties remain in force today.

A second conference was held in 1960 but did not result in any new treaties. By the 1970s, controversies and uncertainties remained and had given rise to a complex range of legal regimes governing territorial control and use of coastal zones. These arrangements were the subject of negotiation at the third Conference on the Law of the Sea, which commenced in 1973 and finalised in 1982. The second conference in 1960 had failed to reach agreement on a uniform breadth for territorial seas or to establish any consensus on sovereign fishing rights. Indeed, not all nations accepted the 1958 Conventions, particularly newly independent states in Asia, Africa and Latin America seeking to control their coastal waters, bringing them into conflict with the major maritime powers. The resulting agreement effectively extended coastal State jurisdiction over increasingly expansive offshore areas, including the continental shelf, in some cases leading to more frequent maritime boundary disputes.[38] In seeking to reach a compromise on an intermediate zone between the territorial sea and high seas, however, delegates to the conference agreed to accept the term 'exclusive economic zone'. The third Conference on the Law of the Sea resulted in the adoption of the final text on the UN Convention on the Law of the Sea (UNCLOS), which finally settled the territorial sea, EEZ, and the high seas maritime zones.[39]

UNCLOS went beyond merely designating spatial boundaries. It also created jurisdictional delimitations, allocating rights and obligations to coastal, flag and port States. A boundary approach was, therefore, evident throughout this treaty. Coastal, flag and port States were given certain rights in relation to the maritime zones under UNCLOS, although these rights were balanced with obligations and the freedom of navigation and access to resources beyond state control. The focus of this chapter is coastal States, with flag States considered in the chapter on shipping (Chapter 5), and port States explored in the context of fishing and living resource harvesting (Chapters 4 and 7).

UNCLOS

Today, UNCLOS is widely accepted as the predominant legal instrument on the law of the sea and known as the 'constitution for the oceans'.[40] It divides the world's oceans into legally defined maritime areas or zones, each with separate rules associated with it. States have specific rights to regulate these areas or their citizens and registered vessels under their jurisdiction operating within them, and/or to exploit resources. These zones include the territorial sea (12 nautical miles seaward of the baseline), a contiguous zone (up to 24 nautical miles seaward), the Exclusive Economic Zone (from 12 to 200 nautical miles seaward), and the continental shelf (an area of seabed and subsoil up to 200 nautical miles beyond the territorial sea which can be extended to 350 nautical miles in some circumstances). Beyond that lies the high seas which, according to UNCLOS, no State can own.

The historical 3 nautical mile limit of the coastal waters is not mentioned in UNCLOS and yet it remains important, demonstrated by its continued reference in some federated States, such as Australia and the US, where domestic legislation provides state or provincial governments with rights and obligations relating to these areas with the federal jurisdiction limited to the balance of the territorial sea.[42]

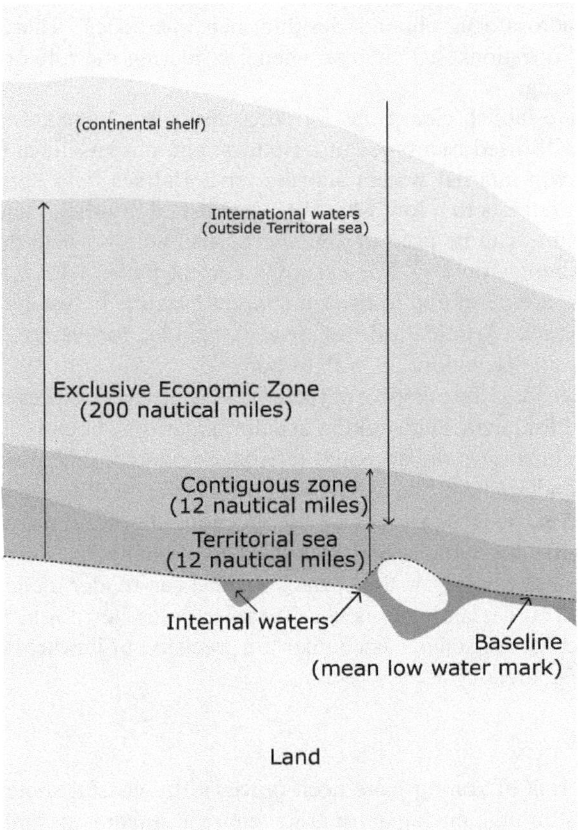

Figure 2.2 Image depicting the limits and spaces under the sovereignty or jurisdiction of the coastal State. (Image courtesy of MJ Smit.)

Source: International Institute for Law of the Sea Studies[41]

Baselines

Under the international law of the sea, each maritime zone is measured from the territorial sea baseline, a boundary defining the shoreward extent of the territorial sea. Given that coastal waters rise and fall with tidal movements, the baseline is fixed at the low-water line along the coast, a line derived from the coastal State's own maritime charts. The geography of coastlines is also extremely varied, making baseline delineation a complex task. So how are these maritime boundaries determined given that, by their very nature, they represent lines artificially imposed onto a dynamic ocean environment? Does a coastline include natural harbours, bays and inlets, and the continental shelf, and how can international laws governing oceans accommodate changes to shorelines caused by rising sea levels? How does international law deal with territorial claims to resources that migrate across ocean boundaries and maritime zones? These are some of the intriguing questions that emerge when considering the role of law in ocean boundary-making.

In order to establish clear rules for determining the boundaries of maritime zones, UNCLOS used two types of baselines: straight baselines indicating the division between internal waters and the territorial sea, and normal baselines where the sea retreats to a low water line (published in official nautical charts). Straight baselines can be used to join appropriate points where the coastline is heavily indented (Article 7). For example, coastal States with rivers emptying into the ocean are permitted to draw a straight baseline between the low-water lines on each bank (Article 9). Rules are also included for features such as bays, reefs and low-tide elevations, as well as ports.

In recent decades, the prospect of rising sea levels has also presented a significant challenge for lawmakers seeking to delimit maritime boundaries. The height of the ocean constitutes the accepted reference point for determining elevation and altitude and is therefore used to determine the limits of many territorial claims. However, rising sea levels are complicating this baseline, with important ramifications for low-lying island States, where a change in elevation of just a metre or two above or below the ocean's surface can render the legal definition of a territorial border ambiguous. As Sammler notes, territorial tensions arise 'when the averages of science encounter the precision of juridical delineation in dynamic coastal areas'.[43]

Maritime zones

Traditional forms of zoning have been practised by coastal societies for thousands of years through customary marine tenure arrangements and by sea farmers cultivating marine organisms such as molluscs, crustaceans, finfish, seaweed and algae. Whilst many coastal societies maintain traditional zoning practices, UNCLOS created the maritime zones that are used today by international and national jurisdictions to determine legal rights and obligations.

The **territorial sea** is defined in Article 3 UNCLOS as extending from the baseline seaward to 12 nautical miles. This maritime zone is the sovereign territory of States, with essentially the same rights as on land, subject only to the right of innocent passage (Article 17). Even then, however, the coastal State can adopt laws specifically relating to innocent passage in the interests of navigational safety and maritime traffic management, protection of cables and pipelines, conservation of living resources and preservation of the environment (Article 21).[44] The **contiguous zone** is a buffer zone directly adjacent to the territorial sea, where the coastal State can exercise particular rights to prevent breaches of customs, immigration, fiscal and sanitary laws (Article 33).

Unlike the other maritime zones whose existence was derived from earlier international law, the **Exclusive Economic Zone** (EEZ) was created by negotiation as part of UNCLOS as a way to settle potential disputes between States over offshore activities such as fishing and energy production by granting certain sovereign rights to coastal States over a greater area of the ocean than the territorial sea.[45] The concept of an exclusive maritime zone for economic purposes derived from the 1945 Truman Proclamation on the right to natural resources of the subsoil and seabed of the continental shelf and coastal fisheries in certain areas of the high seas.[46] The concept was first used in national claims of Chile and Peru and in the Santiago Declaration of 1952, which stated that 'governments are bound to ensure for their peoples access to necessary food supplies and to furnish them with the means of developing their economy'.[47] It also affirmed that the EEZ should extend no less than 200 nautical miles from the coast. In Europe, the concept of an economic zone was more narrowly applied to fisheries and given expression in the 1964 European Fisheries Convention that gave each coastal State the exclusive right to fish in a 6-mile belt measured from the baseline of its territorial sea.[48]

The EEZs introduced by UNCLOS (Articles 56, 58 and 59), extending 200 nautical miles (332 kilometres) from the baseline, effectively incorporated 38% of the ocean previously considered part of the high seas. Coastal States were given the right to explore and exploit their EEZs balanced by an obligation to conserve and manage all resources – both living and non-living – found within the water, on the seafloor, or under the sea floor's subsoil within the zone.[49] Article 56 of the Convention also gave coastal States exclusive rights to engage in offshore energy generation from the waves, currents, and wind within their EEZ, and to establish and use artificial islands, installations and structures, conduct marine scientific research, and protect and conserve the marine environment through marine protected areas.[50] The Convention did not, however, give a coastal State the right to prohibit or limit freedom of navigation or overflight (subject to certain exceptions).

The complexities associated with defining the features and areas of EEZs has led to many delimitation disputes between coastal States.[51] The UNCLOS provisions on the extent of the **continental shelf** proved to be the most challenging to negotiate. Over the course of 30 years, the continental shelf had shifted from a geological concept to a highly specialised area of ocean boundary-making with the determination of seaward limits influenced by political, scientific, technological, industrial and judicial considerations relating to equity, precision and uniformity. Continental shelves make up about 8% of the area covered by the ocean. They are naturally occurring, underwater, seabed features: relatively shallow submarine terraces of continental crust formed at the edge of continental landmasses, typically extending seaward from the coast to depths of 100 to 200 metres before dropping abruptly into the area known as the continental slope.[52] Most of the world's continental shelves were first described in detail in the years after World War II, based on new understandings about the nature of the ocean environment provided by the ocean sciences and undersea technologies emerging in the post-war era.

Governments were already aware in the 1930s that the seabed contained vast reserves of submarine petroleum and that this would soon become available for exploitation with the development of deep-sea platforms and drilling techniques. However, the concept of rights over submerged lands beyond territorial waters remained dormant until 1942, when the United Kingdom and Venezuela signed a treaty dividing the submarine areas of the Gulf of Paria into two parts.[53] As explored earlier in this chapter, until then countries had recognised only two basic maritime zones without any separation of the seabed: a narrow strip of coastal waters that was under the exclusive sovereignty of the coastal State, and an unregulated area beyond that known as the high seas. As noted earlier, the US President, Harry S Truman, issued the second Truman Proclamation in 1945, claiming US jurisdiction over the resources of the continental shelf adjacent to that nation's coastline. This second proclamation represented a radical departure from existing practice by claiming that the resources on the continental shelf contiguous to the US belonged to the US. There was no provision in international law to prevent such a claim on the ocean's resources, and in response a number of States made claims to their adjacent continental shelves. Coastal States in the Arabian and Persian Gulf regions began exploiting offshore oil and gas reserves, while Chile, Peru and Ecuador claimed a 200 nautical mile (320 kilometre) limit well beyond their relatively narrow continental shelves.

The four international conventions adopted in 1958 during the first Conference on the Law of the Sea, included one on the continental shelf. Article 2 of the 1958 Convention gave coastal States the right to exercise sovereign rights over the adjacent continental shelf for the purpose of exploring it and exploiting its natural resources. Nevertheless, the principles around delimiting ocean boundaries between adjacent States remained unclear. In 1969, for example, the International Court of Justice was asked to determine the delimitation of continental shelf areas in the North Sea between Germany and Denmark and Germany and The Netherlands.[54] The Netherlands and Denmark had already drawn partial boundary lines in the North Sea based on the equidistance principle, whereby every point used to measure the territorial sea is equidistant.[55] However, Germany rejected the principle, claiming that it would result in an unequal share due to the length of its North Sea coastline and instead argued that a just and equitable method should be applied. The Court's decision – that the equidistance principle was not part of customary international law – meant that Germany was not bound by it.

With the rapid rise in world oil prices from 1973, the process of determining the seaward limits of a continental shelf – and the sovereign rights to exploit resources within it – became more critical but also highlighted the inequities associated with natural variations in coastal geography around the world. While some coastal States possessed a geographically expansive continental shelf, others had only narrow shelves or were entirely land-locked with no adjacent shelf, creating tensions between those seeking to extend the seaward limits and those demanding equal access and restrictions on the right of coastal States to encroaching further on the ocean floor of the high seas.[56] Ultimately, Article 76 of UNCLOS provided that the continental shelf comprises the seabed and subsoil that extends beyond its territorial sea of a coastal State through

> the natural prolongation of its land territory to the outer edge of the continental margin, or to a distance of 200 nautical miles from the baselines . . . [but] the outer limits of the continental shelf on the seabed shall not exceed 350 nautical miles from the baseline.

It was perhaps the most complex yet technically sophisticated formula ever created for the purposes of ocean boundary-making, requiring provision for a technical advisory committee to review each national interpretation.

The **high seas**, as a maritime zone, pre-existed UNCLOS and are essentially all areas of the ocean that are not territorial sea, EEZ, internal waters or archipelagic waters. The freedom of the seas – for navigation, overflight, laying of submarine cables and pipelines, constructing artificial islands, fishing and conducting scientific research – is preserved under the convention (Article 87). Significantly, the high seas remained an area beyond national jurisdiction, which no State can claim sovereignty over and which must be used for peaceful purposes (Articles 88 and 89).

The seabed under the high seas, known as the **Area**, was contentious in the negotiations. The Area was declared to be the common heritage of (hu)mankind, which means that it cannot be appropriated, must be used for peaceful purposes and, most controversially, the benefits must be shared. Under UNCLOS (Part XI and the *Implementing Agreement*) a new entity was created – the International Seabed Authority – to develop rules for the extraction of resources and the sharing of benefits. The mineral resources in the Area include polymetallic nodules and manganese nodules, but in the intervening decades extraction of them has not proceeded on a commercial basis. The ISA continues to work on rules for extraction, but to date only exploration permits have been issued.[57]

The maritime zones created or codified by UNCLOS remain fundamental to stable and sustainable ocean governance. Their importance lies in their widespread acceptance by almost all nations in the world, and they have provided the underpinnings for many later laws explored in this book.

Conclusion

Borders, zones and jurisdictions are all part of boundary-making on the shoreline and at sea. In geo-political terms this perhaps makes sense, and certainly for lawmakers (and people and corporations bound by laws) such divisions are useful. But for the ocean environment itself, the natural processes that apply within it, and marine living and non-living resources, these anthropocentric conveniences are artificial and unhelpful. They do not align with scientific knowledge of the marine environment and the needs of the ocean. Whilst UNCLOS sought to deliver fair outcomes between nations, such as coastal and landlocked States, it did not provide justice for oceans. The evolution of laws for oceans, seas and shorelines demonstrates a growing awareness of the ineffectiveness of such divisions, and the search for more successful solutions, as the chapters that follow will demonstrate.

Notes

1 Office for Ocean Affairs and the Law of the Sea, *The Baselines: An Examination of the Relevant Provisions of the United Nations Convention on the Law of the Sea* (New York: United Nations, 1989), www.un.org/depts/los/doalos_publications/publicationstexts/The%20Law%20of%20the%20Sea_Baselines.pdf. "The Law of the Sea," *Geoscience Australia*, accessed March 1, 2024, www.ga.gov.au/scientific-topics/marine/jurisdiction/law-of-the-sea
2 See, for example, Paul Alexander, "Sea Tenure in Southern Sri Lanka," *Ethnology* 16, no. 3 (1977): 231–51.
3 In some cases, customary land ownership was returned to local peoples when colonies became independent, such as in the South Pacific. In other cases, customary tenure has been recognised in other ways such as native title rights in Australia.
4 Although 'commons' do still exist.
5 Kenneth M. Cuno, "The Origins of Private Ownership of Land in Egypt: A Reappraisal," *International Journal of Middle Eastern Studies* 12 (1980): 245–75.
6 Real property includes land, houses and other buildings. It is distinguished from personal property, which are other objects such as cars, furniture, clothes and domestic animals.
7 Under English common law, for example, the Crown (representing public ownership) was the owner of the shoreline, foreshore and submerged land under coastal waters and tidal rivers. The Crown had the power to grant private property rights, but this was rarely done and remained subject to public rights of fishing and navigation. As explored later, offshore ocean areas were *res communis* and unable to be owned by any nation.
8 Customary marine tenure is particularly evident in the South Pacific where near-shore marine areas, such as the area out to the nearest reef, are communally owned by adjacent villages under customary law: R. E. Johannes, "Traditional Marine Conservation Methods in Oceania and Their Demise," *Annual Review of Ecology and Systematics*

9 (1978): 349–64. It is also documented in other places in the world: K. K. Baiju et al., "Non-state Legal Systems and Their Role in Governance of Small-scale Marine Fisheries along the South West Coast of India," *Ocean and Coastal Management* 184 (2020): 105020.

9 See, for example "In a Victory for Public Beach Access, Federal Court Rules in Favor of 'Customary Use' of Sands on Private Portions," *Flaglerlive.com* (August 20, 2021), https://flaglerlive.com/customary-use-upheld/#gsc.tab=0.

10 Philip E. Steinberg, *The Social Construction of the Ocean* (Cambridge: Cambridge University Press, 2001), 13.

11 For the full text of UNCLOS, see "United Nations Convention on the Law of the Sea," *United Nations*, accessed March 1, 2024, www.un.org/depts/los/convention_agreements/texts/unclos/closindx.htm.

12 The law of the sea refers to the body of international customs, rules and agreements relating to rights and duties of States in marine areas, whether oceans or seas.

13 For example, the coastline of the United Kingdom is 2,800 km long when measured in 100 km lengths, but 3,400 km long when the measurements are made in lengths of 50 km. See, for example Sophie Weiner, "Why It's Impossible to Accurately Measure a Coastline," *Popular Mechanics* (March 18, 2018), accessed March 1, 2024, www.popularmechanics.com/science/environment/a19068718/why-its-impossible-to-accurately-measure-a-coastline/; and Gerard McNamara and Guilherme Vieira da Silva, "The Coastline Paradox: A New Perspective," *Journal of Coastal Research* 39, no. 1 (2022): 45–54.

14 F. W. Gibson, "The Alaskan Boundary Dispute," *Report of the Annual Meeting of the Canadian Historical Association* 44, no. 1 (1965): 25–41. D. M. L. Farr and Niko Block, "Alaska Boundary Dispute," *The Canadian Encyclopedia* (February 6, 2006), www.thecanadianencyclopedia.ca/en/article/alaska-boundary-dispute.

15 Rachel Carson, *The Edge of the Sea* (Boston: Houghton Mifflin, 1955), 1.

16 For example, where land meets other bodies of water, such as rivers and lakes, rather than tidal waters, riparian law applies based on different rules. Riparian law is not considered here.

17 The Institutes of Justinian, 535 AD.

18 Thomas Ankersen, "Who Owns the Beach? It Depends on State Law and Tide Lines," *The Conversation* (July 19, 2021), https://theconversation.com/who-owns-the-beach-it-depends-on-state-law-and-tide-lines-163405.

19 John Corkill, "Principles and Problems of Shoreline Law," *NCCARF, ACCARNSI Discussion Paper G, Node 1: Coastal Settlements* (December 2012), accessed March 1, 2024, www.wrl.unsw.edu.au/sites/wrl/files/uploads/About_us/ACCARNSI/discussion-papers/Principles%20and%20Problems%20Of%20Shoreline%20Law.pdf, 13.

20 In most places in the world the public has a right of access to shoreline beaches. For the US, for example, see Ankersen, "Who Owns the Beach?"

21 For the US see Ankersen, "Who Owns the Beach?"

22 For Australia see Corkill, "Principles and Problems," 45–51.

23 This is not common although governments do grant leases or licences in some cases.

24 Sean Brennan, "Wet or Dry, It's Aboriginal Land: The Blue Mud Bay Decision on the Intertidal Zone," *Indigenous Law Bulletin* 27, no. 7 (2008), accessed March 1, 2024, https://www8.austlii.edu.au/cgi-bin/viewdoc/au/journals/IndigLawB/2008/27.html#fnB1. "Sea country Rights," *Northern Land Council* (2024), accessed March 1, 2024, www.nlc.org.au/our-land-sea/sea-country-rights.

25 Avani Dias, "Blue Mud Bay: What You Need to Know about Aboriginal People's Hope to Control Intertidal Zone," *ABC News* (June 1, 2017), www.abc.net.au/news/2017-06-01/what-you-need-to-know-about-blue-mud-bay-decision/8573420.

For the full High Court decision see *Northern Territory of Australia & Anor v Arnhem Land Aboriginal Land Trust & Ors* (2008) 236 CLR 24.

26 Laurence Bergreen, *Over the Edge of the World: Magellan's Terrifying Circumnavigation of the Globe* (New York: William Morrow and Company, 2003).

27 Editors of Encyclopaedia, "Treaty of Tordesillas," *Encyclopedia Britannica* (September 21, 2022), www.britannica.com/event/Treaty-of-Tordesillas.

28 Zsofia Korosy, "Whales and the Colonization of the Pacific Ocean," in *Blue Legalities*, ed. Irus Braverman and Johnson, 219.

29 Reiser, "Hugo Grotius, Free Seas . . . .," 203.

30 Christian Pogies, "The Canon: A Tool for Delimiting Maritime Space," *Legal History Insights* (June 14, 2021), www.wrl.unsw.edu.au/sites/wrl/files/uploads/About_us/ACCARNSI/discussion-papers/Principles%20and%20Problems%20Of%20Shoreline%20Law.pdf.

31 House of Lords, *The Law of the Sea in the 21st Century* (London: House of Lords, 2022), accessed March 1, 2024, https://committees.parliament.uk/publications/9005/documents/159002/default/, 7.

32 See Chapter 4 for further discussion about the Nootka Convention and resource extraction.

33 Martin Ira Glassner, *Neptune's Domain: A Political Geography of the Sea* (Abingdon: Routledge, 1990), 5.

34 *Proclamation 2667 of September 28, 1945, Policy of the United States with Respect to the Natural Resources of the Subsoil and Seabed of the Continental Shelf*: "The Truman Proclamation, 1945 (Proclamation 2667 – Policy of the United States with Respect to the Natural Resources of the Subsoil and Sea Bed of the Continental Shelf)," *International Institute for Law of the Sea Studies* (August 30, 2021), accessed March1,2024,http://iilss.net/the-truman-proclamation-1945-proclamation-2667-policy-of-the-united-states-with-respect-to-the-natural-resources-of-the-subsoil-and-sea-bed-of-the-continental-shelf/.

35 Hugo Caminos, "Keynote Address: Harmonization of Pre-Existing 200-Mile Claims in the Latin American Region with the United Nations Convention on the Law of the Sea and Its Exclusive Economic Zone," *University of Miami Inter-American Law Review* 30, no. 1 (2015): 9–30, http://repository.law.miami.edu/umialr/vol30/iss1/3.

36 In some texts, the UN Conferences on the Law of the Sea (of which there were three) are known as UNCLOS I, II and III. These are not to be confused with the UN Convention on the Law of the Sea (UNCLOS) which is the international law treaty.

37 *Convention on the Territorial Sea and the Contiguous Zone* (1958); *Convention on the Continental Shelf* (1958); *Convention on the High Seas* (1958); and the *Convention on Fishing and Conservation of the Living Resources of the High Seas* (1958).

38 Douglas M. Johnston, *The Theory and History of Ocean Boundary-Making* (Kingston and Montreal: McGill-Queen's University Press, 1988), x-2i. In public law, the term 'regime' pertains to the system of principles, rules, procedures and institutions, while the term 'zone' refers to an area that is spatially defined for particular administrative purposes.

39 Johnston, *The Theory and History of Ocean Boundary-Making*, 6.

40 It was Tommy Koh who coined the term 'constitution for the oceans' during the third Conference on the Law of the Sea: Tommy T. B. Koh, "A Constitution for the Oceans," accessed March 1, 2024, www.un.org/depts/los/convention_agreements/texts/koh_english.pdf.

41 "Overlapping Claims to Internal Waters in Law of the Sea and LOSC," *International Institute for Law of the Sea Studies* (August 30, 2021), accessed March 1, 2024, https://iilss.net/overlapping-claims-to-internal-waters-in-law-of-the-sea-and-losc/.

42 See, for example, Australia's *Offshore Constitutional Settlement* and the US *Submerged Lands Act* 43 USC 1301.
43 Katherine G. Sammler, "The Rising Politics of Sea Level: Demarcating Territory in a Vertically Relative World," *Territory, Politics, Governance* (June 30, 2019): 2, https://doi.org/10.1080/21622671.2019.1632219.
44 Innocent passage is defined as 'not prejudicial to the peace, good order or security of the coastal State' with indications given of what might constitute prejudicial behaviour (Article 19) and rights to prevent passage, which is not innocent (Article 25).
45 Michele Metych, "Exclusive Economic Zone," *Encyclopaedia Britannica* (July 13, 2023), accessed March 1, 2024, www.britannica.com/topic/exclusive-economic-zone.
46 *Proclamation 2677 of September 28, 1945.*
47 *Declaration on the Maritime Zone*, accessed March 1, 2024, https://treaties.un.org/doc/publication/unts/volume%201006/volume-1006-i-14758-english.pdf.
48 *Fisheries Convention*, accessed March 1, 2024, www.fao.org/faolex/results/details/en/c/LEX-FAOC032024/.
49 One nautical mile is equal to 1,853 metres, close to the mean length of 1 minute of latitude. This measure was adopted by the International Hydrographic Conference in 1929 and subsequently endorsed by the International Bureau of Weights and Measures.
50 Marine protected areas are explored in detail in Chapter 8.
51 John Burgess et al., eds., *Law of the Sea: A Policy Primer* (Medford, MA: The Fletcher School of Law and Diplomacy, Tufts University, 2017), chapter 2, accessed March 1, 2024, https://sites.tufts.edu/lawofthesea/files/2017/07/LawoftheSeaPrimer.pdf. See 4 for further discussion about the fisheries implications of EEZ declarations.
52 UNCLOS, Article 76.
53 O. P. Sharma, *The International Law of the Sea: India and the UN Convention of 1982* (Oxford: Oxford University Press, 2010).
54 See "North Sea Continental Shelf (Federal Republic of Germany/Netherlands)," *International Court of Justice*, accessed March 14, 2024, www.icj-cij.org/case/52.
55 The 1958 Conventions of UNCLOS defined equidistance 'as the line every point of which is equidistant from the nearest points of the baselines from which the breadth of the territorial sea of each of the two States is measured', and obliged States to use the principle in the absence of an agreement or historical titles.
56 Johnston, *The Theory and History of Ocean Boundary-Making*, 84.
57 "International Seabed Authority," accessed March 1, 2024, www.isa.org.jm/.

Bibliography

Alexander, Paul. "Sea Tenure in Southern Sri Lanka." *Ethnology* 16, no. 3 (1977): 231–51.
Ankersen, Thomas. "Who Owns the Beach? It Depends on State Law and Tide Lines." *The Conversation* (July 19, 2021). https://theconversation.com/who-owns-the-beach-it-depends-on-state-law-and-tide-lines-163405.
Baiju, K. K. et al. "Non-State Legal Systems and Their Role in Governance of Small-Scale Marine Fisheries along the South West Coast of India." *Ocean and Coastal Management* 184 (2020): 105020.
Bergreen, Laurence. *Over the Edge of the World: Magellan's Terrifying Circumnavigation of the Globe*. New York: William Morrow and Company, 2003.
Brennan, Sean. "Wet or Dry, It's Aboriginal Land: The Blue Mud Bay Decision on the Intertidal Zone." *Indigenous Law Bulletin* 27, no. 7 (2008). Accessed March 1, 2024. https://www8.austlii.edu.au/cgi-bin/viewdoc/au/journals/IndigLawB/2008/27.html#fnB1.

Burgess, John et al., eds. *Law of the Sea: A Policy Primer*. Medford, MA: The Fletcher School of Law and Diplomacy, Tufts University, 2017. Accessed March 1, 2024. https://sites.tufts.edu/lawofthesea/files/2017/07/LawoftheSeaPrimer.pdf.

Caminos, Hugo. "Keynote Address: Harmonization of Pre-Existing 200-Mile Claims in the Latin American Region with the United Nations Convention on the Law of the Sea and Its Exclusive Economic Zone." *University of Miami Inter-American Law Review* 30, no. 1 (2015): 9–30. http://repository.law.miami.edu/umialr/vol30/iss1/3.

Carson, Rachel. *The Edge of the Sea*. Boston: Houghton Mifflin, 1955.

Corkill, John. "Principles and Problems of Shoreline Law." NCCARF, ACCARNSI Discussion Paper G, Node 1: Coastal Settlements (December 2012). Accessed March 1, 2024. www.wrl.unsw.edu.au/sites/wrl/files/uploads/About_us/ACCARNSI/discussion-papers/Principles%20and%20Problems%20Of%20Shoreline%20Law.pdf.

Cuno, Kenneth M. "The Origins of Private Ownership of Land in Egypt: A Reappraisal." *International Journal of Middle Eastern Studies* 12 (1980): 245–75.

Declaration on the Maritime Zone. Accessed March 1, 2024. https://treaties.un.org/doc/publication/unts/volume%201006/volume-1006-i-14758-english.pdf.

Dias, Avani. "Blue Mud Bay: What You Need to Know about Aboriginal People's Hope to Control Intertidal Zone." *ABC News* (June 1, 2017). www.abc.net.au/news/2017-06-01/what-you-need-to-know-about-blue-mud-bay-decision/8573420.

Editors of Encyclopaedia Britannica. "Treaty of Tordesillas." *Encyclopedia Britannica* (September 21, 2022). www.britannica.com/event/Treaty-of-Tordesillas.

Farr, D. M. L., and Niko Block. "Alaska Boundary Dispute." *The Canadian Encyclopedia* (February 6, 2006). www.thecanadianencyclopedia.ca/en/article/alaska-boundary-dispute.

Fisheries Convention. Accessed March 1, 2024. www.fao.org/faolex/results/details/en/c/LEX-FAOC032024/.

FlaglerLive. "In a Victory for Public Beach Access, Federal Court Rules in Favor of 'Customary Use' of Sands on Private Portions." *Flaglerlive.com* (August 20, 2021). https://flaglerlive.com/customary-use-upheld/#gsc.tab=0.

Geoscience Australia. "The Law of the Sea." Accessed March 1, 2024. www.ga.gov.au/scientific-topics/marine/jurisdiction/law-of-the-sea.

Gibson, F. W. "The Alaskan Boundary Dispute." *Report of the Annual Meeting of the Canadian Historical Association* 44, no. 1 (1965): 25–41.

Gibson, Jano. "Leaked Draft Documents Trigger Threat of Injunction by NT Government Over Blue Mud Bay Fishing Deal." *ABC News* (October 5, 2022). www.abc.net.au/news/2022-10-05/nt-blue-mud-bay-fishing-document/101498340.

Glassner, Martin Ira. *Neptune's Domain: A Political Geography of the Sea*. Abingdon: Routledge, 1990.

House of Lords. *The Law of the Sea in the 21st Century*. London: House of Lords, 2022. Accessed March 1, 2024, https://committees.parliament.uk/publications/9005/documents/159002/default/.

International Court of Justice. "North Sea Continental Shelf (Federal Republic of Germany/Netherlands)." Accessed March 14, 2024. www.icj-cij.org/case/52.

International Institute for Law of the Sea Studies (IILSS). "Overlapping Claims to Internal Waters in Law of the Sea and LOSC." (August 30, 2021). Accessed March 1, 2024. https://iilss.net/overlapping-claims-to-internal-waters-in-law-of-the-sea-and-losc/.

International Institute for Law of the Sea Studies. "The Truman Proclamation, 1945 (Proclamation 2667 – Policy of the United States with Respect to the Natural Resources of the Subsoil and Sea Bed of the Continental Shelf)." (August 30 2021). Accessed March 1, 2024. http://iilss.net/the-truman-proclamation-1945-proclamation-2667-policy-of-the-united-states-with-respect-to-the-natural-resources-of-the-subsoil-and-sea-bed-of-the-continental-shelf/.

International Seabed Authority. Accessed March 1, 2024. www.isa.org.jm/.

Johannes, R. E. "Traditional Marine Conservation Methods in Oceania and Their Demise." *Annual Review of Ecology and Systematics* 9 (1978): 349–64.

Johnston, Douglas M. *The Theory and History of Ocean Boundary-Making*. Kingston and Montreal: McGill-Queen's University Press, 1988.

Koh, Tommy T. B. "A Constitution for the Oceans." Accessed March 1, 2024. www.un.org/depts/los/convention_agreements/texts/koh_english.pdf.

McNamara, Gerard, and Guilherme Vieira da Silva. "The Coastline Paradox: A New Perspective." *Journal of Coastal Research* 39, no. 1 (2022): 45–54.

Metych, Michele. "Exclusive Economic Zone." *Encyclopaedia Britannica* (July 13, 2023). Accessed March 1, 2024. www.britannica.com/topic/exclusive-economic-zone.

Northern Land Council. "Sea Country Rights." Accessed March 1, 2024. www.nlc.org.au/our-land-sea/sea-country-rights.

Northern Territory of Australia & Anor v Arnhem Land Aboriginal Land Trust & Ors (2008) 236 CLR 24.

Office for Ocean Affairs and the Law of the Sea. *The Baselines: An Examination of the Relevant Provisions of the United Nations Convention on the Law of the Sea*. New York: United Nations, 1989. Accessed March 14, 2024. www.un.org/depts/los/doalos_publications/publicationstexts/The%20Law%20of%20the%20Sea_Baselines.pdf.

Pogies, Christian. "The Canon: A Tool for Delimiting Maritime Space." *Legal History Insights* (June 14, 2021). www.wrl.unsw.edu.au/sites/wrl/files/uploads/About_us/ACCARNSI/discussion-papers/Principles%20and%20Problems%20Of%20Shoreline%20Law.pdf.

Sammler, Katherine G. "The Rising Politics of Sea Level: Demarcating Territory in a Vertically Relative World." *Territory, Politics, Governance* (June 30, 2019): 2. https://doi.org/10.1080/21622671.2019.1632219.

Sharma, O. P. *The International Law of the Sea: India and the UN Convention of 1982*. Oxford: Oxford University Press, 2010.

Steinberg, Philip E. *The Social Construction of the Ocean*. Cambridge: Cambridge University Press, 2001.

United Nations. "United Nations Convention on the Law of the Sea." Accessed March 1, 2024. www.un.org/depts/los/convention_agreements/texts/unclos/closindx.htm.

Weiner, Sophie. "Why It's Impossible to Accurately Measure a Coastline." *Popular Mechanics* (March 18, 2018). Accessed March 1, 2024. www.popularmechanics.com/science/environment/a19068718/why-its-impossible-to-accurately-measure-a-coastline/.

3 Disorder at Sea

Piracy, war and illegality

The most important thing I saw from ships all around the world . . . was an ocean woefully under-protected and the mayhem and misery often faced by those who work these waters.

Ian Urbina, 2019

Overview

In 2017 Admiral James Stavridis, a former leader of the NATO alliance in global operations, wrote that piracy, together with illegal fishing and marine environmental damage, represented the biggest threats to the future of the world's oceans, seas and shorelines. The scale and impacts of these activities, he noted, have led to the maritime environment being called 'the biggest crime scene in the world'.[1]

The oceanic realm has long been the setting for human conflict. For coastal societies, for example, the shoreline was a place where first encounters often led to bloodshed between local peoples and foreign colonisers. From the bronze age naval raids of the 'Sea Peoples' in the Mediterranean[2] to contemporary naval wars and informal maritime conflicts, many a human life has been lost on shorelines and at sea. The breadth of these activities ranges from individual events, such as the death of the British navigator Captain James Cook on the shoreline in Hawai'i,[3] to conflicts that have impacted whole continents such as the state-sanctioned plundering of Latin America. This chapter focuses on piracy, war and illegality at sea and how legal regimes have distinguished between legitimate and unlawful violence over time. It also considers the implications of oceanic crimes for the future of the world's oceans, seas and shorelines.

Maritime piracy

Outlaws of the sea – pirates and buccaneers

For many people the mention of pirates or buccaneers conjures up images of swashbuckling adventurers on the high seas, attacking ships and killing their

DOI: 10.4324/9781003005261-5

crews before seizing their treasured cargo.[4] This romanticised view of piracy originated in the 18th century with writers chronicling the exploits of notorious pirates during the so-called 'golden age of piracy' between around 1690 to 1730.[5] The romantic stereotype of pirates as charming if villainous criminals has become well established in western popular culture, even though the violent reality of piracy is far removed from the rogue heroes of Hollywood movies.[6]

Sea piracy is arguably the oldest universal crime on Earth. It also holds a special place under customary international law as one of the few crimes where States have the jurisdiction to prosecute piracy under domestic law, irrespective of the nationality of the pirate or the victim.[7] Piracy is regarded as a universal crime, and pirates – in the words of the 1st century BCE statesman Cicero – are *hostis humani generis* (the enemy of all humankind) and not entitled to legal protection.[8] Piracy is essentially an act of robbery or criminal violence against another ship, or a coastal area outside of the jurisdiction of a State, and without State authority, although as explored later in the chapter it has a specific definition under international law.

The term 'pirate' originated with the Greek *peirates*, referring to those who raided ships, robbing, kidnapping or murdering those on board. Indeed, some of the earliest references to pirates came from ancient Greece and Rome, where they threatened key trading routes in the Mediterranean Sea. Over time, pirate 'cultures' emerged in a wide range of localities, including the Arabs of the Red Sea, the Vikings of early medieval Europe, along the so-called 'pirate coast' of the Persian Gulf, and in the Strait of Malacca and South China Sea. In Asia, for example, piracy may have arisen as early as the 2nd century after the fall of the Chinese Han dynasty.[9] By the 14th century the English and French fleets were joining forces to battle African corsairs.[10] In the 16th century Spanish galleons were regularly targeted by pirates as they transported their cargoes of silver, gold and gems plundered from the newly discovered lands of the Americas back to Europe.[11] Madame Zheng (or Cheng), arguably the most successful pirate of all time, was active during the 19th century after inheriting a pirate fleet from her husband on his death.[12] Sea piracy was prevalent wherever ships were engaged in military or commercial activities. As Gosse observed in his history of piracy, trade followed the flag and robbery followed trade.[13]

Piracy became a criminal offence under English law with the *Acte for the Punysshement of Pyrotes and Robbers of the Sea* passed in 1536.[14] The law initially granted those with the King's commission the authority to prosecute pirates, but a proclamation in 1569 transferred the jurisdiction to the English courts to conduct trials of pirates captured anywhere on the high seas, regardless of the territory in which the piracy occurred.[15] However, the English Parliament considered the evolving common law to be inadequate in dealing with the crime of piracy, and in the 17th and 18th centuries sought to extend the types of activities considered to be illegal.[16] It also extended the jurisdiction of English law to cover offences committed by or to English ships or British subjects anywhere on the high seas, including foreign waters and navigable rivers to the first bridge.[17]

Following an accident in 1878 involving a foreign ship in Britain's territorial waters (within three nautical miles off the English shoreline at that time), the Parliament extended the jurisdiction further to include offences on foreign ships within Britain's territorial sea limit.[18] Simultaneously, pirates often took advantage of the different laws that existed between English colonies, and sometimes the colonies of different nations, for example seeking refuge from one by hiding in another and by cleverly using the law when it suited them.[19] Amendments to the law removed some of the procedural and substantive obstacles to prosecuting pirates in order to facilitate their capture and trial.[20] As Baer notes, the suppression of some common law protections afforded to the accused in the interests of eradicating piracy is reminiscent of contemporary terrorism laws, which are sometimes used to elevate national interests above individual rights and freedoms.[21]

State-sanctioned piracy – privateers and corsairs

Prior to the development of large navies, many States authorised private individuals known as 'privateers' to conduct quasi-military operations against a rival State, issuing them with a licence or 'letters of marque' to effectively wage war by seizing an enemy merchant vessel. Privateering was a useful strategy for enabling a monarch or government to extend its maritime dominance across the world's oceans and seas. The English admiral Francis Drake, for example, was a privateer under a commission issued by Elizabeth I in 1572. He made his fortune plundering Spanish ships and settlements in the Americas on behalf of the English monarchy.[22] The distinction between privateers and pirates was often blurred, however, with privateers sometimes acting beyond their commission or pirates given tacit encouragement by a State without issuing the necessary legal papers.[23] In times of war, when it suited governments of the day, some pirates were commissioned as privateers only to be outlawed during peacetime.[24]

Corsairs represented another form of State-sanctioned piracy. From the late 14th century to the early 19th century, the Ottoman Empire and the Christian empires of Europe were engaged in a protracted battle for maritime supremacy in the Mediterranean Sea using both conventional navies and corsairs. Muslim corsairs such as the Barbarossa (red beard) brothers were based along North Africa's Barbary coast and, whilst aligned with the Ottoman Empire, they often operated beyond the Empire's control. Meanwhile, pirates living on the Caribbean islands of Hispaniola and Tortuga, and along the Pacific coast of Central America, were known as buccaneers (from the French *boucan*), a disparate group of pirates engaged in protracted battles with the Spanish, sometimes with the support of Spain's enemies, England and France, and sometimes attacking any ship that might be carrying valuable cargo. Buccaneers such as William Dampier were renowned for their exploits and inspired romanticised stories by fiction writers such as Robert Louis Stevenson.[25]

In the days of sail, both naval vessels and privateers operated under an ancient judicial proceeding known as 'prize law'. Under customary international law, a ship and its crew could be legally seized at sea and brought to a friendly port, usually flying the sovereign flag of the 'prize' ship. Once ashore, a local tribunal called 'a prize court' would determine the legality of the seizure. If a ship was considered a lawful prize, the victorious captain and crew would share the value of the vessel in 'prize money'. If not, the captain could be responsible for damages to the owner of the captured vessel and cargo. Such arrangements may seem strange today, but in early modern Europe public officials or private individuals acting under State sanction could personally profit from their activities. In the case of naval captains and privateers, acquiring the proceeds of a legally captured enemy ship was accepted. Nevertheless, different practices prevailed regarding the application of prize law, leading to escalating tensions and armed conflict between States. The 1856 *Paris Declaration Respecting Maritime Law* brought an end to privateering under international law, although instances of privateering continued into the 20th century albeit with far fewer opportunities for seizing an enemy vessel for personal profit.[26]

Modern sea piracy

The scourge of sea piracy has continued unabated to the present day. In 1997 alone, more than 229 violent pirate attacks were reported across the globe resulting in 51 seamen being killed, 30 injured and 412 taken hostage. Typically, these attacks involved a group of pirates boarding a merchant vessel from a small powerboat under cover of darkness, restraining the captain, stealing valuables and disembarking before the alarm could be raised.[27] By 2017 modern piracy was estimated to be costing the global maritime transport network upwards of USD20 billion a year, taking into account insurance ransoms, legal fees, security guards, rerouting ships to avoid certain routes and technology required to prevent pirate attacks.[28] It remains one of the great challenges for commercial shipping, particularly in locations where coastal topography and political or economic circumstances have conspired to create favourable conditions for attack by sea pirates. During the 1990s, for example, commercial ships plying the sea lanes off southeast Asia reported 506 attacks over five years.[29] In recognition of the prevalence of sea piracy in the region, the International Maritime Bureau (a subsidiary of the International Chamber of Commerce) established the Regional Piracy Centre in Kuala Lumpur to monitor pirate attacks on merchant shipping.[30] By 2000, this region was seeing the greatest number of attacks against merchant ships in the world.[31] More recently, the International Maritime Bureau reported 115 piracy and robbery at sea incidents in 2022, and 120 in 2023, including increasing numbers of crew taken hostage and the first successful hijacking of a vessel off the coast of Somalia since 2017.[32]

Sea piracy and international law

Maritime piracy continues to be regarded as a criminal activity involving robbery or other violence at sea, although acts of unlawful warfare, revolution, mutiny or slave trading are also defined as piracy under various treaties and in some State laws. So how does the international law of the sea tackle the age-old problem of sea piracy? While piracy has long been regarded as an international crime, and one of the few crimes where States are empowered to prosecute pirates under domestic law regardless of the nationality of those involved, it presents challenges for international legal regimes.

Under international law, piracy is defined as 'any illegal acts of violence or detention, or any act of depredation, committed for private ends by the crew or the passengers of a private ship . . . on the high seas, against another ship' as well as voluntary participation or inciting or facilitating such acts.[33] Many cases of maritime robbery or violence would fall short of this definition but may still constitute armed robbery at sea, or another crime under State law, depending upon the location of the offence, the registration of the vessels involved and the nationality of personnel and offenders. In commercial law, however, piracy is interpreted more widely and includes attacks in port or from the shoreline.[34] As Paul Todd has noted:

> Th[e] idea of piracy, as a violent criminal act committed at sea, is central to all the definitions, and is probably quite close to its definition for private civil law purposes, for example where the term appears in a carriage or insurance contract. In international law, piracy is defined far more narrowly, but there are reasons for this, which do not extend to defining piracy for criminal or contractual purposes.[35]

Modern piracy is also shaped by different conditions including local geography, economic opportunity and governance. The result is a complex and overlapping arrangement of anti-violence and counter-piracy measures involving an array of government organisations such as military and law enforcement agencies, United Nations agencies, and specialist counter-piracy organisations.[36] As Douglas Guilfoyle notes, the legal responses to piracy have always been subject to a tension between international and State actions to police piracy on the high seas.[37]

The United Nations (UN) General Assembly has repeatedly encouraged States to cooperate in combating sea piracy as part of their maritime security measures.[42] The *UN Convention on the Law of the Sea* (UNCLOS) (1982) offers a legal framework for combating piracy under international law (Articles 100 to 107 and 110) based largely on customary international law. The main provision relating to piracy is contained in Article 105:

Combating sea piracy

Incidents of modern piracy continue to threaten the safety of ships and their crews, disrupt maritime industries, and adversely affect local and regional economies. Some regions and States are more prone to sea piracy than others, particularly those that are close to busy shipping routes and have poor and marginalised communities, weak law enforcement, and corruption.[38] Somalia became an international hot spot for pirate attacks between the 1990s and 2010s, often involving crew members being held hostage in appalling conditions. Somalia has the longest coastline in mainland Africa and lies adjacent to one of the world's busiest shipping routes. The rise of Somali piracy coincided with a prolonged civil war and increasing desperation amongst the Somali people, whose traditional reliance on fishing was under threat from degradation of the marine environment.[39] Initially, the attacks were conducted in the territorial sea by armed groups who claimed to be protecting Somali's fishing resources from foreign exploitation and its coastal waters from waste dumping. However, Somali pirates became more organised and bolder in their attacks, threatening ships passing through navigational 'choke-points' in the narrow waters of the Suez Canal, the Gulf of Aden and the sea between the Horn of Africa and Arabian Peninsula. Their activities posed challenges for international efforts to prosecute the offenders, since many of those apprehended held no formal identification papers and had to be handed back to local authorities for prosecution.[40] Incidents of piracy in the region declined for a time following a concerted international effort led by the United Nations but, in late 2023, pirates from Yemen attacked merchant vessels transiting through the Red Sea, provoking an international military response to safeguard global supply chains.[41]

> On the high seas, or in any place outside the jurisdiction of any State, every State may seize a pirate ship or aircraft, or a ship or aircraft taken by piracy and under the control of pirates, and arrest the persons and seize the property on board. The courts of the State which carried out the seizure may decide upon the penalties to be imposed, and may also determine the action to be taken with regard to the ships, aircraft or property, subject to the rights of third parties acting in good faith. (UNCLOS, Article 105)

In response, States have established multi-national maritime missions such as the Combined Task Force 151, which was formed to suppress pirate attacks in the Gulf of Aden and off the coast of Somalia.[43] However, piracy remains a global issue with some critics of international law arguing that the UNCLOS has failed to deter piracy.[44] In 2021 the UN Secretary-General's Chef de Cabinet advocated for stronger international cooperation, noting that piracy was most prevalent in West Africa, the Straits of Malacca and Singapore. She reported that piracy and armed robbery of ships had risen by nearly 20% over the first half of 2020 and that incidents had nearly doubled in the South China Sea. There was also increasing concern over maritime security in the Gulf of Guinea, the Persian Gulf and Arabian Sea.[45] Attention continues to be drawn to the lack of any single, comprehensive international law instrument to prevent, suppress and respond to incidences of piracy.[46]

Some States have introduced their own security measures to discourage piracy, including deploying warships to escort convoys of commercial ships in dangerous areas, while some commercial shipowners have taken to employing Privately Contracted Armed Security Personnel (PCASP) operating outside internationally recognised 'rules of engagement'.[47] Whilst these actions have significantly reduced incidences of piracy, they tend to shift the problem to another region.[48] The International Maritime Organization and other groups have opposed the use of private military and security companies aboard commercial vessels, arguing that their involvement will serve to escalate an already volatile situation.[49] Furthermore, the technical definition of piracy – involving two or more ships and private rather than political motives – means that much violence and robbery at sea is not counted as piracy and not recorded in official data, potentially masking the extent of the problem.

Naval warfare

Whilst sea piracy is widely condemned as a criminal activity, the legality of other kinds of violence at sea – including maritime warfare, terrorism, contraband operations and slavery – are less clear cut. Just how should international law be applied during armed conflicts at sea between belligerent States? The principles of the law of armed conflict are enshrined in both customary international law and international agreements such as treaties, conventions and protocols. Article 2 of the UN Charter requires all States to settle their international disputes by peaceful means and to refrain from the threat or use of force against other States except as a measure of self-defence.[50] The law of neutrality defines the legal relationship between States engaged in an armed conflict (belligerents) and nations not taking part (neutrals). This law aims to limit the conduct of military conflict and lessen the impact internationally. Regardless of whether the use of armed force is considered lawful or otherwise under the UN Charter, the laws of war are designed to regulate the manner in which an armed conflict is conducted including preventing unnecessary suffering and destruction by mitigating harm to combatants and civilians alike.[51] While the principles of international humanitarian law apply to conflicts on both land and sea, maritime warfare has compelled the development of specific rules and these have, of necessity, evolved over the course of the 20th century in response to changing methods and weapons.[52]

The laws of naval warfare date back to ancient civilisations and customary international law evolved over the course of centuries. Most of the work to codify the law of war at sea was undertaken in the early 20th century, beginning with the Hague Conventions adopted in 1907.[53] Eight of these Conventions addressed different aspects of naval warfare, including the conduct of hostilities such as laying underwater mines, bombing naval forces, protecting sick, wounded and shipwrecked sailors, and protecting certain ships such as merchant vessels, the right of capture and the rights and duties of neutral powers. A year later, and in a further attempt to codify the law of naval warfare, participants at the London Naval Conference of 1908–9 agreed to the *London Declaration Concerning the Laws of Naval War*. The Declaration sought to address controversial aspects of naval warfare including blockades, contraband and 'prize'. It largely restated customary international laws of war at sea but, while several maritime powers (Austria-Hungary, France, Germany, Italy, Japan, Russia, the United Kingdom and the US) signed the Declaration, it was never ratified[54] by any State and consequently never came into force.[55]

In 1913, a year before the outbreak of World War I, the Institute of International Law adopted *The Oxford Manual on the Laws of Naval War Governing the Relations Between Belligerents* but, during the course of World War I, it became clear that the Hague Conventions had not succeeded in limiting the number of victims of naval warfare. In any event, the rules were soon out of date because of the development of new submarine technologies and, during World War II, naval warfare regularly involved the use of torpedoes and underwater mines that indiscriminately targeted neutral vessels as well as merchant and hospital ships.

Protecting the victims of naval warfare

In March 1944, the German submarine No. 852 attacked and killed the captain and crew of the Greek steamship *Peleus*.[56] The incident focused public attention on the inadequacy of laws protecting wounded, sick or shipwrecked members of armed forces at sea. When the attackers were brought before the British Military Court at Hamburg at the end of the war, the judge found that, after sinking the enemy ship, the German captain and crew had killed most of the survivors as they sought refuge in lifeboats. He found the accused guilty of violating a rule of warfare whereby the killing of unarmed enemies was a 'grave breach of the law of nations'.[57] Rules for the protection of victims of naval warfare were subsequently codified in the 1949 *Geneva Convention for the Amelioration of the Condition of the Wounded, Sick, and Shipwrecked Members of Armed Forces at Sea*, replacing the older Hague Convention of 1907.[58]

During the second half of the 20th century, developments in international law of the sea, and in the technology and conduct of naval warfare more generally, led to a comprehensive review of international laws governing armed conflicts at sea. In 1977, the *Geneva Convention Protocol I* was implemented to clarify that the effect of naval hostilities applied to all naval operations affecting the civilian population, including those on land.[59] However, the conduct of hostilities at sea remained a grey area, with controversial tactics employed during conflicts such as the Falklands/Malvinas War between Britain and Argentina in 1982 and war between Iraq and the Islamic Republic of Iran in 1980–8.[60] Such controversies led to the International Institute of Humanitarian Law, with the support of the International Red Cross, convening a series of Round Tables between 1987 and 1994 involving a group of legal and naval experts from 24 States. The initiative resulted in the drafting of the *San Remo Manual on International Law Applicable to Armed Conflicts at Sea* modelled on the 1913 Oxford Manual.[61] Whilst restating customary laws of war at sea, the *San Remo Manual* also provided clarity on how the key principles of the law of war on land also applied to armed conflicts at sea in a contemporary context. Whilst it is a non-binding document, the *San Remo Manual* remains the main point of reference regarding the law of modern naval warfare.

Warfare against trade such as blockades, the capture of contraband, and the capture or destruction of enemy property at sea have also posed challenges for States seeking to regulate methods and weapons of naval warfare.[62] In legal terms, a blockade is defined as an act of war whereby a vessel, acting under authority of a belligerent State, blocks entry to or departure from a defined part of an enemy's coast to achieve a specific military objective such as preventing goods (or contraband) from reaching the enemy.[63] Customary law regarding blockades derives from ancient principles laid down in prize courts. Parties to an armed conflict are permitted to enforce and maintain a blockade, provided they do not violate the laws of war and that the blockade is publicly declared and enforced. A blockade is considered unlawful, however, (1) if it has the sole purpose of starving the civilian population on land, (2) if it denies goods that are indispensable for its survival, or (3) if it has a disproportionate impact on the civilian population compared to the military advantage of the blockade itself. Under the laws of war, a blockade cannot be used to stop humanitarian assistance. Indeed, a blockading party must ensure free passage of food and other essential supplies and may have permission to visit and search vessels carrying such goods. In addition, there are specific rules about 'contraband' that may be confiscated on board a neutral merchant vessel if such goods are likely to be used in armed conflict.[64]

Other incidences of criminal activity at sea

There are multiple examples of violent and/or criminal activities at sea that cause harm but fall outside of the definitions of piracy or war. These include, for example, robbery on the high seas involving only one vessel, or violent attacks

Figure 3.1 Map showing German submarine operations around the British Isles during World War I. (Published by Daily East Oregonian, 13 September 1915, page 1.)

on vessels located within the waters of any given State. These crimes would not meet the definition of piracy set out in UNCLOS and instead State criminal laws apply depending on whether the events occurred within national waters or, on the high seas, in involving State-registered vessels or nationals. The sea has long been used as a means of transport of human cargoes. The first documented instances of human trafficking date to the 16th century when Portugal began capturing African people and taking them to Europe, and the first slave voyage from Africa to the Americas was in 1525.[65] Slavery was legal until the 19th century, when it became prohibited,[66] although forced migration continued from Asia to the Americas.[67] There have been multiple international laws adopted to address the challenge of forced labour, movements and trafficking of people. The *International Agreement for the Suppression of "White Slave Traffic"* (1904) was the first international agreement on human trafficking, followed later by the *International Convention for the Suppression of Traffic in Women and Children* (1921), *ILO No 29 Forced Labour Convention* 1930, *Convention for the Suppression of the Traffic in Persons and of the Exploitation of the Prostitution of*

Others (1949) and the *Protocol to Prevent, Suppress and Punish Trafficking in Persons, Especially Women and Children* (2000).[68] Yet it is known that instances of slavery at sea continue today.[69] Forced migration and human trafficking, sometimes for labour on board illegal fishing vessels that remain at sea, have been well-documented in recent times.[70] The sea is also used to transport people willing to risk their lives as illegal immigrants. The global community continues to respond to these issues with specific regimes (such as the *United Nations Convention against Transnational Organized Crime* (2000) and its *Protocol Against the Smuggling of Migrants by Land, Sea and Air* (2000) and *Protocol to Prevent, Suppress and Punish Trafficking in Persons, Especially Women and Children* (2000)) and cooperative initiatives (including through the UN Office of Drugs and Crime and the International Criminal Police Organization (INTERPOL)) seeking to curb such activities.

More broadly, oceans and seas are also used as transport routes for the smuggling of legal goods (to avoid taxes, tariffs, customs duties, etc.) and/or the smuggling of illicit goods (such as drugs and weapons). These crimes, as well as human trafficking and illegal migration, are difficult to detect as the open ocean is vast making surveillance problematic. UNCLOS provided two relevant responses: First is the designation of the contiguous zone, explained in Chapter 2 as extending to 24 nautical miles from the shoreline, which permits a coastal State to exercise control within that zone to prevent infringement of customs, fiscal, immigration or sanitary laws.[71] Second, is the right of hot pursuit, which permits a coastal State to pursue a vessel believed to have breached the laws of that State.[72] Hot pursuit must be commenced when the foreign ship is still within the territorial sea or contiguous zone but may be continued beyond those waters provided the pursuit has not been interrupted.[73] Therefore, hot pursuit is a broad right that can apply to any illegal activity and extend to any maritime zone, as long as the specific conditions are met. Both the contiguous zone and the right of hot pursuit extend the jurisdiction of the coastal State, enabling it to better enforce the law to address crimes at sea.

In some cases, transnational criminal syndicates conduct illegal activities at sea, involving complex networks of actors with state-of-the-art equipment and technologies. International law of the sea is poorly equipped to respond to such sophisticated offenders and networks, although the UN Office of Drugs and Crime works to address the challenge focusing on cooperative arrangements that have worked well in addressing maritime piracy.[74]

Maritime piracy and war at sea are longstanding examples of violent activities carried out in the ocean, with legal responses evolving over hundreds of years. Yet, as with other topics explored in this book, new challenges continue to emerge and the global community must find ways to respond to those that operate outside the law. Illegal fishing at sea, for example, is a matter of significant global concern. It is estimated that the annual economic impact of illegal fishing

The hijacking of the MS *Achille Lauro*

In 1985 members of the Palestine Liberation Front, posing as tourists, seized a cruise ship carrying the Italian flag – MS *Achille Lauro* – off the coast of Egypt. The hijackers held the passengers and crew hostage, and threatened to kill the passengers unless Israel released 50 Palestinian prisoners. They killed one passenger the following day after their demands were not met.[75] The US considered the incident an act of piracy, although some legal experts argued that it did not qualify as piracy under international law because there was no second vessel involved and the hijackers were not acting for 'private ends'.[76] Nevertheless, the hijacking prompted the International Maritime Organization to draft a convention on maritime terrorism that was subsequently adopted in 1988.[77]

diverted from legitimate trade is US$26 to US$50 billion.[78] Illegal fishing is defined by the FAO as involving breaches of any fishing regulations; however, it is not usually a crime under State legislation and it is not considered so under international law.[79] As a civil offence it may be punishable with fines or loss of legitimate fishing licences, and hot pursuit can still be used in the context of illegal fishing.[80]

Regardless of the type of criminal activity involved, surveillance and enforcement at sea involves the use of considerable resources, including specialist vessels, qualified personnel and surveillance and tracking technologies. Some navies are engaged in constabulary services, but in many cases, it is a coast guard that is utilised. For developing nations, and in particular small island developing States with very large maritime areas to monitor, the cost of such services is prohibitive. A novel legal arrangement to address some of these challenges is the use of fisheries enforcement shiprider agreements. These agreements involve a host and foreign nation, where the foreign State uses its vessels to patrol national waters with fisheries officers of the host State 'riding' on board to carry out law enforcement functions.[81]

As noted earlier, the narrow definition of piracy requires that acts must be committed for 'private ends'. Terrorism is frequently for political or other purposes. Although there are only limited instances of terrorism being facilitated by at sea logistical support, this is certainly a risk.[82] In addition, a vessel could be used as a weapon by being sunk or deliberately run aground to create a navigational hazard or an environmental catastrophe. The global community has since adopted the *Rome Convention on the Suppression of Unlawful Acts Against the Safety of Maritime Navigation* (1988) and the *Protocol for the Suppression of*

Unlawful Acts Against the Safety of Fixed Platforms Located on the Continental Shelf (2005),[83] and the *International Convention on the Suppression of Acts of Nuclear Terrorism* (2005).[84]

Conclusion

Conflicts at sea, including piracy, war and maritime crime, are complex areas with differing motivators and participants. Unsurprisingly, the legal responses have been challenging. International law has taken a dominant role in humanitarian law and the laws of war and maritime piracy. Key features include the long evolution of customary norms, their later codification in treaties and the high level of international cooperation including through legal agreements. The relatively narrow international law definitions of piracy and war, however, reflect the compartmentalisation and categorisation that is common in the laws that have been developed for oceans, seas and shorelines. In addition, the focus on crimes that affect people and economies, as opposed to marine species or the ocean environment itself, highlights the anthropocentric nature of this area of law and the lack of engagement with ocean-centred perspectives. Conflicts led by non-State actors, including terrorism and other crimes at sea that fall short of piracy and war, are largely matters left to individual States to outlaw and criminalise albeit with some measures being adopted at the international level. This adds to complexity in the field as various States have responded in different ways depending on their socio-legal context. Nevertheless, cooperative forces and some novel developments such as shiprider agreements provide potential models for the other challenges in oceans, seas and shorelines.

Notes

1 Admiral James Stavridis, *Sea Power: The History and Geopolitics of the World's Oceans* (New York: Penguin Press, 2017), 274.
2 The Sea Peoples confederacy of naval raiders operated between 1276 and 1178 BCE and are considered a major contributor to the Bronze Age collapse.
3 Captain James Cook was killed in 1779 on the beach at Kealakekua Bay, Hawaiʻi.
4 The vast majority of pirates were men, yet there have been many female pirates throughout history. For further details see, John C. Appleby, *Women and English Piracy 1540–1720: Partners and Victims of Crime* (Martlesham: Boydell &Brewer, 2013); Laura Sook Duncombe, *Pirate Women: The Princesses, Prostitutes, and Privateers Who Ruled the Seven Seas* (Chicago: Chicago Review Press, 2019); Brittany Gilmer, "Invisible Pirates: Women and the Gendered Roles of Somali Piracy," *Feminist Criminology* 14, no. 3 (2019): 371–88; and Robert C. Ritchie, "Piracy," in *The Oxford Encyclopedia of Maritime History*, ed. John J. Hattendorf (Oxford: Oxford University Press, 2007).
5 See Captain Charles Johnson [Daniel Defoe], *A General History of the Robberies and Murders of the Most Notorious Pirates* (London: Charles Rivington, J. Lacy and J. Stone, 1724). 'Blackbeard', for example, was a particularly notorious pirate who operated off the North American coast between 1716 and 1718.

6 Katherine Waite, "The Radical Romanticism of Piracy," *British Online Archives* (July 10, 2019), https://microform.digital/boa/posts/category/articles/352/the-radical-romanticism-of-piracy.
7 Customary international laws are rules coming from general and consistent practice that are accepted as law (*opinion juris*). It applies regardless of whether it is codified in a treaty. In the case of piracy, customary international law predated UNCLOS because of the long history of piracy as discussed earlier.
8 B. H. Dubner, *The Law of International Sea Piracy* (The Hague: Martinus Nijhoff, 1980), 1. John Kavanagh, "The Law of Contemporary Sea Piracy," *Australian International Law Journal* 8 (1999): 127–57, 135.
9 Robert J. Antony, "Bloodthirsty Pirates? Violence and Terror on the South China Sea in Early Modern Times," *Journal of Early Modern History* 16, no. 6 (2012): 481–501, https://doi.org/10.1163/15700658-12342337.
10 G. N. Clark, "The Barbary Corsairs in the Seventeenth Century," *The Cambridge Historical Journal* 8, no. 1 (1944): 22–35.
11 Stavridis, *Sea Power*, 277.
12 She commanded over 1,800 ships and 80,000 men, and operated for longer making more money than any other pirate. Duncombe, *Pirate Women*.
13 Philip Gosse, *The History of Piracy* (New York: Dover Publications, Inc., 2007, first pub. 1932), 1.
14 *Acte for the Punysshement of Pyrotes and Robbers of the Sea* (1536) 28, Hen VIII c 15.
15 Kavanagh, "The Law of Contemporary Sea Piracy," 129–30.
16 Ibid., 132. These included trading with pirates and carrying or confining slaves on board ships.
17 Kavanagh, "The Law of Contemporary Sea Piracy," 133.
18 Ibid., 134.
19 Joel Baer, "Pirates and the Law," in *Pirates* (Stroud: Tempus Publishing, 2007). Pirates also had strict codes by which they operated including rules for distribution of plunder, punishments for crimes and compensation for injuries. See Paul H. Robinson and Sarah M. Robinson, *Pirates, Prisoners and Lepers: Lessons from Life Outside the Law* (Lincoln, NE: Potomac Books, 2015), 29.
20 Baer, "Pirates and the Law," 224.
21 Ibid., 225.
22 Britannica, The Editors of Encyclopaedia, "Sir Francis Drake," *Encyclopedia Britannica* (November 16, 2023), www.britannica.com/biography/Francis-Drake.
23 Britannica, The Editors of Encyclopaedia, "Pirates, Privateers, Corsairs, Buccaneers: What's the Difference?" *Encyclopedia Britannica* (September 18, 2017), www.britannica.com/story/pirates-privateers-corsairs-buccaneers-whats-the-difference
24 Alexander Tabarrok, "The Rise, Fall, and Rise Again of Privateers," *The Independent Review* 11, no. 4 (Spring 2007): 565–77.
25 Dampier, whilst operating as a privateer, also made detailed and influential observations of Indigenous peoples, marine species and ocean currents which, when published, helped to popularise travel writing. See for example Diana Preston and Michael Preston, *A Pirate of Exquisite Mind: The Life of William Dampier, Explorer, Naturalist and Buccaneer* (Ealing: Corgi Books, 2005).
26 Timothy Steigelman, "The Promise and Perils of Prize Law," *World History Connected* 19, no. 1 (February/March 2022): 2–3.
27 Anonymous, "Those in Peril on the Sea," *The Economist* (August 9, 1997): 40.
28 Stavridis, *Sea Power*, 277–80.
29 Kavanagh, "The Law of Contemporary Sea Piracy," 127.

30 "Piracy Reporting Centre, Kuala Lumpur," *Union of International Associations*, accessed January 11, 2024, https://uia.org/s/or/en/1100002897.
31 Robert Beckman, "Combating Piracy and Armed Robbery against Ships in Southeast Asia: The Way Forward," *Ocean Development and International Law*, 33 (2002): 317–41.
32 "New IMB Report Reveals Concerning Rise in Maritime Piracy Incidents in 2023," *International Chamber of Commerce*, accessed January 11, 2024, https://iccwbo.org/news-publications/news/new-imb-report-reveals-concerning-rise-in-maritime-piracy-incidents-in-2023/
33 *UN Convention on the Law of the Sea* (UNCLOS) Article 101(a). For the full text of UNCLOS see "United Nations Convention on the Law of the Sea," *UN*, accessed March 1, 2024, www.un.org/depts/los/convention_agreements/texts/unclos/closindx.htm.
34 Aref Fakhry, "Piracy across Maritime Law: Is There a Problem of Definition?" in T*he Regulation of International Shipping: International and Comparative Perspectives, Essays in Honor of Edgar Gold*, ed. Aldo Chircop, Norman Letalik, Ted L. McDorman, and Susan Rolston (Leiden: Brill Publishing, 2012), 97–117,
35 Paul Todd, *Maritime Fraud and Piracy*, 2nd ed. (London: Lloyd's List, 2010), para. 1.018.
36 Christian Bueger, "Responses to Contemporary Piracy: Disentangling the Organizational Field," in *Modern Piracy*, ed. Douglas Guilfoyle (Cheltenham: Edward Elgar Publishing Limited, 2013), 91–116.
37 Douglas Guilfoyle, "Policy Tensions and the Legal Regime Governing Piracy," in *Modern Piracy*, ed. Douglas Guilfoyle (Cheltenham: Edward Elgar Publishing Limited, 2013), 325–36.
38 Martin Placek, "Pirate Attacks – Statistics & Facts," *Statista* (January 10, 2024), www.statista.com/topics/1290/pirate-attacks/#topicOverview.
39 Edward R. Lucas, "Somalia's 'Pirate Cycle': The Three Phases of Somali Piracy," *Journal of Strategic Security* 6, no. 1 (Spring 2013): 55–63.
40 Stavridis, *Sea Power*, 278–79; Douglas Guilfoyle, "Introduction: Piracy, Law and Lawyers," in *Modern Piracy*, ed. Guilfoyle, 1–10.
41 The Red Sea, between the Mediterranean Sea and Indian Ocean, accounts for 15% of global maritime trade. See "Alarmed by Attacks on Ships in Red Sea, Top UN Officials Urge Protection of Global Supply Chains, Avoiding Deeper Regional Tensions, in Security Council Briefing," *United Nations Security Council*, 9525th meeting, SC/15552 (January 3, 2024), https://press.un.org/en/2024/sc15552.doc.htm. These regional tensions were unresolved at the time of writing.
42 See, for example, UNGA, *Oceans and the Law of the Sea* (A/RES/64/71, December 4, 2009).
43 Piracy increased in this region from 1991 after the fall of the national government when gangs became emboldened to commit violence under the leadership of local warlords. CTF51, in conjunction with the European Union Naval Force Somalia (EUNAVFOR) and independently deployed naval ships from other nations, patrol the Internationally Recommended Transit Corridor to directly address the piracy crisis in the Gulf of Aden and Indian Ocean more generally, and promotes Best Management Practices guidelines for commercial shipping in order to deter piracy in the region. See Combined Maritime Forces, "CTF 151: Counter-Piracy," https://combinedmaritimeforces.com/ctf-151-counter-piracy/. BIMCO et al., *Best Management Practices to Deter Piracy and Enhance Maritime Security in the Red Sea, Gulf of Aden, Indian Ocean and Arabian Sea* (Edinburgh: Witherby Publishing Group, 2018), www.maritimeglobalsecurity.org/media/1038/bmp5-high_res.pdf

44 Paul Hallwood, "Piracy and the Law of the Sea," *The SAIS Review of International Affairs* 33, no. 2 (Summer–Fall 2013): 117–26.
45 United Nations, "Global Response Needed to Counter Rising Security Threats at Sea," *United Nations News* (August 9, 2021), https://news.un.org/en/story/2021/08/1097432.
46 "Concluding Cluster 2 of International Law Commission Report, Sixth Committee Speakers Deliberate over Definitions for International Organizations, Piracy," *UN Meetings Coverage and Press Releases* (October 31, 2023), https://press.un.org/en/2023/gal3702.doc.htm.
47 Gregory DeAngelo and Taylor Leland Smith, "Private Security, Maritime Piracy and the Provision of International Public Safety," *Journal of Risk and Uncertainty* 50 (2020): 77–97. Jessica N. M. Schechinger, "Responsibility for Human Rights Violations Arising from the Use of Privately Contracted Armed Security Personnel against Piracy, Re-emphasizing the Primary Role and Obligations of Flag States," *SHARES Research Paper Series*, 58, Amsterdam Center for International Law (2014).
48 Stavridis, *Sea Power*, 282–84. The UN reported in 2021 that the last two successful piracy attacks off the coast of Somalia were in the spring of 2017, the first since 2012. See UN, "Global Response Needed to Counter Rising Security Threats at Sea."
49 Joel Christopher Coito, "Pirates vs. Private Security: Commercial Shipping, the Montreux Document and the Battle for the Gulf of Aden," *California Law Review* 101, no. 1 (February 2013): 173–226.
50 The full text of the UN Charter can be found at www.un.org/en/about-us/un-charter.
51 War law, or the law of armed conflict, is also known as international humanitarian law.
52 US Naval War College, *The Commander's Handbook on the Law of Naval Operations* (NWP 1–14M) (Office of the Chief of Naval Operations, 2022), https://usnwc.libguides.com/ld.php?content_id=66281931
53 "Convention (XIII) Concerning the Rights and Duties of Neutral Powers in Naval War," *The Hague* (October 18, 1907), https://ihl-databases.icrc.org/en/ihl-treaties/hague-conv-xiii-1907.
54 For many (but not all) nations in the world, being bound by an international treaty involves a two-step process. First the State representative signs the treaty. Then they must follow a process for parliamentary endorsement. Only at that stage is the treaty ratified and becomes binding upon that State. This process prevents a government representative from unilaterally joining a treaty without endorsement through a democratic process.
55 See International Committee of the Red Cross, "Treaties, State Parties and Commentaries," *Declaration Concerning the Laws of Naval War, London* (February 26, 1909), https://ihl-databases.icrc.org/en/ihl-treaties/london-decl-1909.
56 "The 'Peleus' Trial," *Hansard*, UK Parliament 166 (April 25, 1950), https://hansard.parliament.uk/Lords/1950-04-25/debates/cdcb8faa-9721-43df-8e08-62b9202a79ee/ThePeleusTrial.
57 The United Nations War Crimes Commission, *Law Reports of Trials of War Criminals* 1 (1947): 1–21, cited in Marco Sassòli, Antoine Bouvier, Anne Quintin, and Julia Grignon, "British Military Court at Hamburg, the Peleus Trial," *How Does Law Protect in War?* (2022), https://casebook.icrc.org/case-study/british-military-court-hamburg-peleus-trial. Wolff Heintschel von Heinegg, "Maritime Warfare," in *The Oxford Handbook of International Law in Armed Conflict*, ed. Andrew Clapham and Paola Gaeta (Oxford: Oxford University Press, 2014), 145–82.
58 The United Nations War Crimes Commission, "Naval Warfare," *How Does Law Protect in War?* (2022), https://casebook.icrc.org/law/naval-warfare#_ftnref_002.

59 For a summary of the Geneva Conventions and links to the full text, see: "The Geneva Conventions of 1949 and Their Additional Protocols," *ICRC* (January 2014) www.icrc.org/en/document/geneva-conventions-1949-additional-protocols.
60 Charles W. Koburger Jr., *Sea Power in the Falklands* (Westport: Praeger, 1983). Ray Takeyh, "The Iran-Iraq War: A Reassessment," *Middle East Journal* 64, no. 3 (Summer 2010): 365–83.
61 International Committee of the Red Cross, *San Remo Manual on International Law Applicable to Armed Conflicts at Sea*, 31–12–1995 Article, International Review of the Red Cross 309 (December 31, 1995), www.icrc.org/en/doc/resources/documents/article/other/57jmsu.htm.
62 Phillip Drew, *The Law of Maritime Blockade: Past, Present, and Future* (Oxford: Oxford University Press, 2018).
63 Magne Frostad, "Naval Blockade," *Arctic Review on Law and Politics* 9 (2018): 195–225.
64 The Editors of Encyclopaedia, "Blockade," *Encyclopedia Britannica* (August 21, 2019), www.britannica.com/topic/blockade-warfare. Elem Khairullin, "'Yemen, Naval Blockade', How Does Law Protect in War?" *ICRC Online Casebook* (2022), https://casebook.icrc.org/case-study/yemen-naval-blockade-0. US Naval War College, *The Commander's Handbook*.
65 For a summary of the history, see Thomas Lewis, "Transatlantic Slave Trade," *Brittanica*, updated February 29, 2024, www.britannica.com/topic/transatlantic-slave-trade.
66 In 1807 in Britain and 1820 in the US, but the last reported slave voyage to America occurred in 1866.
67 This was outlawed by the US *Page Act* (1875).
68 For the text of these and other related instruments, see "Human Rights Instruments," *UN Human Rights*, accessed March 1, 2024, www.ohchr.org/en/instruments-listings.
69 "Slavery at Sea," *Human Rights at Sea*, accessed January 11, 2024, www.humanrightsatsea.org/what-we-do/slavery-sea.
70 Urbina, *The Outlaw Ocean*.
71 UNCLOS Article 33.
72 UNCLOS Article 111.
73 Particular conditions must be met for hot pursuit: (1) the pursuit must be commenced in internal waters, territorial sea or contiguous zone; (2) hot pursuit cannot commence until a visual or auditory signal is given; (3) the right of hot pursuit can only be exercised by warships, military aircraft or a vessel marked as being on government service; and (4) it ceases when the foreign ship enters the territorial sea of its own State. See further uses of hot pursuit discussed in Chapter 4.
74 See, for example, United Nations, *UNODC Combating Transnational Organized Crime Committed at Sea: Issue Paper* (2013), www.unodc.org/documents/organized-crime/GPTOC/Issue_Paper_-_TOC_at_Sea.pdf.
75 Malvina Halberstam, "Terrorism on the High Seas: The Achille Lauro, Piracy and the IMO Convention on Maritime Safety," *American Journal of International Law* 82, no. 2 (1988): 269–310.
76 *Convention on the High Seas*, Geneva (April 29, 1958).
77 IMO, *Convention for the Suppression of Unlawful Acts Against the Safety of Maritime Navigation*, 1988 (in force 1992).
78 U. R. Sumaila et al., "Illicit Trade in Marine Fish Catch and Its Effects on Ecosystems and People Worldwide," *Science Advances* 6, no. 9 (2020), https://doi.org/10.1126/sciadv.aaz3801. See Chapter 4 for further discussion of illegal fishing.
79 See the work of the FAO such as the *International Plan of Action on IUU Fishing*: "Illegal, Unreported and Unregulated (IUU) Fishing," *FAO*, accessed March 1, 2024, www.fao.org/iuu-fishing/background/what-is-iuu-fishing/.

80 Illegal, unreported and unregulated fishing is discussed further in Chapter 4.
81 Lt. Cmdr. Warren N. Wright, U.S. Coast Guard, "Shiprider Program," *Indo-Pacific Defense Forum* (January 27, 2020), https://ipdefenseforum.com/2020/01/shiprider-program/. These arrangements are explored further in chapter 4.
82 Halberstam, "Terrorism on the High Seas."
83 These instruments can be found through the International Maritime Organization at "List of IMO Conventions," *IMO*, accessed March 1, 2024, www.imo.org/en/About/Conventions/Pages/ListOfConventions.aspx.
84 Rüdiger Wolfrum, "Fighting Terrorism at Sea: Options and Limitations under International Law," *International Tribunal for the Law of the Sea*, The 28th Doherty Lecture (April 13, 2006), www.itlos.org/en/main/press-media/statements-of-the-president/statements-of-president-wolfrum/#c94.

Bibliography

Anonymous. "Those in Peril on the Sea." *The Economist* (August 9, 1997).

Antony, Robert J. "Bloodthirsty Pirates? Violence and Terror on the South China Sea in Early Modern Times." *Journal of Early Modern History* 16, no. 6 (2012): 481–501. https://doi.org/10.1163/15700658-12342337.

Appleby, John C. *Women and English Piracy 1540–1720: Partners and Victims of Crime*. Martlesham: Boydell &Brewer, 2013.

Baer, Joel. "Pirates and the Law." In *Pirates*. Stroud: Tempus Publishing, 2007.

Beckman, Robert. "Combating Piracy and Armed Robbery Against Ships in Southeast Asia: The Way Forward." *Ocean Development and International Law* 33 (2002): 317–41.

BIMCO et al. *Best Management Practices to Deter Piracy and Enhance Maritime Security in the Red Sea, Gulf of Aden, Indian Ocean and Arabian Sea*. Edinburgh: Witherby Publishing Group, 2018. www.maritimeglobalsecurity.org/media/1038/bmp5-high_res.pdf

Bueger, Christian. "Responses to Contemporary Piracy: Disentangling the Organizational Field." In *Modern Piracy*, edited by Douglas Guilfoyle. Cheltenham: Edward Elgar Publishing Limited, 2013.

Clark, G. N. "The Barbary Corsairs in the Seventeenth Century." *The Cambridge Historical Journal* 8, no. 1 (1944): 22–35.

Coito, Joel Christopher. "Pirates vs. Private Security: Commercial Shipping, the Montreux Document and the Battle for the Gulf of Aden." *California Law Review* 101, no. 1 (2013): 173–226.

Combined Maritime Forces. "CTF 151: Counter-Piracy." Accessed March 15, 2024. https://combinedmaritimeforces.com/ctf-151-counter-piracy/.

"Concluding Cluster 2 of International Law Commission Report, Sixth Committee Speakers Deliberate over Definitions for International Organizations, Piracy." *UN Meetings Coverage and Press Releases* (October 31, 2023). https://press.un.org/en/2023/gal3702.doc.htm.

DeAngelo, Gregory, and Taylor Leland Smith. "Private Security, Maritime Piracy and the Provision of International Public Safety." *Journal of Risk and Uncertainty* 50 (2020): 77–97.

Drew, Phillip. *The Law of Maritime Blockade: Past, Present, and Future*. Oxford: Oxford University Press, 2018.

Dubner, B. H. *The Law of International Sea Piracy*. The Hague: Martinus Nijhoff, 1980.

Duncombe, Laura Sook. *Pirate Women: The Princesses, Prostitutes, and Privateers Who Ruled the Seven Seas*. Chicago: Chicago Review Press, 2019.

Editors of Encyclopaedia Britannica. "Blockade." *Encyclopedia Britannica* (August 21, 2019). www.britannica.com/topic/blockade-warfare.
Editors of Encyclopaedia Britannica. "Pirates, Privateers, Corsairs, Buccaneers: What's the Difference?" *Encyclopedia Britannica* (September 18, 2017). www.britannica.com/story/pirates-privateers-corsairs-buccaneers-whats-the-difference.
Editors of Encyclopaedia Britannica. "Sir Francis Drake." *Encyclopedia Britannica* (November 16, 2023). www.britannica.com/biography/Francis-Drake.
Fakhry, Aref. "Piracy Across Maritime Law: Is There a Problem of Definition?" In *The Regulation of International Shipping: International and Comparative Perspectives, Essays in Honor of Edgar Gold*, edited by Aldo Chircop, Norman Letalik, Ted L. McDorman, and Susan Rolston. Leiden: Brill Publishing, 2012.
FAO. "Illegal, Unreported and Unregulated (IUU) Fishing." Accessed March 1, 2024. www.fao.org/iuu-fishing/background/what-is-iuu-fishing/.
Frostad, Magne. "Naval Blockade." *Arctic Review on Law and Politics* 9 (2018): 195–225.
Gilmer, Brittany. "Invisible Pirates: Women and the Gendered Roles of Somali Piracy." *Feminist Criminology* 14, no. 3 (2019): 371–88.
Gosse, Philip. *The History of Piracy*. New York: Dover Publications, Inc., 2007, first pub. 1932.
Guilfoyle, Douglas. "Introduction: Piracy, Law and Lawyers." In *Modern Piracy*, edited by Douglas Guilfoyle. Cheltenham: Edward Elgar Publishing Limited, 2013.
Guilfoyle, Douglas. "Policy Tensions and the Legal Regime Governing Piracy." In *Modern Piracy*, edited by Douglas Guilfoyle. Cheltenham: Edward Elgar Publishing Limited, 2013.
Halberstam, Malvina. "Terrorism on the High Seas: The Achille Lauro, Piracy and the IMO Convention on Maritime Safety." *American Journal of International Law* 82, no. 2 (1988): 269–310.
Hallwood, Paul. "Piracy and the Law of the Sea." *The SAIS Review of International Affairs* 33, no. 2 (2013): 117–26.
Human Rights at Sea. "Slavery at Sea." Accessed January 11, 2024. www.humanrightsatsea.org/what-we-do/slavery-sea.
International Chamber of Commerce. "New IMB Report Reveals Concerning Rise in Maritime Piracy Incidents in 2023." Accessed January 11, 2024. https://iccwbo.org/news-publications/news/new-imb-report-reveals-concerning-rise-in-maritime-piracy-incidents-in-2023/
International Committee of the Red Cross. *San Remo Manual on International Law Applicable to Armed Conflicts at Sea*, 31–12–1995 Article, International Review of the Red Cross 309 (December 31, 1995). www.icrc.org/en/doc/resources/documents/article/other/57jmsu.htm.
International Committee of the Red Cross. "Treaties, State Parties and Commentaries." *Declaration Concerning the Laws of Naval War, London, 26 February 1909*. https://ihl-databases.icrc.org/en/ihl-treaties/london-decl-1909.
Johnson, Captain Charles [Daniel Defoe]. *A General History of the Robberies and Murders of the Most Notorious Pirates*. London: Charles Rivington, J. Lacy and J. Stone, 1724.
Kavanagh, John. "The Law of Contemporary Sea Piracy." *Australian International Law Journal* 8 (1999): 127–57, 135.
Khairullin, Elem. "Yemen, Naval Blockade', How Does Law Protect in War?" *ICRC Online Casebook* (2022). https://casebook.icrc.org/case-study/yemen-naval-blockade-0.
Koburger Jr., Charles W. *Sea Power in the Falklands*. Westport: Praeger, 1983.
Lewis, Thomas. "Transatlantic Slave Trade." *Brittanica*. www.britannica.com/topic/transatlantic-slave-trade, updated February 29, 2024.
Lucas, Edward R. "Somalia's 'Pirate Cycle': The Three Phases of Somali Piracy." *Journal of Strategic Security* 6, no. 1 (2013): 55–63.

Placek, Martin. "Pirate Attacks – Statistics & Facts." *Statista* (January 10, 2024). www.statista.com/topics/1290/pirate-attacks/#topicOverview.

Preston, Diana, and Michael Preston. *A Pirate of Exquisite Mind: The Life of William Dampier, Explorer, Naturalist and Buccaneer*. Ealing: Corgi Books, 2005.

Ritchie, Robert C. "Piracy." In *The Oxford Encyclopedia of Maritime History*, edited by John J. Hattendorf. Oxford: Oxford University Press, 2007.

Robinson, Paul H., and Sarah M. Robinson. *Pirates, Prisoners and Lepers: Lessons from Life Outside the Law*. Lincoln, NE: Potomac Books, 2015.

Schechinger, Jessica N. M. "Responsibility for Human Rights Violations Arising from the Use of Privately Contracted Armed Security Personnel against Piracy, Re-emphasizing the Primary Role and Obligations of Flag States." *SHARES Research Paper Series*, 58, Amsterdam Center for International Law (2014).

Stavridis, Admiral James. *Sea Power: The History and Geopolitics of the World's Oceans*. New York: Penguin Press, 2017.

Steigelman, Timothy. "The Promise and Perils of Prize Law." *World History Connected* 19, no. 1 (2022): 2–3.

Sumaila, U. R. et al. "Illicit Trade in Marine Fish Catch and its Effects on Ecosystems and People Worldwide." *Science Advances* 6, no. 9 (2020). https://doi.org/10.1126/sciadv.aaz3801.

Tabarrok, Alexander. "The Rise, Fall, and Rise Again of Privateers." *The Independent Review* 11, no. 4 (Spring 2007): 565–77.

Takeyh, Ray. "The Iran-Iraq War: A Reassessment." *Middle East Journal* 64, no. 3 (Summer 2010): 365–83.

"The 'Peleus' Trial." *Hansard*, UK Parliament 166 (April 25, 1950). https://hansard.parliament.uk/Lords/1950-04-25/debates/cdcb8faa-9721-43df-8e08-62b9202a79ee/ThePeleusTrial.

Todd, Paul. *Maritime Fraud and Piracy*. 2nd ed. London: Lloyd's List, 2010.

UN. "United Nations Convention on the Law of the Sea." Accessed March 1, 2024. www.un.org/depts/los/convention_agreements/texts/unclos/closindx.htm.

UNGA. *Oceans and The Law of the Sea* (A/RES/64/71, December 4, 2009).

Union of International Association. "Piracy Reporting Centre, Kuala Lumpur." Accessed January 11, 2024. https://uia.org/s/or/en/1100002897.

United Nations. "Global Response Needed to Counter Rising Security Threats at Sea." *United Nations News* (August 9, 2021). https://news.un.org/en/story/2021/08/1097432.

United Nations. "UNODC Combating Transnational Organized Crime Committed at Sea: Issue Paper." (2013). www.unodc.org/documents/organized-crime/GPTOC/Issue_Paper_-_TOC_at_Sea.pdf.

United Nations Security Council. "Alarmed by Attacks on Ships in Red Sea, Top UN Officials Urge Protection of Global Supply Chains, Avoiding Deeper Regional Tensions, in Security Council Briefing." *9525th Meeting*, SC/15552 (January 3, 2024). https://press.un.org/en/2024/sc15552.doc.htm.

United Nations War Crimes Commission. *Law Reports of Trials of War Criminals* 1 (1947), 1–21, cited in Marco Sassòli, Antoine Bouvier, Anne Quintin, and Julia Grignon. "British Military Court at Hamburg, The Peleus Trial." *How Does Law Protect in War?* (2022). https://casebook.icrc.org/case-study/british-military-court-hamburg-peleus-trial.

United Nations War Crimes Commission. "Naval Warfare." *How Does Law Protect in War?* (2022). https://casebook.icrc.org/law/naval-warfare#_ftnref_002.

Urbina, Ian. *The Outlaw Ocean*. New York City: Alfred A Knopf Inc, 2019.

US Naval War College. *The Commander's Handbook on the Law of Naval Operations* (NWP 1–14M). Office of the Chief of Naval Operations, 2022. https://usnwc.libguides.com/ld.php?content_id=66281931

von Heinegg, Wolff Heintschel. "Maritime Warfare." In *The Oxford Handbook of International Law in Armed Conflict*, edited by Andrew Clapham and Paola Gaeta. Oxford: Oxford University Press, 2014.

Waite, Katherine. "The Radical Romanticism of Piracy." *British Online Archives* (July 10, 2019). https://microform.digital/boa/posts/category/articles/352/the-radical-romanticism-of-piracy.

Wolfrum, Rüdiger. "Fighting Terrorism at Sea: Options and Limitations under International Law." *International Tribunal for the Law of the Sea.* The 28th Doherty Lecture (April 13, 2006). www.itlos.org/en/main/press-media/statements-of-the-president/statements-of-president-wolfrum/#c94

Wright, Lt. Cmdr. Warren N. (U.S. Coast Guard). "Shiprider Program." *Indo-Pacific Defense Forum* (January 27, 2020). https://ipdefenseforum.com/2020/01/shiprider-program/

Part II

The ocean as resource

4 An 'inexhaustible' bounty

Fishing and farming of marine life

With the establishment of 200-mile EEZs, the nations of the world have acquired an area of sea surface amounting to about 25% of the globe . . . these enlarged sovereignties now begin to post management problems that can greatly benefit from marine science for their solution.

John Bardach

Overview

From the earliest of times humans have used the sea as a source of food and livelihoods. Fishing as an activity for subsistence, livelihood and/or recreation has persisted across millennia and in almost all places in the world. From neolithic fish hooks to ancient Greek nets, fish rattles, Inuit ice-fishing spears, and Polynesian kites, there is a wealth of evidence of fishing practices that date back to early seafood harvesting.[1] With the development of rudimentary vessels over 6,000 years ago, it became possible for humans to harvest oceanic fish and other marine life.[2] Fishing expanded as equipment and techniques such as catfish noodling and flounder tramping became more specialised, and seafood was bartered, sold in local markets or traded further afield.[3]

Fishing became an increasingly commercial activity in Europe from the Middle Ages and included whaling and sealing as well as fin fishing. From the 19th century, the development of larger and more technologically advanced vessels enabled fishers to increase their capacity to harvest species in large numbers. Industrialisation fundamentally changed the nature of fishing, and technological advances in gear and equipment, as well as refrigeration, proved to be the turning points that enabled distant water fishing and the expansion of trading markets. Such 'quantum jumps' included 'steel vessels and steam engines, then diesel motors, synthetic yarns for nets and electronic fish finding devices'.[4] The post-World War II era brought greater innovations, with fish being caught further offshore or at greater depths, changing the pattern and scale of harvesting and allowing 'fishing in all but the most extreme environments'.[5] Paradoxically, the

DOI: 10.4324/9781003005261-7

creation of more efficient fishing gear and methods also meant that harvesting became increasingly less discriminate, and the problem of bycatch – the unintended capture of non-target species – and wasteful discards grew with significant impacts on some species, ecosystems and the ocean environment itself.[6]

This chapter examines fisheries regulations through time at different scales and in separate marine areas to demonstrate that, despite significant influences and developments, fishing has been, and remains, largely regulated according to just five categories of rules: where fishing can occur, how much can be harvested, who can fish, when fishing can take place, and what gear and equipment is permitted. The simplicity of these five rule types belies the complexity of the global regulatory landscape yet shows that, at least in this area of activity, there is considerable commonality.

Early fisheries rules and practices

Traditional fishing customs and norms

Customary marine tenure rules were some of the first traditional sea laws to evolve, and these established who could control or access certain waters for fishing and other purposes.[7] Historical and anthropological research has demonstrated that many Indigenous and traditional coastal communities – particularly in small island nations – owned and controlled inshore waters in similar ways to land. In Oceania, for example, village land included marine areas adjacent to the shore out to the seaward side of the outer reef, and sometimes beyond the reef.[8] Traditional fishing rules included restrictions on access and use of these communal areas, imposed by village chiefs or leaders. Johannes suggests that these centuries-old systems were 'in the best interest of those who controlled a given area' in order 'to harvest in moderation . . . so they could maintain high sustained yields'.[9] Of course, this logic also applied in other nations but '[i]n the West, recognition that there were practical limits to the sea's productivity developed only around the turn of the [20th] century'.[10] Other rules also supported sustainability, explicitly and/or implicitly, as some customary rules ensured all parts of a species were utilised. In Hawai'i, for example, sharks are considered *'aumakua* (gods), and if a shark is killed all parts must be used – the meat for food, the teeth for weapons and tools, the skin for drums and sanding tools.[11]

Access rights and resource pressures underpin many fisheries laws, including traditional and customary rules. Some communities developed detailed practices, which became customary law based on the fishing methods of the time, and included hand gathering, small nets, and pole and line fishing. In some cases, women were involved in reef gleaning and collecting shellfish in shallow waters, while men could fish for high-status species such as bonito, tuna and turtle and from boats beyond the reef.[12] In other cases, certain people were knowledge holders about species life cycles, sites of fidelity and harvest times.[13] Customary practices often surrounded the making of fishing equipment, harvesting of species and fishing methods – including bans on poisoning and dynamiting reefs and fish.[14]

Mariculture was simultaneously practised by early communities. This was mostly in inlets, coves or very close to shore. In the South Pacific, fish traps and ponds were commonly used to keep small fish and other species such as turtles allowing them to grow before harvesting them.[15] In Hawai'i, for example, these included seawater ponds (*loko kuapa*) some of which have now been restored,[16] and in Australia, Aboriginal people also utilised fish traps and weirs.[17] For many years traditional marine and fisheries laws were seen as historical and outdated, and traditional tenure and marine management rules crumbled as western influences dominated. Yet, with the rise of the environmental movement in the 1970s and simultaneous independence of many former colonies, some places have revived these customary rules. In Samoa, for example, the State has formally recognised the traditional village council (*fono*) as a local governance institution and empowered it to pass fisheries by-laws enforceable against villagers and outsiders.[18] Yet in places such as Fiji the *qoliqoli* (traditional fishing rights) have never been given their former binding status.[19] At the international level, traditional ecological knowledge, customs and practices have been recognised in the *Convention on Biological Diversity*[20] and the *Declaration on the Rights of Indigenous Peoples*.[21] But these traditional legal approaches have not been embraced in fisheries treaties adopted as international law nor in the regional fisheries bodies explored later in the chapter. Much work, therefore, remains to be done to acknowledge and harness the benefits of traditional fisheries governance.

Early western fishing restrictions

Whilst traditional and island communities had early awareness of resource limits and the consequences of unsustainability, the legal landscape evolved quite differently elsewhere. As outlined in Chapter 1, attitudes towards the ocean and marine life were different in societies where marine areas were, and remain, under public ownership with governments regulating access and use. Furthermore, many continental coastal communities were only partially reliant on the ocean as a source of protein given other terrestrial resources available to them which, in part, led to a perception that the ocean was boundless and inexhaustible – unlike many small island communities that depended upon protein from the ocean, which made sustainability a necessity.[22] Nevertheless, rules around fishing practices developed and were relatively simple to administer while populations were low, livelihoods were restricted to subsidence or artisanal fishing, and markets were local.

As communities grew, however, access to fishing grounds and rights to fish often led to conflict between different groups of fishers, and damaging and destructive fishing practices began to raise concerns. Some of the first European laws, for example, sought to restrict the use of certain gear and equipment.

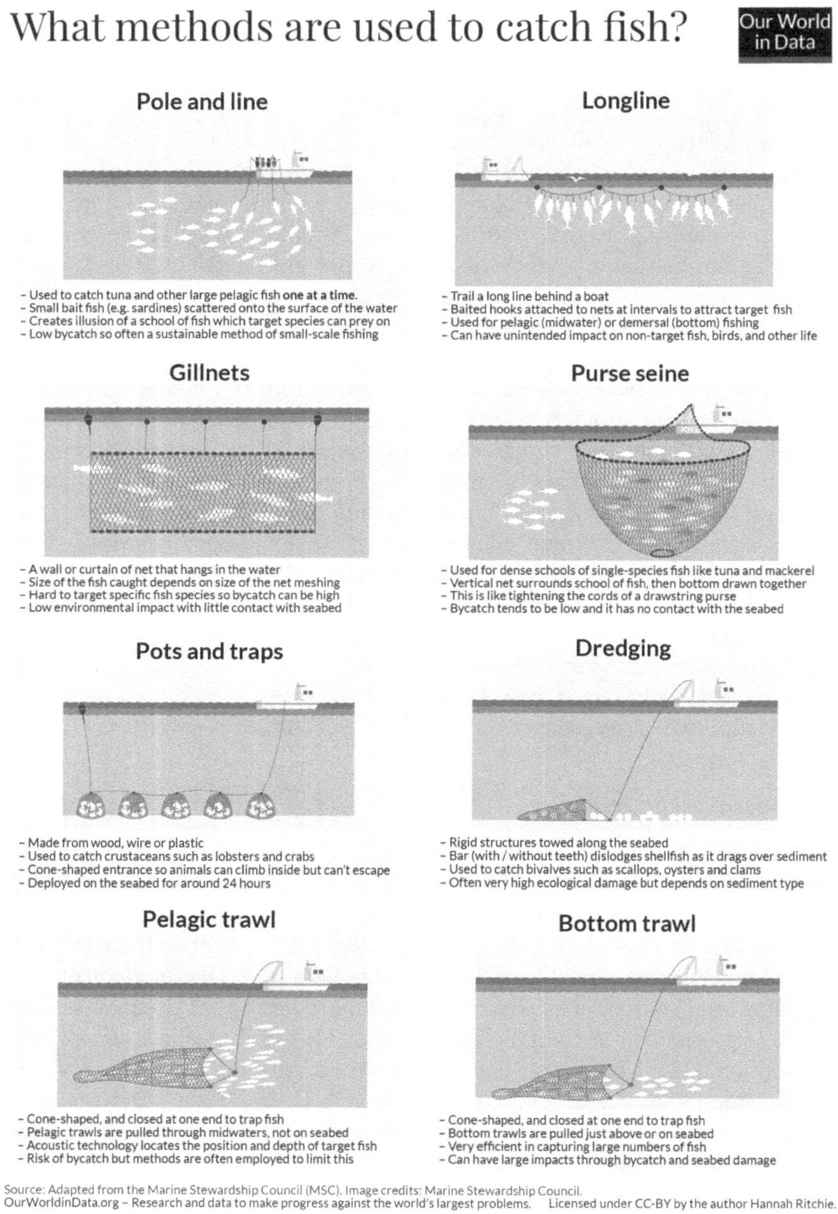

Figure 4.1 Types of fishing and equipment used around the world. (Image courtesy of Hannah Ritchie and Max Roser, 'Fish and Overfishing: How are fish stocks changing across the world? How much is overfished?', October 2021.)

Trawling – whereby a net is dragged along by a vessel – dates to at least the 14th century, and problems arose remarkably early. In 1376, for example, a petition presented to the English Parliament called for the prohibition of a particular piece of equipment – the 'wondyrchoum'.[23] The matter was referred to a Commission and the Court of Chancery on account of the mesh size of the trawl net, because 'no manner of fish which enters can escape, however small it may be, but is forced to stay and be caught',[24] leading to harvesting of a 'great abundance of small fish' and 'great damage . . . and the destruction of the fisheries'.[25] So great was the concern in some places that trawling was prohibited, for example in waters off Marseille in 1793, resulting in greatly increased catches once the area was reopened.[26] There are many examples of the introduction of different restrictions in the 19th century, such as the *Seal Fishery Act 1875* (Northern Ireland), establishing a closure period for the seal fishery adjacent to Greenland.[27]

Fisheries law in national contexts

Fishing practices began to change during the Industrial Revolution, but it was not until the 19th century that fishing became a widespread commercial enterprise and laws emerged to deal with competing uses and users.[28] At this time, more comprehensive fisheries legislation began to be developed that included the regulation of fishing methods, rights, gear and seasons.[29] Often, the focus was on growing commercial fisheries, with subsistence fishing (and sometimes artisanal and small-scale fishing) excluded. Sometimes, these laws provided regulation only for fishing itself, but in other cases they included conservation measures such as prohibitions on catching certain species, and the establishment of aquatic reserves to protect particular marine areas. Nevertheless, despite differences, the five categories of fishing rules referred to earlier were commonly applied across traditional, artisanal and small-scale commercial fisheries. As will be seen later in the chapter, these approaches continue to dominate today at national and international levels.

Over time increasingly intensive commercial fishing practices, as well as market demand as population grew, led to greater harvests both within national waters and beyond. Fisheries law evolved in response to the pressures on species and stocks,[30] yet fishing for personal consumption remained largely unregulated. Humans, however, appear disinclined to give up their remaining wild-caught foods. Indeed, over the past two decades the impact of recreational fishing has been felt, particularly in places such as Australia where there is a strong culture of fishing. So, it is the combined and cumulative effect of all fishers that risk the long-term health of oceans and the sustainability of marine life. As will be seen later in the chapter, the United Nations Food and Agricultural Organization (FAO) has provided much guidance to nation States in developing and enhancing their domestic fisheries regulation, taking into account larger-scale commercial fishing as well as local harvesting practices.[31] In response, contemporary national fisheries regulation seeks to account for all of these matters. In Kenya, for example, the *Fisheries Management and Development Act 2016* covers fishing and aquaculture, establishes a government fisheries service and a fish marketing authority, licences and registration (including subsistence, non-commercial, commercial and foreign fishing), conservation measures (such as fisheries management plans, marine protected areas, prohibited gear and methods, endangered species and fisheries impact assessments), data and record keeping, monitoring, control and surveillance, as well as enforcement.[32] Although comprehensive in the coverage of fish harvesting, these statutes are rarely combined with wildlife conservation laws or marine protected area legislation.

The global regulation of commercial fisheries

During the late 19th century, new fishing techniques and equipment were increasingly transforming traditional fishing grounds into large-scale commercial fisheries. By the mid-20th century, the scale and scope of commercial fishing continued to expand, intensifying competition and conflicts over legal rights to exploit the ocean's bounty.[33] The 'Cod Wars'[34] of the 1960s and 1970s exemplified these emerging tensions. They began when the United Kingdom objected to Iceland's decision in 1952 to increase its territorial waters from three to four nautical miles.[35] The tension soon escalated into a prolonged diplomatic crisis over the right to fish for Atlantic cod (*Gadus morhua*), a species that lives near the seabed in the cold deep ocean waters of the North Atlantic and an important source of food and wealth in the region since the Viking era. Over the next two decades, Iceland brazenly asserted its sovereign interests by expanding its fishery limits and employing disruptive tactics to deter foreign fishing trawlers from operating in its territorial waters. When participants at the 1974 Third Law of the Sea Conference (including the UK) endorsed the principle of a 200-mile Exclusive Economic Zone (EEZ), Iceland grasped the opportunity and extended its waters accordingly.[36] Indeed (as discussed in Chapter 2) the right to control and manage maritime zones would be a key trigger for negotiations as participants sought to find a compromise between the doctrine of freedom of the seas and the right to exploit marine resources.

Although some early treaties and regional collaborative agreements were in place, the UN Convention on the Law of the Sea (1982) (UNCLOS) represented the first global effort to regulate fishing by clarifying the rights and duties of States, including some fisheries rules as explored later in the chapter.[37] Since then, States have implemented UNCLOS provisions in relation to their national waters and built upon flag, port and coastal State responsibilities under the treaty, as well as adopted further global and regional mechanisms to implement its provisions on the high seas.[38]

Regional fisheries bodies, including Regional Fishery Management Organisations (RFMOs), have been established to control and manage high seas fisheries.

The RFMOs, comprised of member States, are the most significant actors in high seas fisheries, adopting legally binding rules for specific migratory species (such as tuna) and particular geographic areas. These RFMOs are all different, shaped and influenced by their mandate and member States. The *Commission on the Conservation of Antarctic Marine Living Resources* (CCAMLR) is at one end of the spectrum, being largely a conservation agreement with some RFMO features. Some organisations deal with a particular species such as the *Western Central Pacific Fisheries Commission* (WCPFC) and the *Indian Ocean Tuna Commission* (IOTC), for example, that focus only on tuna. Others such as the *South Indian Ocean Fisheries Agreement* and *North East Atlantic Fisheries Commission* cover a wide range of species.[39] Only the *General Fisheries Commission for the Mediterranean* (GFCM) has a broad mandate covering fishing and aquaculture in the high seas, EEZs and territorial sea areas of the Mediterranean and Black Seas.[40]

The international community has adopted UN General Assembly (UNGA) resolutions on fishing, and a number of legal instruments under the auspices of the FAO, recognising the need for more sustainable fisheries management that places conservation and environmental protection alongside socio-economic considerations. The *Code of Conduct for Responsible Fisheries* (1995), for example, is one of the most well-known and widely endorsed instruments (although not legally binding). It highlighted best practice for sustainable fisheries management to provide guidance to States seeking to improve their domestic fisheries management.[41] Significantly, two binding global instruments have also been adopted: the *FAO Compliance Agreement* (addressing flag State responsibility in the high seas) and the *Port State Measures to Prevent, Deter and Eliminate Illegal, Unreported and Unregulated Fishing* (Port State Measures Agreement).[42] These two instruments seek to address the growing problem of unauthorised fishing – commonly known as illegal, unreported and uncontrolled (IUU) fishing. Throughout these developments, which have undoubtedly expanded and enriched international fisheries law, the five fisheries rules have persistently been utilised, and are explained in further detail next.

Rule 1: Where can fishing occur?

As noted in Chapter 2, the customary concept of a territorial sea was enshrined in UNCLOS and extended to 12 nautical miles out from the shoreline. The convention granted the coastal State the same sovereignty over this area as on land, with the result that domestic fisheries legislation could be applied, regulating fishing in whatever way the State wished.[43] The only limit imposed by UNCLOS was that all States had an overriding obligation to protect and preserve the marine environment.[44] UNCLOS also created the Exclusive Economic Zone (EEZ), and within these coastal States were granted the right to 'explore and exploit' the ocean, subject to the obligation to 'conserve and manage' the marine environment.[45] Essentially, this means that coastal States – with their geographical advantage – were granted sovereign rights to fish in the EEZ and also to impose regulations relating to harvesting.[46]

Some fishing nations were drawn to the potentially lucrative species that live or migrate through the high seas. UNCLOS gave all nations the right to fish on the high seas[47] and, because it could not be owned or regulated by any one nation, the treaty called upon all States to cooperate in conserving and managing the living resources in these areas.[48] As noted earlier, the RFMOs respond to this need and cover the majority of the world's high seas areas. The FAO has supported many of these organisations, establishing some and assisting with implementation of others in their particular fisheries areas.[49]

Rule 2: How much may be caught?

UNCLOS required that decisions about which species and how many fish are able to be caught must be based upon 'best scientific evidence'.[50] Using that data, coastal States are obliged to determine the 'total allowable catch' of living resources in their EEZs, to prevent over-exploitation and maintain populations at levels which produce the 'maximum sustainable yield'.[51] Furthermore, UNCLOS required the coastal State to promote 'optimum utilization' of living resources within its EEZ and, if it did not have the capacity to harvest the total allowable catch, it must offer the opportunity to other nations to do so.[52] Palau's *Fishing Act*, for example, has implemented this provision, giving power to the Minister to negotiate agreements to harvest within the EEZ and to issue foreign fishing permits.[53]

UNCLOS also created obligations to determine the total allowable catch and establish conservation measures for fisheries on the high seas, based on the best scientific evidence available.[54] The RFMOs have undertaken this work largely by setting upper catch limits and quotas, and imposing technical measures – known as Conservation and Management Measures (CMMs) – on their member States.[55] For example, the IOTC has adopted an array of measures to prohibit the harvesting of certain species and providing for the targeted conservation of other species, mechanisms to reduce incidental catch and safely release bycatch, restricted areas and equipment, use of fish aggregating devices (floating objects such as ropes or lines strategically placed in the open ocean to attract pelagic fish) and vessel monitoring programmes, and seasonal closures, as well as market-related measures, demonstrating the application of the five main fisheries rules.[56] Ultimately, however, these RFMOs focus on commercial exploitation of marine species, and the management measures that have been adopted are for the purpose of sustainable management of industry rather than protection or conservation of marine life.

The UNCLOS regime depends heavily on accurate scientific information and locks in an exploitative regime for the EEZ and the high seas. Such concerns were raised by scientists even as nations were finalising negotiations for the UNCLOS treaty. Bardach, for example, claimed in 1981 that '200-mile economic zones will not augment the biological productivity of edible fish and shell-fish, but they will strongly influence patterns of their exploitation'.[57] While exploitation required the precise number of fish to be accurately estimated, the mobility of species and the three-dimensional nature of the ocean made such precision nearly impossible. To complicate matters further, some fish species move freely between the imaginary zones that humans imposed on the oceanic realm for management purposes. UNCLOS negotiators recognised this problem and inserted a requirement that States should coordinate measures to ensure conservation and development of these stocks.[58] Nevertheless, calculating total allowable catches and maximum sustainable yields with any precision has remained problematic.

Rule 3: Who can fish?

UNCLOS did not specify what legal mechanism member States must use in determining who can fish yet, as noted earlier, it encouraged cooperative arrangements. In EEZs and territorial seas, States often use fishing licences or permits to authorise fishing, sometimes for separate classes – subsistence, recreational, artisanal, small-scale and commercial – and/or 'individual transferable quotas'. On the high seas, the RFMOs manage fishing by setting catch quotas and allocating them to member States (which include adjacent coastal States and distant water nations fishing in the RFMO area). In 2017 the FAO noted that 152 nations were members of RFMOs and some were members of several organisations.[59] The International Whaling Commission had the most members (87), followed by the *International Commission for the Conservation of Atlantic Tunas* (ICCAT) (52).[60] Quotas are then divided amongst licence holders at the domestic level. The RFMO usually requires its member States to report on the vessels flagged to its nation that undertake fishing in the RFMO area.[61]

Overcapacity, involving too many fishers and/or fishing vessels, is a major global concern, with overcapitalisation of fishing fleets and excess harvesting power exceeding what is needed to fish within catch limits. The problem is due, in part, to the unlimited issue of fishing permits in the past, compounded by government subsidies that incentivised industry growth. Much work has been done by the FAO to address the issue of subsidies (in collaboration with other bodies such as the World Trade Organisation),[62] and the global community has set soft law targets, including through the UN Sustainable Development Goal, to prohibit certain types of subsidies and to eliminate others that work against sustainability or facilitate IUU fishing.[63] Nevertheless, blue economy goals involving the fisheries sector risk further expansions of fishing fleets.

Rule 4: When can fishing occur?

Periodic closures of waters to fishing represent another critical tool used in sustainable fisheries management. Seasonal closures are commonly used by States to restrict fishing during particular periods in fish stocks' lifecycles, or simply to restrict the take to a short period in response to a drop in catch rates or concern about fish stocks. Many of the RFMOs have adopted closure periods during which fishing cannot take place – some are voluntary and others for mandatory specific time periods or particular dates. The IOTC, for example, has adopted CMMs on voluntary closure of fishing tropical tuna in the Indian Ocean for an unspecified 31 days.[64] It has also explored temporarily closing the use of fish aggregating devices.[65]

Rule 5: What gear and methods can be legally used?

With the expansion and increasing sophistication of global industrial fishing from the mid-20th century, a key concern was the use of less selective fishing gear and practices resulting in bycatch and discards.[66] Catching and killing unwanted, non-target species, or rejecting fish because they exceed catch quotas or are not economically valuable, can impact upon species that play an important role in marine ecosystems.

Other equipment and methods were found to wreak unacceptable damage on the marine environment. Driftnets, for example, were found to be devastatingly efficient but unacceptably damaging. They entangled fish in a sheet of netting that freely drifted in the water column with a mesh size that did not allow smaller fish to escape. Driftnets were introduced as early as the 11th century in the North Sea, and Dutch fishers expanded their use in the 16th and 17th centuries. Their use expanded further during the 18th and 19th centuries and became widespread during the 20th century. However, their use was increasingly controversial because of the wastefulness involved in bycatch. When Japanese and Taiwanese fishers in the South Pacific began using excessively long driftnets, UN member States negotiated the 'Wellington Convention' prohibiting the use of nets over 2.5 km long.[67] The UN General Assembly later adopted a Resolution calling for a worldwide moratorium on driftnet fishing.[68] The FAO *Code of Conduct on Responsible Fisheries* (1995), called for 'selective and environmentally safe fishing gear and practices'.[69] The FAO also championed other actions, such as encouraging States to adopt national plans to mitigate the impacts of longlines through hook modification, increasing sinking rates of baited hooks and utilising bird-scaring curtains to reduce the risk to seabirds.[70]

Bottom trawling is one fishing method that has attracted particular controversy, in part because benthic species tend to be long-lived, reproduce and grow slowly, making them particularly vulnerable to overfishing.[71] Bottom trawling developed as early as the 14th century, but technological developments in the second half of the 20th century enabled it to be extended into the deep ocean, particularly around seamounts and deep sea ridges.[72] Scientists raised concern even then, yet bottom trawling was largely unrestricted until the 1990s when some countries took action. Surprisingly, despite calls for a moratorium, no global ban is yet in place although there are some regional restrictions in Antarctic waters, the Northeast Atlantic and South Pacific.[73] This demonstrates the challenge of implementing piecemeal approaches with varying rules in different fishing areas.

The RFMOs have also played a key role in restricting the use of destructive gear and methods through the application of CMMs, such as prohibitions on the use of data buoys[74] and restrictions on fish aggregating devices (FADs).[75] Other initiatives have demonstrated the potential for more effective regulation of gear and equipment, ranging from advocating the use of specific types of fish hooks and nets that are more selective and reduce bycatch,[76] to banning super trawlers (large fishing vessels with onboard processing facilities capable of staying at sea for several weeks) and electric pulse trawling.[77]

Regulating aquaculture, mariculture and farming marine life

Aquaculture (the breeding and harvesting of organisms in all types of water) and mariculture (marine-based aquaculture) have ancient origins dating back over 5,000 years, and they continue to be practised in many parts of the world.[78] Indeed, estimates indicate that mariculture is steadily increasing, making up 7% of fish for human consumption in 1974, 26% in 1994, and 39% in 2004.[79] In 2020 the contribution of aquaculture was 49%, although less than half of this was from ocean-based mariculture.[80]

Few global analyses of mariculture laws have been published, and further research is needed to analyse best practice.[82] Some jurisdictions combine mariculture rules under general fisheries regulation, while in other nations aquaculture is regulated under specific legislation.[83] There is no international treaty for mariculture, perhaps because the majority of activities take place within waters under national jurisdiction (e.g., in a State's territorial sea or Exclusive Economic Zone) and domestic legislation applies. Nevertheless, some RFMOs do have a mandate to regulate aquaculture as well as fishing. As noted earlier the GFCM regulates mariculture in the Mediterranean, Adriatic and Black Seas. As with fisheries regulation, there are commonalities in the regulatory measures included, usually involving a licence or permit to operate an aquaculture facility, a leasing arrangement for the site and/or zoning arrangements for aquaculture development, and management and control measures (such as water quality monitoring, regulations to prevent introduction of aquatic organisms, reporting of diseases, handling and marketing of products).

It is clear that the farming of marine life provides communities with the opportunity to supplement reduced wild harvests, provide food security, and sustain livelihoods, yet it has been controversial around the world, raising concerns about the health of farmed products and the impacts on the marine environment. In Australia, Canada and Norway, for example, salmon farming has

Learning from the past

Marine mammal exploitation occurred throughout the world. Indigenous peoples in the Arctic, as well as Norwegian and Japanese fishers, have hunted whales and seals for millennia. Commercial whaling was commenced by the Basques in the 11th century, and later by British, Dutch and then American fishers. In the Caribbean, marine mammals were harvested from the 19th century. Whilst dolphin fisheries were rare (but were an activity in Venezuela), manatees were hunted by Indigenous peoples up until colonial times. But it was in the 18th and 19th centuries that whaling and sealing industries rapidly expanded. The *International Convention for the Regulation of Whaling* (1945) followed on from even earlier instruments and was adopted to ensure the sustainable continuation of the whaling industry, later morphing into a conservation instrument with the adoption of a moratorium on whaling in the 1980s. It was successful in as much as it ceased the fishing of large whales, together with other conservation efforts in international environmental law. Yet it continues to generate controversy and is one of few international cases on marine species dealt with by the International Court of Justice when Australia successfully argued that Japan's harvest of whales was not for legitimate scientific research. Overharvesting to the point of extinction was not limited to whales, and other marine mammals (such as sirenians) suffered considerably. Overharvesting of seals, sea lions and other species led to the demise of Steller's Sea Cow – one of the first marine species to become extinct due to anthropocentric causes. Marine mammals have more recently been treated differently in law than fish. UNCLOS, for example, includes a specific Article focused on marine mammals. UNCLOS identified a few other specific categories of marine life including anadromous and catadromous species such as turtles. UNCLOS also refers to dependent and associated species and so does much domestic legislation. Many other nations have sought to protect other charismatic marine megafauna that had previously been harvested, such as turtles. The story of whales and whaling demonstrates that action can be taken with profound effects, but many other marine species such as sharks and tuna fail to attract the same level of interest and remain vulnerable to over-exploitation.[81]

attracted heavy criticism.[84] Interestingly, it is often the environmental impacts that raise public concern, at levels unseen in wild capture fisheries. At the same time, mariculture has also become a focal point for the emergence of concern about animal welfare. Whether fish feel pain has been a matter of some contention, but increasingly attention has been drawn to the need for regulations around the humane killing of farmed fish as for other farmed animals.[85] Rather than the United Nations leading the way in raising standards, however, it is the Aquaculture Stewardship Council – the peak certification body for farmed fish – that is imposing welfare rules.[86] Perhaps this heralds a new era of concern for the humane treatment of wild-caught fish, which have traditionally not attracted such attention and which often die by asphyxiation on the deck of a boat or are disembowelled whilst still alive.[87]

Overcoming the myth of the inexhaustible ocean

Underpinning these laws has been the long-held belief in the inexhaustibility of the ocean's living resources, a belief that continues to dominate western approaches to commercial fishing.[88] Marine scientists have been warning of the vulnerability of some species to overfishing since at least the 1970s, and there has been a growing realisation that irreversible damage is being done without sufficient interventions to ensure that harvesting practices are sustainable.[89] At the same time, there is growing public criticism of the scale of commercial harvesting practices, which impoverishes the marine environment as well as the communities that depend on it for their survival.[90]

During the course of the 20th century, several important fisheries collapsed as a result of overfishing. The North Atlantic herring stocks, for example, dramatically declined in the 1950s and 1960s and global herring populations fell almost to extinction levels in the late 20th century, largely due to several decades of overfishing facilitated by larger commercial trawl nets and vessels and assisted by advanced navigation and location technologies. Similarly, Far East Asian Kamchatka salmon crashed in the 1950s, Peruvian anchoveta in the 1960s, and North Atlantic cod populations partially collapsed in the 1970s.[91] In 1992, cod populations fell to 1% of historical levels and have not recovered to this day. These collapses have not only impacted on the species themselves but also on their ecosystems and on the communities that have relied on them. Overfishing by commercial fishers has had particularly devastating impacts on artisanal and small-scale fisheries. In the Bay of Bengal, for example, where millions of people depend upon fishing for livelihoods and fish remains the primary source of protein, commercial fishing has depleted stocks available to local fishers.[92] The emergence of blue economy strategies in the 21st century is also likely to produce further increases in fishing capacity, as noted earlier, which may have short-term economic gains but risk long-term fisheries collapse.[93]

While unlimited fishing licences were once issued without any catch limits being imposed, this is no longer the case. However, attitudes to fishing have not demonstrably changed, and fishing enterprises – and many governments – still operate as though the ocean's living resources are bountiful and endless. In part, this misplaced faith in the ocean's inexhaustible bounty may be due to the syndrome of 'shifting baselines', in which generations of fisheries scientists have accepted the stock size and composition at the time they commence their careers without reference to historical data, masking the gradual disappearance of fishery resources over time.[94] The result has been a failure to appreciate the time frame, scale and impact of human-driven change.[95] Recent scholarship has called for a renewed effort to address the syndrome by drawing on multidisciplinary research across the biophysical and social sciences and humanities in order to encourage more informed and just responses to global environmental change.[96]

Fisheries data

The issue of how to accurately calculate catch and stock rates has attracted significant attention amongst fisheries researchers, who persistently point to inaccurate data – including that published by the FAO – and query whether catch rates are a reasonable measure to use when assessing species abundance.[97] However, the FAO's data and statistics are based on official State reports, and the FAO can only publish the information it receives. In turn, States can only report the total of the catch data collected at the national level. So, a first step to improving data is to enhance the accuracy of what is reported.[98] At the national level, for example, there are myriad ways in which States are seeking to improve fish stock and catch data in different scales and contexts (unsurprisingly) supported by technologies including deep learning,[99] forensic technology[100] and smartphone apps.[101]

Another issue of concern for fisheries governance is that reporting frequently only involves landed catches and legitimate fisheries but excludes discarded bycatch (fish captured in nets, for example, but discarded at sea dead or dying), and illegal fishing. This clearly skews any efforts to set an appropriate total allowable catch that might ensure sustainable harvests, because many more fish are being caught than reported. The RFMOs have adopted CMMs focused on reducing bycatch, and similar measures have been implemented in many nations, with efforts likely to be ongoing as emerging new technologies facilitate more selective harvesting.

Illegal, unreported and uncontrolled fishing (IUU fishing)

The FAO and RFMOs, as well as member States, have also focused on combatting illegal, unreported and uncontrolled (IUU) fishing. Addressing gaps in fisheries regulation (uncontrolled fishing) and reducing unreported fishing are important aspects of this response, but the third piece of the puzzle is combatting illegal fishing. In some cases, illegal fishing is carried out by licenced fishers who might catch more than permitted, extend their fishing activities into unapproved waters or otherwise breach their licence conditions. Addressing this problem is largely about monitoring and compliance with fisheries regulation (explored later). Yet there is little doubt that some illegal fishing involves unlicensed activities in waters, for species or with gear and equipment that is prohibited – sometimes these activities take place on unregistered vessels with forced labour – undermining fisheries management and breaching multiple areas of law including human rights.[102]

Estimates of the global extent of illegal fishing suggest the problem is extensive: about 10% to 20% of global reported catches,[103] with the FAO indicating that one in five fish caught originates from IUU fishing.[104] Regardless of the precise figures, the amount of IUU fishing is significant and considerable efforts have been made to eradicate, or at least to reduce, the problem. The FAO has built on more general obligations under UNCLOS by providing a toolbox for combatting IUU fishing.[105] It has also developed binding agreements requiring flag States to strengthen controls to ensure that all registered fishing vessels are authorised to fish on the high seas and comply with international law, and to enhance port States powers of inspection to control illegal catches from being landed and facilitate the exchange of information on compliance and fishing vessels.[106] Sustainable Development Goal 14.6 focuses on combating IUU fishing and SDG Indicator 14.6.1 captures global implementation of the five key instruments in this area. It is clear that, whilst progress has been made, full implementation has yet to be achieved.[107]

Technology has also been used to track illegal fishing vessels and activities at sea. One of the well-known NGOs, *Global Fishing Watch*, uses satellite data and machine learning to track and process vessel movements, and expose (and make publicly available) all industrial human activity at sea.[108] This organisation has also been involved in tracking forced labour on board vessels engaging in illegal fishing.[109] This raises the issue of confidentiality and data sharing, such as who owns satellite data and how it could be better used to monitor oceans. Several RFMOs use this type of data,[110] and some regional data-sharing arrangements exist, although issues remain regarding the use of common standards.[111]

In addition to responses aimed at reducing the incidence of IUU fishing, removing access to available markets for fish caught is important. Catch documentation schemes are critical in combatting IUU fishing, as well as facilitating better management of supply chains. Again, the FAO has sought to harmonise systems across different member States including through the *Voluntary Guidelines for Catch Documentation Schemes* (2017) and, more recently, the *FAO Voluntary Guidelines for Transshipment* (2021) seek to ensure that movements of catches prevent IUU fish harvests from being laundered through legitimate supply chains.

Monitoring and surveillance

Fishing is an activity that is inherently difficult to monitor, given the mobility of fish and the vastness of the ocean. Even where fishers are engaged in legal fishing (with appropriate licences, legitimate gear and equipment, working in authorised areas and harvesting permitted species), ensuring fisheries regulations are being met is tricky. Both active and passive monitoring has been used, through, for example, the use of onboard fish observers to monitor and report on activities being undertaken. The FAO encourages and provides guidance on observer programmes,[112] and RFMOs have adopted CMMs for such arrangements.[113] Yet observer programmes are expensive and piecemeal, and the role is not without risks as fisheries observers remain vulnerable to abuse, violence and even death.[114]

Other active arrangements include patrols by national coast guards, with naval vessels sometimes also being involved in constabulary services. UNCLOS Article 111 provides coastal States with the right of 'hot pursuit', allowing a fleeing ship to be followed and intercepted in circumstances where it is believed to have violated the law.[115] This is a longstanding exception to the freedom of the seas, because it allows for the pursuit and apprehension in areas beyond the coastal State's territorial sea and EEZ.[116] Although it is an ancient legal mechanism, it continues to be utilised including in several high-profile fisheries enforcement situations.[117] Nonetheless, maintaining a pursuit across vast ocean areas and gathering proof and evidence once a vessel is apprehended remain problematic.

Some States do not have naval or coast guard vessels and have sought to build capacity through Shiprider Agreements. These arrangements involve fishery enforcement officers of one nation 'riding' on board the vessels of another nation in order to police their waters. The US has been a particular advocate of this approach in the South Pacific.[118] In this sense the vastness of the ocean combined with a shared legal problem have caused States to cooperate in new and innovative ways. In some regions, multinational cooperative surveillance arrangements are in place, such as those in the South Pacific.[119] This is one of the few regions in the world to have adopted a legally binding treaty on surveillance and enforcement.[120]

Passive surveillance can also be undertaken with the use of remote sensing technologies. Satellite systems – such as Automatic Identification Systems (AIS) and Vessel Monitoring Systems (VMS) – are mandated under various maritime laws for safety purposes, and used by government regulators to track vessel movements (see Chapter 5). These technologies are now being utilised to track fishing vessels for fisheries data collection and compliance purposes. As noted earlier, NGOs such as *Global Fishing Watch* acquire satellite data and demonstrate movements, and in some cases illegal behaviour, to support enforcement efforts.[121]

Compliance and enforcement

Despite the plethora of fisheries regulation, prosecutions for illegal activity are uncommon, largely due to the cost and practicality of proving that offences have occurred. There is no doubt that most domestic fisheries regulation includes offence provisions, and these frequently result in a civil penalty such as a fine rather than criminal penalties.[122] Some of the headline-grabbing stories of oceanic pursuits and apprehensions of illegal fishing vessels have resulted in less spectacular and successful court proceedings.[123] Some RFMOs have brought enforcement proceedings, although again these are uncommon.[124] Nevertheless, the *UN Office of Drugs and Crime* has explored the possibility of establishing criminal fishing offences in the broader context of growing concerns about global maritime crime and transnational organised crime.[125]

In essence, enforcement of fisheries laws is a response to non-compliance, which can take several forms from administrative non-compliance involving misplaced paperwork on board a fishing vessel to incorrectly reporting catches, fishing locations, vessel registrations and transhipment breaches. Some nations, and several RFMOs, have developed non-compliance mechanisms aimed at encouraging fulfilment of obligations through a soft approach, before enforcement or sanctions are considered. CCAMLR is one such RFMO which has adopted compliance measures associated with vessel licensing, movement and transhipment monitoring, inspection and catch documentation systems.[126] These measures ensure legitimate fishers are complying with fisheries regulation and also expose those that are not. Because of the significance of the threat of IUU fishing, further initiatives focus on identifying and sharing lists of IUU fishing vessels and nationals to expose them in circumstances where softer non-compliance measures are unlikely to be effective.

Shrimp/Turtle Case

In 1997 India, Malaysia, Pakistan and Thailand brought proceedings against the US relating to an import ban on shrimp and shrimp products that had been harvested without using turtle excluder devices (TEDs). The US had passed domestic legislation requiring shrimp trawlers to use TEDs. The argument was that the US had breached World Trade Organization (WTO) rules in imposing an environmental measure that was in effect a trade ban. Although WTO and *General Agreement on Tariffs and Trade* (GATT) Articles XI and XX allow a State to take action to protect the environment, such measures cannot discriminate unfairly between nations. The WTO found that the US had breached these rules because it had provided assistance and extra time to other WTO member States to meet the TED requirement but had not given the same advantage to the claimant States. This decision demonstrates that issues at the intersection of trade and environment raise complex issues that often favour trade events, although the conservation measure is clearly necessary.[127]

Trade, consumers and seafood supply chains

International law includes obligations for flag, port and coastal States, but not for market States. As noted earlier, the FAO has adopted guidelines to reduce illegal harvests entering the seafood supply chain. Ultimately, fish (whether wild caught or farmed) must find a market and consumers can be a powerful influence. Traceability, certification schemes and ecolabelling can also assist, both with food safety (a particular concern in aquaculture) and IUU fishing. The FAO *Agreement on Port State Measures* permits nations to impose trade restrictions at the port of entry where IUU fishing has taken place. This is an important development as the World Trade Organization regime has often been seen to favour trade over environmental protection (see text box).

Finding ways to harness shifting community attitudes and human values may also reap rewards and, arguably, the law could play a greater role here. Where once whales were hunted, now they are conserved but, while similar hopes are held for sharks and charismatic marine megafauna such as turtles and marine mammals, the future for tuna looks bleak. Nevertheless, consumers may be persuaded to change their preferences if governments established sustainable seafood labelling schemes. Surprisingly, there is no international law to guide governments in this area, and NGOs such as the *Marine Stewardship Council* and the *Aquaculture Stewardship Council* have sought to establish trusted labels with transparent certification and monitoring requirements.[128] However, the use of labels such as 'dolphin safe' is largely unregulated and often serves to undermine consumer awareness and confidence.[129]

Holistic approach to food webs and ecosystems

Beyond monitoring human activities and marketing sustainable products, fisheries regulation must better address the interconnectedness of species and ecosystems and facilitate holistic approaches to marine management – even within an exploitative context. UNCLOS does not mention ecosystems, but it does refer to best scientific evidence (as noted earlier), which supports ecosystem-based management, and the need for States to take into account the impacts on species associated with or dependent upon harvested species.[130] The subsequent UN Fish Stocks Agreement included the application of a precautionary approach and requirement that conservation and management measures should take into account species belonging to the same ecosystem, associated with or dependent upon target stocks.[131]

As noted earlier, the FAO adopted the ecosystem approach to fisheries in 2003, highlighting that all fisheries should be managed on a precautionary and participatory basis taking into account best available science including ecological dimensions.[132] Yet concerns are being raised about catch quotas for Antarctic krill (*Euphausia superba*), for example, set through CCAMLR on a precautionary basis, given significant declines since the 1970s and increasing harvests.

Antarctic krill are regarded as a keystone species in the Southern Ocean, as they form a significant part of the diet of many marine mammals and seabirds, and also play an important role in drawing down carbon from the atmosphere.[133] This example calls into question whether, and to what extent, ecosystem approaches are genuinely being applied in fisheries regulation.

The warming ocean

Adding to the aforementioned complexity is the fact that the ocean environment is rapidly changing. Waters are warming, acidifying and in some cases de-oxygenating. This directly affects some fish stocks and indirectly impacts others. Either way, biological and ecological stressors must be monitored and predictions made about change in, for example, fish stock reproduction rates, migratory paths and ranges. Some coastal States have developed their own climate change mitigation and adaptation plans under the *Paris Agreement* (explored in other chapters of this book). Yet this is also an area where fisheries regulation can play a role – beyond the climate law regimes – in minimising the impacts of climate change on fish stocks. For example, in 2019 the WCPFC adopted a non-binding resolution on climate change, and in 2022 the IOTC became the first RFMO to adopt a binding CMM.[134] The CMM includes a provision requiring the potential impact of climate change to be taken into account, not just on tuna and tuna-like species but also on species in the same ecosystem or dependent on or associated with tuna stocks. It also paves the way for the future development of climate change-related CMMs.

Conclusion

The five fisheries rules explored throughout this chapter have stood the test of time. They emerged in ancient and traditional contexts and continue to be applied today. Their value lies in their flexibility to meet new challenges. Licence numbers can be reduced, for example, catch rates can be lowered, marine areas and seasons can be closed to harvesting and particular gear and methods can be prohibited if highly damaging or mandated if more selective and beneficial. Thus, the majority of fisheries regulations at domestic, regional and international levels remain fit for purpose as industry-based measures, albeit heavily reliant upon accurate scientific evidence and data if sustainability is to be achieved.

A significant challenge for governments and the commercial fishing industry is to ensure that existing law is implemented, complied with and, where necessary, enforced. Gross wild-caught harvests have remained stable since the 1990s, but fish are being caught in more parts of the world's oceans and the production takes greater fishing effort. This is because wild fish stocks in many places are already harvested at capacity, some are over-harvested, and unauthorised IUU fishing complicates the picture and exacerbates unsustainability. Seafood currently remains one of the only wild-caught meals for many people – the question is for how long this will remain the case. The critical issue is to make existing law work far more effectively. In addition, while ensuring that laws for sustainable fish farming deliver food and livelihood security, they come at environmental costs. Governments will therefore need to consider other strategies, such as encouraging people to consume different sources of protein, and shifting consumers away from charismatic fish species.

Although the global community has recognised the need to regulate and constrain unsustainable fishing, it is clear that UNCLOS and the RFMOs are squarely focused on exploitation of marine living resources rather than protection. Indeed, fisheries and mariculture legislation more generally are designed to regulate anthropocentric activities and, although oceanic and marine living resource limits are taken into account, the focus is on development of extractive industries, maximum yields and optimum utilisation of 'fish stocks' and 'marine living resources'. There is little regard for the needs of marine life or the oceanic realm as a whole. While much effort has been made by lawmakers to ensure that nations and peoples have equal access to these resources, with measures designed to achieve equity and justice amongst peoples, they do not provide justice for the oceans themselves.

As discussed in Chapter 7, there have been some areas where rights have been granted to nature and, although nascent, calls have been made for the adoption of a Universal Declaration of Ocean Rights.[135] In recent years, rivers have been granted rights and oceans could be afforded similar rights in the future.[136] Advocating for ocean justice has become increasingly critical in the face of global population growth, blue economy plans to expand fisheries, and ever-advancing technologies, which are likely to place further pressures on wild species and the marine environment.[137] Nevertheless, a fundamental shift in global environmental ethics seems unlikely, as does a global shift towards the traditional ethic of stewardship in the marine environment. Yet it is imperative that we find better ways to conserve and manage living marine resources before planetary boundaries are crossed and tipping points reached.

Notes

1 "Traditional Fishing Techniques Around the World," *Fishing Booker Blog* (October 11, 2023), https://fishingbooker.com/blog/traditional-fishing-techniques-around-the-world/.

2 The earliest known sea-going vessel was discovered in modern Kuwait and estimated to be around 7,000 years old: "A History of Sea Vessels," *Bridgeman Images Blog* (December 16, 2021), https://blog.bridgemanimages.com/blog/a-history-of-sea-vessels.

3 Dietrich Sahrhage and Johannes Lundbeck, *A History of Fishing* (Heidelberg: Springer Berlin, 2012).

4 John E. Bardach and Regina Miranda Santerre, "Climate and the Fish in the Sea," *BioScience* 31, no. 3 (1981): 205–31, 213.

5 Reg A. Watson and A. Tidd, "Mapping Nearly a Century and a Half of Global Marine Fishing: 1869–2015," *Marine Policy* 93 (2018): 171–77, 171.
6 R. W. D. Davies et al., "Defining and Estimating Global Marine Fisheries Bycatch," *Marine Policy* 33, no. 4 (2009): 661–72.
7 R. E. Johannes, "Traditional Marine Conservation Methods in Oceania and Their Demise," *Annual Review of Ecology and Systematics* 9 (1978): 349–64. Some of these practices persist today.
8 Johannes, "Traditional Marine Conservation Methods," 350.
9 Ibid.
10 Ibid.
11 L. Taylor, *Sharks of Hawai'i – Their Biology and Cultural Significance* (Honolulu: University of Hawai'i Press, 1993), 19; and P. V. Kirch, *Feathered Gods and Fishhooks: An Introduction to Hawaiian Archaeology and Pre-history* (Honolulu: University of Hawai'i Press, 1985), 116 and 142.
12 Margaret D. Chapman, "Women's Fishing in Oceania," *Human Ecology* 15, no. 3 (1987): 267–88; R. E. Johannes, "The Renaissance of Community-Based Marine Resource Management in Oceania," *Annual Review of Ecology and Systematics* 33 (2002): 317–40.
13 Johannes, "Traditional Marine Conservation Methods . . ."
14 Johannes, "The Renaissance of Community-Based Marine Resource Management . . ." In some nations, such as Australia, early laws imposed during colonial times also regulated these practices such as the *Fisheries Act 1881* (NSW) regulated the use of torpedoes and dynamite.
15 Daniella LoScerbo et al., "Fish Traps of the Society Islands," accessed January 31, 2024, www.seagardens.net/society-islands; Kekuewa Kikiloi, "A New Synthesis in Oceanic Domestication: The Symbiotic Development of Loko i'a Aquaculture in Pre-contact Oceania," *SPC Traditional Marine Resource Management and Knowledge Information Bulletin* 15 (2003): 1–36.
16 Josh McDaniel, "The Return of Kū'ula: Restoration of Hawaiian Fishponds," accessed January 31, 2024, https://seagrant.soest.hawaii.edu/the-return-of-kuula/.
17 "A Brief Introduction to Indigenous Fishing," *AIATSIS*, accessed January 31, 2024, https://aiatsis.gov.au/brief-introduction-indigenous-fishing.
18 Erika J. Techera, *Marine Environmental Governance: From International Law to Local Practice* (Abingdon: Routledge, 2012).
19 Ibid.
20 "Convention on Biological Diversity," accessed January 31, 2024, www.cbd.int. This is a legally binding treaty negotiated and adopted by nation States.
21 "United Nations Declaration on the Rights of Indigenous Peoples," *United Nations*, accessed January 31, 2024, www.un.org/development/desa/indigenouspeoples/declaration-on-%20the-rights-of-indigenous-peoples.html. This is not legally binding on nations but is a very persuasive document as it sets out key principles.
22 Johannes, "Traditional Marine Conservation Methods in Oceania . . .," 350. See also, Chapman, "Women's Fishing in Oceania."
23 Peter Jones, "The Long 'Lost' History of Bottom Trawling in England, c.1350–1650," *International Journal of Maritime History* 30, no. 2 (2018): 201–17.
24 Ibid., 205, quoting from the Parliamentary Rolls of Medieval England.
25 John Philip Hore and Edward Jex, *The Deterioration of Oyster and Trawl Fisheries of England: Its Cause and Remedy* (United Kingdom: E Stock, 1880), 55–56.
26 Callum Roberts, *An Unnatural History of the Sea* (Washington, DC: Island Press, 2007), 351.
27 "World Legal Information Institute," *Worldlii*, accessed January 31, 2024, www.worldlii.org/nie/legis/num_act/sfa1875137/.

28 John R. Gillis, *The Human Shore* (Chicago: University of Chicago Press, 2012), 25.
29 For example, *Fisheries Act 1881* (New South Wales, Australia) and the *Fisheries Act 1868* (Canada).
30 The term 'stock' is used in fisheries management to mean a population of fish within a particular area (sometimes isolated from other stocks of the same species). This term is commonly used yet implies – or perhaps highlights – that fish are often considered only as a resource rather than wildlife with intrinsic value.
31 The FAO is the UN body that has taken the lead on supporting sustainable fishery management through its mandate on food security. See for example, *Code of Conduct for Responsible Fisheries*, *FAO Voluntary Guidelines on the Responsible Governance of Tenure of Land, Fisheries and Forests in the Context of National Food Security* and the *FAO Voluntary Guidelines for Securing Sustainable Small-Scale Fisheries in the Context of Food Security and Poverty Eradication*: "Fisheries and Aquaculture," *FAO*, accessed January 31, 2024, www.fao.org/fishery/en.
32 Interestingly, it defines 'fish' as including all marine or aquatic animals or plants and includes shells, coral, reptiles and marine mammals: s.2. National fisheries legislation is accessible via the FAOLEX database: "FAOLEX," accessed March 1, 2024, www.fao.org/faolex/en/.
33 Helen M. Rozwadowski, *Vast Expanses: A History of the Oceans* (Chicago: University of Chicago Press, 2018), 131–32.
34 These were not wars in a conventional sense, but they were militarised international conflicts at sea.
35 Conflicts had been common between these nations. Even as early as the 15th century, English catch rates were so extensive that they resulted in conflict, the imposition of trade restrictions and ultimately only settled through international licensing agreements.
36 Kevin Bilms, "The Cod Wars and Lessons for Maritime Counterinsurgency," *Proceedings: US Naval Institute* 149, no. 2 (February 2023): 1440; Gudni Thorlacius Johannesson, "Troubled Waters: Cod War, Fishing Disputes, and Britain's Fight for the Freedom of the High Seas, 1948–1964" (PhD, University of London, 2007).
37 For a summary of the history, see Mark Zacharias, *Marine Policy* (Abingdon: Earthscan, 2014), 190–91. For the full text, see *United Nations Convention on the Law of the Sea*, accessed March 1, 2024, www.un.org/depts/los/convention_agreements/texts/unclos/closindx.htm.
38 One of the most significant developments was the adoption of the global *Agreement for the Implementation of the Provisions of the United Nations Convention on the Law of the Sea of 10 December 1982 Relating to the Conservation and Management of Straddling Fish Stocks and Highly Migratory Fish Stocks* (UN Fish Stocks Agreement) "UNFSA Overview," *United Nations*, accessed January 31, 2024, www.un.org/oceancapacity/unfsa. Straddling stocks refers to those species that live in areas that cross a nation's waters and the adjacent high seas. Highly migratory species travel long distances through both national waters and the high seas. For an excellent summary (including a table of fisheries instruments), see Julia Nakamura, "International Fisheries Law: Past to Future," in *Oceans Governance*, ed. S. Partelow, M. Hadjimichael, and A-K. Hornidge (Cham, Switzerland: Springer, 2023).
39 These different fisheries organisations and governance arrangements are summarised by the FAO: "Fisheries and Aquaculture," *FAO*, accessed January 31, 2024, www.fao.org/fishery/en/governance.
40 "General Fisheries Commission for the Mediterranean," *FAO*, accessed January 31, 2024, www.fao.org/gfcm/en/.
41 "Code of Conduct for Responsible Fisheries," *FAO*, accessed January 31, 2024, www.fao.org/3/v9878e/v9878e00.htm.

42 Ibid.
43 UNCLOS Article 2.
44 UNCLOS Article 192 and 193.
45 UNCLOS Article 56.
46 Although landlocked States were given the right to participate in fishing any surplus living resources in EEZs under UNCLOS Article 69. See further discussion later.
47 UNCLOS Articles 87 and 116.
48 UNCLOS Articles 117 and 118.
49 T. Terje Løbach, M. Petersson, E. Haberkon, and P. Mannini, *Regional Fisheries Management Organizations and Advisory Bodies. Activities And Developments, 2000–2017* (Rome: FAO Fisheries and Aquaculture Technical Paper No. 651, 2020).
50 For example, UNCLOS Articles 61 and 119; UNFSA Article 5. Best scientific evidence includes information about the species and their abundance, biological information about their reproduction rates, habitats and ranges, as well as catch and fishing effort data.
51 UNCLOS Article 61.
52 UNCLOS Article 62.
53 "Fishing Title 27, Division 1 Foreign Fishing," *Republic of Palau*, accessed January 31, 2024, www.worldlii.org/paclii/pw/legis/consol_act/ft27126/.
54 UNCLOS Article 119.
55 Conservation and management measures (CMMs) are usually adopted by consensus and therefore conservation measures can be vetoed and derailed by just one member State.
56 See, for example, "Conservation and Management Measures," *IOTC*, accessed January 31, 2024, www.iotc.org/cmms.
57 Bardach, "Living Marine Resources and the Law of the Sea."
58 UNCLOS Article 64 and Annex I; and the UNFSA. For an excellent overview see Terje Løbach et al., *Regional Fisheries Management Organizations and Advisory Bodies*.
59 Terje Løbach et al., *Regional Fisheries Management Organizations and Advisory Bodies*, 11.
60 ICCAT also has cooperators who agree to follow procedures but are not a contracting party: "Contracting Parties," *ICCAT*, accessed January 31, 2024, www.iccat.int/en/contracting.html.
61 See for example the "Record of Vessels," *ICCAT*, accessed January 31, 2024, www.iccat.int/en/VesselsRecord.asp.
62 "The WTO Agreement on Fisheries Subsidies and the Role of FAO," *FAO*, accessed January 31, 2024, www.fao.org/documents/card/en/c/cc9063en.
63 SDG 14.6: "Sustainable Development Goals," *United Nations*, accessed January 31, 2024, https://sdgs.un.org/goals.
64 IOTC Resolution 23/03 on Establishing a Voluntary Fishing Closure in the Indian Ocean for the Conservation of Tropical Tunas: see Compendium.
65 IOTC Resolution 15/09 on a Fish Aggregating Devices (FADS) Working Group.
66 By-catch are non-target species inadvertently caught in nets and other fishing gear. Discards is a portion of the catch thrown back into the sea.
67 *Convention for the Prohibition of Fishing with Long Driftnets in the South Pacific* (Wellington Convention) (1989), accessed March 1, 2024, https://ecolex.org/details/treaty/convention-for-the-prohibition-of-fishing-with-long-driftnets-in-the-south-pacific-tre-001043/.
68 UNGA Resolution 46/215, UN Doc A/RES/46/215.
69 FAO, "Code of Conduct for Responsible Fisheries" (1995), accessed January 31, 2024, www.fao.org/3/a-v9878e.pdf.

70 FAO, *International Plan of Action for Reducing Incidental Catch of Seabirds in Longline Fisheries* (Rome: FAO, 1998): see S. D. Good et al., "National Plans of Action (NPOAs) for Reducing Seabird Bycatch: Developing Best Practice for Assessing and Managing Fisheries Impacts," *Biological Conservation* 247 (2020): 108592.
71 Bottom trawling involves a net being dragged through the water weighted down by a boom that is scraped along the ocean floor, indiscriminately scooping up fish and other marine life, including deep sea corals and sponges.
72 Lissette Victorero et al., "Out of Sight, but Within Reach: A Global History of Bottom-Trawled Deep-Sea Fisheries from >400 m Depth," *Frontiers in Marine Science* 5 (2018), accessed January 31, 2024, https://doi.org/10.3389/fmars.2018.00098. See also, Peter Jones, "The Long 'Lost' History of Bottom Trawling in England."
73 Through CCAMLR, NEAFC and the South Pacific Regional Fisheries Management Organisation (SPRFMO), "Conservation and Management Measure for the Management of Bottom Fishing in the SPRFMO Convention Area," accessed January 31, 2024, www.sprfmo.int/assets/Fisheries/Conservation-and-Management-Measures/2021-CMMs/CMM-03-2021-Bottom-Fishing-12Mar2021.pdf.
74 "Conservation and Management Measures," *SPRFMO*, accessed January 31, 2024, www.sprfmo.int/assets/Fisheries/Conservation-and-Management-Measures/7fe67e4f02/CMMs-Booklet-13Dec2016-downloaded-from-website.pdf; and accessed January 31, 2024, www.wcpfc.int/system/files/booklets/31/CMM%20and%20Resolutions.pdf.
75 Some RFMOs in the Pacific prohibit the use of FADs for certain types of fishing or specific periods because they attract many types of marine life, not just target species: "Conservation and Management Measure on the Application of High Seas FAD Closures and Catch Retention, Conservation and Management Measure 2009–02," *WCPFC*, accessed January 31, 2024, www.wcpfc.int/system/files/booklets/31/CMM%20and%20Resolutions.pdf. Nevertheless, recent research suggests that they can be utilised beneficially inside marine reserves to attract fish into the area: Michael Bode et al., "Fish Aggregating Devices Could Enhance the Effectiveness of Blue Water Marine Protected Areas," *Conservation Letters* 16 (2023): 12984.
76 F. Poisson et al., "New Technologies to Improve Bycatch Mitigation in Industrial Tuna Fisheries" *Fish and Fisheries* 23, no. 3 (2021): 545–63.
77 David Wroe, "Super Trawler Banned from Fishing in Australian Waters," *Sydney Morning Herald* (September 11, 2012), www.smh.com.au/environment/conservation/super-trawler-banned-from-fishing-in-australian-waters-20120911-25q3i.html.
78 Mariculture involves small- or industrial-scale farming of marine fish, crustaceans, and molluscs for food and other products in the open ocean or in land- or sea-based enclosures, as well as more localised farming of species such as kelp and seaweed in coastal waters.
79 FAO, *The State of the World's Fisheries and Aquaculture* (Rome: FAO, 2016).
80 FAO, *The State of the World's Fisheries and Aquaculture* (Rome: FAO, 2022).
81 Aldemaro Romero et al., "Environmental History of Marine Mammal Exploitation in Trinidad and Tobago, W.I., and Its Ecological Impact," *Environment and History* 8, no. 3 (2002): 255–74.
82 David R. Percy, Nathaniel Hishamunda, and Blaise Kuemlangan, "Governance in Marine Aquaculture: The Legal Dimension," accessed January 31, 2024, www.fao.org/fishery/docs/CDrom/P24/master/root/13.pdf.
83 For example, Liberia's *National Fisheries and Aquaculture Act 2019*; Tonga's *Aquaculture Management Act 2003* and Namibia's *Aquaculture Act 2002*.
84 Tonje C. Osmundsen and Marit Schei Olsen, "The Imperishable Controversy Over Aquaculture," *Marine Policy* 76 (2017): 136–42.

85 Jon Ungoed-Thomas, "Farmed Fish Feel Pain, Stress and Anxiety and Must Be Killed Humanely, Global Regulator Accepts," *The Guardian* (October 9, 2022), www.theguardian.com/world/2022/oct/08/farmed-fish-feel-pain-stress-and-anxiety-and-must-be-killed-humanely-global-regulator-admits.
86 "Fish Welfare Project," *Aquaculture Stewardship Council*, accessed March 1, 2024, www.asc-aqua.org/programme-improvements/fish-welfare/.
87 Ungoed-Thomas, "Farmed Fish Feel Pain."
88 Larry A. Nielsen, "The Evolution of Fisheries Management Philosophy," *Marine Fisheries Research* 38 (1976): 15–23.
89 See generally, Max Nicholson, *The Environmental Revolution* (London: Hodder and Stoughton, 1970).
90 Kira Gee, "The Ocean Perspective," in *Maritime Spatial Planning: Past, Present, Future*, ed. Jacek Zaucha and Kira Gee (New York: Springer International Publishing, 2019), 35.
91 Gregory Ferguson-Cradler, "Fisheries' Collapse and the Marking of a Global Event, 1950s-1970s," *Journal of Global History* 13 (2018): 399–424.
92 "Bangladesh Overfishing: Almost All Species Pushed to Brink," *BBC News* (April 16, 2020), www.bbc.com/news/world-asia-52227735.
93 The blue economy concept is explored in Chapter 1.
94 Daniel Pauly, "Anecdotes and the Shifting Baseline Syndrome of Fisheries," *Trends in Ecology and Evolution* 10, no. 1 (1995): 430.
95 Heidi K. Alleway et al., "The Shifting Baseline Syndrome as a Connective Concept for More Informed and Just Responses to Global Environmental Change," *People and Nature* 5 (2023): 885–96.
96 Ibid.
97 Dirk Zeller et al., "Still Catching Attention: *Sea around Us* Reconstructed Global Catch Data, Their Spatial Expression and Public Accessibility," *Marine Policy* 70 (2016): 145–52. "Catch Reconstruction: Concepts, Methods, and Data Sources," *Sea around Us*, www.seaaroundus.org/catch-reconstruction-and-allocation-methods/. Daniel Pauly, Ray Hilborn, and Trevor A Branch, "Fisheries: Does Catch Reflect Abundance?" *Nature* 494 (2013): 303–6.
98 The FAO *State of the World's Fisheries and Aquaculture* report includes information on data collection and guidance provided to States to improve data collection and curation.
99 Jamie Shaffer, "Leveraging Deep Learning to Facilitate Fish Counts" (January 31, 2024), https://github.com/jshaffer94247/Counting-Fish.
100 University of Tasmania, "Tasmanian Fisheries Forensics Technology Set to Improve Global Catch Management" (December 18, 2023), www.utas.edu.au/about/news-and-stories/articles/2023/tasmanian-fisheries-forensics-technology-set-to-improve-global-catch-management.
101 See, for example, in Australia and Iceland: Catherine Norwood, "Smartphone Option to Add Critical Recreational Catch Data," *FRDC* (December 13, 2023), www.frdc.com.au/smartphone-option-add-critical-recreational-catch-data and "iCatch: Fish Catch Reporting App for Smartphones," *Icefish Connect* (November 15, 2021), https://icefishconnect.is/newfront/news/1834
102 "Forced Labour and Human Trafficking in Fisheries International Labour Organization," accessed March 1, 2024, www.ilo.org/global/topics/forced-labour/policy-areas/fisheries/lang–en/index.htm. See also, Ian Urbina, *The Outlaw Ocean* (London: Penguin/Random House, 2019).
103 David J. Agnew et al., "Estimating the Worldwide Extent of Illegal Fishing," *PLOS One* 4, no. 2 (2009): e4570. This research estimated that in West Africa, total catches

were 40% higher than reported catches. Watson and Tidd, "Mapping Nearly a Century."

104 "The Global Fight against Illegal, Unreported and Unregulated Fishing Reaches a New Milestone," *Food and Agriculture Organization of the United Nations* (November 7, 2022), www.fao.org/newsroom/detail/the-global-fight-against-illegal-unreported-and-unregulated-fishing-reaches-a-new-milestone/en.

105 "International Plan of Action to Prevent, Deter and Eliminate Illegal, Unreported and Unregulated Fishing," *FAO*, accessed January 31, 2024, www.fao.org/iuu-fishing/international-framework/ipoa-iuu/en/.

106 "Illegal, Unreported and Unregulated (IUU) fishing: International Framework," *FAO*, accessed January 31, 2024, www.fao.org/iuu-fishing/international-framework/en/.

107 The 2022 assessment indicates that the aggregated score globally is implementation of four out of the five instruments: FAO, *State of the World's Fisheries and Aquaculture* (2022), 164.

108 The initiative was established as a collaboration between Oceana, SkyTruth and Google and its projects are philanthropically funded: "Revolutionizing Ocean Monitoring and Analysis," *Global Fishing Watch*, accessed March 1, 2024, https://globalfishingwatch.org/.

109 "Following Forced Labor in the World's Fishing Fleets," *Global Fishing Watch*, accessed January 31, 2024, https://globalfishingwatch.org/blog/new-study-unveils-risk-of-forced-labor-in-fisheries.

110 Terje Løbach et al., *Regional Fisheries Management Organizations and Advisory Bodies*.

111 Quentin Bates, "EU to Use Global Standards For Fisheries Data Sharing," *FiskerForum* (September 20, 2023), https://fiskerforum.com/eu-to-use-global-standards-for-fisheries-data-sharing/.

112 FAO, *Code of Conduct for Responsible Fisheries* (1999) and FAO, *Guidelines for Developing an At-sea Fishery Observer Programme* (Rome: FAO, 2003).

113 See for example, SPRFMO, *Conservation and Management Measure Establishing the SPRFMO Observer Programme* (CMM16–2022).

114 Karen McVeigh, "Disappearances, Danger and Death: What Is Happening to Fishery Observers?" *The Guardian* (May 22, 2020), www.theguardian.com/environment/2020/may/22/disappearances-danger-and-death-what-is-happening-to-fishery-observers; and Awudu Salami Sulemana Yoda, "Fisheries Observer Turns Up Dead in Latest Incident in Ghana Waters," *Mongabay* (December 28, 2023), https://news.mongabay.com/2023/12/fisheries-observer-turns-up-dead-in-latest-incident-in-ghana-waters/. "Efforts Have Been Made to Improve Safety: Association for Professional Observers," *RFMO Observer Safety Measures*, www.apo-observers.org/observer-safety/rfmo-observer-safety-measures/.

115 UNCLOS Article 111 includes specific rules for hot pursuit.

116 Caroline C. Coombs, "The Doctrine of Hot Pursuit under International Law" (PhD, The University of Western Australia, 2016).

117 Randall Walker, "International Law of the Sea: Applying the Doctrine of Hot Pursuit in the 21st Century," *Auckland University Law Review* 17 (2011): 194–218.

118 Warren N. Wright, "Shiprider Program," *Indo-Pacific Forum* (January 27, 2020), https://ipdefenseforum.com/2020/01/shiprider-program/

119 Peter Griffin, "An Eye on the Pacific: The Regional Fisheries Surveillance Centre," *Pacific Islands Forum Fisheries Agency* (August 25, 2023), https://tunapacific.ffa.int/2023/08/25/an-eye-on-the-pacific-the-regional-fisheries-surveillance-centre/.

120 *Niue Treaty on Cooperation in Fisheries Surveillance and Law Enforcement in the South Pacific Region* (1992), accessed January 31, 2024, www.fao.org/faolex/results/details/en/c/LEX-FAOC005116/.

121 Global Fishing Watch, "Understanding Fishing Activity Using AIS and VMS Data," https://globalfishingwatch.org/wp-content/uploads/Understanding-Fishing-Activity.pdf.
122 European Commission, "Infringements and Sanctions," accessed March 1, 2024, https://oceans-and-fisheries.ec.europa.eu/fisheries/rules/enforcing-rules/infringements-and-sanctions_en.
123 "Fishermen Caught in Epic Chase Acquitted," *Sydney Morning Herald* (November 6, 2005), www.smh.com.au/national/fishermen-caught-in-epic-chase-acquitted-20051106-gdmdzr.html.
124 For an examination of two Spanish cases brought in relation to breaches of CCAMLR rules, see Mercedes Rosello, "Regional Fishery Management Organisation Measures and the Imposition of Criminal and Administrative Sanctions in Respect of High Seas Fishing," *Marine Policy* 144 (2022): 105213.
125 "Crimes in the Fisheries Sector," *UNODC*, accessed January 31, 2024, www.unodc.org/unodc/en/ccp/activities/crimes-in-the-fisheries-sector.html?testme.
126 "Compliance," *CCAMLR*, accessed March 1, 2024, www.ccamlr.org/en/compliance/compliance.
127 "India etc versus US: 'Shrimp-turtle'," *WTO*, accessed January 31, 2024, www.wto.org/english/tratop_e/envir_e/edis08_e.htm.
128 "Marine Stewardship Council," accessed January 31, 2024, www.msc.org/; and "Aquaculture Stewardship Council," accessed January 31, 2024, https://asc-aqua.org/.
129 The US has taken steps to regulate the use of the label: "Dolphin-Safe," *NOAA*, accessed March 1, 2024, www.fisheries.noaa.gov/national/marine-mammal-protection/dolphin-saf
130 UNCLOS Articles 61, 63 and 119. Ecosystem based management is explored in Chapter 1.
131 UN Fish Stocks Agreement Article 5.
132 FAO, *The State of the World's Fisheries and Aquaculture* (2022), 130.
133 "Krill Fisheries and Sustainability," *CCAMLR*, accessed January 31, 2024, www.ccamlr.org/en/fisheries/krill-fisheries-and-sustainability.
134 Md Saiful Karim, "Indian Ocean Tuna Commission Climate Change Resolution: A Quiet Interaction of Ocean and Climate Change Legal Regimes," *Marine Policy* 148 (2023): 105434.
135 The Ocean Race, "Towards a Universal Declaration of Ocean Rights (UDOR): Concept Note," accessed March 1, 2024, https://static1.squarespace.com/static/55914fd1e4b01fb0b851a814/t/646523cd9c8b6d4f55abaa3c/1684349908559/UDOR_Concept+Note+%281%29.pdf
136 In Australia and the US, legislation provides a person or corporation (such as an expert or group) legal standing to bring proceedings on behalf of the environment. Granting specific rights to the ocean could be achieved in similar ways to freshwater, yet granting rights to particular species will require new legal developments.
137 Blue justice is a term that has come to mean eradicating fisheries crime in the context of blue economy and blue growth initiatives: "Blue Justice," accessed January 31, 2024, https://bluejustice.org/. Ocean justice is a broader term, although not yet commonly used, and connotes an approach to oceans governance that involves moving beyond extractive conceptions of oceans based on fungible resources, and re-imagining oceans and harnessing marine stewardship and ecological thinking: see for example "Ocean Justice: Imagining with the Seas," accessed January 31, 2024, https://oceanjustice.com.au/.

Bibliography

"A History of Sea Vessels." *Bridgeman Images* (December 16, 2021). https://blog.bridgemanimages.com/blog/a-history-of-sea-vessels.

Agnew, David J. et al. "Estimating the Worldwide Extent of Illegal Fishing." *PLOS One* 4, no. 2 (2009): e4570.

AIATSIS. "A Brief Introduction to Indigenous Fishing." Accessed January 31, 2024. https://aiatsis.gov.au/brief-introduction-indigenous-fishing.

Alleway, Heidi K. et al. "The Shifting Baseline Syndrome as a Connective Concept for More Informed and Just Responses to Global Environmental Change." *People and Nature* 5 (2023): 885–96.

Aquaculture Stewardship Council. Accessed January 31, 2024. https://asc-aqua.org/.

Aquaculture Stewardship Council. "Fish Welfare Project." Accessed March 1, 2024. www.asc-aqua.org/programme-improvements/fish-welfare/.

Association for Professional Observers. "RFMO Observer Safety Measures." Accessed March 1, 20204. www.apo-observers.org/observer-safety/rfmo-observer-safety-measures/.

"Bangladesh Overfishing: Almost All Species Pushed to Brink." *BBC News* (April 16, 2020). www.bbc.com/news/world-asia-52227735.

Bardach, John E. "Living Marine Resources and the Law of the Sea." *BioScience* 31, no. 3 (1981): 191.

Bardach, John E., and Santerre, Regina Miranda. "Climate and the Fish in the Sea." *BioScience* 31, no. 3 (1981): 205.

Bates, Quentin. "EU to Use Global Standards for Fisheries Data Sharing." *FiskerForum* (September 20, 2023). https://fiskerforum.com/eu-to-use-global-standards-for-fisheries-data-sharing/.

Bilms, Kevin. "The Cod Wars and Lessons for Maritime Counterinsurgency." *Proceedings: US Naval Institute* 149, no. 2 (February 2023): 1440.

"Blue Justice." Accessed January 31, 2024. https://bluejustice.org/.

Bode, Michael et al. "Fish Aggregating Devices Could Enhance the Effectiveness of Blue Water Marine Protected Areas." *Conservation Letters* 16 (2023): 12984.

CCAMLR. "Compliance." Accessed March 1, 2024. www.ccamlr.org/en/compliance/compliance.

CCAMLR. "Krill Fisheries and Sustainability." Accessed January 31, 2024. www.ccamlr.org/en/fisheries/krill-fisheries-and-sustainability.

Chapman, Margaret D. "Women's Fishing in Oceania." *Human Ecology* 15, no. 3 (1987): 267.

Convention for the Prohibition of Fishing with Long Driftnets in the South Pacific (Wellington Convention) (1989). Accessed March 1, 2024. https://ecolex.org/details/treaty/convention-for-the-prohibition-of-fishing-with-long-driftnets-in-the-south-pacific-tre-001043/.

"Convention on Biological Diversity." Accessed January 31, 2024. www.cbd.int.

Coombs, Caroline C. "The Doctrine of Hot Pursuit under International Law." PhD, University of Western Australia, 2016.

Davies, R. W. D. et al. "Defining and Estimating Global Marine Fisheries Bycatch." *Marine Policy* 33, no. 4 (2009): 661–72.

European Commission. "Infringements and Sanctions." Accessed March 1, 2024. https://oceans-and-fisheries.ec.europa.eu/fisheries/rules/enforcing-rules/infringements-and-sanctions_en.

FAO. "Code of Conduct for Responsible Fisheries." Accessed January 31, 2024. www.fao.org/3/v9878e/v9878e00.htm.

FAO. "Fisheries and Aquaculture." Accessed January 31, 2024. www.fao.org/fishery/en.

FAO. "General Fisheries Commission for the Mediterranean." Accessed January 31, 2024. www.fao.org/gfcm/en/.
FAO. *Guidelines for Developing an At-Sea Fishery Observer Programme*. Rome: FAO, 2003.
FAO. "Illegal, Unreported and Unregulated (IUU) Fishing: International Framework." Accessed January 31, 2024. www.fao.org/iuu-fishing/international-framework/en/.
FAO. "International Plan of Action to Prevent, Deter and Eliminate Illegal, Unreported and Unregulated Fishing." Accessed January 31, 2024. www.fao.org/iuu-fishing/international-framework/ipoa-iuu/en/.
FAO. *The State of the World's Fisheries and Aquaculture*. Rome: FAO, 2016.
FAO. *The State of the World's Fisheries and Aquaculture*. Rome: FAO, 2022.
FAO. "The WTO Agreement on Fisheries Subsidies and the Role of FAO." Accessed January 31, 2024. www.fao.org/documents/card/en/c/cc9063en.
"FAOLEX." Accessed March 1, 2024. www.fao.org/faolex/en/.
Ferguson-Cradler, Gregory. "Fisheries' Collapse and the Marking of a Global Event, 1950s-1970s." *Journal of Global History* 13 (2018): 399–424.
"Fishermen Caught in Epic Chase Acquitted." *Sydney Morning Herald* (November 6, 2005). www.smh.com.au/national/fishermen-caught-in-epic-chase-acquitted-20051106-gdmdzr.html.
Gee, Kira. "The Ocean Perspective." In *Maritime Spatial Planning: Past, Present, Future*, edited by Jacek Zaucha and Kira Gee. New York: Springer International Publishing, 2019.
Gillis, John R. *The Human Shore*. Chicago: University of Chicago Press, 2012.
Global Fishing Watch. "Following Forced Labor in the World's Fishing Fleets." Accessed January 31, 2024. https://globalfishingwatch.org/blog/new-study-unveils-risk-of-forced-labor-in-fisheries.
Global Fishing Watch. "Revolutionizing Ocean Monitoring and Analysis." Accessed March 1, 2024. https://globalfishingwatch.org/.
Global Fishing Watch. "Understanding Fishing Activity Using AIS and VMS Data." Accessed March 1, 2024. https://globalfishingwatch.org/wp-content/uploads/Understanding-Fishing-Activity.pdf.
Good, S. D. et al. "National Plans of Action (NPOAs) for Reducing Seabird Bycatch: Developing Best Practice for Assessing and Managing Fisheries Impacts." *Biological Conservation* 247 (2020): 108592.
Griffin, Peter. "An Eye on the Pacific: The Regional Fisheries Surveillance Centre." *Pacific Islands Forum Fisheries Agency. News* (August 25, 2023). https://tunapacific.ffa.int/2023/08/25/an-eye-on-the-pacific-the-regional-fisheries-surveillance-centre/.
Hore, John Philip, and Jex, Edward. *The Deterioration of Oyster and Trawl Fisheries of England: Its Cause and Remedy*. United Kingdom: E Stock, 1880.
"iCatch: Fish Catch Reporting App for Smartphones." *Icefish Connect* (November 15, 2021). https://icefishconnect.is/newfront/news/1834.
ICCAT. "Contracting Parties." Accessed January 31, 2024. www.iccat.int/en/contracting.html.
ICCAT. "Record of Vessels." Accessed January 31, 2024. www.iccat.int/en/VesselsRecord.asp.
International Labour Organization. "Forced Labour and Human Trafficking in Fisheries." Accessed March 1, 2024. www.ilo.org/global/topics/forced-labour/policy-areas/fisheries/lang – en/index.htm.
IOTC. "Conservation and Management Measures." Accessed January 31, 2024. www.iotc.org/cmms.

Johannes, R. E. "The Renaissance of Community-Based Marine Resource Management in Oceania." *Annual Review of Ecology and Systematics* 33 (2002): 317.
Johannes, R. E. "Traditional Marine Conservation Methods in Oceania and Their Demise." *Annual Review of Ecology and Systematics* 9 (1978): 349.
Johannesson, Gudni Thorlacius. "Troubled Waters: Cod War, Fishing Disputes, and Britain's Fight for the Freedom of the High Seas, 1948–1964." PhD, University of London, 2007.
Jones, Peter. "The Long 'Lost' History of Bottom Trawling in England, c.1350–1650." *International Journal of Maritime History* 30, no. 2 (2018): 201.
Karim, Md Saiful. "Indian Ocean Tuna Commission Climate Change Resolution: A Quiet Interaction of Ocean and Climate Change Legal Regimes." *Marine Policy* 148 (2023): 105434.
Kikiloi, Kekuewa. "A New Synthesis in Oceanic Domestication: The Symbiotic Development of Loko I'a Aquaculture in Pre-Contact Oceania." *SPC Traditional Marine Resource Management and Knowledge Information Bulletin* 15 (2003): 1.
Kirch, P. V. *Feathered Gods and Fishhooks: An Introduction to Hawaiian Archaeology and Pre-history*. Honolulu: University of Hawai'i Press, 1985.
LoScerbo, Daniella et al. "Fish Traps of the Society Islands." Accessed January 31, 2024. www.seagardens.net/society-islands.
"Marine Stewardship Council." Accessed January 31, 2024. www.msc.org/.
McDaniel, Josh. "The Return of Kū'ula: Restoration of Hawaiian Fishponds." Accessed January 31, 2024. https://seagrant.soest.hawaii.edu/the-return-of-kuula/.
McVeigh, Karen. "Disappearances, Danger and Death: What Is Happening to Fishery Observers?" *The Guardian* (May 22, 2020). www.theguardian.com/environment/2020/may/22/disappearances-danger-and-death-what-is-happening-to-fishery-observers.
Nakamura, Julia. "International Fisheries Law: Past to Future." In *Oceans Governance*, edited by S. Partelow, M. Hadjimichael, and A-K. Hornidge. Cham, Switzerland: Springer, 2023.
Nicholson, Max. *The Environmental Revolution*. London: Hodder and Stoughton, 1970.
Nielsen, Larry A. "The Evolution of Fisheries Management Philosophy." *Marine Fisheries Research* 38 (1976): 15–23.
"Niue Treaty on Cooperation in Fisheries Surveillance and Law Enforcement in the South Pacific Region." (1992). Accessed January 31, 2024. www.fao.org/faolex/results/details/en/c/LEX-FAOC005116/.
NOAA. "Dolphin-Safe." Accessed March 1, 2024. www.fisheries.noaa.gov/national/marine-mammal-protection/dolphin-saf.
Norwood, Catherine. "Smartphone Option to Add Critical Recreational Catch Data." *FRDC* (December 13, 2023). www.frdc.com.au/smartphone-option-add-critical-recreational-catch-data.
"Ocean Justice: Imagining with the Seas." Accessed January 31, 2024. https://oceanjustice.com.au/.
Osmundsen Tonje, C., and Marit Schei Olsen. "The Imperishable Controversy Over Aquaculture." *Marine Policy* 76 (2017): 136–42.
Pauly, Daniel. "Anecdotes and the Shifting Baseline Syndrome of Fisheries." *Trends in Ecology and Evolution* 10, no. 1 (1995): 430.
Pauly, Daniel, Ray Hilborn, and Trevor A. Branch. "Fisheries: Does Catch Reflect Abundance?" *Nature* 494 (2013): 303–6.
Percy, David R., Nathaniel Hishamunda, and Blaise Kuemlangan. "Governance in Marine Aquaculture: The Legal Dimension." Accessed January 31, 2024. www.fao.org/fishery/docs/CDrom/P24/master/root/13.pdf.
Poisson, F. et al. "New Technologies to Improve Bycatch Mitigation in Industrial Tuna Fisheries." *Fish and Fisheries* 23, no. 3 (2021): 545–63.

Republic of Palau. "Fishing Title 27, Division 1 Foreign Fishing." Accessed January 31, 2024. www.worldlii.org/paclii/pw/legis/consol_act/ft27126/.

Roberts, Callum. *An Unnatural History of the Sea*. Washington, DC: Island Press, 2007.

Romero, Aldemaro et al. "Environmental History of Marine Mammal Exploitation in Trinidad and Tobago, W.I., and Its Ecological Impact." *Environment and History* 8, no. 3 (2002): 255–74.

Rosello, Mercedes. "Regional Fishery Management Organisation Measures and the Imposition of Criminal and Administrative Sanctions in Respect of High Seas Fishing." *Marine Policy* 144 (2022): 105213.

Rozwadowski, Helen M. *Vast Expanses: A History of the Oceans*. Chicago: University of Chicago Press, 2018.

Sahrhage, Dietrich, and Lundbeck, Johannes. *A History of Fishing*. Heidelberg: Springer Berlin, 2012.

Salami Sulemana Yoda, Awudu. "Fisheries Observer Turns Up Dead in Latest Incident in Ghana Waters." *Mongabay* (December 28, 2023). https://news.mongabay.com/2023/12/fisheries-observer-turns-up-dead-in-latest-incident-in-ghana-waters/.

Sea around Us. "Catch Reconstruction: Concepts, Methods, and Data Sources." Accessed March 1, 2024. www.seaaroundus.org/catch-reconstruction-and-allocation-methods/.

Shaffer, Jamie. "Leveraging Deep Learning to Facilitate Fish Counts." Accessed January 31, 2024. https://github.com/jshaffer94247/Counting-Fish.

SPRFMO. "Conservation and Management Measures." Accessed January 31, 2024. www.sprfmo.int/assets/Fisheries/Conservation-and-Management-Measures/7fe67e4f02/CMMs-Booklet-13Dec2016-downloaded-from-website.pdf.

SPRFMO. "Conservation and Management Measure Establishing the SPRFMO Observer Programme." (CMM16–2022). https://sprfmo.int/assets/Fisheries/Conservation-and-Management-Measures/2023-CMMs/CMM-16-2023-Observer-Programme_29Mar23.pdf

SPRFMO. "Conservation and Management Measure for the Management of Bottom Fishing in the SPRFMO Convention Area." Accessed January 31, 2024, www.sprfmo.int/assets/Fisheries/Conservation-and-Management-Measures/2021-CMMs/CMM-03-2021-Bottom-Fishing-12Mar2021.pdf.

Taylor, L. *Sharks of Hawai'i – Their Biology and Cultural Significance*. Honolulu: University of Hawai'i Press, 1993.

Techera, Erika J. *Marine Environmental Governance: From International Law to Local Practice*. Abingdon: Routledge, 2012.

Terje Løbach, T., M. Petersson, E. Haberkon, and P. Mannini. *Regional Fisheries Management Organizations and Advisory Bodies. Activities and Developments, 2000–2017*. Rome: FAO Fisheries and Aquaculture Technical Paper No. 651, 2020.

"The Global Fight against Illegal, Unreported and Unregulated Fishing Reaches a New Milestone." *FAO Newsroom* (November 7, 2022). www.fao.org/newsroom/detail/the-global-fight-against-illegal-unreported-and-unregulated-fishing-reaches-a-new-milestone/en.

The Ocean Race. "Towards a Universal Declaration of Ocean Rights (UDOR): Concept Note." Accessed March 1, 2024. https://static1.squarespace.com/static/55914fd1e4b01fb0b851a814/t/646523cd9c8b6d4f55abaa3c/1684349908559/UDOR_Concept+Note+%281%29.pdf.

"Traditional Fishing Techniques around the World." *FishingBooker Blog* (October 11, 2023). https://fishingbooker.com/blog/traditional-fishing-techniques-around-the-world/.

Ungoed-Thomas, Jon. "Farmed Fish Feel Pain, Stress and Anxiety and Must Be Killed Humanely, Global Regulator Accepts." *The Guardian* (October 9, 2022). www.theguardian.com/world/2022/oct/08/farmed-fish-feel-pain-stress-and-anxiety-and-must-be-killed-humanely-global-regulator-admits.

United Nations. "Sustainable Development Goals." Accessed January 31, 2024. https://sdgs.un.org/goals.

United Nations. "UNFSA Overview." Accessed January 31, 2024. www.un.org/oceancapacity/unfsa.

United Nations. "United Nations Declaration on the Rights of Indigenous Peoples." Accessed January 31, 2024. www.un.org/development/desa/indigenouspeoples/declaration-on-%20the-rights-of-indigenous-peoples.html.

"United Nations Convention on the Law of the Sea." Accessed March 1, 2024. www.un.org/depts/los/convention_agreements/texts/unclos/closindx.htm.

University of Tasmania. "Tasmanian Fisheries Forensics Technology Set to Improve Global Catch Management." Accessed December 18, 2023. www.utas.edu.au/about/news-and-stories/articles/2023/tasmanian-fisheries-forensics-technology-set-to-improve-global-catch-management.

UNODC. "Crimes in the Fisheries Sector." Accessed January 31, 2024. www.unodc.org/unodc/en/ccp/activities/crimes-in-the-fisheries-sector.html?testme.

Urbina, Ian. *The Outlaw Ocean*. London: Penguin/Random House, 2019.

Victorero, Lissette et al. "Out of Sight, But Within Reach: A Global History of Bottom-Trawled Deep-Sea Fisheries from >400 m Depth." *Frontiers in Marine Science* 5 (2018). Accessed January 31, 2024. https://doi.org/10.3389/fmars.2018.00098.

Walker, Randall. "International Law of the Sea: Applying the Doctrine of Hot Pursuit in the 21st Century." *Auckland University Law Review* 17 (2011): 194–218.

Watson, Reg A., and A. Tidd. "Mapping Nearly a Century and a Half of Global Marine Fishing: 1869–2015." *Marine Policy* 93 (2018): 171.

WCPFC. "Conservation and Management Measure on the Application of High Seas FAD Closures and Catch Retention, Conservation and Management Measure 2009–02." Accessed January 31, 2024. www.wcpfc.int/system/files/booklets/31/CMM%20and%20Resolutions.pdf.

Worldlii. "World Legal Information Institute." Accessed January 31, 2024. www.worldlii.org/nie/legis/num_act/sfa1875137/.

Wright, Warren N. "Shiprider Program." *Indo-Pacific Forum* (January 27, 2020). https://ipdefenseforum.com/2020/01/shiprider-program/

Wroe, David. "Super Trawler Banned from Fishing in Australian Waters." *Sydney Morning Herald* (September 11, 2012). www.smh.com.au/environment/conservation/super-trawler-banned-from-fishing-in-australian-waters-20120911-25q3i.html.

WTO. "India etc versus US: 'Shrimp-turtle'." Accessed January 31, 2024. www.wto.org/english/tratop_e/envir_e/edis08_e.htm.

Zacharias, Mark. *Marine Policy*. Abingdon: Earthscan 2014.

Zeller, Dirk et al. "Still Catching Attention: *Sea around Us* Reconstructed Global Catch Data, Their Spatial Expression and Public Accessibility." *Marine Policy* 70 (2016): 145–52.

5 Seafaring

Ships and shipping in law

Even now my heart
Journeys beyond its confines, and my thoughts
Over the sea, across the whale's domain,
Travel afar the regions of the earth
'The Seafarer', eleventh century[1]

Overview

Oceans and seas have been used as a means of transport and trade since ancient times. When vessels were relatively small and powered by sail, navigation and safety of life at sea were the primary concerns. As larger vessels began plying the oceans, rescue obligations and rules around commercial salvage evolved. The global shipping industry has changed dramatically over the past half century, spurred on by growth in the carriage of petroleum products and containerisation. Over that time, the total weight of transported cargo has increased 20 times and accidents involving container ships have also increased, with significant impacts on people and animals on board, as well as the marine environment.[2] In response, it has been the International Maritime Organization (IMO) that has adopted more robust regulations for the shipping industry to address specific problems.[3]

This chapter focuses primarily on commercial shipping and traces the development of maritime laws, particularly in relation to three key areas: the prevention of maritime accidents, safety and security of ships including design and navigation; responses to maritime incidents including safety of life at sea and rescue obligations; and the rules governing cargo, maritime goods and salvage.[4] Legal efforts to address operational and accidental oil spills and other waste from ships, transport of hazardous waste, and the deliberate dumping of material at sea, as well as emerging issues including shipbreaking and the release of ballast water, are explored in the pollution chapter. While significant achievements improvements

DOI: 10.4324/9781003005261-8

have been achieved through legal and regulatory regimes, issues continue to plague the industry and its impacts on the world's oceans, seas and shorelines.

The origins of maritime law

Around 70% of Earth's surface is covered by oceans and seas of which around two-thirds are considered 'international waters', perhaps better known as the 'high seas'. No one country or individual owns these waters. They are regarded as a 'global commons', but they are far from lawless. Indeed, the need for international cooperation in relation to the safety of ships on the high seas has long been recognised in maritime traditions such as ships going to the aid of other ships in distress. Over the centuries, these traditions have evolved into international rules, agreements and conventions, collectively known as maritime law, governing the activities of ships, shipping companies, and seafarers.

What is maritime law?

Maritime law is designed to give all countries the right to use the oceans for navigation, fishing, commercial shipping and other activities without interference from other parties It regulates activities including maritime navigation, disputes, offences and the welfare of seafarers on board a vessel in any oceanic location. Maritime law is different from the international Law of the Sea: on the one hand, maritime law is a system of legal rules, conventions and regulations governing private maritime business and nautical matters and includes both domestic laws relating to maritime activities, including navigation, seafarer welfare, piracy, fishing, marine salvage, pollution and conservation, and private international law governing the relationship between private parties operating ocean-going ships. The law of the sea, on the other hand, is a body of international public law governing how States should behave in maritime environments.[5] As Philip Steinberg has written: 'private ocean law (or maritime law) is a set of rules (including national legislation and international agreements) regulating the economic and commercial aspects of marine transport. Public ocean law (or the Law of the Sea) governs the sea itself, particularly with reference to control of ocean-space and access to its living and nonliving resources'.[6] Nevertheless, these two areas of law are connected because they depend upon common rules of access and navigation, as well as specific vessel-related obligations.

The earliest commercial activities in human history involved the transporting of goods and people by sea and, whilst there is no consensus amongst legal experts on the precise origins of law relating to maritime activities, the earliest known example can be found in the ancient Babylonian Code of Hammurabi (c 2050–1750 BCE). Some experts claim that maritime law was first developed on the island of Rhodes in the Mediterranean, possibly around 800 BCE. Whilst no ancient texts survive, 'The Sea-Law of the Rhodians' (known as The Rhodian Sea-Law) is thought to have been based on a rule in the Digest of the Code of Justinian (commissioned in the 6th century) and maritime customary law that had evolved over previous centuries. The Rhodian Sea-Law focused on the legal regulation of sea trade and established standards for the treatment of merchant ships sailing between ports. It also required that disputes at sea must be decided by Rhodian maritime law rather than in local courts.[7] Far from obsolete, some of the legal principles derived from The Rhodian Sea-Law, such as the principle of General Average – whereby all stakeholders share the losses if part of the cargo or vessel is sacrificed in a seafaring emergency – is still used in civil codes today.[8]

Irrespective of the precise point of origin, this ancient maritime code subsequently influenced the development of Roman maritime law in the region and portions were also incorporated into the *Basilica* – the Byzantine legal code – in the Eastern Empire. Even after the collapse of the Roman Empire, Rome's maritime code continued to shape the laws of early European States, including the

Figure 5.1 Engraving of Phoenician sailors and merchants who were renowned for their achievements in maritime navigation and trade in the Mediterranean region. (Published in *The Illustrated History of the World for the English People. From the Earliest Period to the Present Time, Ancient-Mediaeval-Modern. With Many Original High-Class Engravings*, New York Ward: Lock, 1881?-84?, Volume 1.)

most famous of these – the Rolls (or Laws) of Oléron – which formed the basis for all Atlantic and Baltic codes in continental Europe. They were introduced to England in about 1190 and codified in the Black Book of the Admiralty in 1336. They mainly dealt with the rights and responsibilities of ships' captains on board their ships in relation to matters such as discipline, mutiny, pay, cargoes, sickness, piloting and accidents.[9]

Whilst maritime law evolved through different codes that addressed the local circumstances in various States, the principle and application of court judgments in transnational commercial cases – broadly known as *lex maritima et mercatoria* – were generally adhered to by merchants and mercantile traders from the Middle Ages.[10] The same could not be said of English law, however, where courts applied two different types of law: the medieval English treatise *Lex mercatoria* relating to disputes amongst merchants in seaport towns, and, from 1291, rulings made by the office of admiral to hear matters 'done upon the sea'. Admirals were appointed to prevent shipwreck, suppress piracy and the unlawful taking of royal fish, and secure maritime property forfeited to the crown. They were assisted by deputy admirals who, under the admiral's authority, heard maritime cases such as piracy and homicide at sea in regional courts of England.[11] The jurisdiction of the Admiralty Court continued to grow over the following centuries as the scale of England's imperial reach and maritime trade expanded. By the 17th century, the Admiralty Court was hearing cases relating to a wide range of matters including collision at sea, pillaging of vessels, piracy, shipwreck, salvage, hostage-taking and issues affecting pilots, masters, seamen and fishermen.[12]

With the increase of international maritime activity from the 18th century came attempts by jurists in different States to codify the various maritime customs and mercantile rules that had accrued in different regions over the preceding centuries. In the Mediterranean, for example, the Book of the Consulate of the Sea (*Catalan Llibre del Consolat de Mar*), published in 1494, contained a collection of local maritime customs and ordinances in the Catalan language.[13] It was not until the early 19th century that maritime nations agreed to a legal regime governing the navigation of ocean-going ships. Concerns remained, however, over different navigation rules between States that caused confusion. For example, the seemingly straightforward matter of vessel navigation lights, in use from at least the 16th century, were not standardised leading to a heightened risk of collisions at sea between ships of different nations.

The risk was exacerbated by the rise of steam-powered ships from the mid-19th century, leading to the introduction of new rules – initially in Britain and the US – governing navigation lights and fog signals to be used on steamships and sailing vessels, respectively. In 1889 the US convened the first international maritime conference in Washington DC in an effort to find consensus on an international regime for shipping. It resulted in the adoption in 1890 (in effect in 1897) of rules binding all ships, regardless of nationality, to the same rules in order to avoid the risk of collision at sea.[14] These 'Rules of the Road' remained essentially unchanged until the IMO adopted the *Convention on the International Regulations for Preventing Collisions at Sea*, 1972 (COLREGs), which included arrangements for navigation lights, daymarks, sound signals and how to avoid action for vessels approaching each other.[15]

The business of marine insurance

Arguably, hull and cargo insurance is the oldest form of insurance in the world, with early forms possibly dating back to 1200 BC when Phoenician traders operated in the Mediterranean.[16] There were some relevant clauses in the Rules of Oléron, and risk-transfer agreements in 16th-century Europe. In the late 17th century, London's coffee houses had become popular as informal meeting places for different groups of entrepreneurs and merchants involved in Britain's expanding maritime empire. In 1688, the *London Gazette* noted that Edward Lloyd's Coffee House was the favoured meeting place for merchants, bankers, and seafarers engaged in the maritime trade and, in 1696, Edward Lloyd began publishing news about shipping movements, the cargo aboard each ship, and where pirates were known to be active. The first edition of *Lloyd's List* published in 1734 drew on Lloyd's reputation for reliable intelligence, and it continues to provide weekly international shipping news today.[17]

Lloyd's Coffee House was also popular with sailors, merchants and shipowners seeking insurance against risks associated with the maritime trade. Members of the coffee house would take a share of the risk by signing their names one after the other on a policy for an agreed amount – a process that became known as 'underwriting'.[18] In 1760, merchants and 'underwriters' formed the Society for the Registry of Shipping, the world's first 'classification society', employing retired sea captains to inspect, rate and classify the materials and condition of vessels docking in British ports with the aim of establishing construction and maintenance standards for merchant ships.[19] The Society subsequently merged with a rival group in 1834 to form Lloyd's Register of British and Foreign Shipping and, by the 1880s, Lloyd's had classified almost half of the world's shipping and was recognised as the world's leading classification society.[20] Since then, classification societies have continued to play a key role in improving safety in the maritime industry, gathering scientific data and developing rules and standards to ensure that, as vessels become increasingly more complex and technologically advanced, they remain seaworthy and compliant with national and international regulations.[21]

The risks associated with international maritime trade also gave rise to legal principles governing disputes between the various parties engaged in the maritime industry. The concept of limited liability, for example, evolved at a time when shipowners had no means to ensure safety of navigation or to forecast the weather and could be liable for massive claims or bankruptcy from a shipping accident involving damage to people, property or the environment. Limited liability was introduced to ensure that shipping and trade could prosper while allowing for compensation to be claimed by those suffering loss or damage caused by shipowners or their representatives. As with many maritime arrangements, it was the IMO that took the lead in developing and codifying international laws in the 20th century. The IMO addressed the matter of liability of shipowners in the *Convention on Limitation of Liability for Maritime Claims* in 1976, replacing an earlier international convention signed in 1957.[22] In modern limited liability and insurance regimes, most contracts governing the carriage of goods by sea are supported by shipping charters (known as 'charter parties') or bills of lading.[23] Under maritime law, the liability of a shipowner and, in some instances, the charterer, is limited by the maximum amount of compensation that a court can order the shipowner to pay.[24]

Salvaging ships and cargo

Unlike land-based laws, the salvage of maritime property – including both ships and their cargo – provides for the salvaging party to receive remuneration. This 'right of recovery' has a long history, possibly dating to Rhodian law, and was first recognised as a code of maritime law in the Middle Ages.[25] According to the first modern textbook on maritime law, *Abbott on Law of Merchant Shipping*

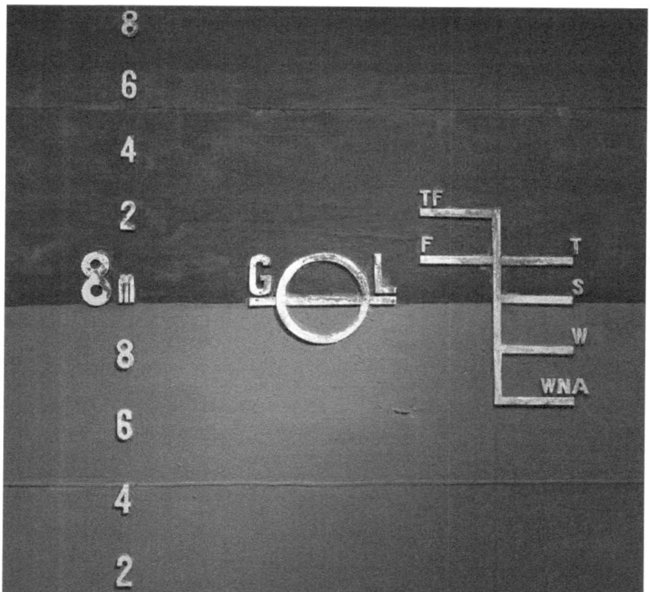

Figure 5.2 The Plimsoll mark on the side of a ship. (Photo courtesy of Hannes Grobe.)

published in 1802, salvage rights were recognised in maritime codes as a way of deterring lawless plunder of shipwrecks, offering instead a financial incentive to provide assistance to those in distress. In England, salvage rights were first recognised in the 17th century when fishermen, having rescued a ship that ran aground on the coast of Essex, claimed their right to 'a verie good and sufficient reward' from the King for having saved his property.[26]

Salvage claims continued to be a distinctive area of maritime law although, by the early 20th century, sailing ships had largely been replaced by steam-powered vessels which were capable of towing ships in distress, and salvage activities increasingly became the domain of commercial salvage operators using tugs and specialised vessels for salvage operations. In 1908, Lloyds established a standard procedure to be used by insurers in relation to parties involved sharing the proceeds of salvage claims and, two years later, an international group of maritime lawyers and insurers founded the Comité Maritime International (CMI) with the aim of unifying maritime law beginning with a legal convention governing salvage.[27]

Salvage rights were, until recent decades, restricted to a reward for the saving of life and property at sea. A convention on salvage adopted in 1910 provided for a 'no cure, no pay' principle, whereby a salvage operator was only rewarded for services if the operation was a success in terms of saving the vessel and commercially valuable cargo. However, a series of maritime disasters involving oil pollution after World War II resulted in some States refusing to provide refuge for stricken vessels to enable salvage work to be completed, fearing the impacts of pollution in their coastal waters. As a result, salvage operators were often forced to tow stricken ships out into the ocean to be sunk and were discouraged from such operations because the salvage rules at that time meant they could not claim a salvage reward or recover their expenses.[28] The environmental damage wrought by oil pollution focused international attention on the need for financial incentives that encouraged salvage operators to actively prevent grounded tankers and their cargo from impacting on the marine environment. This increasing concern for the environment gave rise to the IMO introducing the International Convention on Salvage in 1989 (in force 1996), which required that the assessment of salvage remuneration must take into account the skill and efforts of salvage operators in preventing or minimising damage to the environment (Article 13), and introducing Special Compensation (Article 14) to enable salvage operators to recover their expenses where there was a threat of environmental damage preventing them from earning a reward from a salving ship and cargo in the normal way.[29]

As with other areas of maritime law, legal arrangements relating to salvaging ships and cargo have continued to evolve in response to changes in global shipping and new technologies such as wind farms and offshore drilling. With the development of new underwater exploration equipment, for example, humans have been exploring the ocean at greater depths and gaining access to shipwrecks and their cargo on the seafloor. Whilst these developments were not foreseen in early salvage laws, the 1989 Convention did provide for parties to exclude the recovery of historic wrecks and property on the seabed where these had cultural significance to them.[30]

Shipping disasters and safety at sea

The sea has long been feared as a dangerous environment. Beyond insurance arrangements for vessels and cargo discussed earlier, there was an ever-present risk of injury or death for crew and passengers from natural hazards such as wind, weather, rocks and shoals, as well as from human interference including piracy, privateering, wartime attacks and terrorist assaults, not to mention the seaworthiness of the vessel itself. The oldest known shipwreck is more than 4,000 years old (see Chapter 10), and shipwreck narratives have long featured in western literature, from epic stories such as Homer's *Odyssey* in the 8th century BCE to popular novels like *Robinson Crusoe*, drawing on accounts from shipwreck survivors reflecting prevailing cultural attitudes to maritime voyaging and the sense of powerlessness felt by those on board.[31]

As maritime nations ventured beyond coastal seas and into the open oceans, their ships invariably faced the prospect of accidents and disasters at sea and the loss of the lives of crew and passengers. With the development of larger vessels and increasing demand for the transport of high volumes of goods by sea came increasing numbers of maritime disasters and loss of life. It became clear to maritime nations that there was a need for more consistent rules to ensure that ships could travel from port to port with a reasonable expectation of seafarer safety, seaworthiness of vessels and fair trade. Customary maritime laws such as the Rhodian Sea Code or Rolls of Oléron had been designed to resolve disputes over commercial shipping activities, but they did not address the matter of safety of life at sea.

Amongst the earliest safety measures for ships at sea concerned navigation. For example, as noted earlier, it was common practice from the 16th century for ships to display a light at the highest point of the vessel to alert nearby ships to their presence.[32] It was not until the nineteenth century, however, that the safety of those on board began to attract serious attention, particularly with the increasing incidence of fatalities involving migrants on long-distance voyages to far-flung British and European colonies. Many of the problems stemmed from the failure to address basic safety requirements. A British parliamentary inquiry conducted in 1836, for example, identified numerous reasons for such disasters, from poor construction and maintenance of ships to incompetent masters, drunkenness, inadequate navigation charts and the lack of attention to safety by shipowners.[33] Such inquiries led to agitation for reform in the merchant shipping industry including, for example, campaigns to improve the working conditions of seamen, the need for compulsory inspection of vessels and the establishment of a maximum load line to address the problem of overloading promoted, most notably, by the British parliamentarian, Samuel Plimsoll.[34] Reforms were slow, however, and depended on national governments making their own arrangements for maritime safety and security – a pattern that continues today through the establishment of Maritime Safety Agencies and Authorities.

By the 20th century, maritime safety measures were still largely the responsibility of individual maritime nations and driven by public calls for reform in response to shipping disasters. By then too, as Sarah Palmer has noted, the old idea that humans were powerless in the face of nature on the high seas had given way to new cultural attitudes towards the ocean, manifested in the belief that new shipping technologies and better training of crews could overcome the hazards of ocean voyaging.[35] The folly of this belief in the invincibility of technology was nowhere more apparent than when the RMS *Titanic* – hailed as the 'unsinkable' ship – sank on its pioneer voyage in 1912 after colliding with an iceberg in the North Atlantic Ocean, resulting in the deaths of more than 1,500 passengers and crew. The sheer scale of the disaster shocked the world, exposing the vulnerability of even the most technologically advanced vessel of its day. The disaster also had a dramatic impact on the global shipping industry, focusing attention on the lack of mandatory international rules governing the safety of shipping including the requirement for adequate lifesaving equipment aboard passenger vessels. In the immediate aftermath of the disaster, maritime nations gathered in London in 1914 to produce the first *International Convention on Safety of Life at Sea* (SOLAS Convention), although the outbreak of World War I before the convention came into force delayed the implementation until 1929.[36] The most recent version of SOLAS, adopted in 1974 (in force 1980), is considered to be the most important of all international treaties relating to the safety of merchant ships. It now applies to 98% of world shipping and includes safety standards for construction, equipment design and personnel aboard vessels and covers safety issues such as fire protection, life-saving appliances, radio communications, navigation safety, carriage of cargoes and dangerous goods, safe management and maritime security.[37]

Safety of life at sea

The inherent dangers of ocean and sea environments for humans mean that safety of life at sea has become one of the cornerstones of international law. Customary obligations aimed at saving lives at sea had their origins in Roman law when vessels in distress had few ways to communicate danger once away from shorelines and had to rely on themselves or other vessels for rescue. Rules were also developed to address the widespread problem of plundering of wrecked ships and the murder or enslavement of those on board.[38] These customary obligations to save life at sea formed a key principle of international law as it emerged in the 16th and 17th centuries. The principle included the right of vessels in distress to seek refuge in coasts or ports of other States, as well as rules requiring coastal people to assist the shipwrecked. It also prohibited looting or taking any action that could cause a ship to be wrecked and, as one 17th-century treatise on maritime commerce noted, those who did not offer help to the shipwrecked could even be punished as murderers. Curiously, however, the obligation of the master to rescue vessels in distress remained a custom of the 'common law of the sea' until it was accepted as a duty in international law in the 19th century.[39]

With the development of steamships in the 19th century came an increase in the number of vessels capable of carrying large numbers of people, navigating the world's oceans and seas over much longer distances and at greater speeds. Inevitably, these technological advances also brought a sharp increase in maritime incidents involving ships colliding or running aground in poor weather, resulting in large numbers of lives lost at sea.[40] The sheer scale of maritime disasters involving loss of life set the scene for the development of international law codifying not only the right of vessels in distress to seek refuge and the duty to assist those shipwrecked but also the duty of shipmasters to assist other vessels in distress.

By the time the *UN Convention on the Law of the Sea* (1982) (UNCLOS) was drafted, these customary obligations had evolved into a detailed set of international obligations that required the ship's master to provide assistance to other vessels in distress at sea; coastal States to rescue vessels in distress off their coasts or in their ports; and flag States to ensure safe navigation practices.[41] Indeed, Article 98 of UNCLOS specifically requires flag States to provide an 'adequate and effective search and rescue service', and to ensure that the masters of their ships render assistance to anyone found in danger at sea, including those who may be lost at sea because their ship is endangered or has been involved in a collision.[42] The only exception to this duty is where it is necessary for the rescue party to avoid endangering the rescuing vessel, its crew and its passengers. In these circumstances, the ship's master is required to record the reasons for not rendering assistance and to alert the relevant rescue services accordingly.

The duty to rescue life at sea is also a core principle of the 1979 *International Convention on Maritime Search and Rescue* (SAR Convention). The aim of SAR was to establish an international system for coordinating search and rescue operations involving seafarers, fishermen or other passengers working on board vessels. In 1994, one of the worst peacetime maritime disasters occurred when the ferry *Estonia* sank in the Baltic Sea, killing 852 of the 989 passengers and crew on board. As with the *Titanic*, the incident led to urgent reviews of safety regulations and the design of life rafts for ferries. It also motivated European maritime States to undertake systematic studies of previous passenger ship accidents in order to mitigate future risks.[43] Such studies have shown considerable improvement in navigation safety since the implementation of the SOLAS and SAR Conventions, with a significant reduction in the frequency of serious accidents involving commercial passenger vessels.[44] However, in recent decades, the focus has shifted, with search and rescue operations increasingly involving people aboard cruise ships, leisure yachts and migrant boats who, for the most part, are not trained or experienced seafarers, posing new obligations and challenges for States with jurisdiction over those rescued, particularly where shipping activities are unconventional or illicit.[45]

Unconventional and illicit activities

The proliferation of ships carrying flags of convenience involving a lack of enforcement of safety conventions, the prevalence of substandard ships and poorly trained crews mean that shipping accidents will continue to put lives – and the marine environment – at risk. As noted in Chapter 3, maritime piracy continues to flare up in different seas from time to time. The world is also witnessing increasing numbers of maritime incidents involving migrants and refugees seeking sanctuary by resorting to sea travel in overcrowded and unsafe boats, often leading to capsized boats and desperate rescue efforts. This predicament highlights a tension that exists for flag States that seek to control their borders and refuse entry to migrants while claiming to be operating under the SAR Convention.[46]

The SAR Convention states that, following a rescue, the master of the rescue ship is required to treat the rescued parties humanely in accordance with international human rights law, to 'provide for the initial medical or other needs of the rescued individuals and to deliver them to a place of safety within a reasonable time'.[47] The guidelines also explicitly recognised that States not only have rescue obligations under the law of the sea; they must also meet their obligations under human rights and refugee law.[48] As some legal scholars have observed, uncertainty remains over this aspect of international law, in part because the notion of a 'place of safety' has no single meaning for those being rescued and will differ according to their circumstances. In some instances, for example, those rescued need to avoid disembarkation in places where their lives would be put at risk. There are also no consistent rules about how coastal States should respond when ships in distress reach their shores. As a result, some States have interpreted their duty to save life at sea in different ways, particularly in response to the increasing numbers of desperate migrants who seek asylum in another State and who 'voluntarily' embark on dangerous sea voyages.[49]

One such incident in 2001 involved the rescue of asylum-seekers by a Norwegian-flagged container ship MV *Tampa*. On 24 August 2001, the *Palapa*, a small Indonesian fishing boat overloaded with 433 asylum-seekers from Afghanistan, became stranded in international waters about 140 kilometres north of Christmas Island in the maritime zone between Indonesia and Australia. The captain of the container ship, MV *Tampa*, rescued those on board the stricken vessel under direction by the Australian Maritime Safety Authority. The captain set a course for the Indonesian port city of Merak, but some of the refugees threatened to commit suicide if they were returned to Indonesia and the captain, under pressure to take his rescued passengers to safety, headed instead for the nearby Australian territory of Christmas Island.[50]

However, the Australian government refused entry into Australian waters, advising the captain to dock in Indonesia. With many of those rescued in poor health, the *Tampa* captain made repeated requests to Australia for assistance to no avail. He decided to enter Australian waters, but the Australian authorities responded by advising that he was in 'flagrant breach' of the law and, three days after the rescue operation, the Australian government dispatched 45 Special Air Service troops to board the ship, administer medical assistance, and assert control over the ship's movements. On the same day, the Australian Prime Minister made an unsuccessful bid to introduce a new law enabling the government to remove any foreign ship in Australian territorial waters.[51] Instead, within eight days of the rescue, the Australian government had secured agreements with Nauru and New Zealand to take responsibility for the asylum-seekers in 'offshore' detention centres. The Australian government's handling of the '*Tampa* Affair' drew international condemnation, although the government claimed that its policy was saving lives by deterring people from seeking asylum in unseaworthy boats. In addition to raising questions about the adequacy of international refugee and human rights laws, the so-called Tampa Affair also drew international attention to how States addressed their obligations to asylum-seekers arriving by sea. In the aftermath of the incident, the IMO sought to clarify State obligations in the SOLAS and SAR Conventions by issuing *Guidelines on the Treatment of Persons Rescued at Sea* to provide greater guidance to governments and shipmasters particularly relating to humanitarian obligations.[52]

Flag states and 'flags of convenience'

Flags have been used to signal the origin of a ship at sea since at least 1000 BCE when Egyptians used them to identify their ships. Over time it became part of customary law for a ship to fly the flag of a country in return for receiving protection and permission to dock in its ports. With the rise of nation States in the 17th and 18th centuries, merchant ships began to fly a flag to identify the State that had jurisdiction over them and, as maritime trade expanded, the flag became a potent symbol of a State's sovereignty at sea.[53] Until the mid-20th century, flag States dominated maritime trade, offering ships tax, port access and regulation incentives as well as naval protection from pirates and privateers to encourage them to register with them and fly their flag. They also exercised exclusive control over their vessels and were able to close their ports to ships of other flag States.[54]

In the aftermath of World War II, however, the Allied powers determined that there was a need for greater coordination of maritime affairs including regulations relating to the safety of both passenger and cargo vessels. The IMO set about developing international standards for maritime safety and security, including the design and equipment of ships, safety of navigation, radio communication, search and rescue, training and certification of mariners, carriage of cargoes, flag State responsibilities, port State control measures, and facilitation of international maritime traffic.[55] These conventions were designed to be enforced when a ship sailed in international waters or in the waters of a member country.[56]

The customary right of States to sail ships under their flag on the high seas was formally recognised in the 1958 *Convention on the High Seas* (Article 4), and the introduction of UNCLOS in 1982 (Articles 90 and 92) provided for flag States to have exclusive jurisdiction over their vessels on the high seas. In return, States were required to ensure that vessels sailing under their flag complied with international regulations, including those dealing with safety, navigation, and protecting the marine environment.[57] With the expansion of transoceanic maritime trade from the 1960s, some ship owners resorted to registering their vessels in States with minimum regulatory oversight and low taxes. This practice became known as flying 'flags of convenience'.[58] This practice has flourished, with the number of ships of unknown origin and ownership, and not being maintained and operated in accordance with international safety standards, having steadily increased. By 2002, fewer than half of the world's shipping tonnage was registered to flag States and, in 2022, the United Nations reported that the vast majority of global shipping was carried out under flags of convenience, with Panama, Liberia and the Marshall Islands accounting for 44.3% of the world's cargo capacity.[59]

The erosion of the flag State system has created significant problems in a number of areas. According to the International Transport Workers' Federation, for example, the combination of flags of convenience shipping and intense competition in global maritime trade has fuelled a 'rush to the bottom' in shipping safety, with seafarers working on board flags of convenience ships more likely to experience low wages and unsafe conditions as ship owners seek the cheapest way to operate their vessels.[60] Flags of convenience have also increased the likelihood of terrorist groups using a vessel where the ownership is unknown, and they create challenges for the control of illegal fishing with flag States having to undertake expensive surveillance and inspection of foreign fishing vessels in territorial waters in order to enforce international environmental law (see Chapter 4).[61] In 2016, for example, authorities in Spain arrested six members of an organisation responsible for illegal fishing of the Patagonian toothfish, a protected species, in the Southern Ocean in 2003. The fishing vessel had originally been flagged to Belize, but the captain changed the flag to that of Uruguay before being apprehended by the Australian coast guard. The hunt for the vessel cost the Australian government some $10 million and, even then, it would be another 13 years before the organisation involved was brought to justice.[62] The case of the *Ever Given*, a container ship that became stuck in the Suez Canal in 2021, similarly drew international attention to the legal complexities of flags of convenience. The vessel, owned by a Japanese company, operated by a

Taiwan-based conglomerate, and flying the flag of Panama, became stranded in Egyptian territorial waters. Under UNCLOS, Panama had jurisdiction over the vessel while Egypt was obliged to respect a ship's innocent passage in its territorial seas and may not have the right to withhold the *Ever Given* to enable Egypt's Suez Canal Authority to investigate the incident.[63] It remains unclear as to which party can be held responsible for the significant financial damage caused by the blockage of a major shipping route.

The tragic case of Gulf Livestock 1

On 14 August 2020, the animal transport ship *Gulf Livestock 1* departed from New Zealand bound for China carrying 5,867 live cattle and a crew of 43 men, including 39 from the Philippines, two from New Zealand and two from Australia. On 2 September, the Panamanian-registered vessel sent an emergency message having sustained engine failure during a typhoon. The ship had capsized after being struck by a large wave, and all but two of the men and all of the animals aboard perished. A subsequent investigation by the Australian Broadcasting Commission revealed that Indonesian and Australian maritime authorities had recorded multiple safety breaches and mechanical issues relating to the ship, including concerns about navigational safety, engine failure, the reliability of its safety systems, faulty gauges and thermometers, and working conditions on board.[64]

The ship, an old container transport vessel, had been converted to carry livestock. Using shipping data captured from the vessel's Automatic Identification System (AIS) transponder and released by Spire Global, a space-based data and analytics provider, the ABC observed that a tropical depression had formed east of the Philippines, strengthening into a typhoon given the name 'Julian' or 'Maysak'. Other commercial vessels operating in the area detoured to avoid the oncoming storm, but the *Gulf Livestock 1* did not change its course and entered the East China Sea just as the typhoon strengthened. Messages received by families of the two Australians on board indicate that the engine control room had flooded and the motor failed, leaving the ship adrift. As the vessel was hit by huge waves, one of the two survivors – Chief Officer Eduardo Sareno – made the decision to abandon the ship. He was later rescued by the Japanese coastguard, together with another crew member, who was found adrift in a lifeboat. Neither the ship nor the other 40 men on board have ever been found.[65]

Public outrage following the sinking of the *Gulf Livestock 1*, as well as other incidents such as the sinking of the *Al Badri 1* off Sudan in June 2022, with 15,000 sheep drowned, resulted in the New Zealand government legislating to permanently ban the export of livestock by sea from April 2023. The Australian Labor Party also pledged to phase out live sheep exports by sea prior to winning the Australian federal election in May 2022, although the live export of cattle would remain.[66] The problems surrounding 'flag of convenience' ships remain with ships continuing to operate without regulatory oversight of the safety of vessels, equipment or crew.[67] The fact remains that livestock export by sea is a valuable industry for countries like Australia, although trade unions and animal welfare groups continue to raise concerns about the welfare of both humans and animals aboard the ships.[68]

New maritime technologies and practices

The development of new maritime technologies and practices has long played a key role in shaping the maritime industry and maritime law. Advances in ship design, for example, have enabled larger vessels to travel safely through more dangerous waters,[69] and containerisation has transformed maritime trade.[70] However, the application of new technologies in the marine environment has been a double-edged sword for international law. On the one hand, some technological innovations have enabled greater efficiencies, reduced costs and improved safety, but they may also increase the risk of environmental damage and facilitate illicit activities to go undetected.[71] On the other hand, many technological developments have delivered significant benefits to the marine environment, including the potential to mitigate environmental harm and enable more effective monitoring and enforcement of maritime activities.[72] Scientists have used satellite technology, for example, to monitor 'ship track' pollution clouds emitted from shipping fuel and found that international shipping was a significant source of greenhouse gases, including CO_2 and sulphur. In an effort to mitigate this pollution, the International Maritime Organization introduced upper limits for sulphur emissions in 2020.[73]

The increasing number of large commercial vessels traversing the world's oceans and seas since World War II, for example, was accompanied by a heightened risk of catastrophic environmental damage (see Chapter 9). Some of the more infamous incidents have involved tankers carrying large quantities of oil, such as the *Torrey Canyon* (1967), *Amoco Cadiz* (1978), *Exxon Valdez* (1989), *Erika* (1999), and *Prestige* (2002). Prior to the *Exxon Valdez* accident, shipmasters were generally reliant on visual navigation, analogue radar and voice communications to avoid accidents. In the aftermath, several States began to develop and test tracking systems to monitor ship movements, particularly those sailing in high-risk seas, straits and canals. It was soon clear, however, that the international shipping community needed a single tracking system for use across the world's oceans and seas. Under the auspices of the IMO, and with input from the International Telecommunications Union, the maritime Automatic Identification System (AIS) became the standard international tracking system from the 1990s to increase safety at sea and avoid collisions. Initially, the AIS was used to ensure the safe passage of ships through the Panama Canal and was subsequently used in other 'chokepoints' such as the Strait of Gibraltar. Since the 1990s, the AIS has become increasingly important as a tool for identifying and monitoring vessels in the face of increasing concerns over port security and illegal, unreported and unregulated fishing activities, particularly on the high seas.[74] The AIS is also playing a pivotal role in international maritime security more broadly. In the aftermath of the terrorist attacks in the US in 2001, for example, the IMO amended the SOLAS Convention to require all ships 300 gross tons or greater or carrying 12 or more passengers on international voyages, to carry AIS (effective from 31 December 2004).[75]

The Vessel Monitoring System (VMS) is a form of satellite tracking using transmitters on board fishing vessels. As with the AIS, the VMS is used to monitor compliance, collect data and provide evidence for prosecution of violations under international or domestic law including, for example, unlawful discharges. UNCLOS does not specify the use of VMS but recognises the sovereign rights of coastal States to protect their coastal waters. However, some organisations have mandated their use including the North-East Atlantic Fisheries Commission (1999) and the Commission for the Conservation of Antarctic Marine Living Resources (2000). The VMS has become an important tool for States to monitor the location and movement of commercial fishing and other vessels in territorial seas and exclusive economic zones, and some States have made it a mandatory requirement for certain vessels to carry one (see Chapter 4 for further discussion of the regulatory framework for fishing vessels).[76]

In recent decades, such sophisticated digital and satellite technologies have revolutionised traditional maritime practices such as navigation and mapping. But while digital platforms and automated systems have undoubtedly improved the efficiency of operations, they have also made them more complex and vulnerable to cybersecurity risks, as well as creating new challenges for maritime law in relation to liability, safety regulations and the role of humans in an industry being transformed by drones, artificial intelligence and underwater robots that 'blur the lines between traditional maritime boundaries and jurisdictions'.[77] Remotely operated vehicles (ROVs) and autonomous underwater vehicles (AUVs), for example, perform deep-water scientific and industrial operations such as seawater sampling and cable-laying without the need for an umbilical cable connected to a support vessel.[78] Autonomous ships (known as Maritime Autonomous Surface Ships), a technology still in its infancy, are designed to operate with little or no human involvement and are capable of being controlled from shore or by onboard computers using artificial intelligence, which present new challenges for flag States seeking to comply with international law.[79]

Conclusion

Maritime law (also known as Admiralty Law) has its origins in ancient practices and customs from at least 2050 BCE involving ships transporting cargo and passengers by sea. Over the centuries, it has evolved into a complex body of legal rules and international treaties relating to a wide range of issues, including maritime disputes, accidents, oil spills, insured seafarers or passengers, piracy, salvage and marine insurance. The history of maritime law serves to demonstrate the complexity and fragmentation of the international legal framework relating to human uses of oceans, seas and shorelines. The result is that some laws overlap or impose different rules based on the type of activities involved. Fishing labour laws, for example, differ from merchant labour laws, even though the vessels and activities involved are comparable in size and scale.

Maritime law also contains certain principles that distinguish it from other areas of law. The obligation of the master to rescue vessels in distress, for example, is a custom of the 'common law of the sea' that was accepted into international law in the 19th century. It remains the only area of law relating to oceans, seas and shorelines where legal responsibility has been imposed on an individual – in this case the skipper or master of a vessel. Another distinctive feature of maritime law concerns limitation of liability first introduced in English laws in 1733 to encourage shipping and trade. This is a privilege accorded to a shipowner and, in some cases, the charterer, master and crew, limiting the amount of their liability in respect of claims arising from damage caused by their ship.

Whilst much progress has been made by the IMO since the mid-20th century in relation to the regulation of ships and shipping, including over 50 conventions and protocols dealing with maritime accidents, the safety and security of ships, prevention of pollution, and rules governing salvage, the whole area of safety and security at sea continues to be fraught. The global nature and complexity of modern maritime trade, for example, has led to a proliferation of substandard ships and the failure of flag States to enforce regulations. Changes in maritime law since the late 20th century reflect a shift in focus, from the preoccupation with regulating shipping and salvage operations to improve economic and social outcomes, to the relatively recent emphasis on preventing or minimising environmental damage in marine and coastal environments. Nevertheless, the divisions between maritime, marine pollution and piracy laws are arguably unhelpful, particularly in the context of growing blue economy plans by many nations, which will increase shipping traffic. Perhaps the last word should be left to the oceans themselves, but there is limited, if any, reference to the intrinsic values of oceans in maritime law.

Notes

1 "The Seafarer," in *Codex Exoniensis: A Collection of Anglo-Saxon Poetry*, trans. Benjamin Thorpe (London: Society of Antiquaries, 1842), fols 81v–83r.

2 A 2022 study of container ship accidents found that they had increased significantly in the previous decade, mainly involving collisions, groundings and fires. See Shuyan Wan et al., "Emerging Marine Pollution from Container Ship

Accidents: Risk Characteristics, Response Strategies, and Regulation Advancements," *Journal of Cleaner Production* 376 (2022): 134266, https://doi.org/10.1016/j.jclepro.2022.134266.

3 In 1948 the United Nations Maritime Conference adopted a convention to create the Intergovernmental Maritime Consultative Organisation (in force in 1958), and in 1982 it became the International Maritime Organization (IMO), the lead UN agency responsible for promoting maritime safety.

4 This chapter does not provide a comprehensive overview of maritime law as many excellent texts fulfil this role. For example, Yvonne Baatz, *Maritime Law*, 5th ed. (Abingdon: Routledge, 2023); Melis Özdel, ed., *Commercial Maritime Law* (London: Bloomsbury, 2020); and Francis D. Rose, *Kennedy & Rose Law of Salvage* (London: Sweet & Maxwell/Thomson Reuters, 2017).

5 Simon Baughen, *Shipping Law*, 8th ed. (London: Taylor & Francis Ltd, June 27, 2023).

6 Philip Steinberg, *The Social Construction of the Ocean* (Cambridge: Cambridge University Press, 2001), 15.

7 "General average" is a principle of maritime law that establishes that all sea cargo stakeholders evenly share any damage or losses that may occur as a result of the voluntary sacrifice of part of the vessel or cargo to save the whole during an emergency. See Daphne Penna, "General Average in Byzantium," in *General Average and Risk Management in Medieval and Early Modern Maritime Business*, ed. M. Fusaro, A. Addobbati, and L. Piccinno (Cham: Palgrave Macmillan, 2023), https://doi.org/10.1007/978-3-031-04118-1_4; Editors of Encyclopaedia, "Rhodian Sea Law," *Encyclopaedia Britannica* (July 29, 2012), www.britannica.com/event/Rhodian-Sea-Law; Wolfgang Graf Vitzthum, "From the Rhodian Sea Law to UNCLOS III," *Ocean Yearbook Online* (2003): 56–57.

8 Frank L. Wiswall Jr., "Law," in *The Oxford Encyclopedia of Maritime Law*, ed. John J. Hattendorf (Oxford: Oxford University Press, 2007).

9 "Laws of Oleron," in *Oxford Companion to Ships and the Sea*, 2nd ed., ed. I. C. B. Dear and Peter Kemp (Oxford: Oxford University Press, 2006), www.oxfordreference.com/display/10.1093/oi/authority.20110803100248626. Surviving parts of the original book were published in 1871 by Sir Travers Twiss.

10 David J. Bederman, "Private International Law: International Commercial Usage," in *Custom as a Source of Law* (Cambridge: Cambridge University Press, 2010), 117–34.

11 Wiswall, "Law."

12 Over the next 300 years, three key doctrines of international maritime law emerged: freedom of the seas which rejected extensive claims to sovereignty over the ocean (see Chapter 1), the concept of territorial waters over which the coastal State was entitled to exercise its authority (see Chapter 2), and the establishment of an outer limit of territorial waters (one marine league or three miles) (see Chapter 2).

13 The title comes from "consuls", the commercial judges of the maritime cities on the Mediterranean coast. See Editors of Encyclopaedia, "Book of the Consulate of the Sea," *Encyclopedia Britannica* (February 22, 2016), www.britannica.com/topic/Book-of-the-Consulate-of-the-Sea.

14 Frank L. Wiswall Jr., "Shipping Conventions," in *The Oxford Encyclopedia of Maritime Law*, ed. John J. Hattendorf (Oxford: Oxford University Press, 2007).

15 Editors of Encyclopaedia, "The Rules of the Road at Sea," *Encyclopedia Britannica* (July 20, 2017), www.britannica.com/topic/rules-of-the-road-at-sea. The *Convention on the International Regulations for Preventing Collisions at Sea* (COLREGs) updated and replaced the Collision Regulations of 1960, which were adopted at the same time as the *International Convention for the Safety of Life at Sea* (SOLAS). All Convention signatories must adopt the rules contained in the international regulations

within their State jurisdiction. See IMO, "Convention on the International Regulations for Preventing Collisions at Sea (COLREGs)" (1972), accessed May 24, 2023, www.imo.org/en/About/Conventions/Pages/COLREG.aspx.

16 Gregory D. L. Morris, "A Brief History of Marine Insurance," *Risk & Insurance* (January 3, 2024), https://riskandinsurance.com/brief-history-marine-insurance/.

17 From 1734 this was published as Lloyd's List. Lloyd's of London has subsequently become an internationally recognised corporate entity (not an insurance company) where risk is shared amongst members. The entity is governed by the Lloyd's Act of 1871 and subsequent Acts of Parliament.

18 Underwriters included corporations as well as private individuals (called "Names") whose liability was unlimited. The foundations of the modern marine insurance industry can be traced to 1764 when a merchant vessel insured by Lloyd's – the *Mills Frigate* – became the subject of a court case when it was found to be leaking and unable to return from the West Indies. The court determined that a ship must be seaworthy before leaving shore, and that an insurance claim would not be paid on defective ships even if it was unknown to both parties to a contract. Lloyd's held a monopoly on maritime insurance related to the slave trade until its abolition in 1807.

19 *Lloyd's Register Book*, first published in 1764, is still issued annually and lists all merchant ships of 100 or more tons gross.

20 The Society's name was changed to *Lloyd's Register of Shipping* in 1914. "Our History," *Lloyd's Register*, accessed June 2, 2023, www.lr.org/en/about-us/who-we-are/our-history/.

21 Denise Micallef, "A Legal Analysis of the Limitation of Liability of Classification Societies," *CMI Yearbook 2014* (2014): 223–24, https://comitemaritime.org/wp-content/uploads/2018/05/Dr-Denise-Micallef-A-Legal-Analysis-CMI-YB-2014-pp-275.pdf.

22 IMO, "Convention on Limitation of Liability for Maritime Claims," accessed June 2, 2023, www.imo.org/en/About/Conventions/Pages/Convention-on-Limitation-of-Liability-for-Maritime-Claims-(LLMC).aspx.

23 There are three different types of charter – time, voyage and demise or bareboat charter – according to the particular contractual arrangements between the shipowner, the charter and the master and crew.

24 A seminal text on this issue is *Scrutton on Charterparties and Bills of Lading*, first published in 1886 and now in its 25th edition: The Hon Mr Justice Foxton et al., *Scrutton on Charterparties and Bills of Lading*, 25th ed. (Mytholmroyd: Sweet & Maxwell, 2024).

25 Salvage was regarded as part of the *lex mercatoria* (the law of the maritime world), and rules relating to salvage claims can be found in the Laws of Oléron (960 C.E.), the code of the Hanseatic League (1597) and the Ordonnances de la Marine of Louis XIV (1681). See Richard A. A. Shaw, 'Salvage," in *The Oxford Encyclopedia of Maritime History*, ed. John J. Hattendorf (Oxford: Oxford University Press, 2007).

26 Cited in Shaw, 'Salvage."

27 This process is still followed by salvage contractors today. In addition, Lloyds now issue summaries of salvage cases, although the details remain confidential for commercial reasons.

28 Archie Bishop, "The Development of Environmental Salvage and Review of the Salvage Convention 1989," *International Salvage Union* (February 9, 2012): 1–2, www.marine-salvage.com/environmental/Tulane%20-%20The%20Development%20of%20Environmental%20Salvage.pdf.

29 IMO, "International Convention on Salvage" (1989), accessed May 2, 2023, www.imo.org/en/About/Conventions/Pages/International-Convention-on-Salvage.aspx. This legal convention proved cumbersome to implement because of the need to establish how much environmental damage was averted in each incident. To address

this problem, the salvage insurance industry introduced its own measures known as Special Compensation P & I Clubs. See Bishop, The Development of Environmental Salvage, 11.

30 The adoption of UNESCO's Convention on the Protection of Underwater Cultural Heritage in 2001 provides protection of maritime cultural property (see Chapter 10). See for example Jessica Moran and Bec Pridham, 'Salvage Fight over Sydney to Hobart yacht Huntress as Aboriginal Land Council Claims Ownership," *ABC News* (January 10, 2023), www.abc.net.au/news/2023-01-09/sydney-to-hobart-yacht-huntress-salvage-fight-indigenous-claim/101836372?utm_source=abc_news_app&utm_medium=content_shared&utm_campaign=abc_news_app&utm_content=mail.

31 UNESCO notes that there are some 3 million known shipwreck sites recorded around the world. Steve Mentz, *Shipwreck Modernity: Ecologies of Globalisation, 1550–1719* (Minneapolis: University of Minnesota Press, 2015), 25; Alan G. Jamieson, *Out of the Depths: A History of Shipwrecks* (London: Reaktion Books, 2022). Steven Mentz, "Towards a Blue Cultural Studies: The Sea, Maritime Culture and Early Modern Literature," *Literature Compass 6*, no. 5 (2009): 997–1013. John Mack, *The Sea: A Cultural History* (London: Reaktion Books Ltd, 2011).

32 Apostolos Delis, 'Seafaring Lives at the Crossroads of Mediterranean Maritime History," *International Journal of Maritime History* 32, no. 2 (May 2020): 464–78.

33 See for example Hansard, "Shipwrecks and Collisions of Merchant Vessels," *Debates*, House of Commons (February 15, 1848): 96, cc668–73, accessed March 15, 2024, https://api.parliament.uk/historic-hansard/commons/1848/feb/15/shipwrecks-and-collisions-of-merchant.

34 Plimsoll was a divisive figure amongst those involved in the British maritime industry, but his agitation for reform eventually led to a new British law in 1890 governing the compulsory load line and now known as the "Plimsoll Line". See "Samuel Plimsoll and Ship Safety," *Royal Museum Greenwich*, accessed March 15, 2024, www.rmg.co.uk/stories/topics/samuel-plimsoll-ship-safety#:~:text=In%20the%2019th%20century%2C%20MP,without%20the%20risk%20of%20sinking.

35 Sarah Palmer, "Safety Regulations for Shipping," in *The Oxford Encyclopedia of Maritime History*, ed. John J. Hattendorf (Oxford: Oxford University Press, 2007). As Palmer notes, by the late 20th century there was a further shift in cultural attitudes with increasing concern about the environmental damage wrought by substandard ships and the need to protect the oceans and its creatures from human activities.

36 Subsequent conferences on the safety of life at sea were conducted in 1948, 1960 and 1974, each producing a new SOLAS convention. See James Kraska and Raul A Pedrozo, *International Maritime Security Law* (Leiden: Martinus Nijhoff Publishers, 2013), 369. Anish Joseph and Dimitrios Dalaklis, "The International Convention or the Safety of Life at Sea: Highlighting the Interrelations of Measures Towards Effective Risk Mitigation," *Journal of International Maritime Safety, Environmental Affairs and Shipping* 5, no. 1 (2021): 1–11.

37 IMO, "International Convention for the Safety of Life at Sea (SOLAS)" (1974), accessed June 2, 2023, www.imo.org/en/About/Conventions/Pages/International-Convention-for-the-Safety-of-Life-at-Sea-(SOLAS),-1974.aspx

38 The Rolls of Oléron, for example, set out punishment for those who robbed or murdered survivors of shipwrecks, while others offered compensation as an incentive to rescue ships in distress. Irini Papanocolopulu, "The Historical Origins of the Duty to Save Life at Sea in International Law," *Journal of the History of International Law* 24 (2022): 149–88, 155–56.

39 Charles Molloy, *De jure maritimo et navali, or, A Treatise of Affairs Maritime and of Commerce*, printed for John Bellinger . . . George Dawes . . . and Robert Boulter . . . (London, 1676), book II, 238, cited in Papanocolopulu, "The Historical Origins," 158.
40 According to one study, for example, more than 2,000 vessels were wrecked in the North Sea in the winter of 1820 alone, resulting in 20,000 deaths. See Dracos Vassalos and Donald Paterson, "Reconfiguring Passenger Ship Internal Environment for Damage Stability Enhancement," *Journal of Marine Science and Engineering* 8 (2020): 2, cited in Papanicolopulu, "The Historical Origins," 162.
41 Irini Papanicolopulu, "The Duty to Rescue at Sea, in Peacetime and in War: A General Overview," *International Review of the Red Cross* 98, no. 2 (2016): 491–514.
42 UNCLOS Article 98. Unlike conventions relating to salvage, the duty to rescue at sea applies to all ships including warships.
43 An official inquiry after the incident found that the probable cause was the failure of locks on the bow visor, which caused water to flood the car deck and capsize the ship, although subsequent investigations revealed flaws in construction of the vessel's bow missed during certification. "MS Estonia Sinking: One of the Deadliest Accidents in European Waters," *Safety4Sea* (October 4, 2019), https://safety4sea.com/cm-ms-estonia-sinking-one-of-the-deadliest-accidents-in-european-waters/; Andrius Sytas, "New Probe into Estonia Ferry Sinking Reveals Construction Flaws – Officials," *Reuters* (January 24, 2023), www.reuters.com/world/europe/new-probe-into-estonia-ferry-sinking-reveals-construction-flaws-officials-2023-01-23/.
44 Eleftheria Eliopoulou, Aimilia Alissafaki, and Apostolos Papanikolaou, 'Statistical Analysis of Accidents and Review of Safety Level of Passenger Ships," *Journal of Marine Science and Engineering* 11, no. 2 (2023), https://doi.org/10.3390/jmse11020410. Allianz, "Shipping Losses Lowest This Century But Numbers Remain High," accessed March 15, 2024, www.agcs.allianz.com/news-and-insights/news/safety-shipping-review-2019.html.
45 Francesco Munari, "Search and Rescue at Sea: Do New Challenges Require New Rules?" in *Governance of Arctic Shipping: Rethinking Risk, Human Impacts and Regulation*, ed. Aldo Chircop, Floris Goerlandt, Claudio Aporta, and Ronald Pelot (Cham: Springer Polar Sciences), 63–81.
46 Erik Røsæg, "The Duty to Rescue Refugees and Migrants at Sea," *Faculty of Law, University of Oxford* (March 25, 2020), https://blogs.law.ox.ac.uk/research-subject-groups/centre-criminology/centreborder-criminologies/blog/2020/03/duty-rescue.
47 This provision is a rare example where an individual, rather than a State, has the responsibility to fulfil certain obligations under international law. The right to life is codified in various human rights treaties such as the International Covenant on Civil and Political Rights (ICCPR), Article 6; and the European Convention for the Protection of Human Rights and Fundamental Freedoms (ECHR), Article 2.
48 Between 2014 and 2020, an estimated 40,000 migrants perished at sea while attempting to move to another country, with around half of those drowning in the Mediterranean Sea. See Missing Migrants Project, accessed May 4, 2023, https://missingmigrants.iom.int/. Also see Richard Barnes, "Refugee Law at Sea," *The International and Comparative Law Quarterly* 53, no. 1 (2004): 47–77, www.jstor.org/stable/3663136. For a detailed discussion of State obligations under the law of the sea and intersection with human rights and refugee law obligations, see Violeta Moreno-Lax, "The Interdiction of Asylum Seekers at Sea: Law and (Mal)practice in Europe and Australia," *Policy Brief* 4, Kaldor Centre for International Refugee Law, May 2017, 8–9, www.kaldorcentre.unsw.edu.au/sites/kaldorcentre.unsw.edu.au/files/Policy_Brief4_Interdiction_of_asylum_seekers_at_sea.pdf.
49 Papanocolopulu, "The Historical Origins of the Duty to Save Life," 150–51.

50 Francine Feld, "The Tampa Case: Seeking Refuge in Domestic Law," *Australian Journal of Human Rights* 8, no. 1 (2002): 11, https://classic.austlii.edu.au/au/journals/AUJlHRights/2002/11.html.
51 The Border Protection Bill 2001 was backdated to specifically include the *Tampa* rescue operation, and worded to ensure that no Australian court could review the actions or directions of an Australian military officer. See, for example, Commonwealth of Australia, *A Select Committee on a Certain Maritime Incident*, Canberra (October 23, 2002), www.aph.gov.au/binaries/senate/committee/maritime_incident_ctte/report/report.pdf; National Museum of Australia, "Tampa Affair" (September 28, 2022), www.nma.gov.au/defining-moments/resources/tampa-affair.
52 For the full Guidelines see IMO Maritime Safety Committee, Guidelines on the Treatment of Persons Rescued at Sea (Res. MSC.167(78), https://wwwcdn.imo.org/localresources/en/OurWork/Facilitation/Documents/MSC.167%20(78).pdf. IMO, International Chamber of Shipping (ICS), and Office of the UN High Commissioner for Refugees (UNHCR), *Rescue at Sea: A Guide to Principles and Practice as Applied to Refugees and Migrants* (n.d.), https://wwwcdn.imo.org/localresources/en/OurWork/Facilitation/Documents/MSC.167%20(78).pdf; Sophie Roden, *Turning Their Back on the Law? The Legality of the Coalition's Maritime Interdiction and Return Policy* (Canberra: Australian National University, n.d.), https://law.anu.edu.au/sites/all/files/acmlj/turning_their_back_on_the_law_v2.pdf
53 A merchant vessel must be registered and can only be registered in one jurisdiction although the jurisdiction may be changed.
54 Philipp Wendel, *State Responsibility for Interferences with the Freedom of Navigation in Public International Law* (Berlin: Springer, 2007), 6; Seafarers Rights International (SRI), "Flag State Responsibilities and Seafarers' Rights," *Strategic Research for the Maritime Industry* (September 29, 2014), https://seafarersrights.org/flag-state-responsibilities-and-seafarersrights/.
55 The standards are set out in over 50 international conventions and protocols, and over 800 codes, recommendations and guidelines. See Kraska and Pedrozo, *International Maritime Security Law*, 362–64; IMO, "Registration of Ships and Fraudulent Registration Matters," accessed March 15, 2024, www.imo.org/en/OurWork/Legal/Pages/Registration-of-ships-and-fraudulent-registration-matters.aspx.
56 Admiralty law, which is sometimes used interchangeably with maritime law, applies to the private law of navigation and shipping in both inland waters and the ocean, and its jurisdiction may overlap with the international law of the sea regime and maritime law. International Maritime Conventions, "List of IMO Conventions" (2019), accessed March 15, 2024, www.imo.org/en/About/Conventions/Pages/ListOfConventions.aspx; P. Hoagland, J. Jacoby, and M. E. Schumacher, "Law of the Sea," in *Encyclopedia of Ocean Sciences*, 2nd ed. (Cambridge, MA: Academic Press, 2001), 1481–92.
57 Under UNCLOS, each flag State is required to maintain its own flag State control system to implement and enforce international maritime regulations for all ships flying their flag. It provides for a State to grant its nationality to ships and for those ships to be surveyed before registration. See Nivedita M. Hosanee, *A Critical Analysis of Flag State Duties as Laid Down under Article 94 of the 1982 United Nations Convention on the Law of the Sea* (New York: UN Division for Ocean Affairs and the Law of the Sea, 2009), https://static.un.org/depts/los/nippon/unnff_programme_home/fellows_pages/fellows_papers/hosanee_0910_mauritious.pdf.
58 "Flags of convenience" or open registries refers to commercial vessels that fly flags of States that are unconnected to the shipowner's place of residence to gain financial advantage by evading restrictions on their commercial freedom. Many of these flags belong to small or developing countries that permit foreign-owned vessels to operate

under their jurisdiction to attract foreign investment. Anthony van Fossen, "Flags of Convenience and Global Capitalism," *International Critical Thought* 6, no. 3 (2016): 359–77; Robert G. Greenhill, "Shipping," in *The Oxford Encyclopedia of Maritime History*, ed. John J. Hattendorf (Oxford: Oxford University Press, 2007).

59 Anna Fleck, "Flags of Convenience Dominate Maritime Freight," *Statista* (January 11, 2023), www.statista.com/chart/29086/flags-of-convenience/.

60 International Transport Workers' Federation, "What Are Flags of Convenience?" accessed November 4, 2023, www.itfglobal.org/en/sector/seafarers/flags-of-convenience.

61 Md Saiful Karim, "Flag State Responsibility for Maritime Terrorism," *SAIS Review of International Affairs* 33, no. 2 (Summer–Fall 2013): 127–34.

62 Greg Noone, "Flags of Convenience: Could the Threat of Lawsuits Put an End to the Practice?" *Hakai Magazine* (July 25, 2022), https://hakaimagazine.com/news/flags-of-convenience-could-the-threat-of-lawsuits-put-an-end-to-the-practice/.

63 Marcelo Molina Villalobos, "The Ever Given and the Problem with Flags of Convenience in International Shipping," *Berkeley Journal of International Law* (April 18, 2021), www.berkeleyjournalofinternationallaw.com/post/the-ever-given-and-the-problem-with-flags-of-convenience-in-international-shipping.

64 Alison McClymont and Dan Harrison, "Into the Storm," *ABC News* (December 11, 2022), www.abc.net.au/news/2022-12-11/why-did-gulf-livestock-1-sail-into-typhoon-maysak/101739560. The ABC team found that Tokyo MOU had recorded 34 breaches or deficiencies against Gulf Livestock 1; the Australian Maritime Safety Authority had also raised a number of concerns about the vessel's stability and navigation system, including detaining the ship in Broom in 2019; while Indonesian authorities had detected problems with the engine propulsion system. According to New Zealand authorities, the vessel was not due for an inspection until at least October 2020, and had not been identified as a "high risk" vessel in the Port State Control system.

65 Between 2011 and 2020, 876 vessels were lost at sea. See "Facts + Statistics: Marine accidents," *Insurance Information Institute*, www.iii.org/fact-statistic/facts-statistics-marine-accidents. According to data from Lloyds and Allianz insurance companies, 94 ships over 100 gross tons were lost at sea in 2013 alone, of which more than a third were cargo ships and the most common cause was foundering (sinking or submerging). On average, less than one ship a year disappears without a trace. For example, between 2002 and 2013 a total of seven ships were listed as missing or overdue. Allianz, "Allianz Study: Shipping Losses, Decline, New Risks Emerge" (2014), accessed March 15, 2024, www.allianz.com/en/press/news/studies/news-2014-03-13.html. Cargo ships also lose containers at sea. In 2022, for example, cargo ships lost 661 of 250 million containers. While the numbers are relatively small, drifting containers pose a significant hazard to shipping. World Shipping Council, "Containers Lost at Sea 2023 Update," May 2023, https://mb.cision.com/Public/20134/3772700/9f81b7bcd3582277.pdf.

66 The decision to ban live sheep exports was based in part on animal welfare issues, although the move was strongly opposed by the National Farmers' Federation because of the economic impacts on the industry. In 2019, the Australian industry alone was worth over $800 million per year. For a timeline of Australia's live export trade see Claire Petrie, "Live Export: A Chronology," updated September 6, 2019, www.aph.gov.au/About_Parliament/Parliamentary_Departments/Parliamentary_Library/pubs/rp/rp1920/Chronologies/LiveExport.

67 *Gulf Livestock 1* was registered in Panama, and legal responsibility for investigating the incident lay with the Panama Maritime Authority. The Authority completed its investigation into the sinking in April 2022 and released its report to the families of

those who died, but it has not been made public. *Gulf Livestock 1* was one of 876 vessels lost at sea between 2011 and 2021.

68 See, for example, Stephanie Hing, Sue Foster, and Di Evans, "Animal Welfare Risks by Live Cattle Export from Australia to China by Sea," *Animals (Basel)* 11, no. 10 (October 2021): 2862, www.ncbi.nlm.nih.gov/pmc/articles/PMC8532794/.

69 K. J. Rawson and E. C. Tupper, "Ship Design," in *Basic Ship Theory*, 5th ed. (Amsterdam: Elsevier, 2001), 617–54.

70 Brian J. Cudahy, *Box Boats: How Container Ships Changed the World* (New York: Fordham University Press, 2007).

71 See Chapter 11 for further discussion of emerging technologies and industries such as marine bioprospecting. International Council for the Exploration of the Sea (ICES), "Request from the Netherlands Regarding the Impacts of Pulse Trawling on the Ecosystem and Environment from the Sole (Solea solea) Fishery in the North Sea," *ICES Advice, Special Requests* (2020), https://doi.org/10.17895/ices.advice.6020; Bloom Association, "Electric 'Pulse' Fishing: Why It Should Be Banned" (January 2018), https://our.fish/wp-content/uploads/2018/06/electric-fishing-advocacy.pdf; Australian Government, See "Regulation Impact Statement: Future Status of Super Trawlers," Department of Agriculture, OBPR Reference number 17021, https://oia.pmc.gov.au/sites/default/files/posts/2019/05/1_ris_future_status_of_super_trawlers.docx;

72 Hilde J. Woker, Rozemarijn J. Roland Host, and Harriet Harden-Davies, "New Technology and the Protection of the Marine Environment," in *Research Handbook on International Marine Environmental Law*, 2nd ed., ed. R. Rayfuse, A. Jaeckel, and N. Klein (Cheltenham: Edward Elgar Publishing, 2023), chapter 18.

73 International Maritime Organization, "Global Limit on Sulphur in Ships' Fuel Oil Reduced from 01 January 2020," *Media Release* (London: IMO, December 20, 2019), www.imo.org/en/MediaCentre/PressBriefings/pages/34-IMO-2020-sulphur-limit-.aspx. However, recent research suggests that the sulphur particles have been counteracting some of the warming from greenhouse gases and that reduced emissions are inadvertently contributing to increased global temperatures. See, for example, Zeke Hausfather and Piers Forster, "Analysis: How Low-Sulphur Shipping Rules are Affecting Global Warming," *Carbon Brief* (July 3, 2023), www.carbonbrief.org/analysis-how-low-sulphur-shipping-rules-are-affecting-global-warming/.

74 Kimbra Cutlip, "AIS for Safety and Tracking: A Brief History," *Global Fishing Watch* (March 31, 2017), https://globalfishingwatch.org/data/ais-brief-history/.

75 The AIS requires shipmasters to report the ship's identity, type, position, course, speed, navigational status and other safety-related information to shore stations and other ships or aircraft as required, as well as providing certain pre-arrival information to port officials, unless the master believes the safety of the ship would be compromised by, for example, imminent attack in high-risk areas.

76 As of 2012, for example, the VMS was mandated for all EU, Faroese and Norwegian vessels exceeding 12 metres overall length. See Scottish Government, "Marine and Fisheries Compliance: Vessel Monitoring System Fact Sheet" (May 31, 2018), accessed January 5, 2024, www.gov.scot/publications/marine-and-fisheries-compliance-vessel-monitoring-system/.

77 Muhammad Bilawal Khaskheli et al., "Technology Advancement and International Law in Marine Policy, Challenges, Solutions and Future Prospective," *Marine Affairs and Policy* 10 (2023): 1258924, https://doi.org/10.3389/fmars.2023.1258924.

78 C. Guitart, J. W. Readman, and J. M. Bayona, "Seawater Organic Contaminants," in *Encyclopaedia of Comprehensive Sampling and Sample Preparation* (Oxford: Elsevier, 2012), 297–316.

79 Paul Dean and Henry Clack, "Autonomous Shipping and Maritime Law," in *New Technologies, Artificial Intelligence and Shipping Law in the 21st Century*, ed. Bariş Soyer and Andrew Tettenborn (Abingdon: Informa Law from Routledge, 2020), 73–74.

Bibliography

Allianz. "Allianz Study: Shipping Losses, Decline, New Risks Emerge." Accessed March 15, 2024. www.allianz.com/en/press/news/studies/news-2014-03-13.html.

Allianz. "Shipping Losses Lowest This Century but Numbers Remain High." *Safety & Shipping Review* (2019). www.agcs.allianz.com/news-and-insights/news/safety-shipping-review-2019.html.

Australian Government. "Regulation Impact Statement: Future Status of Super Trawlers." Department of Agriculture, OBPR Reference number 17021. https://oia.pmc.gov.au/sites/default/files/posts/2019/05/1_ris_future_status_of_super_trawlers.docx.

Baatz, Yvonne. *Maritime Law*. 5th ed. Abingdon: Routledge, 2023.

Barnes, Richard. "Refugee Law at Sea." *International and Comparative Law Quarterly* 53, no. 1 (2004): 47–77.

Baughen, Simon. *Shipping Law*. 8th ed. London: Taylor & Francis Ltd, 2023.

Bederman, David J. "Private International Law: International Commercial Usage." In *Custom as a Source of Law*. Cambridge: Cambridge University Press, 2010.

Bishop, Archie. "The Development of Environmental Salvage and Review of the Salvage Convention 1989." Accessed April 30, 2024. www.marine-salvage.com/environmental/Tulane%20-%20The%20Development%20of%20Environmental%20Salvage.pdf.

Commonwealth of Australia. *A Select Committee on a Certain Maritime Incident*. Canberra, October 23, 2002. www.aph.gov.au/binaries/senate/committee/maritime_incident_ctte/report/report.pdf.

Cudahy, Brian J. *Box Boats: How Container Ships Changed the World*. New York: Fordham University Press, 2007.

Cutlip, Kimbra. "AIS for Safety and Tracking: A Brief History." *Global Fishing Watch* (March 31, 2017). https://globalfishingwatch.org/data/ais-brief-history/.

Dean, Paul, and Henry Clack. "Autonomous Shipping and Maritime Law." In *New Technologies, Artificial Intelligence and Shipping Law in the 21st Century*, edited by Bariş Soyer and Andrew Tettenborn. Abingdon: Informa Law from Routledge, 2020.

Delis, Apostolos. "Seafaring Lives at the Crossroads of Mediterranean Maritime History." *International Journal of Maritime History* 32, no, 2 (May 2020): 464–78.

Editors of Encyclopaedia Britannica. "Book of the Consulate of the Sea." *Encyclopedia Britannica* (February 22, 2016). www.britannica.com/topic/Book-of-the-Consulate-of-the-Sea.

Editors of Encyclopaedia Britannica. "Rhodian Sea Law." *Encyclopaedia Britannica* (July 29, 2012). www.britannica.com/event/Rhodian-Sea-Law.

Editors of Encyclopaedia Britannica. "The Rules of the Road at Sea." *Encyclopedia Britannica* (July 20, 2017). www.britannica.com/topic/rules-of-the-road-at-sea.

Eliopoulou, Eleftheria, Aimilia Alissafaki, and Apostolos Papanikolaou. "Statistical Analysis of Accidents and Review of Safety Level of Passenger Ships." *Journal of Marine Science and Engineering* 11, no. 2 (2023). https://doi.org/10.3390/jmse11020410.

Feld, Francine. "The Tampa Case: Seeking Refuge in Domestic Law." *Australian Journal of Human Rights* 8, no. 1 (2002). https://classic.austlii.edu.au/au/journals/AUJlHRights/2002/11.html.

Fleck, Anna. "Flags of Convenience Dominate Maritime Freight." *Statista* (January 11, 2023). www.statista.com/chart/29086/flags-of-convenience/.

Foxton the Hon Mr. Justice et al. *Scrutton on Charterparties and Bills of Lading*. 25th ed. Mytholmroyd: Sweet & Maxwell, 2024.
Greenhill, Robert G. "Shipping." In *The Oxford Encyclopedia of Maritime History*, edited by John J. Hattendorf. Oxford: Oxford University Press, 2007.
Guitart, C., J. W. Readman, and J. M. Bayona. "Seawater Organic Contaminants." In *Encyclopedia of Comprehensive Sampling and Sample Preparation*, edited by J. Pawliszyn and J. M. Bayona, 297–316. Oxford: Elsevier, 2012.
Hansard. "Shipwrecks and Collisions of Merchant Vessels." Debates, House of Commons (February 15, 1848), 96, cc668–73. https://api.parliament.uk/historic-hansard/commons/1848/feb/15/shipwrecks-and-collisions-of-merchant.
Hausfather, Zeke, and Piers Forster. "Analysis: How Low-Sulphur Shipping Rules Are Affecting Global Warming." *Carbon Brief* (July 3, 2023). www.carbonbrief.org/analysis-how-low-sulphur-shipping-rules-are-affecting-global-warming/.
Hing, Stephanie. Sue Foster, and Di Evans. "Animal Welfare Risks by Live Cattle Export from Australia to China by Sea." *Animals (Basel)* 11, no. 10 (October 2021): 2862. www.ncbi.nlm.nih.gov/pmc/articles/PMC8532794/.
Hoagland, P., J. Jacoby, and M. E. Schumacher. "Law of the Sea." In *Encyclopedia of Ocean Sciences*, 2nd ed. Cambridge, MA: Academic Press, 2001.
Hosanee, Nivedita M. "A Critical Analysis of Flag State Duties as Laid Down under Article 94 of the 1982 United Nations Convention on the Law of the Sea." *UN Division for Ocean Affairs and the Law of the Sea* (New York, 2009). https://static.un.org/depts/los/nippon/unnff_programme_home/fellows_pages/fellows_papers/hosanee_0910_mauritious.pdf.
ICES. *Request from the Netherlands Regarding the Impacts of Pulse Trawling on the Ecosystem and Environment from the Sole (Solea solea) Fishery in the North Sea*. ICES Advice, Special Requests, 2020. https://doi.org/10.17895/ices.advice.6020.
IMO. "Convention on the International Regulations for Preventing Collisions at Sea (COLREGs)." Accessed May 24, 2023. www.imo.org/en/About/Conventions/Pages/COLREG.aspx.
IMO. "Convention on Limitation of Liability for Maritime Claims." Accessed June 2, 2023. www.imo.org/en/About/Conventions/Pages/Convention-on-Limitation-of-Liability-for-Maritime-Claims-(LLMC).aspx.
IMO. "Global Limit on Sulphur in Ships' Fuel Oil Reduced from 01 January 2020." *Media Release* (2019). www.imo.org/en/MediaCentre/PressBriefings/pages/34-IMO-2020-sulphur-limit-.aspx.
IMO. "International Chamber of Shipping (ICS), and Office of the UN High Commissioner for Refugees (UNHCR), Rescue at Sea: A Guide to Principles and Practice as Applied to Refugees and Migrants." (n.d.). https://wwwcdn.imo.org/localresources/en/OurWork/Facilitation/Documents/MSC.167%20(78).pdf.
IMO. "International Convention for the Safety of Life at Sea (SOLAS)." (1974). Accessed June 2, 2023. www.imo.org/en/About/Conventions/Pages/International-Convention-for-the-Safety-of-Life-at-Sea-(SOLAS),-1974.aspx.
IMO. "International Convention on Salvage." Accessed May 2, 2023. www.imo.org/en/About/Conventions/Pages/International-Convention-on-Salvage.aspx.
IMO. "List of IMO Conventions." Accessed March 15, 2024. www.imo.org/en/About/Conventions/Pages/ListOfConventions.aspx;
IMO. "Registration of Ships and Fraudulent Registration Matters." Accessed March 15, 2024. www.imo.org/en/OurWork/Legal/Pages/Registration-of-ships-and-fraudulent-registration-matters.aspx.
IMO Maritime Safety Committee. *Guidelines on the Treatment of Persons Rescued at Sea* (Res. MSC.167(78)). Accessed March 15, 2024. https://wwwcdn.imo.org/localresources/en/OurWork/Facilitation/Documents/MSC.167%20(78).pdf.

International Transport Workers' Federation. "What Are Flags of Convenience?" Accessed November 4, 2023. www.itfglobal.org/en/sector/seafarers/flags-of-convenience.

Jamieson, Alan G. *Out of the Depths: A History of Shipwrecks*. London: Reaktion Books, 2022.

Joseph, Anish, and Dimitrios Dalaklis. "The International Convention or the Safety of Life at Sea: Highlighting the Interrelations of Measures towards Effective Risk Mitigation." *Journal of International Maritime Safety, Environmental Affairs and Shipping* 5, no. 1 (2021): 1–11.

Karim, Md Saiful. "Flag State Responsibility for Maritime Terrorism." *SAIS Review of International Affairs* 33, no. 2 (Summer–Fall 2013): 127–34.

Khaskheli, Muhammad Bilawal, Shumin Wang, Xin Zhang, Imran Haider Shamsi, Chenghua Shen, Sanober Rasheed, Zakir Ibraham, and Dost Muhammad Baloch. "Technology Advancement and International Law in Marine Policy, Challenges, Solutions and Future Prospective." *Marine Affairs and Policy* 10 (2023): 1258924, https://doi.org/10.3389/fmars.2023.1258924.

Kraska, James, and Raul A. Pedrozo, *International Maritime Security Law*. Leiden: Martinus Nijhoff Publishers, 2013.

"Laws of Oleron." In *Oxford Companion to Ships and the Sea*, 2nd ed., edited by I. C. B. Dear and Peter Kemp. Oxford: Oxford University Press, 2006.

Lloyd's Register. "Our History." Accessed June 2, 2023. www.lr.org/en/about-us/who-we-are/our-history/.

Mack, John. *The Sea: A Cultural History*. London: Reaktion Books Ltd, 2011.

McClymont, Alison, and Dan Harrison. "Into the Storm." *ABC News* (December11,2022).www.abc.net.au/news/2022-12-11/why-did-gulf-livestock-1-sail-into-typhoon-maysak/101739560.

Mentz, Steve. *Shipwreck Modernity: Ecologies of Globalisation, 1550–1719*. Minneapolis: University of Minnesota Press, 2015.

Mentz, Steven. "Towards a Blue Cultural Studies: The Sea, Maritime Culture and Early Modern Literature." *Literature Compass* 6, no. 5 (2009): 997–1013.

Micallef, Denise. "A Legal Analysis of the Limitation of Liability of Classification Societies." *CMI Yearbook* (2014): 223–41.

"Missing Migrants Project." Accessed May 4, 2023. https://missingmigrants.iom.int/.

Moran, Jessica, and Bec Pridham. "Salvage Fight over Sydney to Hobart Yacht Huntress as Aboriginal Land Council Claims Ownership." *ABC News* (January 10, 2023). www.abc.net.au/news/2023-01-09/sydney-to-hobart-yacht-huntress-salvage-fight-indigenous-claim/101836372?utm_source=abc_news_app&utm_medium=content_shared&utm_campaign=abc_news_app&utm_content=mail.

Moreno-Lax, Violeta. "The Interdiction of Asylum Seekers at Sea: Law and (mal)practice in Europe and Australia." *Policy Brief* 4. Sydney: Kaldor Centre for International Refugee Law, May 2017. www.kaldorcentre.unsw.edu.au/sites/kaldorcentre.unsw.edu.au/files/Policy_Brief4_Interdiction_of_asylum_seekers_at_sea.pdf.

Morris, Gregory D. L. "A Brief History of Marine Insurance." Accessed January 3, 2024. https://riskandinsurance.com/brief-history-marine-insurance/.

"MS Estonia Sinking: One of the Deadliest Accidents in European Waters." *Safety-4Sea* (October 4, 2019). https://safety4sea.com/cm-ms-estonia-sinking-one-of-the-deadliest-accidents-in-european-waters/.

Munari, Francesco. "Search and Rescue at Sea: Do New Challenges Require New Rules?" In *Governance of Arctic Shipping: Rethinking Risk, Human Impacts and Regulation*, edited by Aldo Chircop, Floris Goerlandt, Claudio Aporta, and Ronald Pelot. Cham: Springer Polar Sciences, 2020.

National Museum of Australia. "Tampa Affair." Accessed March 15, 2024. www.nma.gov.au/defining-moments/resources/tampa-affair.

Noone, Greg. "Flags of Convenience: Could the Threat of Lawsuits Put an End to the Practice?" *Hakai Magazine* (July 25, 2022). https://hakaimagazine.com/news/flags-of-convenience-could-the-threat-of-lawsuits-put-an-end-to-the-practice/.
Özdel, Melis, ed. *Commercial Maritime Law*. London: Bloomsbury, 2020.
Palmer, Sarah. 'Safety Regulations for Shipping." In *The Oxford Encyclopedia of Maritime History*, edited by John J. Hattendorf. Oxford: Oxford University Press, 2007.
Papanicolopulu, Irini. "The Duty to Rescue at Sea, in Peacetime and in War: A General Overview." *International Review of the Red Cross* 98, no. 2 (2016): 491–514.
Papanocolopulu, Irini. "The Historical Origins of the Duty to Save Life at Sea in International Law." *Journal of the History of International Law* 24 (2022): 149–88.
Penna, Daphne. "General Average in Byzantium." In *General Average and Risk Management in Medieval and Early Modern Maritime Business*, edited by M. Fusaro, A. Addobbati, and L. Piccinno. Cham: Palgrave Macmillan, 2023. https://doi.org/10.1007/978-3-031-04118-1_4.
Petrie, Claire. "Live Export: a Chronology." Accessed March 15, 2024. www.aph.gov.au/About_Parliament/Parliamentary_Departments/Parliamentary_Library/pubs/rp/rp1920/Chronologies/LiveExport.
Rawson, K. J., and E. C. Tupper. "Ship Design." In *Basic Ship Theory*, 5th ed. Amsterdam: Elsevier, 2001.
Roden, Sophie. *Turning Their Back on the Law? The Legality of the Coalition's Maritime Interdiction and Return Policy*. Canberra: Australian National University, n.d. https://law.anu.edu.au/sites/all/files/acmlj/turning_their_back_on_the_law_v2.pdf
Røsæg, Erik. "The Duty to Rescue Refugees and Migrants at Sea." *Faculty of Law, University of Oxford* (March 25, 2020). https://blogs.law.ox.ac.uk/research-subject-groups/centre-criminology/centreborder-criminologies/blog/2020/03/duty-rescue.
Rose, Francis D. *Kennedy & Rose Law of Salvage*. London: Sweet & Maxwell/Thomson Reuters, 2017.
Royal Museum Greenwich. "Samuel Plimsoll and Ship Safety." Accessed March 15, 2024. www.rmg.co.uk/stories/topics/samuel-plimsoll-ship-safety#:~:text=In%20the%2019th%20century%2C%20MP,without%20the%20risk%20of%20sinking.
Shaw, Richard A. A. "Salvage." In The Oxford Encyclopedia of Maritime History, edited by John J Hattendorf. Oxford: Oxford University Press, 2007.
Scottish Government. "Marine and Fisheries Compliance: Vessel Monitoring System Fact Sheet." (May 31, 2018). Accessed January 5, 2024. www.gov.scot/publications/marine-and-fisheries-compliance-vessel-monitoring-system/.
Seafarers Rights International (SRI). "Flag State Responsibilities and Seafarers' Rights." *Strategic Research for the Maritime Industry* (September 29, 2014). https://seafarersrights.org/flag-state-responsibilities-and-seafarersrights/.
Steinberg, Philip. *The Social Construction of the Ocean*. Cambridge: Cambridge University Press, 2001.
Sytas, Andrius. "New Probe into Estonia Ferry Sinking Reveals Construction Flaws – Officials." *Reuters* (January 24, 2023).
"The Seafarer." In *Codex Exoniensis: A Collection of Anglo-Saxon Poetry*, translated by Benjamin Thorpe. London: Society of Antiquaries, 1842.
van Fossen, Anthony. "Flags of Convenience and Global Capitalism." *International Critical Thought* 6, no. 3 (2016): 359–77.
Vassalos, Dracos, and Donald Paterson. "Reconfiguring Passenger Ship Internal Environment for Damage Stability Enhancement." *Journal of Marine Science and Engineering* 8 (2020): 2.
Villalobos, Marcelo Molina. "The Ever Given and the Problem with Flags of Convenience in International Shipping." *Berkeley Journal of International Law* (April 18, 2021). www.

berkeleyjournalofinternationallaw.com/post/the-ever-given-and-the-problem-with-flags-of-convenience-in-international-shipping.

Vitzthum, Wolfgang Graf. "From the Rhodian Sea Law to UNCLOS III." *Ocean Yearbook Online* (2003): 56–57.

Wan, Shuyan, Xiaohan Yang, Xinya Chen, Zhaonian Qu, Chunjiang An, Baiyu Zhang, Kenneth Lee, and Huifang Bi. "Emerging Marine Pollution from Container Ship Accidents: Risk Characteristics, Response Strategies, and Regulation Advancements." *Journal of Cleaner Production* 376 (2022): 134266. https://doi.org/10.1016/j.jclepro.2022.134266.

Wendel, Philipp. *State Responsibility for Interferences with the Freedom of Navigation in Public International Law*. Berlin: Springer, 2007.

Wiswall Jr., Frank L. "Law." In *The Oxford Encyclopedia of Maritime Law*, edited by John J. Hattendorf. Oxford: Oxford University Press, 2007.

Wiswall Jr., Frank L. "Shipping Conventions." In *The Oxford Encyclopedia of Maritime Law*, edited by John J. Hattendorf. Oxford: Oxford University Press, 2007.

Woker, Hilde J., Rozemarijn J. Roland Host, and Harriet Harden-Davies. "New Technology and the Protection of the Marine Environment." In *Research Handbook on International Marine Environmental Law*, 2nd ed., edited by R. Rayfuse, A. Jaeckel, and N. Klein. Cheltenham: Edward Elgar Publishing, 2023.

World Shipping Council. "Containers Lost at Sea 2023 Update." May 2023. https://mb.cision.com/Public/20134/3772700/9f81b7bcd3582277.pdf.

6 Disrupting the flow

Construction and extraction in the deep ocean

Who has known the ocean? Neither you nor I, with our earth-bound senses, know the foam and surge of the tide that beats over the crab hiding under the seaweed of his tide-pool home. . . . Even less is it given to man to descend those six incomprehensible miles into the recesses of the abyss, where reign utter silence and unvarying cold and eternal night.

Rachel Carson, "Undersea"

Overview

The deep ocean is the largest habitat on Earth but, for most of human history, its depths have been inaccessible and unknowable, the source of myths and legends in many different cultures. In 1823, the *Encyclopædia Britannica* simply noted that, for 'want of proper instruments, beyond a certain depth, the sea has hitherto been found unfathomable'.[1] Across different cultures, humans dwelling in coastal areas traditionally hunted or collected food, fibre and other living and non-living resources from shallower waters on the surfaces and shorelines of oceans and seas although, in some cases such as the mining of guano, rock phosphate and coral, these traditional activities did have an impact on marine and coastal areas.[2] During the 19th century, however, the world's oceans and seas became the focus of scientific interest and, with the development of new forms of submarine technology in the mid-20th century, humans gained access to the deep ocean, transforming it into a setting for new types of human uses, structures, and exploitative practices. This chapter explores the ways in which legal regimes have addressed the construction of artificial structures in oceans and seas, including drilling platforms to extract oil and minerals from the seabed, laying extensive submarine networks of telecommunication cables, and introducing artificial reefs and islands to the ocean environment. It also considers some of the recent challenges that face States and the international community in relation to ageing or deteriorating structures and how international law serves to regulate their operation, removal or alternative uses.

DOI: 10.4324/9781003005261-9

Communicating from the depths

Amongst the earliest structures to be installed on the seabed of the high seas were transoceanic telegraph cables. Initially laid beneath the coastal waters of Great Britain and the US from the early 1850s, submarine telegraph cables enabled messages to be exchanged over long distances in minutes rather than days. Several attempts were also made to establish a submarine telegraph cable across the Atlantic Ocean, but laying a cable that could survive the rigours of the deep ocean environment required a detailed understanding of the physical geography of the seabed. In his efforts to promote a transatlantic link, Matthew Fontaine Maury, an American oceanographer and naval officer, led several surveys of the North Atlantic basin between 1849 and 1853, undertaking systematic depth soundings along the popular steamship route between Europe and North America.[3] From these deep-sea soundings, he was able to produce the first bathymetric map of an ocean basin, paving the way for the successful installation, in 1866, of the North Atlantic submarine telegraphic cable on the deep seabed between Great Britain and the US. Newspapers of the day heralded the cable as the eighth wonder of the world, revolutionising communication between continents separated by vast expanses of ocean.[4]

By the 1880s, the importance of protecting submarine cable infrastructure and maintaining transoceanic communications between States was soon reflected in

Figure 6.1 Landing the shore end of the Atlantic cable. Painting by Robert Charles Dugley, 1866 [oil on canvas]. (From Metropolitan Museum of Art Collection.)

international law. In 1884 several coastal States signed the international *Convention for the Protection of Submarine Telegraph Cables* (Paris Convention, in force from 1888), requiring all ships to keep a distance of one nautical mile (1.9 kilometres) from cable laying ships when in operation.[5] This was followed by State laws such as the US *Submarine Cable Act* in 1886 that imposed a penalty for anyone found to have damaged a cable intentionally or unintentionally (including accidental damage caused by fishing nets) in a way that might interrupt or obstruct telegraphic communications.

The original intention of the 1884 Convention to preserve submarine communications continued to underpin subsequent international law involving the ocean environment. Two of the four conventions proposed at the first UN Conference of the Law of the Sea in 1958, for example, addressed the safety of submarine cables, while the Geneva Convention on the High Seas affirmed the right of all States to lay submarine cables on the bed of the high seas outside of territorial waters in accordance with the concept of freedom of the high seas, and the Geneva Convention on the Continental Shelf required coastal States to not impede the laying or maintenance of cables on the shelf. Similar protections were embraced in the historic 1982 UNCLOS, including the duty of States to punish those responsible for breaking or injuring a submarine cable, either wilfully or through 'culpable negligence'.[6]

Submarine communication technology has changed dramatically since the copper wires of the 19th century. Today, fibre-optic cables traverse the seabed of the world's oceans and seas, transmitting 95% of all international data between continents and islands, involving over 300 submarine cables and covering more than 1.2 million kilometres of ocean floor.[7] These cables are critical to maintaining international communications – including the World Wide Web – surpassing even satellite communications for reliability and capacity.[8] However, whilst the original intention of the Convention to preserve communications networks remains, new risks have emerged in relation to national security, economic activities and the marine environment. Indeed, any disruption to the submarine cable global network today would have severe consequences for the flow of digital information across the world, and all human activities dependent on it.[9]

Extracting wealth from the seabed

The world's oceans and seas play a crucial role in meeting humanity's energy needs. With the development of modern extraction techniques enabling the infrastructure for drilling and production to be installed on the seafloor, offshore extraction of oil and natural gas has become one of the world's major industries.[10] Coastal communities have long extracted sand and gravel from shallow shelf and beach areas, but mining activities on the deep seabed have a much more recent history. In the late 19th century, western ships exploring the vast oceans beyond established shipping routes were attracting scientific and commercial interest in the samples of minerals they dredged up from the seabed.[11] Early efforts to extract oil from shallow seas began in this period, with one of the earliest wells drilled off a wooden pier in a Californian canal. The first freestanding drilling platform was constructed in the Gulf of Mexico in 1938 although, even after World War II, oil rigs were generally still small structures cantilevered over the side of old wartime barges, susceptible to wave action and limited in how far they could drill into sand.

BP Horizon drilling platform explosion

In 2010 the Deepwater Horizon oil drilling platform operated by British Petroleum in the Gulf of Mexico, exploded, killing 11 workers and injuring 17. The rig capsized and sank, rupturing the riser and spewing nearly 134 million gallons of oil into the surrounding water over the course of 87 days. Subsequent investigations revealed the cause to be a malfunction in the drilling equipment. The disaster drew global attention to the vulnerability of such installations to accidental or intentional damage, including acts of terrorism. The cost to wildlife was incalculable and far-reaching. The oil slick extended over more than 149,000 square kilometres of ocean and an estimated 65,000 turtles died in 2010 alone, while a study ten years later found fish continued to show evidence of contamination. The US Government imposed a six-month moratorium on offshore drilling on the continental shelf, and the oil well involved was capped three months after the incident. Five US states launched a legal battle that lasted six years, and BP eventually pleaded guilty to 14 criminal charges and agreed to compensate the victims. It resulted in the largest environmental damage settlement in US history.[12]

With shifting conceptions of the ocean as 'frontier' in the second half of the 20th century, underpinned by the emerging science of oceanography and the development of new submarine technologies, the world's oceans and seas seemed to promise a vast, untapped, limitless resource awaiting exploitation for human benefit. As one promoter of the mineral potential of oceans and seas put it in 1964, here was 'a boundless, inexhaustible storehouse of the material stuff of civilization'.[13] In the process, this cultural transformation also heightened international competition for these new sources of food and minerals as States increasingly sought to stake their claim to the seabed. In 1954, the American Petroleum Institute promoted offshore oil drilling in a magazine advertisement, drawing parallels with the settler 'frontier' of the American West: 'In the open waters of the Gulf of Mexico, against every hazard of wind, wave, and sudden storm, sea-going oilmen are opening up a new American frontier'.[14] The first floating offshore drilling rig was installed in the Santa Barbara Channel in 1955 following California's decision to introduce oil and gas exploration leases, and a surge of new commercial operations followed with new types of floating drilling platforms and production facilities that could be moored or mounted on the seabed in deeper ocean waters.[15]

Petroleum companies were in a race to adopt new technologies and practices that would make offshore drilling cheaper and simpler. However, these new practices involved significant risk of accidents. In 1969, for example, the largest oil spill in the US at that time, and one of the largest in the world even today, occurred near the city of Santa Barbara when an oil drilling platform blew out 10 kilometres from the coast. Public outrage over the damage wrought on the marine environment resulted in a number of new environmental laws being passed in the US, effectively laying the foundations for the current legal and regulatory framework.[16] By 1982, amid increasing public agitation for better regulation, the US Congress imposed a moratorium on new leases for the US West Coast, Mid-Atlantic and eastern region of the Gulf of Mexico. Tragically, the environmental damage from offshore exploration activities continued, this time in the oil-rich seabed off Alaska. In 1989, the vessel *Exxon Valdez* ran aground, and the resulting oil spill had a catastrophic impact on this ecologically sensitive environment, provoking international outrage and drawing attention to the failure of environmental and safety regulation of oil transportation vessels more broadly (see Chapter 9 and the Exxon Valdez case study).[17]

In Europe, the first commercial oil wells began operating on land from the 1850s, but they were generally small in scale and dug by hand. The demand for fuel during the world wars of the 20th century, however, greatly accelerated the search for new sources of gas and oil in Europe. In the early postwar years new offshore drilling technologies developed during Britain's first 'oil boom' made possible construction of the first offshore well in Europe in 1959, transforming the process of extracting fossil fuels from the seabed. The discovery of huge deposits of petroleum beneath the North Sea by the United Kingdom and the Netherlands in the 1960s has led to that region being one of the largest offshore drilling areas in the world.[18] Today one-quarter of the world's oil reserves are thought to be offshore, with the most productive areas located in the North Sea, Gulf of Mexico, Atlantic Ocean off Brazil and West Africa, the Arabian Gulf, and the seas off Southeast Asia. At the same time, the potential of the ocean to be used as the source of renewable energy has become a matter of international interest, raising expectations that wind, waves, tides and ocean currents could provide a substantial proportion of the world's electricity needs in the future.

As the world's appetite for oil and gas has continued to grow, so too has public concern about the environmental impact of oil extraction, particularly offshore operations, which are known to pose a high risk of accidental oil spills and contamination from the release of chemicals and other pollutants to the marine environment, quite apart from the indirect impacts on the world's atmospheric and oceans from CO_2 emissions released during the burning of fossil fuels.[19] Rightly or wrongly, the regulation of construction and operation of offshore infrastructure has been separated from legal frameworks for shipping and maritime transport. From a legal perspective, given that surprisingly there is no treaty related to non-living resource extraction at sea, there are significant gaps and weaknesses in the international regulatory regime in relation to offshore installations including, for example, the legal status of oil rigs, environmental problems, decommissioning issues, conflicts with navigation, and the protection of offshore facilities from, for example, collision or other accidents involving ships.[20]

Offshore extraction activities

The UNCLOS defines the rights and responsibilities of all nations in their use of the world's oceans, including the protection of the marine environment and exploitation of offshore living and non-living natural resources. It is the main international regulatory regime for offshore exploration and production activities in the world's oceans and covers artificial islands, installations and structures on the continental shelf (Article 80) and international obligations towards decommissioning any installations or structures that are abandoned or disused to ensure the safety of navigation, fishing and protecting the marine environment (Article 60(3)).[21] The International Maritime Organisation, which is responsible for the safety and security of shipping and prevention of pollution by ships, endorsed the *International Convention on Oil Pollution Preparedness, Response and Cooperation* in 1990 requiring States to establish measures for preventing and responding to pollution from ships and offshore units under the jurisdiction of treaty parties. However, this Convention only addressed response measures for spills caused by blowouts on oil rigs, not measures to prevent them.[22]

These weaknesses in international law relating to offshore extraction activities have become a matter of international concern, particularly in sensitive marine environments such as the Arctic Ocean, where controversial State plans and approvals for oil and gas drilling projects are being met with condemnation by environmental organisations.[23] Human activities in the Arctic Ocean are subject to several treaties and agreements but, in the absence of an Arctic Treaty, their implementation depends on international cooperation and national implementation.[24] In any event, despite the efforts of the Arctic Council to support best practice, critics of the existing legal regime argue that it does little to ensure the prevention of large-scale oil spills or to address the unique challenges of cleaning up an oil spill in the Arctic environment.[25]

In the absence of an international regulatory regime governing offshore extraction activities, regional organisations sought to regulate offshore oil and gas activities to prevent pollution in sensitive marine environments. In the Arctic Ocean, for example, the eight States bordering the Arctic Ocean signed the *Agreement on Cooperation on Marine Oil Pollution, Preparedness and Response in the Arctic* in 2013 with the intention to 'strengthen cooperation, coordination and mutual assistance among the Parties on oil pollution preparedness and response in the Arctic in order to protect the marine environment from pollution by oil'.[26] The Arctic Council also introduced a number of non-binding guidelines and standards specifically aimed at preventing offshore oil spills in Arctic conditions although, while some Arctic States have incorporated these 'soft laws' into national legislation governing offshore drilling in the Arctic, they are not legally enforceable by the Arctic Council.[27] In other instances, regional conventions primarily focused on preventing pollution in the marine environment have been expanded to include offshore extraction activities. For example, the *Convention for the Protection of the Marine Environment of the North-East Atlantic* (OSPAR), originating in 1972 with the Oslo Convention against dumping, was subsequently amended to address the prevention and elimination of pollution from land-based sources of marine pollution and pollution from offshore sources.[28] Similarly, the *Malabo Protocol*, under the *Abidjan Convention for Cooperation in the Protection and Development of the Marine and Coastal Environment of the West and Central African Region* (1981), focuses on environmental norms and standards related to offshore oil and gas activities.[29] In the enclosed Caspian Sea, the *Aktau Protocol* (2011) under the 2003 *Convention for the Protection of the Marine Environment of the Caspian Sea* (Tehran Convention), addresses oil spill preparedness and response covers offshore fixed and floating structures (see Chapter 9 for further discussion of pollution and dumping waste at sea).[30] In the search for non-fossil fuel energy options, blue energy or renewable energy from the oceans has grown in popularity. Although commercial-scale wave and tidal energy technologies are still developing, offshore wind infrastructure is established in many jurisdictions. There are no specific global regulatory frameworks that would provide standards for offshore renewable energy, and therefore the provisions in UNCLOS, the *London Convention* and Protocol, and the general obligations noted earlier remain relevant.[31] There has been some scientific and public concern about the impacts of such technology with misinformation adding to the controversy.[32]

Marine mining

Post-war developments in submarine technology not only opened the seabed up to exploitation of its oil and gas resources. They also put mineral deposits known to exist in the sediments of the deep ocean floor within human reach. Amongst these were manganese nodules (also known as polymetallic nodules) found in large numbers in the sediments of the seabed in both shallow and deep ocean waters. Deep-sea manganese nodules were first discovered in the sediments of the world's ocean basins during the scientific voyage of HMS *Challenger* in 1872–76, and the expedition chemist recognised their potential for use in products such as bleaching powder.[33] It would be another century before systematic studies of deep-sea minerals commenced with an eye to their commercial value, and books like John L Mero's *The Mineral Resources of the Sea* in 1964 helped to generate enthusiasm for seabed mining of manganese and other minerals to meet the world's future needs.[34]

Such enthusiasm, however, overlooked the logistical difficulties of mining manganese nodules, typically found between 4,500 and 5,200 metres.[35] It also served to highlight the fact that the deep seabed did not lie within the jurisdiction of any State and that mining it would require international agreement. As John Bardach noted in his 1968 book *Harvest of the Sea*: 'New legal concepts will have to be developed for the sharing of resources in and under the sea before we can colonize the oceans'.[36] Tensions had already emerged in the first UN Conference on the Law of the Sea in 1958 between the major maritime powers, on the one hand, seeking to preserve the long tradition of freedom of the seas and smaller coastal States, on the other hand, defending their customary rights to the living and non-living resources of adjacent coastal waters and sea floor.[37] (See Chapter 2 for further discussion of the four conventions adopted at the first UN Conference on the Law of the Sea in 1958.) The Maltese ambassador, Arvid Pardo, proposed a way to address this problem in a landmark speech to the UN General Assembly in 1967, calling for the resources of the oceans to be beyond national jurisdiction and arguing that they should be designated as the 'common heritage of mankind'. He envisaged that the wealth derived from the high seas could be used to address global social and economic problems in land-locked and developing nations, and he urged the nations of the world to create a system of international regulation to prevent technologically advanced countries from wresting control of the seabed and its resources.[38]

The 'common heritage of mankind'

Arvid Pardo summed up his argument for a new regime of international cooperation, beginning with reserving the deep seabed and its subsoil exclusively for peaceful purposes:

> Traditionally, international law has been essentially concerned with the regulation of relations between states. In ocean space, however, the time has come to recognise as a basic principle of international law the overriding common interest of mankind in the preservation of the quality of marine environment and in the rational and equitable development of its resources lying beyond national jurisdiction. This does not imply disregard of the interest of individual states, but rather the recognition of the fact that in the long term these interests can be protected only within the framework of a stable international regime of close co-operation between states.[39]

The UN General Assembly embraced Pardo's vision in 1970, declaring the mineral resources of the seabed as the 'common heritage of mankind' and adopting the *Declaration of Principles Governing the Sea-Bed and the Ocean-Floor, and the Subsoil Thereof: Beyond the Limits of National Jurisdiction*.[40] This was a decisive move by the UN to reserve the seabed exclusively for peaceful purposes. As it happened, marine mining was slow to materialise, in part because of the prohibitive costs and logistics of extracting them from great depths, the collapse of world metal prices in the 1970s and an increase in land-based mining in developing nations.[41] Nevertheless, negotiations continued for a new framework for deep seabed mining beyond national jurisdiction, resulting in the inclusion of a controversial regulatory regime within the 1982 UNCLOS (Part XI) that reflected many developing nations' ('G-77 States') proposals.[42] Issues included cost-effectiveness and decision-making processes of the independent International Seabed Authority (ISA), as well as production restrictions and requirements to transfer technology. The US objected to the final text and did not ratify the Convention, but by then the parties to UNCLOS realised that the deep seabed mining regime was unworkable since most of the industrialised countries were precluded from benefiting from it. Further negotiations followed, led by a group of the most industrialised States (the 'G-10') and other interested countries, and in 1994 concluded with the adoption of the Agreement relating to the implementation of Part XI. Operating together, UNCLOS and the Part XI Agreement created a seabed mining regime to be governed by the ISA. The ISA's role was to authorise and control the extraction of seabed minerals found beyond 'the Area' (beyond the limits of national jurisdiction) representing about half of the entire ocean floor of the planet.[43]

Since then, there has been a resurgence of government and private sector interest in the commercial exploitation of marine minerals, driven in part by the technological advances in marine mineral extraction and processing, and the increasing commercial value of minerals such as manganese nodules, cobalt crusts and the sulphur-rich ore that form at submarine plate boundaries.[44] The ISA's regulatory role is central to this boom, with the Secretary-General envisaging that seabed mining will drive the global transition to clean energy. Drawing on Arvid Pardo's vision, he declared that the economic benefits of deep seabed mining will be shared for the 'benefit of mankind as a whole', particularly 'for landlocked and geographically disadvantaged States, and small island developing States that are heavily reliant on the ocean and its resources for economic development'.[45]

Nevertheless, the prospect of deep-sea mining has become highly controversial. Critics argue, for example, that the ISA has a conflict of interest in acting as both mining regulator and custodian of the seabed environment,[46] that the ISA's concept of distributing the economic benefits of deep-sea mining is untested, and that an international legal regime is urgently needed to address new issues and concerns that have emerged since the 1970s, particularly in relation to environmental and national security.[47] By the beginning of 2022 the ISA had awarded 31 contracts for prospecting and exploring but, in the absence of an agreed Mining Code to regulate exploitation of the seabed, it had not approved any applications for commercial mining.[48] When the island nation of Nauru notified the ISA in June 2021 of its intention to apply for seabed mining approval, it triggered a treaty provision known as the 'two-year rule' that obliged the ISA to finalise and adopt regulations for deep seabed mining within 24 months. That deadline expired in July 2023 without the Mining Code being finalised and, although member States of the ISA agreed to continue negotiations with the aim of adopting a Code in 2025, the agreement itself was not legally binding. The consequences of the ISA's failure to finalise a Mining Code are presently unclear. The Implementation Agreement requires the ISA to provisionally consider mining applications based on existing provisional rules, regulations, procedures and norms but, despite consensus on some of the draft regulations, differences remain over provisions relating to the quantity of mining allowed and the collection of mining royalties. The future of deep-sea mining is highly controversial. On the one hand, the seafloor is known to have vast reserves of rare earth metals necessary for the global transition to clean energy technologies. On the other hand, scientific knowledge of the seabed environment and how the extraction of minerals from it might affect it are limited.[49] Environmental organisations have been urging governments to ban deep-sea mining fearing massive biodiversity loss, disruption of the ocean's 'biological pump' and the loss of microbes necessary for storing carbon. Indeed, the rare scaly-foot snail (*Chrysomallon squamiferm*) found in deep-sea hydrothermal vents has become the first marine species to be listed as endangered by the International Union for Conservation of Nature (IUCN) as a result of deep-sea mining activity.[50] Furthermore, the current legal regime in areas of the seabed beyond national jurisdiction has left a 'critical gap' in the protection of the high seas.[51]

Decommissioned seabed structures

In addition to the risk of pollution from offshore extraction activities, the problem of removing end-of-life and abandoned artificial structures from the seabed has emerged as a significant environmental and legal problem closely related to the issue of dumping at sea.[52] There are an estimated 7,000 oil and gas installations and platforms on the continental shelves of more than 53 countries, and many have been operational for 15 to 20 years. Others have already been abandoned and await decommissioning and removal.[53]

Early installations of seabed structures in the mid-20th century failed to consider how and when decommissioned structures ought to be removed, although the 1958 Geneva Convention on the Continental Shelf (Article 5) did specify that 'any installations which are abandoned or disused must be entirely removed' so as to not interfere with navigation, a rule subsequently adopted in the 1982

UNCLOS (Articles 60 and 80).[54] In 1989, the International Maritime Organisation (IMO) developed soft law (non-binding) *Guidelines and Standards for the Removal of Offshore Installations and Structures on the Continental Shelf and in the Exclusive Economic Zone*.[55] Section 1.1 of the Guidelines repeats the UNCLOS position on removal, except where non-removal or partial removal is consistent with the Guidelines and Standards. Section 2.1 requires a case-by-case evaluation to allow offshore infrastructure to remain on the seabed. Evaluation criteria include safety of navigation, the rate of deterioration of the infrastructure and risk of movement, the potential effect on the marine environment, costs, technical feasibility, risks of injury associated with removal and 'determination of a new use or other reasonable justification for allowing the installation or structure or parts thereof to remain on the seabed'.

Even so, the international legal framework for decommissioning offshore installations is fragmented and the decision to remove (or partly remove) decommissioned structures is largely at the discretion of individual States because most structures and extraction activities take place within State waters and on the continental shelf.[56] UNCLOS (Article 60), for example, allows a State to make its own decision regarding structures on the seabed within its EEZ or continental shelf and provides no specific rules relating to structures that lie within a State's territorial sea, nor to similarly contentious practices linked to pollution in the marine environment including waste disposal at sea and shipbreaking.[57] Any authorised activities are, however, subject to the general obligation to protect and preserve the marine environment (Article 192) and the specific Articles on various forms of pollution at sea. (See Chapter 9 for a discussion of ocean pollution and the effectiveness of international agreements such as the London Convention and the 2009 International Convention for the Safe and Environmentally Sound Recycling of Ships (Hong Kong Convention).)[58] In short, leaving offshore infrastructure in place could be considered to be a form of ocean dumping. Although the 1972 *Convention for the Prevention of Marine Pollution by Dumping Wastes and Other Matter* (London Convention) outlaws deliberate disposal at sea, the 1996 Protocol provides an exception if 'placement of matter[is] for a purpose other than . . . mere disposal' (Article 4). So, if a decommissioned rig, platform or pipeline is left in place as an artificial reef (see later in the chapter), it could satisfy the exception.

The problem of what to do with decommissioned structures has assumed a greater urgency in recent years as increasing numbers of offshore oil rigs, platforms and pipelines reach the end of their useful life. The IMO's Guidelines do suggest the possibility of re-using installations as artificial reefs for the development of fisheries consistent with the UNCLOS requirement to protect the marine environment and its living resources, although they may also be considered a form of marine pollution.[59] The idea of a 'rigs-to-reef' program in the deep ocean has attracted wide debate. There is some evidence, for example, that artificial reefs made from decommissioned rigs in shallower waters have been effective in attracting fishes and invertebrates.[60] Marine anglers in the US recognised the value of artificial reefs to enhance fish catches from at least the 1850s. According to William Elliott of Beaufort, sheepshead – a species of fish – were:

> formerly taken in considerable numbers among our various inlets, into which large trees had fallen to which the barnacles soon became attached; but as the lands have been cleared for cultivation of sea-island cotton, the trees have disappeared, and with them the fish; and it has been found necessary to renew their feeding grounds by artificial means. Logs of oak or pine are formed into a sort of hut without a roof, five or six feet high; it is floored, and then floated to the place desired, and sunk in eight feet of water, by casting stones or live oak timber within; as soon as barnacles are formed, which will happen in a few weeks, the fish will begin to resort to the ground.[61]

Since that time, many different materials have been used to create artificial reefs, including shipwrecks, tyres, light poles, cement blocks and even fly ash from coal combustion. But while such artificial structures have been beneficial in providing habitats for marine species and, ultimately for human fishers, they have also created environmental problems such as damage to benthic habitats, facilitating the spread of invasive species, and the release of contaminants as the structures corrode.[62] From a legal perspective, for example, there is no globally endorsed approach with the EU favouring artificial reefs constructed from new materials and the US approving a rigs-to-reefs approach.[63]

The 'age of artificial islands'?

Humans have been reclaiming land from lakes, rivers and oceans for thousands of years, and the evidence is everywhere, from ancient crannogs in the lochs of the Outer Hebrides to the Solomon Islands, where the Lau people built 80 artificial islands in a lagoon over the course of several hundred years by raising the height of existing reefs or islets.[64] Asian countries also have a long history of dredging and land reclamation practices, including the construction of extensive canal networks to facilitate trade. However, the modern practice of land reclamation is on a far larger scale and involves significant terraforming of seabed sediments and adjacent coasts, as well as major impacts on the surrounding waters and marine ecosystems.[65]

The construction of artificial islands, for example, is increasingly undertaken as a way of creating new areas of dry land to accommodate a country's population needs, attract tourists, or as a means by which States seek to extend their sovereignty into adjacent oceans and seas.[66] Some of the world's largest artificial islands are currently being built off the coastal city of Dubai in the United Arab Emirates, a favoured destination for wealthy tourists. This is land reclamation on a vast scale, with sand dredged from the Persian Gulf, relocated to desirable new

The 'Great Wall of Sand' – artificial islands in the South China Sea

The South China Sea, a major global shipping route with rich oil and gas resources, is at the centre of conflicting territorial claims. In recent years, the People's Republic of China has built artificial islands on seven reefs in the Spratly Islands within a tri-state maritime boundary zone, and installed structures, runways and military defences on them in support of its sovereign claims in the South China Sea.

In 2015, the Commander of the US Pacific Fleet dubbed China's island-building exercise as the 'great wall of sand', arguing that China's actions were inconsistent with the 2002 China-ASEAN Declaration of Conduct committed parties to 'exercise self-restraint in the conduct of activities that would complicate or escalate disputes and affect peace and stability'. Some ASEAN member states pursued various non-legal strategies to demonstrate their own territorial claims in the region. The Philippines turned to The Hague for arbitration, seeking a special tribunal to rule on the matter in accordance with UNCLOS. In 2016, the tribunal ruled that China's claim was not valid and that the Spratlys did not meet the legal definition of islands (able to sustain a human community). China was therefore not entitled to claim the surrounding seas within its territory under international law. While China rejected the ruling, diplomatic negotiations have continued to address competing territorial claims in the South China Sea.[68]

locations and deposited on the seafloor. Projects include 'The World Islands', an archipelago of 300 islands arranged to resemble a map of Earth's continents, and islands purpose-built to accommodate luxury hotels, a night souk (bazaar) and the world's largest Ferris wheel.[67]

These projects are mostly close to shore or on the shoreline, where well-settled law provides rules around the acquisition of property rights through accretion. As noted in Chapter 2, these onshore additions, or newly constructed islands, are intended to attract property rights and be considered as 'land'. Offshore construction is an entirely different proposition. The UNCLOS gives coastal States the right to construct or install artificial structures on the seabed within the areas of the EEZ and continental shelf under their national jurisdiction. The current trend towards building artificial islands has, however, highlighted the different motivations across different regions, presenting a conundrum for the international community. On the one hand, States in the Pacific region are designing artificially constructed islands as a response to dealing with the impacts of climate change, creating new land for island populations threatened by sea-level rise. On the other hand, artificial islands being constructed in disputed oceans and seas such as the South China Sea highlight how the modern scale of land reclamation can trigger serious geopolitical tensions over State entitlements to maritime territories, particularly in regional seas bounded by multiple coastal States (see Chapter 2). While the recent enthusiasm for island-building offers a way forward for many island and coastal States facing an uncertain future, it also demonstrates how creating new land in contested waters has the potential to disrupt international trade, communication and freedom of navigation, and create new challenges for policymakers and legal institutions.

Conclusion

Since the mid-20th century, the development of new submarine technologies and installations has given humans access to the deep ocean as never before. Scientists estimate that humans have only explored and charted 5% of the planetary ocean, although the advent of seafloor mapping and robotic submersibles is yielding new knowledge about the ocean depths on a daily basis. Nevertheless, despite the dearth of information about the ocean depths, humans have found enterprising ways of using it for a range of purposes, from the installation of telecommunication cables between continents to the extraction of oil and natural gas from the seabed via offshore drilling and production platforms, and the construction of artificial islands.

UNCLOS has become the primary international legal mechanism for regulating activities associated with the construction, use and decommissioning of offshore installations globally, while the IMO is responsible for regulating shipping safety and pollution. However, the international regime for regulating construction and extraction activities in the marine environment is fragmented and, in some cases, ineffective. The laws governing oil and gas operations in sensitive marine environments, for example, rely on international cooperation to prevent a recurrence of the catastrophic oil spills that have devastated marine ecosystems and haunted coastal communities. Accidents associated with offshore extractive industries have also cast a long shadow over renewed interest in the commercial exploitation of marine minerals, particularly those required to fuel the global transition to clean energy, while the failure of the International Seabed Authority to finalise a Mining Code highlights the inevitable tensions between mining and environmental interests. Technological interventions in the marine environment are delivering many benefits – both economic and social – but, perhaps inevitably, they are also creating new problems that are proving to be both controversial and challenging to address in existing regulatory regimes. There are, clearly, technological developments that can benefit ocean protection and conservation, as well as restoration and recovery. The critical issue is whether legal frameworks are equipped to ensure that their application is fair and equitable for ocean as well as human communities.

Notes

1 "Sea," in *Encyclopædia Britannica* XIX (Edinburgh, 1823), 64 cited in Helen Rozwadowski, *Vast Expanses: A History of the Oceans* (London: Reaktion Books, 2018), 105.
2 See, for example, G. Ben Daley and Peter Griggs, "Mining the Reefs and Cays: Coral, Guano and Rock Phosphate Extraction in the Great Barrier Reef, Australia, 1844–1940," *Environment and History* 12, no. 4 (2006): 395–433.
3 Known as the 'pathfinder of the seas', Maury developed an extensive knowledge of the winds and currents of the world's oceans and began publishing navigational charts for mariners from 1847.
4 See *The Eighth Wonder of the World – the Atlantic Cable* (New York: Kimmel & Forster, 1866) featuring an allegorical scene showing Neptune with a trident in foreground, and lion representing Great Britain holding one end of the Atlantic cable and eagle representing the US holding the other end of the cable, with ocean between them and cities behind them. This image, and the 1851 edition of Maury's *Explanations and Sailing Directions to Accompany the Wind and Current* Charts, are held by the US Library of Congress, www.loc.gov/item/13016495/ and www.loc.gov/pictures/item/93510355/.
5 M. Wynn Tranfield, "Unspooling the Legacy of Submarine Cables," *DttP: Documents to the People* (Chicago: American Library Association, 2018), https://journals.ala.org/index.php/dttp/article/view/6826/9185.
6 UNCLOS, Article 113.
7 "Submarine Cables," *National Oceanic and Atmospheric Administration (US)*, accessed April 30, 2024, www.noaa.gov/submarine-cables#:~:text=It%20is%20a%20 common%20 misconception,See%20U.N.
8 The first submarine fibre optic (the science of transmitting data, voice and images by passing light through thin, transparent fibres) cables were laid across the Pacific Ocean in 1996.
9 See for example Lowell C. McAdam, "On the Law of the Sea Conventions: Benefits for Submarine Cable Systems," *Testimony before the US Senate Foreign Relations Committee* (June 28, 2012), 2, www.foreign.senate.gov/imo/media/doc/McAdamTestimony2.pdf. Tranfield, "Unspooling the Legacy of Submarine Cables."
10 Around one-quarter of global oil production comes from offshore oil fields, and about 60% of oil sold internationally is carried by oil tankers. See Nathan Andrews et al., "Oil, Fisheries and Coastal Communities: A Review of Impacts on the Environment, Livelihoods, Space and Governance," *Energy Research & Social Science* 75 (May 2021), www.sciencedirect.com/science/article/pii/S221462962100102X.
11 Britain's HMS *Challenger* voyage in 1872–76 was the first scientific expedition to explore the depths of the world's oceans. Over three and a half years the *Challenger* circumnavigated the globe collecting information about the water and seabed. The scientific reports were hailed as the most comprehensive study of the world's oceans and seas, laying the foundations for the science of oceanography. See, for example, Helen Rozwadowski, *Fathoming the Ocean: The Discovery and Exploration of the Deep Sea* (Cambridge, MA: Harvard University Press, 2005), 104–5.
12 "US and Five Gulf States Reach Historic Settlement with BP to Resolve Civil Lawsuit Over Deepwater Horizon Oil Spill," *US Department of Justice, Office of Public Affairs Press Release* (October 5, 2015), www.justice.gov/opa/pr/us-and-five-gulf-states-reach-historic-settlement-bp-resolve-civil-lawsuit-over-deepwater.
13 John L. Mero, *The Mineral Resources of the Sea* (Amsterdam: Elsevier Publishing Company, 1964), vi. Rozwadowski, *Vast Expanses*, 186–87.

14 Advertisement by American Petroleum Institute, "US Oilmen Challenge the Sea," *Life* XXXVI, no. 23 (June 7, 1954): 152, cited in Rozwadowski, *Vast Expanses*, 163.

15 R. J. Howe, "Evolution of Offshore Drilling and Production Technology," *Paper presented to Offshore Technology Conference, Texas*, 1986, https://onepetro.org/OTCONF/proceedings-abstract/86OTC/All-86OTC/OTC-5354-MS/49288. By 2019 offshore oil extraction in the Gulf of Mexico produced 692 million barrels or 15% of the total US oil production.

16 K. C. Clarke and Jeffrey J. Hemphill, "The Santa Barbara Oil Spill, a Retrospective," in *Yearbook of the Association of Pacific Coast Geographers*, 64, no. 1, ed. Darrick Danta (Honolulu: University of Hawai'i Press, January 2002), 152–57, http://dx.doi.org/10.1353/pcg.2002.0014.

17 See overview in "Oil Pollution Act of 1990 (OPA)," *United States Coast Guard, US Department of Homeland Security*, accessed April 30, 2024. www.uscg.mil/Mariners/National-Pollution-Funds-Center/About_NPFC/opa/.

18 The North Sea oil fields currently involve 184 rigs. The North Sea oil boom peaked in the UK in 1999 and in Norway in 2001. See John Chandler, *Petroleum Resource Management: How Governments Manage Their Offshore Petroleum Resources* (Cheltenham: Edward Elgar Publishing, 2018). Jonathan Craig, Francesco Derali, Fiona MacAulay, and Rasoul Sorkhabi, "The History of the European Oil and Gas Industry (1600s–2000s)," *Geological Society, London, Special Publications*, 465, no. 218 (2018): 1–24.

19 In 2010 it was estimated that 147 billion tonnes of oil had been pumped from reserves around the world, of which half was extracted since 1990. The extraction of offshore deposits of natural gas has also grown steadily, accounting for around one-third of the world's total production. The Persian Gulf is regarded as the world's largest reserve. "Energy," *World Ocean Review*, accessed April 30, 2024, https://worldoceanreview.com/en/wor-1/energy/fossil-fuels/.

20 The 1958 Continental Shelf Convention, for example, specified a 500-metre maximum safety zone around rigs to damage to underwater infrastructure from fishing gear or collisions and to prevent fire accidentally igniting as a result of people smoking on private yachts. Hossein Esmaeili, "The Protection of Offshore Oil Rigs in International Law (Part I), in *Australian Mining and Petroleum Law Journal* 18 (1999): 241–42.

21 John Chandler, David White, Erika J. Techera, Susan Gourvenec, and Scott Draper, "Engineering and Legal Considerations for Decommissioning of Offshore Oil and Gas Infrastructure in Australia," *Ocean Engineering* 131 (2017): 338–47, http://dx.doi.org/10.1016/j.oceaneng.2016.12.030. Erika J. Techera and John Chandler, "Offshore Installations, Decommissioning and Artificial Reefs: Do Current Legal Frameworks Best Serve the Marine Environment?" *Marine Policy* 59 (2015): 53–60.

22 Seline Trevisanut, "Decommissioning of Offshore Installations: A Fragmented and Ineffective International Regulatory Framework," in *The Law of the Seabed: Access, Uses, and Protection of Seabed Resources*, ed. Catherine Banet (Leiden: Koninklijke Brill, 2020), 431–53.

23 See, for example, "The Case Against Offshore Drilling in the Arctic," *Ocean Conservancy*, accessed January 12, 2024, https://oceanconservancy.org/protecting-the-arctic/risky-drilling/. Will Sullivan, "Massive Arctic Oil Drilling Project Gets the Green Light," *Smithsonian Magazine* (March 14, 2023), www.smithsonianmag.com/smart-news/a-controversial-arctic-oil-drilling-project-is-one-step-closer-to-moving-forward-180981570/#:~:text=A%20 controversial%20plan%20for%20 oil,per%20 CNN's%20Ella%20Nilsen, accessed January 12, 2024.

24 Significantly, the Arctic is not protected as a Special Area under MARPOL, presumably because it is not an area impacted by high shipping traffic. See "Special Areas

under MARPOL," *International Maritime Organization*, accessed April 30, 2024, www.imo.org/en/OurWork/Environment/Pages/Special-Areas-Marpol.aspx and accessed January 12, 2024, www.imo.org/en/ourwork/environment/pages/pssas.aspx.

25 See for example Daria Shapovalova, "Can International Law Protect the Arctic from Oil Spills?" *The Arctic Institute* (March 26, 2019), www.thearcticinstitute.org/international-law-protect-arctic-oil-spills/. C. Redgwell, "Mind the Gap in the GAIRS: The Role of Other Instruments in LOSC Regime Implementation in the Offshore Energy Sector," *The International Journal of Marine and Coastal Law* 29 (2014): 600–21. L. Chabason, "Offshore Oil Exploitation: A New Frontier for International Environmental Law," *Institute for Sustainable Development and International Relations* (2011), accessed April 30, 2024; L. Chabason, "Offshore Oil Exploitation: A New Frontier for International Environmental Law," *Institute for Sustainable Development and International Relations* (2011), accessed April 30, 2024, www.iddri.org/sites/default/files/import/publications/wp-1111_chabason_offshore.pdf.

26 The eight Arctic States are Canada, Kingdom of Denmark, Finland, Iceland, Norway, Russian Federation, Sweden, and the US. Arctic Council Working Group, "Agreement on Cooperation on Marine Oil Pollution Preparedness and Response in the Arctic," accessed January 12, 2024, https://eppr.org/resources/agreements/.

27 Shapovalova, "Can International Law Protect the Arctic?"

28 OSPAR currently involves 15 States and the European Union. See the OSPAR Convention website, accessed January 12, 2024, www.ospar.org/convention, Annex III.

29 "West and Central Africa," *UNEP*, accessed January 12, 2024, www.unep.org/explore-topics/oceans-seas/what-we-do/working-regional-seas/regional-seas-programmes/west-and.

30 "Tehran Convention," *Caspian Environmental Resource Center*, accessed January 12, 2024, https://tehranconvention.org/en.

31 For further discussion see Glen Wright, Sandy Kerr, and Kate Johnson, eds., *Ocean Energy: Governance Challenges for Wave and Tidal Stream Technologies* (Abingdon: Routledge, 2018).

32 Ibon Galparsoro et al., "Reviewing the Ecological Impacts of Offshore Wind Farms," *Ocean Sustainability* 1, no. 1 (2022), https://doi.org/10.1038/s44183-022-00003-5. Tim Fernandez and Melinda James, "Editor of Scientific Journal Says Fake Study Linking Whale Deaths to Wind Farms Is 'Deliberate Misinformation," *ABC News* (November 7, 2023), www.abc.net.au/news/2023-11-07/editor-blasts-fake-study-linking-whale-deaths-to-wind-farms/103069922.

33 They are formed as concentric layers of iron and manganese hydroxides accrete around an object such as a shark's tooth, and they contain valuable metals including cobalt, zirconium and copper. See J. Murray and A. F. Renard, *Report on the Scientific Results of the Voyage of H.M.S. Challenger During the Years 1873–76: Deep-sea Deposits* (London: Johnson Reprint Company Limited, 1891).

34 Mero, *The Mineral Resources of the Sea*. Some coastal States, including the US, Chile, Peru and Ecuador, were quick to introduce national laws claiming the potential ocean resources that might lie within their adjacent continental shelves.

35 "Treasures of the Abyss," *Geoscientist Online*, The Geological Society, London (May 2013), www.geolsoc.org.uk/Geoscientist/Archive/May-2013/Treasures-from-the-abyss.

36 John E. Bardach, *Harvest of the Sea* (New York: Harper and Row, 1968), 10 cited in Rozwadowski, *Vast Expanses*, 183.

37 Rozwadowski, *Vast Expanses*, 182–83.

38 His vision became a major driving factor in efforts by the UN to develop a comprehensive regime for ocean governance between 1967 and 1982.

39 Arvid Pardo, *The Common Heritage: Selected Papers on Oceans and World Order, 1967–1974* (Valetta: Malta University Press, 1975), 176.

40 The common heritage of mankind concept reflected the traditional view of the high seas as *res communis*, belonging to all nations, and was extended in the late 20th century to include new areas such as the deep ocean floor made accessible to humans as the result of new technologies. See Alexandre Kiss, "The Common Heritage of Mankind: Utopia or Reality?" *International Journal* 40, no. 3 (1985): 423–41.

41 Manganese nodules, for example, are usually found at depths below 4,000 metres.

42 Some of the industrialised States rejected these provisions, and it was ultimately considered to be 'unworkable'. See Michael C. Wood, "International Seabed Authority: The First Four Years," *The Max Planck Yearbook of United Nations Law Online* 3 (1999): 175–78.

43 Michael Lodge, "The International Seabed Authority and Deep Seabed Mining," *Our Ocean, Our World: United Nations Chronicle* LIV, nos. 1 and 2 (May 2017).

44 World Ocean Review, "Energy"; Lodge, "The International Seabed Authority."

45 Lodge, "The International Seabed Authority." The ISA issues guidelines and licences for mining exploration, which must be sponsored by a State party to UNCLOS and meet certain standards of technological and financial capacity.

46 See for example Louisa Casson, "Four Reasons Why the International Seabed Authority Probably Won't Protect Our Oceans," *Greenpeace* (July 24, 2019), www.greenpeace.org/international/story/23397/four-reasons-why-the-international-seabed-authority-probably-wont-protect-our-oceans/. "The Main Players in the Push Towards Deep-sea Mining," *Reuters* (April 18, 2023), www.reuters.com/business/environment/main-players-push-towards-deep-sea-mining-2023-04-14/#:~:text=THE%20INTERNATIONAL%20SEABED%20AUTHORITY&text=Critics%20say%20that%20its%20dual,and%20accountability%2C%20claims%20it%20denies.

47 Edward Guntrip, "The Common Heritage of Mankind: An Adequate Regime for Managing the Deep Seabed?" *Melbourne Journal of International Law* 4, no. 2 (October 2003). Guntrip notes for example that there is potential for the deep seabed to be used for intelligence gathering and that this use conflicts with the common heritage of mankind principle.

48 The ISA previously adopted regulations for prospecting and exploring the Area, but it has not been able to finalise a Mining Code for seabed exploitation despite many years of negotiations.

49 A group of 600 experts have called for the ISA to pause its consideration of exploitation until critical knowledge gaps have been addressed. Pradeep A. Singh, "The Invocation of the 'Two-Year Rule' at the International Seabed Authority: Legal Consequences and Implications," *The International Journal of Marine and Coastal Law* 37, no. 3 (2022): 375–412, https://doi.org/10.1163/15718085-bja10098.

50 Jonathan Lambert, "Ocean Snail Is First Animal to Be Officially Endangered by Deep-Sea Mining," *Nature* 22 (July 2019).

51 See, for example, International Union for Conservation of Nature (IUCN), "Deep-sea Mining," *Issues Brief* (May 2022), www.iucn.org/resources/issues-brief/deep-sea-mining. Karen McVeigh, "David Attenborough Calls for Ban on 'Devastating' Deep Sea Mining," *The Guardian* (March 13, 2020), www.theguardian.com/environment/2020/mar/12/david-attenborough-calls-for-ban-on-devastating-deep-sea-mining.

52 In 1950 there were only two offshore drilling rigs in the world. By 2020 this had increased to around 7,000 offshore oil and gas drilling platforms. Part of the controversy is the issue of liability, particularly where the infrastructure has been sold or transferred to an owner without the financial capacity to pay the heavy cost of decommissioning: Erika Techera, "Australian Developments in Decommissioning Law and Policy," *Asia-Pacific Journal of Ocean Law and Policy* 7, no. 1 (2022): 119–22.

53 Techera and Chandler, "Offshore Installations."
54 Trevisanut, "Decommissioning of Offshore Installations," 432.
55 Adopted by the International Maritime Organization on 19 October 1989 (IMO Resolution A.672(16), www.imo.org/environment/mainframe.asp? topic_id=1026.
56 Trevisanut, "Decommissioning of Offshore Installations," 435–38.
57 Under UNCLOS (Article 60) a State has the right to build or authorize construction of artificial islands, installations and structures in its exclusive economic zone and continental shelf; they must give warning of their presence; they must be maintained; and any abandoned or disused structures must be removed to ensure safety of navigation, and must give 'due regard' to fishing, protection of the marine environment and the rights and duties of other States. Trevisanut, "Decommissioning of Offshore Installations," 441–45.
58 Shipbreaking involves recycling parts of decommissioned ships using a technique called 'beaching', where workers drive ships onto sandy beaches for dismantling. The practice, which releases hazardous chemicals into the environment, is typically undertaken by industrialised countries on the shores of developing countries such as Bangladesh, India and Pakistan. See for example "Shipbreaking: Campaign Update," *Center for International Environmental Law*, accessed January 12, 2024, www.ciel.org/project-update/shipbreaking/.
59 Trevisanut, "Decommissioning of Offshore Installations," 452–53. K. Bangert, "Environment Protection – Offshore, Oil and Gas Production," in *Maritime Safety – Current Problems of Use of the Baltic Sea*, ed. U. Karpen (Baden-Baden: Nomos Verlagsgesellschaft, 2005), 88.
60 Mark J. Kaiser, Yunke Yu, and Brian Snyder, '"Economic Feasibility of Using Offshore Oil and Gas Structures in the Gulf of Mexico for Platform-based Aquaculture," *Marine Policy* 34, no. 3 (May 2010): 699–707. Peter Macreadie, Ashley M. Fowler, and David J. Booth, "Rigs to Reef: Will the Deep Sea Benefit from Artificial Habitat?" *Frontiers in Ecology and the Environment* 9, no. 8 (2011): 455–61.
61 The Honorable William Elliott of Beaufort, "Carolina Sports, by Land and Water," cited in Chen-Tung Arthur Chen and Wen-Yan Chiau, "Human Uses of the Oceans," in *Earth and Atmospheric Sciences: Oceanography*, ed. Jacques C. J. Nihoul and Chen-Tung Arthur Chen, in *Encyclopedia of Life Support Systems (EOLSS)*, developed under the auspices of the UNESCO (Paris: EOLSS Publishers), chapter 7, www.eolss.net/sample-chapters/C01/E6-18-07.pdf,
62 Macreadie et al., "Rigs to Reef."
63 Techera and Chandler, "Offshore Installations."
64 Erin Blakemore, "Artificial Islands Older Than Stonehenge Stump Scientists," *National Geographic* (June 12, 2019). Richard Fisher and Javier Hirschfeld, "Why We Are in 'The Age of Artificial Islands'," *BBC Future* (January 7, 2022), www.bbc.com/future/article/20220105-why-were-in-the-age-of-artificial-islands.
65 For an excellent discussion of the legal, social and ecological implications of land reclamation in the South China Sea, see Jennifer L. Gaynor, "Liquid Territory, Shifting Sands," in *Blue Legalities: The Life and Laws of the Sea*, ed. Irus Braverman and Elizabeth R. Johnson (Durham: Duke University Press, 2020), 107–27.
66 Alastair Bonnett, *Elsewhere: A Journey into Our Age of Islands* (Chicago: University of Chicago Press, 2020).
67 "The Artificial Islands of Dubai," *Geology.com*, accessed January 12, 2024, https://geology.com/satellite/artificial-islands-of-dubai/.
68 Gaynor, "Liquid Territory, Shifting Sands"; Matthew Southerland, "China's Island Building in the South China Sea: Damage to the Marine Environment, Implications, and International Law," *US-China Economic and Security Review Commission Staff Research Report* (Washington, DC, April 12, 2016), www.uscc.gov/sites/default/files/Research/China%27s%20Island%20Building%20in%20the%20South%20China%20Sea_0.pdf.

Bibliography

Andrews, Nathan, Nathan J. Bennett, Philippe Le Billon, Stephanie J. Green, Andres M. Cisneros-Montemayor, Sandra Amongin, Noella J. Gray, and U. Rashid Sumaila. "Oil, Fisheries and Coastal Communities: A Review of Impacts on the Environment, Livelihoods, Space and Governance." *Energy Research & Social Science* 75 (May 2021). www.sciencedirect.com/science/article/pii/S221462962100102X.

Arctic Council Working Group. "Agreement on Cooperation on Marine Oil Pollution Preparedness and Response in the Arctic." Accessed January 12, 2024. https://eppr.org/resources/agreements/.

Bangert, K. "Environment Protection – Offshore, Oil and Gas Production." In *Maritime Safety – Current Problems of Use of the Baltic Sea*, edited by U. Karpen. Baden-Baden: Nomos Verlagsgesellschaft, 2005.

Blakemore, Erin. "Artificial Islands Older Than Stonehenge Stump Scientists." *National Geographic* (June 12, 2019).

Bonnett, Alastair. *Elsewhere: A Journey into Our Age of Islands*. Chicago: University of Chicago Press, 2020.

Carson, Rachel. "Undersea." *Atlantic Monthly* 78 (1937): 322.

Caspian Environmental Resource Center. "Tehran Convention." Accessed January 12, 2024, https://tehranconvention.org/en.

Casson, Louisa. "Four Reasons Why the International Seabed Authority Probably Won't Protect Our Oceans." *Greenpeace* (July 24, 2019). www.greenpeace.org/international/story/23397/four-reasons-why-the-international-seabed-authority-probably-wont-protect-our-oceans/.

Center for International Environmental Law. "Shipbreaking: Campaign Update." Accessed January 12, 2024. www.ciel.org/project-update/shipbreaking/.

Chabason, L. "Offshore Oil Exploitation: A New Frontier for International Environmental Law." *Institute for Sustainable Development and International Relations* (2011). Accessed April 30, 2024. www.iddri.org/sites/default/files/import/publications/wp-1111_chabason_offshore.pdf.

Chandler, John. *Petroleum Resource Management: How Governments Manage Their Offshore Petroleum Resources*. Cheltenham: Edward Elgar Publishing, 2018.

Chandler, John, David White, Erika J. Techera, Susan Gourvenec, and Scott Draper. "Engineering and Legal Considerations for Decommissioning of Offshore Oil and Gas Infrastructure in Australia." *Ocean Engineering* 131 (2017): 338–47.

Clarke, K. C., and Jeffrey J. Hemphill. "The Santa Barbara Oil Spill, a Retrospective." In *Yearbook of the Association of Pacific Coast Geographers*, 64, no. 1, edited by Darrick Danta. Honolulu: University of Hawai'i Press, 2002.

Craig, Jonathan, Francesco Derali, Fiona MacAulay, and Rasoul Sorkhabi. "The History of the European Oil and Gas Industry (1600s–2000s)." *Geological Society, London, Special Publications* 465, no. 218 (2018): 1–24.

Daley, G. Ben, and Peter Griggs. "Mining the Reefs and Cays: Coral, Guano and Rock Phosphate Extraction in the Great Barrier Reef, Australia, 1844–1940." *Environment and History* 12, no. 4 (2006): 395–433.

Elliott of Beaufort, The Honorable William. "Carolina Sports, by Land and Water." Cited in Chen-Tung Arthur Chen and Wen-Yan Chiau. "Human Uses of the Oceans." In *Earth and Atmospheric Sciences: Oceanography*, edited by Jacques C. J. Nihoul and Chen-Tung Arthur Chen, in *Encyclopedia of Life Support Systems (EOLSS)*, developed under the auspices of the UNESCO (Paris: EOLSS Publishers), chapter 7. www.eolss.net/sample-chapters/C01/E6-18-07.pdf.

Esmaeili, Hossein. "The Protection of Offshore Oil Rigs in International Law (Part I)." *Australian Mining and Petroleum Law Journal* 18 (1999): 241–42.

Fernandez, Tim, and Melinda James. "Editor of Scientific Journal Says Fake Study Linking Whale Deaths to Wind Farms Is 'Deliberate Misinformation." *ABC News* (November 7, 2023). www.abc.net.au/news/2023-11-07/editor-blasts-fake-study-linking-whale-deaths-to-wind-farms/103069922.

Fisher, Richard, and Javier Hirschfeld. "Why We Are in 'The Age of Artificial Islands'." *BBC Future* (January 7, 2022). www.bbc.com/future/article/20220105-why-were-in-the-age-of-artificial-islands.

Galparsoro, Ibon et al. "Reviewing the Ecological Impacts of Offshore Wind Farms." *Ocean Sustainability* 1, no. 1 (2022). https://doi.org/10.1038/s44183-022-00003-5.

Gaynor, Jennifer L. "Liquid Territory, Shifting Sands." In *Blue Legalities: The Life and Laws of the Sea*, edited by Irus Braverman and Elizabeth R. Johnson. Durham: Duke University Press, 2020.

Geology.com. "The Artificial Islands of Dubai." Accessed Jan 12, 2024. https://geology.com/satellite/artificial-islands-of-dubai/.

Guntrip, Edward. "The Common Heritage of Mankind: An Adequate Regime for Managing the Deep Seabed?" *Melbourne Journal of International Law* 4, no. 2 (October 2003).

Howe, R. J. "Evolution of Offshore Drilling and Production Technology." Paper presented to Offshore Technology Conference, Texas, 1986. Accessed April 30, 2024. https://onepetro.org/OTCONF/proceedings-abstract/86OTC/All-86OTC/OTC-5354-MS/49288.

International Maritime Organization. "Special Areas Under MARPOL." Accessed January 12, 2024. www.imo.org/en/OurWork/Environment/Pages/Special-Areas-Marpol.aspx and www.imo.org/en/ourwork/environment/pages/pssas.aspx.

International Union for Conservation of Nature (IUCN). "Deep-Sea Mining." *Issues Brief* (May 2022). www.iucn.org/resources/issues-brief/deep-sea-mining.

Kaiser, Mark J., Yunke Yu, and Brian Snyder. '"Economic Feasibility of Using Offshore Oil and Gas Structures in the Gulf of Mexico for Platform-based Aquaculture." *Marine Policy* 34, no, 3 (May 2010): 699–707.

Kiss, Alexandre. "The Common Heritage of Mankind: Utopia or Reality?" *International Journal* 40, no. 3 (1985): 423–41.

Lambert, Jonathan. "Ocean Snail Is First Animal to Be Officially Endangered by Deep-Sea Mining." *Nature* 22 (July 2019).

Lodge, Michael. "The International Seabed Authority and Deep Seabed Mining." *Our Ocean, Our World: United Nations Chronicle* LIV, nos. 1 and 2 (May 2017).

Macreadie, Peter, Ashley M. Fowler, and David J. Booth. "Rigs to Reef: Will the Deep Sea Benefit from Artificial Habitat?" *Frontiers in Ecology and the Environment* 9, no. 8 (2011): 455–61.

McAdam, Lowell C. "On the Law of the Sea Conventions: Benefits for Submarine Cable Systems." Testimony before the US Senate Foreign Relations Committee (June 28, 2012). www.foreign.senate.gov/imo/media/doc/McAdamTestimony2.pdf.

McVeigh, Karen. "David Attenborough Calls for Ban on 'Devastating' Deep Sea Mining." *The Guardian* (March 13, 2020). www.theguardian.com/environment/2020/mar/12/david-attenborough-calls-for-ban-on-devastating-deep-sea-mining.

Mero, John L. *The Mineral Resources of the Sea*. Amsterdam: Elsevier Publishing Company, 1964.

Murray, J., and A. F. Renard. *Report on the Scientific Results of the Voyage of H.M.S. Challenger during the Years 1873–76: Deep-sea Deposits*. London: Johnson Reprint Company Limited, 1891.

National Oceanic and Atmospheric Administration (US). "Submarine Cables." Accessed April 30, 2024. www.noaa.gov/submarine-cables#:~:text=It%20is%20a%20 common%20 misconception,See%20U.N.

Ocean Conservancy. "The Case against Offshore Drilling in the Arctic." Accessed January 12, 2024. https://oceanconservancy.org/protecting-the-arctic/risky-drilling/.

OSPAR Convention. Accessed January 12, 2024. www.ospar.org/convention.
Pardo, Arvid. *The Common Heritage: Selected Papers on Oceans and World Order, 1967–1974*. Valetta: Malta University Press, 1975.
Redgwell, C. "Mind the Gap in the GAIRS: The Role of Other Instruments in LOSC Regime Implementation in the Offshore Energy Sector." *The International Journal of Marine and Coastal Law* 29 (2014): 600–21.
Rozwadowski, Helen. *Fathoming the Ocean: The Discovery and Exploration of the Deep Sea*. Cambridge, MA: Harvard University Press, 2005.
Rozwadowski, Helen. *Vast Expanses: A History of the Oceans*. London: Reaktion Books, 2018.
Shapovalova, Daria. "Can International Law Protect the Arctic from Oil Spills?" *The Arctic Institute* (March 26, 2019). www.thearcticinstitute.org/international-law-protect-arctic-oil-spills/.
Singh, Pradeep A. "The Invocation of the 'Two-Year Rule' at the International Seabed Authority: Legal Consequences and Implications." *The International Journal of Marine and Coastal Law* 37, no. 3 (2022): 375–412.
Southerland, Matthew. "China's Island Building in the South China Sea: Damage to the Marine Environment, Implications, and International Law." *US-China Economic and Security Review Commission Staff Research Report, Washington, DC* (April 12, 2016). www.uscc.gov/sites/default/files/Research/China%27s%20Island%20Building%20in%20the%20South%20China%20Sea_0.pdf.
Sullivan, Will. "Massive Arctic Oil Drilling Project Gets the Green Light." *Smithsonian Magazine* (March 14, 2023). Accessed January 12, 2024. www.smithsonianmag.com/smart-news/a-controversial-arctic-oil-drilling-project-is-one-step-closer-to-moving-forward-180981570/#:~:text=A%20 controversial%20plan%20for%20 oil,per%20CNN's%20Ella%20Nilsen,
Techera, Erika J. "Australian Developments in Decommissioning Law and Policy." *Asia-Pacific Journal of Ocean Law and Policy* 7, no. 1 (2022): 119–22.
Techera, Erika J., and John Chandler. "Offshore Installations, Decommissioning and Artificial Reefs: Do Current Legal Framework Best Serve the Marine Environment?" *Marine Policy* 59 (2015): 53–60.
The Eighth Wonder of the World – the Atlantic Cable. New York: Kimmel & Forster, 1866.
The Geological Society. "Treasures of the Abyss." *Geoscientist Online*, London (May2013). www.geolsoc.org.uk/Geoscientist/Archive/May-2013/Treasures-from-the-abyss.
"The Main Players in the Push Towards Deep-sea Mining." *Reuters* (April 18, 2023). www.reuters.com/business/environment/main-players-push-towards-deep-sea-mining-2023-04-14/#:~:text=THE%20INTERNATIONAL%20SEABED%20AUTHORITY&text=Critics%20say%20that%20its%20dual,and%20accountability%2C%20claims%20it%20denies.
Tranfield, M. Wynn. "Unspooling the Legacy of Submarine Cables." *DttP: Documents to the People*. Chicago: American Library Association, 2018. Accessed March 15, 2024. https://journals.ala.org/index.php/dttp/article/view/6826/9185.
Trevisanut, Seline. "Decommissioning of Offshore Installations: A Fragmented and Ineffective International Regulatory Framework." In *The Law of the Seabed: Access, Uses, and Protection of Seabed Resources*, edited by Catherine Banet. Leiden: Koninklijke Brill, 2020.
UNEP. "West and Central Africa." Accessed January 12, 2024. www.unep.org/explore-topics/oceans-seas/what-we-do/working-regional-seas/regional-seas-programmes/west-and.
United States Coast Guard, US Department of Homeland Security. "Oil Pollution Act of 1990 (OPA)." Accessed April 30, 2024. www.uscg.mil/Mariners/National-Pollution-Funds-Center/About_NPFC/opa/.

US Department of Justice. "US and Five Gulf States Reach Historic Settlement with BP to Resolve Civil Lawsuit over Deepwater Horizon Oil Spill." *Office of Public Affairs Press Release* (October 5, 2015). www.justice.gov/opa/pr/us-and-five-gulf-states-reach-historic-settlement-bp-resolve-civil-lawsuit-over-deepwater.

Wood, Michael C. "International Seabed Authority: The First Four Years." *The Max Planck Yearbook of United Nations Law Online* 3 (1999): 175–78.

World Ocean Review. "Energy." Accessed April 30, 2024. https://worldoceanreview.com/en/wor-1/energy/fossil-fuels/.

Wright, Glen, Sandy Kerr, and Kate Johnson, eds. *Ocean Energy: Governance Challenges for Wave and Tidal Stream Technologies*. Abingdon: Routledge, 2018.

Part III

The ocean as ecosystem

7 The fragile ocean

Protecting species and ecosystems

It is a curious situation that the sea, from which life first arose should now be threatened by the activities of one form of that life. But the sea, though changed in a sinister way, will continue to exist; the threat is rather to life itself.

Rachel Carson, The Sea Around Us

Overview

The Steller's Sea Cow (*Hydrodamalis gigas*) was declared extinct in 27 short years after its 'discovery' by Georg Wilhelm Steller.[1] Following this early loss, the fur industry claimed the Japanese sea lion (*Zalophus japonicus*) in the 1950s, and the Caribbean monk seal (*Neomonachus tropicalis*) was declared extinct in 2008 (although it had not been seen for 50 years).[2] Some shoreline species also suffered a similar fate, including the first invertebrate – the Eelgrass Limpet (*Lottia alveus*) – whose demise is linked to the loss of the eelgrass on which it lived and fed.[3]

Although only 15 marine species are said to have become extinct due to human activity,[4] the swift and early eradication of the Steller's Sea Cow should have signalled the fragility of the ocean.[5] By the early 20th century, industrialisation saw the harvesting of marine species expand from small-scale commercial ventures to global enterprises with devastating and growing consequences for marine and coastal species. Since then, oceanic flora and fauna have been most directly impacted by harvesting and hunting, but also indirectly through habitat loss, marine pollution and anthropogenic infrastructure development, both coastal (including houses, hotels, ports, seawalls and groins) and offshore (including shipping, petroleum and mineral extraction and submarine cables) and related construction activities (such as dredging and drilling).

Over time, scientists have acquired considerable knowledge of the marine environment and life within it, yet it is thought that perhaps as many as 90% of oceanic species remain undiscovered.[6] Nevertheless, what scientific research has proven is that escalating damage to known flora, fauna and habitats has become a biodiversity crisis likely to result in a sixth mass extinction,[7] and that urgent

DOI: 10.4324/9781003005261-11

action is needed to prevent marine defaunation.[8] Governments have attempted to control and regulate human activities to limit impacts using law as a policy tool, guided by scientific awareness and emerging knowledge, with varying success. Marine environmental law focused on wildlife conservation has involved two different regulatory approaches: (1) laws that focus on species (and later also ecosystems) with rules for their conservation, management and in some cases, restoration; and (2) area-based laws for specific marine and coastal spaces, habitats and geographic regions.[9] When applied separately, these two approaches involve choices to be made that are not necessarily based on the needs and functions of species and ecosystems. For species, their overall health is inherently linked to habitat areas required for survival and/or dependent upon broader ecosystem interactions. Although early environmental laws separated the two approaches, lawmakers have subsequently applied them in tandem, as will be seen later, in an attempt to approach conservation in more holistic ways.

This chapter journeys through the evolution of species-based marine environmental law from traditional and customary approaches to early conservation laws and more sophisticated and holistic wildlife regimes. The focus of this chapter is squarely on conservation of species and ecosystems, while Chapter 4 explores living resources that are fished or otherwise harvested, and Chapter 8 addresses area-based conservation approaches.

Customary conservation and early legal arrangements

There is little doubt that early human communities adopted traditional resource management practices based on tenure (ownership or control of land and water), traditional knowledge (including ecological knowledge of species) and customary law (unwritten social lores and cultural norms that govern behaviour).[10] These traditional approaches were often based on cultural beliefs about ancestral relationships with the marine environment and its creatures, and 'shared reverence for the sacred'.[11] Where they were underpinned by a strong underlying stewardship ethic, they may have played a part in conservation and/or controlled and sustainable exploitation.[12] In other contexts, they were adopted to avoid conflict and facilitate trade, and sometimes led to over-exploitation and negative marine ecological impacts.[13] Interestingly, the types of legal tools utilised are similar to those used in western legal frameworks today: controlling who can undertake activities, how much can be taken and where and at what times of the year.

During the 17th and 18th centuries, as maritime nations were expanding their international empires and establishing colonies, many of these traditional approaches were supplanted by systems focused on profit-making supported by common and civil (rather than customary) law systems.[15] Although some of these traditional approaches are being restored today in some islands and continental

Case study – marine conservation in the South Pacific

Prior to European colonisation, customary law in the South Pacific involved traditional reef and lagoon tenure. Clans or groups, led by chiefs, controlled and managed land and fishing rights from the beach to the outer reefs, and in some cases beyond the reef into deeper waters. It was the chief who regulated marine resources. A range of customary fishing regulations and conservation measures were used to sustainably manage marine resources. These included harvesting and/or eating of certain species by different groups or genders, closing of areas to fishing and other activities (e.g., *tabu, tapu* and *kapu* areas), seasonal restrictions, allowing some catch to escape or be held in enclosures until needed (e.g., use of fish ponds), prohibitions on taking small or young members of a species, restrictions on taking seabirds or turtles and/or their eggs. This range of rules – who could fish, what could be fished, when fishing or harvesting was allowed and where it could occur – are remarkably similar to fishing and marine conservation rules that all legal jurisdictions still utilise today.[14]

coastal States in common with other customary laws, they rarely operate in isolation and western legislative models are frequently applied alongside them.[16]

In other parts of the world, a few early laws could be said to be conservation-based where they regulated the harvesting or hunting of particular species. These were predominantly related to terrestrial species, although some laws included fish.[17] For the most part, however, these laws focused on restricting harvesting and outlawing poaching so that stocks could be maintained for the future or to benefit another economic sector.[18]

The evolution of species-based laws

Escalating impacts on wildlife in the 18th century led to the extinction of seabirds such as the Great Auk (*Pinguinus impennis*) in 1844,[19] and the Labrador Duck (*Camptorhynchus labradorius*) in 1878.[20] In some cases the cause was habitat loss, but the main impact was hunting for ornamental feathers, which were used to adorn hats. Public outrage in the US led to the establishment of one of the world's first environmental non-governmental organisations (NGO) – the Audubon Society.[21] The legal response was the US *Lacey Act of 1900*, which not only preserved wildlife and outlawed poaching but also controlled movements across state borders, which ultimately prevented the introduction of non-native species.[22]

Figure 7.1 A woman wearing a 'Chanticleer' hat made of bird feathers, circa 1912. (Photo by Bain News Service; George Grantham Bain Collection, US Library of Congress, Prints and Photographs Division, Washington DC, Digital Id: cph 3b08931.)

One of the first multinational agreements was the *International Convention for the Protection of Birds that Are Useful for Agriculture* (1902), which provided unconditional protection for 'useful' birds (e.g., insect-eaters) prohibiting the killing or capturing of them and the destruction, collection, or sale of eggs and nests.[23] Yet simultaneously, the Convention permitted the shooting and destruction of birds 'noxious' to agriculture (e.g., the annexed list refers to some marine-related species such as sea eagles, pelicans and cormorants). This early agreement highlights several regulatory approaches that persist in international conservation agreements today: (1) the use of lists to categorise species into groupings with differing rules for each; (2) the adoption of temporal restrictions such as seasons during which particular rules apply that permit or further restrict certain activities (e.g., hunting/shooting seasons and protections during breeding or nesting); and (3) differing rules during the biological cycle and steps in the supply chain (e.g., protection of habitats, nests, eggs, young and mature animals, as well as regulations on setting traps, killing or harming a species, collecting but not harming, and possessing and/or selling live or dead animals).

In the first half of the 20th century there were other, albeit limited, examples of international agreements for the conservation of certain species. These instruments became necessary for species that crossed jurisdictional boundaries, or where impacts could not be controlled by one State alone. Because of their high mobility, birds (including seabirds) were some of the first subjects. The *Migratory Bird Treaty* (1916) between Canada and the US, for example, utilised species lists with declared refuge areas, seasonal restrictions and export controls, as well as exceptions for harvesting by Indigenous peoples for certain traditional purposes.[24]

The *Antarctic Treaty* (1959) stands out as a regional agreement that took a conservation approach from the outset, focusing on the use of Antarctica for peaceful purposes and scientific investigation.[25] It led to the early adoption of a conservation instrument – the *Agreed Measures for the Conservation of Antarctic Fauna and Flora* (1964).[26] However, the first treaties to specifically focus on conservation were not adopted until the 1970s, triggered in part by growing scientific concern as well as global public pressure and grassroots activism as part of the broader environmental movement that gathered momentum during that decade. Some treaties catalysed new domestic and national laws, and others were themselves triggered by local events and circumstances. For example, growing awareness of hunting pressure on polar bears led to calls for an international agreement in 1965.[27] This eventually led to the adoption of the *Polar Bear Agreement* (1973) by the five States with Arctic territory inhabited by polar bears. The Agreement was innovative for its time, as in addition to prohibiting the capturing, killing and sale of polar bears, for example, it also included novel terminology requiring States to:

> protect the *ecosystems* of which polar bears are a part, with special attention to habitat components such as *denning and feeding sites* and *migration patterns*, and . . . [to] manage polar bear populations in accordance with *sound conservation practices* based on the *best available scientific data* [emphasis added].[28]

It also created exceptions for Indigenous peoples with traditional hunting rights but restricted these local peoples by requiring them to use traditional methods and means (e.g., not high-powered guns and helicopters). The Agreement is an early success story, resulting in polar bears being 'among the few large carnivores that are still found in roughly their original habitat and range – and in some places, in roughly their natural numbers'.[29] The regime also demonstrates how an international agreement can continue to 'live' and evolve to address new threats such as climate change. In this case, parties to the *Polar Bear Agreement* have adopted the *Circumpolar Action Plan* (2015), which facilitates adaptive polar bear management and ongoing research.[30]

International species conservation laws

Convention on International Trade in Endangered Species of Wild Fauna and Flora (1973) (CITES)

The *Polar Bear Agreement* signalled a new international law conservation focus, but it was limited to only one species. The growing market in luxury goods, including animal trophies and skins, ivory products, and exotic plants and animals, led the UN General Assembly to agree in 1963 on the need for a new convention to regulate import, export and transit of rare and threatened wildlife.[31] The *Convention on International Trade in Endangered Species of Wild Fauna and Flora* (1973) (CITES) was the response. CITES was one of the first instruments with the potential to regulate the conservation and sustainable use of all species on Earth.[32] The International Union for the Conservation of Nature (IUCN) NGO became the organisation providing key advice on species conservation status, including through the *IUCN Red List of Threatened Species*, a globally endorsed resource of scientific data.[33]

Although CITES focuses only on species, and not ecosystems or habitats, it has global reach (i.e., 184 States have ratified it, and moreover it covers trade between parties and non-parties), and has the potential to include all species (over 42,000 are currently listed and more are consistently added).[34] CITES listings include many marine animals including all marine turtles, the majority of whales and multiple corals, sharks, rays and other fish, as well as some seabirds and crustaceans. The CITES regime also contains several innovative approaches, protecting look-a-like species (to prevent accidental trade), and including parts or derivatives of the animals or plants (so that end-products, such as jewellery and medicines using bones and teeth, were covered).

However, whilst CITES has been partially effective in protecting species, there is little doubt that illegal trade continues. Ensuring the success of international treaties is difficult given the challenges of enforcement, but the CITES regime includes critically important elements – implementation and compliance measures – not incorporated into many earlier agreements.[35] A step-wise approach is applied where non-compliance is identified: initial identification of compliance issues, support and guidance on implementing measures to achieve compliance, mandated monitoring and reporting, targeted support for parties with persistent compliance challenges, and application of sanctions in the form of suspension of trade where non-compliance persists. In addition, the Secretariat works with other UN agencies through the *International Consortium on Combating Wildlife Crime* to strengthen criminal justice systems.[36] The main limitation of CITES is that it only regulates international trade but does not protect endangered species inside national borders, a task left to individual States to address.

Convention on Migratory Species (1979)

Another critical international law development was the adoption of the *Convention on Migratory Species* (1979).[37] This Convention facilitated State cooperation to conserve animals that migrate across national boundaries on land, in water and in the air. The Convention also used a listing approach with species being included on one or both of Appendices I and II. Endangered migratory species are placed onto Appendix I, with range States[38] obliged to take conservation actions (e.g., prohibit taking and prevent, remove, minimise and/or control activities that have adverse impacts or factors endangering the species). This Convention took a slightly broader approach than CITES by requiring states to endeavour 'to conserve and . . . restore those habitats of the species which are of importance in removing the species from danger of extinction'.[39] Appendix II includes species with an unfavourable conservation status,[40] which need international cooperative agreements for conservation and management. These agreements can take the form of binding conservation instruments amongst relevant nations and/or non-binding memoranda of understanding. The CMS has been ratified by 160 nations and the Appendices include more than 1300 species.[41]

Five of the seven existing CMS Agreements relate to species that migrate in oceans or seas, and/or that are sea- or water-birds.[42] There are 19 MOUs including for sharks, dugongs, manatees, cetaceans, seals, cranes and other migratory birds.[43] Nevertheless, some States are not a party to the Convention leaving regulatory gaps across Asia (Japan, South Korea and China) and North America (Canada, Mexico and the US) although some are participating non-parties. In addition, many migratory species are not listed (e.g., only one butterfly species is included) or are not the subject of agreements (e.g., insects), and these omissions limit the Convention's effectiveness.[44]

More holistic responses

UN Convention on the Law of the Sea (UNCLOS)

As the global environmental movement progressed, and aided by the establishment of UNEP, international environmental law expanded and evolved during the last two decades of the 20th century. The adoption of the *UN Convention on the Law of the Sea* (UNCLOS) in 1982 was a major global victory in terms of settling the law of the sea including disputed maritime zones. As explained in Chapter 2, UNCLOS had taken three decades to negotiate and, although the territorial sea and high seas zones pre-dated it, UNCLOS included several restrictions on previous freedoms and in new maritime areas. For example, States were permitted to pass laws on innocent passage through the territorial sea on the basis of conservation of living resources,[45] and on the high seas, all States are required to cooperate in conserving living resources including in setting catch limits for harvested species[46] and preventing damage to the flora and fauna of the seabed.[47]

The Exclusive Economic Zone (EEZ) was an entirely new invention and refers to coastal States' role in the conservation of living resources largely focusing on fishing restrictions.[48] Relevantly, Part XII UNCLOS obliged all States to protect and preserve the marine environment in all maritime zones[49] whilst also recognising States' sovereign right to exploit natural resources in their territories.[50] This tension remains a key concern and driver of marine degradation and species decline in many areas of the world. The Articles that follow focus on pollution, hazards and alien species but do not explain how sustainability can be achieved – indeed they do not use the word 'sustainability' at all.

International Convention for the Regulation of Whaling (ICRW)

Another key event in 1982 was the setting of zero catch limits for whales adopted as a Resolution of the International Whaling Commission under the *International Convention for the Regulation of Whaling* (ICRW).[51] As explained in Chapter 4, ICRW was (and remains) a fisheries treaty. In 1982 the ICRW decided to 'pause' commercial whale harvesting for the 1985/6 whaling season, and in 1986 adopted a moratorium on whaling.

UN Sustainable Development Goals (SDGs)

Following the 1987 Brundtland Report, *Our Common Future*,[52] and the subsequent adoption of the Rio Declaration and the *UN Conference on Environment and Development* (UNCED),[53] the concept of 'sustainable development' received global endorsement. Sustainable development sought to balance economic, environmental and socio-cultural concerns, and this principle has persisted through the Sustainable Development Goals (SDGs).[54] In practice, however, Earth's terrestrial environments often receive less attention than human-centred economic, social and developmental concerns, and this is equally the case for the marine environment.[55]

Convention on Biological Diversity (1992) (CBD)

Also adopted at UNCED was the *Convention on Biological Diversity* (1992) (CBD) with its goals of conservation of biological diversity (which is much broader than species alone), sustainable use of its components, and the fair and equitable sharing of the benefits.[56] The CBD did not use lists of endangered species and ecosystems with obligations attached but rather encouraged conservation of biodiversity (preferably in the natural environment rather than zoos or wildlife parks), the adoption of national regulations for the use of resources, and the establishment of protected areas and legislation for the protection of threatened species.[57]

The Convention included contemporary principles and scientific concepts such as ecosystem-based approaches, integrated and adaptive management

Case study: Global Biodiversity Framework Targets

Target 4 – Ensure urgent management actions to halt human induced extinction of known threatened species and for the recovery and conservation of species . . .

Target 5 – Ensure that the use, harvesting and trade of wild species is sustainable, safe and legal, preventing overexploitation, minimizing impacts on non-target species and ecosystems . . .

Target 6 – Eliminate, minimize, reduce and or mitigate the impacts of invasive alien species on biodiversity and ecosystem services by . . . reducing the rates of introduction and establishment of other known or potential invasive alien species by at least 50 per cent by 2030 . . .

Target 9 – Ensure that the management and use of wild species are sustainable, thereby providing social, economic and environmental benefits for people, especially those in vulnerable situations and those most dependent on biodiversity . . .

techniques.[58] Importantly, CBD Article 8 recognised the value of Indigenous peoples and their traditional ecological knowledge and practices.[59] Its provisions, however, were broad and in many respects aspirational, with treaty requirements for States to take action as far as 'possible and appropriate'. Nevertheless, the CBD advanced environmental law by requiring States to submit National Reports and develop National Biodiversity and Strategic Action Plans, all of which are publicly accessible.[60] These were relatively novel legal provisions that supported compliance, transparency and accountability of member States.

Furthermore, the CBD has led to the establishment of global, quantitative conservation targets: the Aichi Targets that were to be achieved by 2020,[61] and the more recent Global Biodiversity Framework targets for 2030.[62] Although the targets are not legally binding on nations, they set ambitious goals and, in doing so, incentivise greater action. Neither of these initiatives set quantitative targets for conservation of marine and coastal species, yet several focused on species conservation more broadly (see textbox).

Two global crises

The biodiversity crisis

Whether due to delayed action, the overwhelming complexity of conservation obligations, limited scientific knowledge, and/or mismatches between science and legal responses, by the turn of the 21st century biodiversity indicators were rapidly worsening, including in the world's oceans, seas and shorelines.[63] Although the biodiversity crisis had been identified much earlier,[64] by the 2000s scientific publications increasingly pointed to the severity of the extinction crisis[65] and its effects on coastal and marine ecosystem functions.[66] Not only were marine species being over-harvested, but they were also impacted by habitat loss and environmental degradation more broadly. In addition, new threats were emerging as significant, including climate change and invasive species – both human induced.

Although research suggests that far fewer marine species have gone extinct than terrestrial ones, scientists and others have expressed concern that the pattern of exponential extinctions experienced by land-based species may already (or soon) be occurring in global oceans.[67] This is based in part on findings that several marine species, whilst persisting in small numbers in restricted areas, have already become functionally extinct at local levels (through the loss of species in particular geographic ranges), at ecological scales (where the species is no longer sufficiently abundant to perform their functional role), and commercially (below the level they can be economically harvested).[68] These extinctions have dire consequences for marine and coastal food webs and ecosystems. From a human perspective, they pose serious threats to (1) food insecurity (given the heavy reliance many people place on protein drawn from oceans); (2) related livelihoods and economies; (3) non-consumptive effects (loss of amenity, sacred and religious species, as well as resources for socio-cultural practices and objects); and (4) the contribution they make to mitigating climate change (loss of nature-based mitigation and adaptation). Furthermore, as marine species and ecosystems become extinct, the ability to acquire new knowledge through scientific research is also lost, compounding the existing problem of data deficiencies and limited knowledge of deep seas species and ecosystems.[69]

The climate crisis

The expanding use of fossil fuels during the 20th century has led to rapid increases in greenhouse (GHG) emissions, including significantly higher concentrations of CO_2, in Earth's atmosphere causing long-term shifts in temperature and weather patterns.[70] Scientists now recognise the crucial role that oceans play in absorbing up to 25% of global anthropogenic CO_2 emissions. Increasing CO_2 levels therefore have serious implications for the marine environment, including increased water temperatures, ocean acidification and sea level rise. For shorelines, too, these changes are contributing to more extreme weather events, leading to storm surges, inundation and coastal erosion. In turn, species and ecosystems (and their habitats) are directly impacted by the changing marine and coastal environments, disrupting biological processes and life cycles.[71]

Growing international concerns in the 1980s about the impacts of climate change led to the adoption of the *UN Framework Convention on Climate Change*

(1992)[72] and later *Paris Agreement* (2015).[73] However, neither agreements have as yet resulted in the stabilisation of GHG emissions, although no doubt emissions would be even greater without these instruments. The Nationally Determined Contribution (NDC) documents, which States are obliged to submit under the Paris Agreement, demonstrate that many nations focus quite significantly on the conservation of marine and coastal species as part of nature-based solutions to climate change mitigation. 'Blue carbon', for example, utilises the ability of marine flora to absorb or sequester CO_2, thereby operating as a carbon sink, while adaptation techniques utilise the power of marine flora to absorb energy from the oceans and prevent coastal erosion and storm surges.[74] It is anticipated that the global climate change law regime provides fresh impetus for marine and coastal species conservation, and in particular draws attention to the value of marine plants such as mangroves, seagrasses (for coastal protection and as a carbon sink) and diatoms (the world's smallest plants) in carbon sequestration.

Other impacts on species and ecosystems

Invasive species

Invasive species remain a growing challenge for marine ecosystems and economies as well as posing major risks to public health. Cholera, for example, has long been associated with coastal and estuarine environments, and some experts have speculated that ballast water from Bangladesh was the cause of at least one outbreak of the disease in Peru.[75] It is certainly the case that ballast water was implicated, leading to a new global treaty to better manage ballast water from ships.[76] Nevertheless, implementing the provisions is costly and likely to prove difficult for many port States. This is concerning, given that many nations have adopted a blue economy agenda, which depends, at least in part, on expanding shipping and oceanic transport.[77] In other cases, marine invasive species are transported on the outside hulls of vessels and, beyond regulating the chemicals used to prevent biofouling, limited laws address this issue.[78]

Marine genetic resources

The first seamounts were first discovered in the 19th century, but technology limitations prevented detailed exploration until the late 20th century.[79] Seamounts, found in deep ocean waters, are hotspots of biological diversity, attracting commercial fishers seeking to harvest some of the more valuable species such as migratory tuna and deep water species such as orange roughy. The Global Census of Marine Life on Seamounts has estimated that there may be as many as 100,000 seamounts over 1,000 metres high in the world's oceans, and many more smaller ones. Few of these have been studied, but they are potentially home to many new species, some of which may be scientifically significant.[80]

UNCLOS includes provisions for regulating the exploitation of non-living resources (including nodules of minerals) on the seabed but not living resources. A significant development in 2023 was the adoption of the Implementing Agreement under UNCLOS known as the High Seas Treaty.[81] One part of that agreement relates to marine genetic resources found in the high seas, and another section provides a mechanism for creating high seas marine protected areas.[82] The High Seas Treaty fills an important gap by providing a legal regime for access and benefit sharing of living resources in the high seas, excluding fish stocks already regulated under fishing agreements.[83] Hydrothermal vents, for example, are found in the deep sea, mostly located in mid-oceanic, high seas areas.[84] They are naturally occurring fissures in the seabed from which hot water discharges, which creates a biologically more productive area than other parts of the deep sea. Unique life forms have been discovered around hydrothermal vents, yet no international law exists to protect them, despite concerns about the impact of marine scientific research and potential future impact of mining.[85] It remains to be seen how effective this international law will be, given the ongoing tension between nations favouring extraction over conservation.

Marine-based tourism

Even for species and ecosystems where deliberate abuses of them have ceased – whales, seals, and turtles for example are no longer regularly harvested from the ocean – humans continue to wreak damage upon them through other pursuits such as tourism and recreation. Seaside recreation became increasingly popular from the 19th century. Since then it has grown into a major worldwide industry and has significantly impacted many coastal species and areas.[86] Paradoxically, it was the emergence of ecotourism in the 1980s that resulted in increasing numbers of visitors seeking out marine mammals in their natural habitats.[87] Marine-based tourism has boomed, with activities such as whale watching, swimming with sea lions and sharks, snorkelling and diving becoming increasingly popular. The accessibility and affordability of these activities has hastened the growth of the businesses built upon them.

Protected area management tools are often used to protect 'sites of fidelity' – areas of the ocean that marine species tend to return to (see Chapter 8) – although industry-based codes of conduct have been more effective in preventing negative impacts by controlling participant and vessel numbers, restricting feeding, baiting, touching and flash photography, and limiting the time vessels and tourists can interact with species.[88] No global treaty exists for eco-tourism and, although the CMS and IWC have endorsed some strategies and tools,[89] best practice legal measures have been distilled and shared amongst nations, most often by NGOs.[90] This is an area where international law could play a valuable role in the future, particularly by setting minimum enforceable standards.

Innovations and novel concepts

As outlined earlier, marine conservation law has incrementally changed over the decades since 1972 and continues to do so. While UNCLOS supports an exploitation-based approach to the marine environment, attempts have been made to embed conservation concepts drawn from western science such as ecosystem-based and adaptive management practices, although these have had limited effectiveness to date. There are also opportunities for greater use of satellite and other remote technologies for monitoring and enforcement of law but, as a generalisation, technology has tended to work against conservation and sustainable use of marine environments, as opposed to terrestrial environments.[91] For example, innovations in ship design and advanced navigation equipment have allowed vessels to operate farther offshore and in extreme weather settings; echo locators and fish aggregation devices, along with hook and netting technologies, facilitate larger harvests from deeper waters; and advances in factory ships and refrigeration allow catches to be processed and packaged offshore.[92]

Furthermore, many new technologies have been developed by industrialised nations, which have often reaped the rewards of their use to the detriment of developing nations. This has not gone unrecognised, with several UN treaty regimes and non-binding instruments supporting marine technology transfer to less developed nations, with a goal of encouraging all States to benefit from them.[93] Yet technology has a greater role to play in conservation and sustainable offshore activities, particularly in the collation of existing datasets with tools for data mining,[94] the use of autonomous vehicles to explore, map and depict the bathymetry of the ocean,[95] and remote sensing (from drones or satellites) to track and monitor species and human activities, including surveillance to support law enforcement.[96] Other possibilities include amending the scope of existing treaties. The *World Heritage Convention*, for example, could be expanded to allow for World Heritage species as well as places,[97] and extended to conserve what exists now to include restoring degraded ecosystems and species.[98]

More radical options include giving rights to non-human species as a way to achieve ocean justice.[99] An underlying stewardship ethic, which could provide a basis for animal rights and justice for nature, is absent in many contemporary marine conservation laws, despite being common in traditional systems and having existed at the international level in the 1970s. There have been calls for rights to be given to nature as they are to humans, recognising that species and ecosystems are not merely property to be owned by people or nations. Constitutional rights of nature were adopted in Ecuador in 2008, and rights have been granted, for example, to rivers including the Ganges and Yamuna (India), Rio Altrato (Colombia) and Whanganui (New Zealand).[100] To date, however, no non-human marine species have been given such rights. There have been court proceedings in which it was argued – largely unsuccessfully – that some animals should have similar legal rights as people.[101] Scholars working in the field of the rights of nature have suggested that granting such rights is potentially a way to address the biodiversity crisis.[102] Despite the great reverence for oceans, seas and shorelines in some cultures, and the regard paid to certain charismatic marine fauna, it seems unlikely that the rights of nature will become a widely accepted approach in the foreseeable future. Nevertheless, applying justice principles to extend the right to a healthy environment to a 'human right to nature' may well be possible, albeit challenging.[103]

Conclusion

There is little doubt that global efforts to control and manage human activities to limit impacts have had some positive outcomes and halted the decline of selected marine and coastal species. Success stories include the sea otter, thought to be extinct due to hunting in the early 20th century, which was rediscovered in 1938 and has since been protected and is now thriving.[104] Yet, as the current extinction crisis demonstrates, marine environmental laws are far from fully effective, given the sluggish reactionary nature of law, the persistence of the myth that ocean resources are limitless, and the preference given to industries and economic outputs over conservation.

Evidence of species decline and (near) collapses have brought attention to the plight of animals and plants, and then laws developed that seek to respond to the risks be they harvesting, habitat loss, or trade. This piecemeal approach has led to an 'horrendogram'[105] of marine laws and policies and the need for more integrated responses has been highlighted in environmental law principles.[106] Legal efforts to address marine species conservation and biodiversity loss can best be described as reactive with few proactive measures taken – with the exception perhaps of the principle of environmental impact assessment.[107] Furthermore, cultural attitudes play a significant role, with preference being given to marine megafauna and charismatic species in industrialised nations. As noted earlier, many Indigenous and traditional peoples maintain belief systems involving totem animals that include a wider range of species. Nonetheless, contemporary laws seem to favour species that we use and those we revere over those we fear.[108] Yet species such as zooplankton are ecosystem engineers, critical for marine life, and are impacted by human activities such as seismic survey methods.[109] Harnessing public support for conserving marine species and ecosystems, whether on religious, cultural, ethical or philosophical bases, will be critical. Nevertheless, as noted earlier, while the history of whale conservation may be seen as an outstanding example of successfully harnessing public sentiment, it is proving far more difficult to generate enthusiasm for marine megafauna such as tuna and sharks. Even where there is a history of public affection for species, such as seashells and corals, they can become endangered as a result of indiscriminate harvesting.[110]

As the extinction crisis worsens, it remains to be seen whether the dominant approach of listing species for protection and management based heavily on their conservation status will remain appropriate. Choices may need to be made about which species to conserve, and therefore laws will need to include new ways to prioritise action. One way forward may be to include a criterion based on the breadth of functions that a species delivers: those species that provide multiple functional services to associated or dependent plants, animals and ecosystems (other than humans), as well as contributing to overall marine and coastal health, may need to be conserved and managed ahead of others (see, for example, Antarctic krill conservation in Chapter 8). For example, many top predators play a critical role in maintaining healthy populations of other species (by removing weak individuals and thereby keeping populations strong), coastal plant ecosystems provide breeding and nursery grounds to myriad species, and other animals are critical in removing waste and toxins. It is likely, however, that such an approach would be skewed to favour those species providing ecosystem goods and services of value to humans.

We have already learnt much from species. Biomimicry[111] is a growing field, with researchers continuing to develop new technologies based on, for example, the mechanics of octopus suckers, the antifreeze properties of deep sea fish blood, and the spiral architecture of mantis shrimp clubs.[112] Of course, it is not only what we know, but what we do not know that is at risk. With estimates that hundreds of thousands and maybe millions of species remain undiscovered, a critical question is whether current marine conservation laws are adequate to prevent negative impacts on known and unknown species. We must ensure we have the best regimes in place so that oceanic wildlife remains extant for future generations to explore and discover.

Notes

1 It was 'discovered' in 1741 along coastal areas in the North Pacific Ocean and by 1768 it was declared to be extinct: Josh Davis, "Steller's Sea Cow: The First Historical Extinction of a Marine Mammal at Human Hands," accessed December 1, 2023, www.nhm.ac.uk/discover/stellers-sea-cow-first-historical-extinction-of-marine-mammal-at-human-hands.html. Steller was a German zoologist on a Russian sea otter hunting expedition captained by Vitus Bering, and he is the only scientist to have recorded seeing the animals alive. The Steller's Sea Cow is said to be the first historical extinction of a marine species due to human hunting. Other terrestrial extinctions occurred prior to that, such as the Madagascan hippos 1,000 years ago, moa birds in New Zealand 600 years ago, and the dodo from Mauritius in the 1600s.

2 "The Red List of Threatened Species," *IUCN*, accessed December 1, 2023, www.iucnredlist.org/.

3 J. T. Carlton et al., "The First Historical Extinction of a Marine Invertebrate in an Ocean Basin: The Demise of the Eelgrass Limpet Lottia alveus," *Biological Bulletin* 180, no. 1 (1991): 72–80. Only one marine fish has been completely eradicated – The New Zealand grayling (*Prototroctes oxyrhynchus*) (upokororo) was declared extinct in 2018 although last sighted in 1923. The grayling is amphidromous, meaning that it spawns in freshwater rivers before migrating to the sea and returning to freshwater to reproduce.

4 D. Mccauley et al., "Marine Defaunation: Animal Loss in the Global Ocean," *Science* 347, no. 6219 (2015): 1255641.
5 Larry A. Nielsen, "The Evolution of Fisheries Management Philosophy," *Marine Fisheries Review* (1976): 15–23.
6 Pelagic and coastal life, for example, is far better understood than species and ecosystems in the deep ocean and polar regions.
7 Robert H. Cowie, Philippe Bouchet, and Benoît Fontaine, "The Sixth Mass Extinction: Fact, Fiction or Speculation?" *Biological Reviews* 97 (2022): 640–63.
8 McCauley et al., "Marine Defaunation."
9 Only the first of these is explored in this chapter, with area-based approaches covered in Chapter 8.
10 Brendan Tobin, *The Role of Customary Law in Access and Benefit-Sharing and Traditional Knowledge Governance: Perspectives from Andean and Pacific Island Countries* (Geneva: World Intellectual Property Organization and Shibuya: United Nations University, 2013).
11 LoriKim Alexander, Andrews Agyekumhene, and Phil Allman, "The Role of Taboos in the Protection and Recovery of Sea Turtles," *Frontiers in Marine Science* 4, no. 237 (2017): 1–9.
12 R. E. Johannes, "Traditional Marine Conservation Methods in Oceania and Their Demise," *Annual Reviews of Ecological Systems* 9 (1978): 349–64.
13 Joshua E. Cinner et al., "Trade, Tenure, and Tradition: Influence of Sociocultural Factors on Resource Use in Melanesia," *Conservation Biology* 19, no. 5 (2005): 1469–77.
14 Johannes, "Traditional Marine Conservation Methods in Oceania and Their Demise."
15 Ibid.
16 See Chapter 1 for a discussion on customary law and legally pluralist mixed law systems.
17 For example, the English *Fish Act 1533*, 25 Hen.8 c.4. Also, the *Fish (No. 2) Act 1533*, 25 Hen.8 c.8 – An Act against killing of young spawn or fry of eels and salmon involving a closed season, and the subsequent *Fisheries Act 1558*, 1 Eliz. 1 CAP. XVII. See further discussion in Chapter 4.
18 For example, early laws for the conservation of land-based species for the purposes of hunting: One of the first was the English *Wild-fowl Act 1533*, 25 Hen.8 c.11 – an Act against destruction of wild-fowl.
19 The last known Great Auks were killed in Iceland in 1844 for a museum collection. This raises more questions than it answers including the value of 'collecting' and 'collections' in the context of conservation: Melissa Petruzzello, "6 Animals We Ate Into Extinction," *Britannica*, accessed December 1, 2023, www.britannica.com/list/6-animals-we-ate-into-extinction.
20 "Labrador Duck," *Endangered List*, accessed December 1, 2023, https://endangeredlist.org/animal/labrador-duck/.
21 "The History and Evolution of the Migratory Bird Treaty Act," *Audubon Society*, accessed December 1, 2023, www.audubon.org/news/the-history-and-evolution-migratory-bird-treaty-act.
22 The Act originally covered game and wild birds and was then amended to protect a broader range of animal and plant species. It remains in force today: "Overview of the Lacey Act (16 U.S.C. SS 3371–3378)," *Michigan State University Animal Legal & Historical Center*, accessed December 1, 2023, www.animallaw.info/article/overview-lacey-act-16-usc-ss-3371-3378.
23 "Convention for the Protection of Birds Useful to Agriculture," accessed December 1, 2023, www.ecolex.org/details/treaty/convention-for-the-protection-of-birds-useful-to-agriculture-tre-000067/.

24 "The History and Evolution of the Migratory Bird Treaty Ac."
25 "The Antarctic Treaty," *Secretariat of the Antarctic Treaty*, accessed December 1, 2023, www.ats.aq/e/antarctictreaty.html.
26 See also the later *Protocol on Environmental Protection to the Antarctic Treaty* (1991). For an outline of the conservation provisions, see "Environmental Protection," *Secretariat of the Antarctic Treaty*, accessed December 1, 2023, www.ats.aq/e/environmental.html. See also Chapter 8 of this volume for further discussion of Antarctica and polar law.
27 "The 1973 Agreement on the Conservation of Polar Bears," *Polar Bear Range States*, accessed December 1, 2023, https://polarbearagreement.org/about-us/1973-agreement.
28 Agreement on the Conservation of Polar Bear, Article II.
29 "Polar Bear Population," *WWF*, accessed December 1, 2023, www.arcticwwf.org/wildlife/polar-bear/polar-bear-population/.
30 "Circumpolar Action Plan," *Polar Bear Range States*, accessed December 1, 2023, https://polarbearagreement.org/circumpolar-action-plan.
31 Willem Wijnstekers, *The Evolution of CITES*, 11th ed. (Budapest: International Council for Game and Wildlife Conservation, 2018), https://cites.org/sites/default/files/common/resources/The_Evolution_of_CITES_2018.pdf.
32 "Convention on International Trade in Endangered Species of Wild Fauna and Flora," accessed December 1, 2023, https://cites.org. The Convention works by listing species on one of three hierarchical Appendices, depending upon their conservation status (i.e., their level of vulnerability to extinction). Thereafter, conditions are placed on the international import and export of species with differing rules for each Appendix. The species threatened with extinction are listed on Appendix I and trade is strictly regulated, with lesser conditions placed on trade applying to species listed on Appendix II and III to prevent their deterioration. Species are categorised as Not Evaluated, Data Deficient, Least Concern, Near Threatened, Vulnerable, Endangered, Critically Endangered, Extinct in the Wild and Extinct.
33 "The IUCN Red List of Threatened Species," *IUCN*, accessed December 1, 2023, www.iucnredlist.org/.
34 "The CITES Species," *CITES*, accessed December 1, 2023, https://cites.org/eng/disc/species.php.
35 "CITES Compliance Procedures," *CITES*, accessed December 1, 2023, https://cites.org/eng/prog/compliance.
36 "ICCWC – International Consortium on Combating Wildlife Crime," *CITES*, accessed December 1, 2023, https://cites.org/eng/prog/iccwc.
37 "Convention on the Conservation of Migratory Species of Wild Animals," accessed December 1, 2023, www.cms.int/en/legalinstrument/cms.
38 Being those countries through whose air, land or water the species moves, or a State whose flagged vessel engages in taking migratory species: CMS Article I.
39 CMS Article III (4)(a).
40 Conservation status is defined as meaning the combined influences impacting on the migratory species that may affect its long-term distribution and abundance: CMS Article I.
41 "Species+," *CMS*, accessed December 1, 2023, https://speciesplus.net/species.
42 They relate to cetaceans, albatrosses, petrels, seals and waterbirds: "Agreements," *CMS*, accessed December 1, 2023, www.cms.int/en/cms-instruments/agreements.
43 "Memoranda of Understanding," *CMS*, accessed December 1, 2023, www.cms.int/en/cms-instruments/mou.
44 Christopher Michael Hensz and Jorge Soberón, "Participation in the Convention on Migratory Species: A Biogeographic Assessment," *AMBIO* 47 (2018): 739–46.

45 UNCLOS Article 21. For the full text see "United Nations Convention on the Law of the Sea," *UN*, accessed March 1, 2024, www.un.org/depts/los/convention_agreements/texts/unclos/closindx.htm.
46 UNCLOS Article 117–19.
47 UNCLOS Article 145.
48 UNCLOS Articles 61, 62 and 63.
49 UNCLOS Article 192.
50 UNCLOS Article 193.
51 "History and Purpose," *International Whaling Commission*, accessed December 1, 2023, https://iwc.int/commission/history-and-purpose.
52 *Our Common Future*, World Commission on Environment and Development (UN Doc A/42/427, 1987), accessed December 1, 2023, https://sustainabledevelopment.un.org/content/documents/5987our-common-future.pdf.
53 See Chapter 1 of this volume.
54 Sustainable Development Goals, "SDG14 Life below Water," accessed December 1, 2023, www.un.org/sustainabledevelopment/oceans/.
55 "The Ocean Flows through All 17 of the UN Sustainable Development Goals," *Economist Impact*, accessed December 1, 2023, https://impact.economist.com/ocean/ocean-sustainable-development-goals/.
56 "Introduction," *CBD*, accessed December 1, 2023, www.cbd.int/intro/.
57 CBD Articles 8–9.
58 Outlined in Chapter 1 of this volume.
59 CBD Articles 8 and 10.
60 "National Reports," *CBD*, accessed December 1, 2023, www.cbd.int/reports/; and "Find National Targets," *CBD*, accessed December 1, 2023, www.cbd.int/nbsap/targets/.
61 "Aichi Biodiversity Targets," *CBD*, accessed December 1, 2023, www.cbd.int/sp/targets/.
62 "2030 Targets (with Guidance Notes)," *CBD*, accessed December 1, 2023, www.cbd.int/gbf/targets/.
63 Benjamin S. Halpern et al., "Recent Pace of Change in Human Impact on the World's Ocean," *Nature: Science Reports* 9 (2019): 11609.
64 One of the earliest papers to use the term was by E. O. Wilson, "The Biological Diversity Crisis: A Challenge to Science," *Issues in Science and Technology* 2, no. 1 (1985): 20–29.
65 E.g., Gerado Ceballos and Paul R Ehrlich, "Mammal Population Losses and the Extinction Crisis," *Science* 296 (2002): 904–7.
66 Boris Worm et al., "Impacts of Biodiversity Loss on Ocean Ecosystem Services," *Science* 314, no. 5800 (2006): 787–90.
67 D. Mccauley et al., "Marine Defaunation: Animal Loss in the Global Ocean," *Science* 347, no. 6219 (2015): 1255641.
68 Ibid.
69 See Chapter 11 in this volume for a further discussion of knowledge and data.
70 Scott C. Doney, D. Shallin Busch, Sarah R. Cooley, and Kristy J. Kroeker, "The Impacts of Ocean Acidification on Marine Ecosystems and Reliant Human Communities," *Annual Review of Environment and Resources* 45, no. 1 (2020): 83–112.
71 Bardach and Santerre, "Climate and the Fish in the Sea," 206.
72 "What Is the United Nations Framework Convention on Climate Change?" *United Nations Climate Change*, accessed December 1, 2023, https://unfccc.int/process-and-meetings/what-is-the-united-nations-framework-convention-on-climate-change.
73 "The Paris Agreement," *United Climate Change*, accessed December 1, 2023, https://unfccc.int/process-and-meetings/the-paris-agreement.

74 "NDC Registry," *United Nations Climate Change*, accessed December 1, 2023, https://unfccc.int/NDCREG.
75 Rita R. Colwell, "Global Climate and Infectious Disease: The Cholera Paradigm," *Science* 274, no. 5295 (1996): 2025–31. Although note that there is some controversy about whether it was ballast water or other sources.
76 See Chapter 9.
77 The 'blue economy' refers to increasing wealth from the oceans (through expanded fishing, shipping, and marine tourism) whilst also attempting to achieve environmental and socio-cultural outcomes. See Chapters 1 and 12 of this volume for further discussion.
78 See Chapter 9 of this volume.
79 "Mountains in the Sea," *Hydro International*, accessed December 1, 2023, www.hydro-international.com/content/article/mountains-in-the-sea.
80 "Seamounts: Underwater Oases," *Smithsonian*, accessed December 1, 2023, https://ocean.si.edu/ocean-life/invertebrates/seamounts-underwater-oases; and "Seamounts," *Marine Education Society of Australasia*, accessed December 1, 2023, www.mesa.edu.au/seamounts/seamounts01.asp
81 *Agreement under the United Nations Convention on the Law of the Sea on the Conservation and Sustainable Use of Marine Biological Diversity of Areas beyond National Jurisdiction*, accessed March 1, 2024, https://treaties.un.org/Pages/ViewDetails.aspx?src=TREATY&mtdsg_no=XXI-10&chapter=21&clang=_en#EndDec
82 High Seas Treaty Parts II and III. High seas protected areas are explored further in Chapter 8 in this volume.
83 See High Seas Treaty, Part II.
84 "Global Compilation of Confirmed and Inferred Vent Sites," *NOAA PMEL Earth-Ocean Interactions Program*, accessed December 1, 2023, www.pmel.noaa.gov/eoi/PlumeStudies/global-vents/index.html.
85 Magnus Johnson, "Oceans Need Protection from Scientists Too," *Nature* 433, no. 105 (2005), https://doi.org/10.1038/433105a. As noted earlier, some of the Regional Seas Conventions do protect seamounts in ABNJ.
86 High Seas Treaty, see Chapter 7.
87 Sites of fidelity refers to places where species naturally accumulate in numbers that make tourism viable. Such sites can include 'stops' on migratory routes, feeding, breeding and nursery grounds.
88 For example, "Code of Conduct: Regulating whale Shark Interactions," *Madagascar Whale Shark Project*, accessed December 1, 2023, www.madawhalesharks.org/get-involved/code-of-conduct/.
89 "Whale Shark Interaction Guidelines," *CMS*, accessed December 1, 2023, www.cms.int/en/publication/whale-shark-interaction-guidelines; and "Management Strategies and Tools," *International Whaling Commission*, accessed December 1, 2023, https://wwhandbook.iwc.int/en/responsible-management/management-strategies.
90 "Shark and Ray Tourism Best Practice," *Ocean Earth Foundation*, accessed December 1, 2023, https://tierramar.com.au/portfolio-view/shark-and-ray-tourism-best-practice/; and Sophie Lewis and Dylan Walker, *Global Best Practice Guidance for Responsible Whale and Dolphin Watching: Tourism Activities Involving Wild Cetaceans* (Brighton: World Cetacean Alliance with support from ClubMed, 2018).
91 On land, technology has allowed farmers to grow more crops on less land and more efficiently use water and fertilisers. In the ocean, the efficiencies have come at the cost of sustainable harvests and non-target species and ecosystems. Furthermore, the benefits have mostly flowed to the industrialised nations.
92 Pierre Girard and Thomas Du Payrat, *An Inventory of New Technologies in Fisheries*, Issue Paper (Paris: OECD, 2017).

93 See, for example, UNCLOS Article 62, Fish Stocks Agreement Article 5, FAO Code of Conduct for Responsible Fisheries Article 5.2, and UNESCO, *IOC Criteria and Guidelines for the Transfer of Marine Technology* (Paris: UNESCO, 2005).
94 See, for example, the "Atlas of Marine Protection, Global MPA Database," *Marine Conservation Institute*, accessed December 1, 2023, https://old.mpatlas.org/map/mpas/; and "Protected Areas (WDPA)," *Protected Planet*, accessed December 1, 2023, www.protectedplanet.net/en/thematic-areas/wdpa?tab=WDPA.
95 "Autonomous Underwater Vehicles," *NOAA Ocean Exploration*, accessed December 1, 2023, https://oceanexplorer.noaa.gov/technology/subs/auvs/auvs.html.
96 Gavin Haines, "'No Place to Hide' for Illegal Fishing Fleets as Surveillance Satellites Prepare for Lift-off," *Mongabay* (August 30, 2019), https://news.mongabay.com/2019/08/no-place-to-hide-for-illegal-fishing-fleets-as-surveillance-satellites-prepare-for-lift-off/.
97 Chris Wold, "World Heritage Species: A New Legal Approach to Conservation," *Georgetown International Environmental Law Review* 20 (2008): 337–96.
98 Anastasia Telesetsky, An Cliquet, and Afshin Akhtar-Khavari, *Ecological Restoration in International Environmental Law* (Abingdon: Routledge, 2017).
99 For a discussion of ocean justice and the limitations of current law of the sea to achieve it, see Susan Reid, "Ocean Justice: Reckoning with Material Vulnerability," *Cultural Politics* 19, no. 1 (2023): 107–27.
100 Some councils, provinces and states in North America have also recognised the rights of nature: Global Alliance for the Rights of Nature, accessed December 1, 2023, www.garn.org/. See also Jane Gleeson-White, "It's Only Natural: The Push to Give Rivers, Mountains and Forests Legal Rights," *The Guardian* (April 1, 2018), www.theguardian.com/australia-news/2018/apr/01/its-only-natural-the-push-to-give-rivers-mountains-and-forests-legal-rights.
101 Judge Mendoza, Judgment November 3, 2016, File No. P-72.254/15 "Presented By A.F.A.D.A about the Chimpanzee 'Cecilia' – Non Human Individual," accessed December 1, 2023, www.nonhumanrights.org/wp-content/uploads/2016/12/Chimpanzee-Cecilia_translation-FINAL-for-website.pdf; and David Grimm, "Chimpanzee 'Personhood' Fails on Appeal," *Science Insider* (December 4, 2014), www.science.org/content/article/chimpanzee-personhood-fails-appeal.
102 For example, Lieselotte Viaene, "Can Rights of Nature Save Us from the Anthropocene Catastrophe? Some Critical Reflections from the Field," *Asian Journal of Law and Society* 9, no. 2 (2022): 187–206.
103 Fátima Alves, "The Rights of Nature and the Human Right to Nature: An Overview of the European Legal System and Challenges for the Ecological Transition," *Frontiers in Environmental Science* 11 (2023): 1175143.
104 Mccauley et al., "Marine Defaunation," referring to K. W. Kenyon, "The Sea Otter in the Eastern Pacific Ocean," *North American Fauna* 68 (1969): 1–352.
105 A term coined by Boyes and Elliott: Suzanne J. Boyes and Michael Elliott, "Marine Legislation – The Ultimate 'Horrendogram': International Law, European Directives & National Implementation," *Marine Pollution Bulletin* 86 (2014): 39–47.
106 See Chapter 1 of this volume.
107 Also, introduced in Chapter 1 of this volume.
108 See Vivienne R. Westbrook et al., *Sharks in the Arts: From Feared to Revered* (Abingdon: Routledge, 2018).
109 Reg A. Watson and A. Tidd, "Mapping Nearly a Century and a Half of Global Marine Fishing: 1869–2015," *Marine Policy* 93 (2018): 171–77, 176.
110 The chambered nautilus and giant clam are listed under CITES.

111 Although Leonardo de Vinci is credited with one of the first examples of biomimicry in learning from birds to enable human flight, it was Otto Schmidt who invented the term 'biomimetics' in the 1950s and Benyus who popularised biomimicry: Janine Benyus, *Biomimicry: Innovation Inspired by Nature* (New York: William Morrow & Co, 1997). Biomimicry and biomimetics are explored further in Chapter 11 of this volume.

112 Patrick Aryee, *30 Animals That Made Us Smarter* (London: BBC Books, 2021).

Bibliography

Agreement under the United Nations Convention on the Law of the Sea on the Conservation and Sustainable Use of Marine Biological Diversity of Areas Beyond National Jurisdiction A/CONF.232/2023/4 (June 19, 2023).

Alexander, LoriKim, Andrews Agyekumhene, and Phil Allman. "The Role of Taboos in the Protection and Recovery of Sea Turtles." *Frontiers in Marine Science* 4, no. 237 (2017): 1–9.

Alves, Fátima. "The Rights of Nature and the Human Right to Nature: An Overview of the European Legal System and Challenges for the Ecological Transition." *Frontiers in Environmental Science* 11 (2023): 1175143.

Aryee, Patrick. *30 Animals That Made Us Smarter*. London: BBC Books, 2021.

Audubon Society. "The History and Evolution of the Migratory Bird Treaty Act." Accessed December 1, 2023. www.audubon.org/news/the-history-and-evolution-migratory-bird-treaty-act.

Benyus, Janine. *Biomimicry: Innovation Inspired by Nature*. New York: William Morrow & Co, 1997.

Bouchet, Philippe, and Benoît Fontaine. "The Sixth Mass Extinction: Fact, Fiction or Speculation?" *Biological Reviews* 97 (2022): 640–63.

Boyes, Suzanne J., and Michael Elliott. "Marine Legislation – The Ultimate 'Horrendogram': International Law, European Directives & National Implementation." *Marine Pollution Bulletin* 86 (2014): 39.

Carlton, J. T. et al. "The First Historical Extinction of a Marine Invertebrate in an Ocean Basin: The Demise of the Eelgrass Limpet Lottia alveus." *Biological Bulletin* 180, no. 1 (1991): 72–80.

Carson, Rachel. *The Sea around Us*. Oxford: Oxford University Press, 1951.

CBD. "2030 Targets (with Guidance Notes)." Accessed December 1, 2023. www.cbd.int/gbf/targets/.

CBD. "Aichi Biodiversity Targets." Accessed December 1, 2023. www.cbd.int/sp/targets/.

CBD. "Find National Targets." Accessed December 1, 2023. www.cbd.int/nbsap/targets/.

CBD. "Introduction." Accessed December 1, 2023. www.cbd.int/intro/.

CBD. "National Reports." Accessed December 1, 2023. www.cbd.int/reports/.

Ceballos, Gerado, and Paul R. Ehrlich. "Mammal Population Losses and the Extinction Crisis." *Science* 296 (2002): 904–7.

Cinner, Joshua E. et al. "Trade, Tenure, and Tradition: Influence of Sociocultural Factors on Resource Use in Melanesia." *Conservation Biology* 19, no. 5 (2005): 1469–77.

CITES. "CITES Compliance Procedures." Accessed December 1, 2023. https://cites.org/eng/prog/compliance.

CITES. "ICCWC – International Consortium on Combating Wildlife Crime." *CITES*. Accessed December 1, 2023. https://cites.org/eng/prog/iccwc.

CITES. "The CITES Species." Accessed December 1, 2023. https://cites.org/eng/disc/species.php.

CMS. "Agreements." Accessed December 1, 2023. www.cms.int/en/cms-instruments/agreements.

CMS. "Memoranda of Understanding." Accessed December 1, 2023. www.cms.int/en/cms-instruments/mou.

CMS. "Species+." Accessed December 1, 2023. https://speciesplus.net/species.

CMS. "Whale Shark Interaction Guidelines." Accessed December 1, 2023. www.cms.int/en/publication/whale-shark-interaction-guidelines.

Colwell, Rita R. "Global Climate and Infectious Disease: The Cholera Paradigm." *Science* 274, no. 5295 (1996): 2025–31.

Convention for the Protection of Birds Useful to Agriculture. Accessed December 1, 2023. www.ecolex.org/details/treaty/convention-for-the-protection-of-birds-useful-to-agriculture-tre-000067/.

Convention on International Trade in Endangered Species of Wild Fauna and Flora. Accessed December 1, 2023. https://cites.org.

Convention on the Conservation of Migratory Species of Wild Animals. Accessed December 1, 2023. www.cms.int/en/legalinstrument/cms.

Davis, Josh. "Steller's Sea Cow: The First Historical Extinction of a Marine Mammal at Human Hands." Accessed December 1, 2023. www.nhm.ac.uk/discover/stellers-sea-cow-first-historical-extinction-of-marine-mammal-at-human-hands.html.

Doney, Scott C., Busch D. Shallin, Sarah R. Cooley, and Kristy J. Kroeker. "The Impacts of Ocean Acidification on Marine Ecosystems and Reliant Human Communities." *Annual Review of Environment and Resources* 45, no. 1 (2020): 83–112.

Endangered List. "Labrador Duck." Accessed December 1, 2023. https://endangeredlist.org/animal/labrador-duck/.

Girard, Pierre, and Thomas Du Payrat. *An Inventory of New Technologies in Fisheries*. Paris: OECD, 2017.

Gleeson-White, Jane. "It's Only Natural: The Push to Give Rivers, Mountains and Forests Legal Rights." *The Guardian* (April 1, 2018). www.theguardian.com/australia-news/2018/apr/01/its-only-natural-the-push-to-give-rivers-mountains-and-forests-legal-rights.

"Global Alliance for the Rights of Nature." Accessed December 1, 2023. www.garn.org/.

Grimm, David. "Chimpanzee 'Personhood' Fails on Appeal." *Science Insider* (December 4, 2014). www.science.org/content/article/chimpanzee-personhood-fails-appeal.

Haines, Gavin. "'No Place to Hide' for Illegal Fishing Fleets as Surveillance Satellites Prepare for Lift-Off." *Mongabay* (August 30, 2019). https://news.mongabay.com/2019/08/no-place-to-hide-for-illegal-fishing-fleets-as-surveillance-satellites-prepare-for-lift-off/.

Halpern, Benjamin S. et al. "A Global Map of Human Impact on Marine Ecosystems." *Science* 319 (2008): 948–52.

Halpern, Benjamin S. et al. "Recent Pace of Change in Human Impact on the World's Ocean." *Nature: Science Reports* 9 (2019): 11609.

Hensz, Christopher Michael, and Jorge Soberón. "Participation in the Convention on Migratory Species: A Biogeographic Assessment." *AMBIO* 47 (2018): 739–46.

Hydro International. "Mountains in the Sea." Accessed December 1, 2023. www.hydro-international.com/content/article/mountains-in-the-sea.

International Whaling Commission. "History and Purpose." Accessed December 1, 2023. https://iwc.int/commission/history-and-purpose.

International Whaling Commission. "Management Strategies and Tools." Accessed December 1, 2023. https://wwhandbook.iwc.int/en/responsible-management/management-strategies.

IUCN. "The Red List of Threatened Species." Accessed December 1, 2023. www.iucnredlist.org/.

IUCN. "The IUCN Red List of Threatened Species." Accessed December 1, 2023. www.iucnredlist.org/.

Johannes, R. E. "Traditional Marine Conservation Methods in Oceania and Their Demise." *Annual Reviews of Ecological Systems* 9 (1978): 349–64.

Johnson, Magnus. "Oceans Need Protection from Scientists Too." *Nature* 433, no. 105 (2005). https://doi.org/10.1038/433105a.

Kenyon, K. W. "The Sea Otter in the Eastern Pacific Ocean." *North American Fauna* 68 (1969): 1.

Lewis, Sophie, and Dylan Walker. *Global Best Practice Guidance for Responsible Whale and Dolphin Watching: Tourism Activities Involving Wild Cetaceans*. Brighton: World Cetacean Alliance with support from ClubMed, 2018.

Madagascar Whale Shark Project. "Code of Conduct: Regulating Whale Shark Interactions." Accessed December 1, 2023. www.madawhalesharks.org/get-involved/code-of-conduct/.

Marine Conservation Institute. "Atlas of Marine Protection, Global MPA Database." Accessed December 1, 2023. https://old.mpatlas.org/map/mpas/.

Marine Education Society of Australasia. "Seamounts." Accessed December 1, 2023. www.mesa.edu.au/seamounts/seamounts01.asp

Mccauley, D. et al. "Marine Defaunation: Animal Loss in the Global Ocean." *Science* 347, no. 6219 (2015): 1255641.

Mendoza, Judge. Judgment November 3, 2016, File No. P-72.254/15 "Presented By A.F.A.D.A about the Chimpanzee "Cecilia" – Non Human Individual." Accessed December 1, 2023. www.nonhumanrights.org/wp-content/uploads/2016/12/Chimpanzee-Cecilia_translation-FINAL-for-website.pdf.

Michigan State University Animal Legal & Historical Center. "Overview of the Lacey Act (16 U.S.C. SS 3371–3378)." Accessed December 1, 2023. www.animallaw.info/article/overview-lacey-act-16-usc-ss-3371-3378.

Nielsen, Larry A. "The Evolution of Fisheries Management Philosophy." *Marine Fisheries Review* (1976): 15–23.

NOAA Ocean Exploration. "Autonomous Underwater Vehicles." Accessed December 1, 2023. https://oceanexplorer.noaa.gov/technology/subs/auvs/auvs.html.

NOAA PMEL Earth-Ocean Interactions Program. "Global Compilation of Confirmed and Inferred Vent Sites." Accessed December 1, 2023. www.pmel.noaa.gov/eoi/PlumeStudies/global-vents/index.html.

Ocean Earth Foundation. "Shark and Ray Tourism Best Practice." Accessed December 1, 2023. https://tierramar.com.au/portfolio-view/shark-and-ray-tourism-best-practice/.

Petruzzello, Melissa. "6 Animals We Ate Into Extinction." *Britannica*. Accessed December 1, 2023. www.britannica.com/list/6-animals-we-ate-into-extinction.

Polar Bear Range States. "Circumpolar Action Plan." Accessed December 1, 2023. https://polarbearagreement.org/circumpolar-action-plan.

Polar Bear Range States. "The 1973 Agreement on the Conservation of Polar Bears." Accessed December 1, 2023. https://polarbearagreement.org/about-us/1973-agreement.

Protected Planet. "Protected Areas (WDPA)." Accessed December 1, 2023. www.protectedplanet.net/en/thematic-areas/wdpa?tab=WDPA.

Reid, Susan. "Ocean Justice: Reckoning with Material Vulnerability." *Cultural Politics* 19, no. 1 (2023): 107–27.

Secretariat of the Antarctic Treaty. "Environmental Protection." Accessed December 1, 2023. www.ats.aq/e/environmental.html.

Secretariat of the Antarctic Treaty. "The Antarctic Treaty." Accessed December 1, 2023. www.ats.aq/e/antarctictreaty.html.

Smithsonian. "Seamounts: Underwater Oases." Accessed December 1, 2023. https://ocean.si.edu/ocean-life/invertebrates/seamounts-underwater-oases.

Sustainable Development Goals. "SDG14 Life Below Water." Accessed December 1, 2023. www.un.org/sustainabledevelopment/oceans/.

Telesetsky, Anastasia, An Cliquet, and Afshin Akhtar-Khavari. *Ecological Restoration in International Environmental Law*. Abingdon: Routledge, 2017.

"The Ocean Flows through all 17 of the UN Sustainable Development Goals." *Economist Impact*. Accessed December 1, 2023. https://impact.economist.com/ocean/ocean-sustainable-development-goals/.

Tobin, Brendan. *The Role of Customary Law in Access and Benefit-Sharing and Traditional Knowledge Governance: Perspectives from Andean and Pacific Island Countries*. Geneva: World Intellectual Property Organization and Shibuya: United Nations University, 2013.

UN DOALOS. "United Nations Convention on the Law of the Sea." Accessed March 1, 2024. www.un.org/depts/los/convention_agreements/texts/unclos/closindx.htm.

UNESCO. *IOC Criteria and Guidelines for the Transfer of Marine Technology*. Paris: UNESCO, 2005.

United Nations Climate Change. "NDC Registry." Accessed December 1, 2023. https://unfccc.int/NDCREG.

United Nations Climate Change. "The Paris Agreement." Accessed December 1, 2023. https://unfccc.int/process-and-meetings/the-paris-agreement.

United Nations Climate Change. "What Is the United Nations Framework Convention on Climate Change?" Accessed December 1, 2023. https://unfccc.int/process-and-meetings/what-is-the-united-nations-framework-convention-on-climate-change.

Viaene, Lieselotte. "Can Rights of Nature Save Us from the Anthropocene Catastrophe? Some Critical Reflections from the Field." *Asian Journal of Law and Society* 9, no. 2 (2022): 187.

Watson, Reg A., and A. Tidd. "Mapping Nearly a Century and a Half of Global Marine Fishing: 1869–2015." *Marine Policy* 93 (2018): 171.

Weeks, Linton. "Hats Off to Women Who Saved The Birds." *NPR History Department* (July 15, 2015). www.npr.org/sections/npr-history-dept/2015/07/15/422860307/hats-off-to-women-who-saved-the-birds.

Westbrook, Vivienne R. et al. *Sharks in the Arts: From Feared to Revered*. Abingdon: Routledge, 2018.

Wijnstekers, Willem. *The Evolution of CITES*. 11th ed. Budapest: International Council for Game and Wildlife Conservation, 2018. Accessed March 1, 2024. https://cites.org/sites/default/files/common/resources/The_Evolution_of_CITES_2018.pdf.

Wilson, E. O. "The Biological Diversity Crisis: A Challenge to Science." *Issues in Science and Technology* 2, no. 1 (1985): 20–29.

Wold, Chris. "World Heritage Species: A New Legal Approach to Conservation." *Georgetown International Environmental Law Review* 20 (2008): 337–96.

World Commission on Environment and Development. *Our Common Future* (UN Doc A/42/427, 1987). Accessed December 1, 2023, https://sustainabledevelopment.un.org/content/documents/5987our-common-future.pdf.

Worm, Boris et al. "Impacts of Biodiversity Loss on Ocean Ecosystem Services." *Science* 314, no. 5800 (2006): 787–90.

WWF. "Polar Bear Population." Accessed December 1, 2023. www.arcticwwf.org/wildlife/polar-bear/polar-bear-population/.

8 Ocean space

Protecting marine areas and regions

When it comes to the fluid seas . . . boundaries can be fantastically elusive.
Stacy Alaimo, *Blue Legalities*

Overview

Human societies have a long history of developing rules for regulating activities in geographically delimited areas. As will be seen later in the chapter, traditional and Indigenous communities certainly did so, and they frequently incorporated a conservation-based stewardship element. As western maritime nations became established, they adopted laws for their territorial seas – which were themselves defined ocean areas – although their delimitation did not reflect the characteristics or needs of marine life but rather were founded on politico-legal boundaries. By the 20th century, approaches to oceans, seas and shorelines had succeeded in creating multiple maritime and coastal zones with jurisdiction given to individual States.[1] Various ocean activities (such as fishing, shipping, oil and gas extraction, and tourism) were regulated differently, with control and management often given to specific authorities over particular ocean spaces.[2] Rising concerns about marine degradation from the 1970s onwards led governments to act in favour of conservation and to introduce area-based controls for specific ocean spaces. This 'protected area management' approach was often used in tandem with species-based laws (threatened species and biodiversity rules) and activity-based regulation (such as fishing and shipping law) but had the advantage that, within a defined marine area, the entirety of the natural environment and human activities could be managed together. Sometimes, area-based regimes were adopted because of the specific oceanic environment that required tailored measures or specific threats to particular marine spaces.

This chapter explores area-based legal measures applied in the oceanic realm, such as marine protected areas, marine parks, sanctuary zones, aquatic reserves and safety zones, and focuses on marine protected areas (MPAs)[3] as they are 'one of the most widely used tools for marine conservation'.[4] In other cases, space-based

DOI: 10.4324/9781003005261-12

measures include regional approaches to ocean governance. For example, the Food and Agriculture Organisation (FAO) has divided up the high seas into fishing sectors with Regional Fisheries Bodies (RFBs) and Regional Fishery Management Organisations (RFMOs) established to manage fishery resources within them.[5] UN Environment (UNEP) has also taken a regional approach to marine environmental health through the Regional Seas Programmes (RSPs), which focus particularly on marine pollution.[6] In part, these arrangements have resulted from the strong emphasis on regional approaches encouraged in the *UN Convention on the Law of the Sea* (UNCLOS) and are explored in other chapters of this book.

Evolution of laws for protected area management

Sites of fidelity

Marine species live in all areas of the ocean, but they are not equally distributed. Some ocean spaces are inhabited and returned to more than others. These include 'sites of fidelity', such as breeding, birthing or nursery areas, or feeding grounds and cleaning stations for marine mammals, fish, crustaceans and other ocean and coastal species.[7] Some such places draw one or two key species and other areas, such as coral reefs, are particularly biodiverse. Animals, such as turtles and seabirds, move from the ocean to land and return year after year to lay eggs or rear young, and those sites, as well as routes that form part of their migratory pathways, are critical in their life cycles. Other marine species and ecosystems are sedentary or tied to a site with little or no opportunity for movement. In these places, marine and coastal life is vulnerable and in greater need of protection, or the conservation of these areas is critical to life cycles. These sites frequently become a focal point for research, harvesting or marine-based tourism, precisely because high concentrations of marine life can be found there. Where human activities occur in an overlapping area, significant impacts can have devastating consequences for the inhabitants. Fishing is an obvious example, with historical whaling stations being situated on coastlines close-by migratory pathways and places where whales could predictably be found at particular times of the year or were known to be vulnerable as they travelled with calves. Similarly, high-value 'fishing grounds' were, and continue to be, located where fish can be found regularly and in large numbers, making harvesting more efficient. Other areas of high biodiversity have attracted different extractive industries, such as islands where guano bird droppings were harvested for use as fertiliser.[8] In many cases, these productive areas have been over-exploited resulting in collapses of fish stocks, significant declines in species, degraded areas that ultimately lead to reduced production.[9] Outside these immediate areas, human activities – such as shipping and construction – have had indirect consequences through oil and chemical spills, which can disperse through the movements of currents, and through noise and light pollution.[10] Yet even before that stage was reached, the law often facilitated exploitation without constraint.[11]

Customary and traditional law approaches

Area-based tools to regulate and manage the marine and coastal environment are, perhaps, as old as human uses of these places. They principally involve the designation of geographically delimited spaces, with conditions and/or restrictions placed on access and use within them to limit activities and impacts on the natural environment. As noted in Chapter 7, many Indigenous groups – particularly in island communities but also in other coastal contexts – adopted customary marine governance rules that included area-based tools aligned with traditional worldviews that did not separate land and water in the binary ways in which western societies do. Customary laws restricted access and use of these spaces, using broadly similar approaches to the way we do today. For example, in Polynesia, and other parts of the Pacific, certain marine areas were declared taboo with restricted access and/or limited fishing permitted. These were known as *tabu*, *kapu* or *tapu* areas, often set aside for ritual purposes, to build stocks

Figure 8.1 Whaling on Danes Island, Arctic Ocean. Painting by Abraham Speeck, artist (Dutch), 1634. Oil on canvas. (Skokloster Castle Collection.)

for future harvests or to preserve the area as breeding ground.[12] During colonial times, however, these traditional area-based conservation tools were frequently displaced by the European colonisers who imposed laws based on regimes in their home countries. As with some of the traditional species conservation rules and restrictions, contemporary governance of marine areas has again turned to customary rules.[13]

Locally Managed Marine Areas (LMMA) Network

In the mid-1990s, many community-based marine management projects were underway throughout Southeast Asia and the Pacific. In the early 2000s more than 100 conservation practitioners from 20 projects in 12 countries explored best practices, how to measure and share success and scale-up activities. The LMMA Network was formed and brings together communities, NGOs, government agencies and researchers working to promote food security and livelihoods based on the belief that local communities are best positioned to manage coastal resources if empowered to do so. Today, LMMA supports Networks in Indonesia, the Philippines, Papua New Guinea, Palau, Pohnpei, Fiji and the Solomon Islands, and engages with more than 15 other countries in the Indo-Pacific.[14]

Marine protected area management in western contexts

Individual species were often the first to be protected under western laws. Setting aside specific terrestrial areas with royal protection emerged in medieval times, usually to build stocks for hunting rather than as conservation initiatives.[15] By the late 18th century, attitudes to the natural world were beginning to change,[16] leading to the emergence of protected area management as a tool for conservation of land areas and the creation of the first national parks in the 19th century. In 1872, Yellowstone National Park was designated in the US, the first national park in the world.[17] The second national park was designated in Australia – the Royal National Park, Sydney in 1879 – and included a marine component.[18]

The protected area management model rapidly spread across the world during the early 20th century, and today most nations have some form of national parks legislation. Although many areas included marine and intertidal extensions of terrestrial parks, the declaration of marine protected areas emerged later.[19] Their development lagged behind fisheries regulations, which had evolved by the late 19th century and frequently included the possibility of declaring aquatic reserves in areas where fishing was prohibited or restricted. Standalone marine parks were designated in the 1930s, perhaps as a response to beliefs that fisheries management was failing.[20]

It was not until the environmental movement in the 1970s that the number of marine parks began to increase and the term 'marine protected areas' (MPAs) was introduced.[21] The International Union for the Conservation of Nature and Natural Resources (IUCN) – a global environmental non-governmental organisation – took the lead in 1999 in defining MPAs and classifying them into six management categories ranging from strict nature reserves to protected areas with sustainable use. In 2008 IUCN provided a definition of MPAs that is widely used today: 'a clearly defined geographical space, recognised, dedicated and managed through legal or other effective means, to achieve the long-term conservation of nature with associated ecosystems services and cultural values'.[22]

Nevertheless, ocean-based protected areas today are often referred to as MPAs, even though they do not meet this definition as they are not dedicated to conservation. Fisheries regulations, for example, include aquatic or marine 'reserves' which focus only on restricting fishing, and shipping law also includes rules around areas where species conditions apply to vessels traversing these waters (Particularly Sensitive Seas Areas (PSSAs) for example). Other exclusion zones (such as those around military facilities or oil and gas infrastructure) are usually created for non-conservation purposes but can still have environmental benefits. A further complication is that some protected areas provide a complete 'sanctuary' or 'no take' conservation areas and clearly fall within the IUCN definition of an MPA, but other multi-use zones provide for different industries and activities (including fishing, shipping, tourism, and conservation) with only a percentage of the area dedicated to conservation. This array of terminology has created – and continues to create – confusion, because it requires a detailed examination of the rules and regulations for any given marine area in order to determine the purpose and conservation effect.

MPAs are frequently controversial, particularly where they restrict fishing or other exploitation activities, bringing conservationists and fishers into conflict.[23] MPAs are also difficult to monitor, given the remoteness and invisibility of many offshore and underwater activities, and laws are therefore difficult to enforce. Nevertheless, there have been some successes when human activities, and in many cases people themselves, have been removed from adjacent land with resulting rewards for the marine environment. For example, Bikini Atoll in the Marshall Islands was heavily affected by colonisation and then nuclear testing, being described as a wasteland in the 1950s at which time local communities were relocated off the islands shortly thereafter and have not been permitted to return.[24] Today the coral reef and associated species have now recovered to a great extent.[25] Scientific studies of security zones around oil rigs and offshore infrastructure similarly indicate that, without human activity and fishing pressure, ecosystems can thrive.[26] Temporary reductions in pressures over large ocean areas, such as the cessation of fishing in the Atlantic during World War II[27] and suspension of cruise ship activities during the COVID-19 pandemic, have demonstrated that oceans can recover when anthropogenic impacts are removed.[28] Indeed, there is plenty of evidence of the value of MPAs for ocean health, and they have accordingly been recognised as a key component of marine conservation strategies.[29]

Many nations in the world have adopted legislation that allows governments to designate national and marine parks for conservation purposes. Although each

Figure 8.2 An emperor penguin (*Aptenodytes forsteri*) chick with parent and an unrelated chick on sea ice in the Ross Sea, Antarctica. (Image courtesy of Brocken Inaglory, 27 October 2007.)

nation is different, there are many similarities. For example, most laws establish a government agency or authority to manage the creation of parks and their ongoing care and control. Processes for nominating a new area and criteria for designation are frequently set out. There are provisions on how the parks are to be controlled and managed, often involving different zoning within the park where different activities can take place. Finally, compliance, non-compliance, offence and enforcement provisions and usually included to varying extents. Legislation in this form can be found across the world.[30]

International treaties and marine protected areas

Some of the early fisheries and species-based agreements outlined in Chapters 4 and 7 made specific reference to designated areas associated with species protections. The *International Convention for the Regulation of Whaling* (1946), for example, permitted the International Whaling Commission to adopt 'regulations with respect to the conservation and utilization of whale resources, fixing . . . open and closed waters, including the designation of sanctuary areas'.[31] Similarly, the *Convention for the Conservation of Antarctic Seals* (1972) provided in Article 3 that:

> Contracting Parties may . . . adopt other measures with respect to the conservation . . . of seal resources . . . (d) open and closed areas, including the

designation of reserves, (e) the designation of special areas where there shall be no disturbance of seals.[32]

As noted in Chapter 7, the *Polar Bear Agreement* (1973) also included references to protecting 'denning and feeding sites'.[33] Frequently, however, these laws were adopted to protect resources for future hunting and harvesting rather than for conservation purposes. It was not until the Stockholm Conference in 1972 that the global community collectively recognised that people had a 'special responsibility to safeguard and wisely manage the heritage of wildlife and its habitat, which are now gravely imperilled by a combination of adverse factors' and that 'nature conservation . . . must therefore receive importance'.[34]

The *Convention on Migratory Species* (Convention on Migratory Species) (1979) sought to prevent migratory species from becoming endangered, including by encouraging protection of habitats. Article III (4)(a) required States to endeavour 'to conserve and . . . restore those habitats of the species which are of importance in removing the species from danger of extinction'. Range States[35] for migratory species were encouraged to enter into agreements to restore the species utilising tools including conservation and restoration of habitats and networks of habitats.[36] There are seven agreements under the Convention and all of them include rules for protected areas. The *Agreement on the Conservation of Cetaceans of The Black Sea, Mediterranean Sea and Contiguous Atlantic Area* (ACCOBAMS) (1996), for example, required parties to take coordinated measures to maintain the conservation status of cetaceans including through a network of specially protected areas.[37] This, and the treaties that preceded it, focused more squarely on species protections, with area-based measures as additional components. The two key early treaties that took a purely area-based approach were the Ramsar Convention and the World Heritage Convention.

Ramsar Convention on Wetlands of International Importance (1971)

This Convention was the first international agreement focused purely on protecting habitats. Wetlands were frequently seen as wastelands that could not be used for agriculture or construction. Their dampness was believed to be the source of disease, and they were frequently used as rubbish dumps and/or filled to reclaim land. Their ecological importance was not acknowledged in a treaty until 1971, when the Ramsar Convention was drafted by States and non-governmental organisations in response to concerns that bodies of water were being lost to development that were crucial for migratory birds. To this end, rather than address species, it focused on wetland areas, defined quite broadly as including:

> areas of marsh, fen, peatland or water, whether natural or artificial, permanent or temporary, with water that is static or flowing, fresh, brackish or

> salt, including areas of marine water the depth of which at low tide does not exceed six metres.[38]

This definition was extended further in Article 2.1 for the purpose of protecting 'coherent' sites. Relevant to shorelines, wetlands: 'may incorporate riparian and coastal zones adjacent to the wetlands, and islands or bodies of marine water deeper than six metres at low tide lying within the wetlands'. Such areas are habitats for many fish, molluscs, crustaceans, snakes, corals, seagrasses and mangroves, as well as being frequented by dugongs, turtles and some other marine megafauna. Member States were required to promote the conservation of wetlands, including by establishing nature reserves and as far as possible the wise use of those wetlands.[39] Although the treaty does not include definitions for 'conservation', 'wise use' or 'ecological character', the subsequent *Handbook on Wise Use of Wetlands*, refers to the ecosystem approach, sustainable use and development, as well as restoration, and notes that wise use 'equates with the maintenance of ecosystems and the continued delivery of ecosystem services to maintain human well-being'.[40] It was one of the first Conventions to require States to report to the Secretariat, although Article 3.2 only requires monitoring and reporting of changes in 'ecological character of any wetland in its territory'. Marine areas listed under the Ramsar Convention can be found across the world in industrialised and developing States. Examples include Blue Bay Marine Park (Mauritius), Abrolhos Marine National Park (Brazil), and the Great Barrier Reef (Australia).[41] As well as fully protected MPAs, the flexible definition of wetland in the Ramsar Convention allows not only for oceans but also coastal lagoons and estuaries that meet the shoreline to be globally recognised, conserved and managed.

World Heritage Convention

The WHC was the second area-based treaty adopted in the 1970s. It was triggered by the construction of the Aswan High Dam, which would submerge the temple of Abu Simbel and other Nubian monuments. Relevantly, the Convention seeks to protect both natural and cultural sites of 'outstanding universal value' – of such exceptional value to be of importance for all humanity including future generations.[42] Article 2 provides a framework for Member States to nominate sites, and the World Heritage Committee decides on the listing based on a series of criteria and, with respect to natural areas, the expert advice of IUCN. Outstanding universal value (OUV) is not defined in the treaty but is explained further in *The Operational Guidelines for the Implementation of the World Heritage Convention*:

> [OUV] means . . . natural significance which is so exceptional as to transcend national boundaries and to be of common importance for present and future

> generations of all humanity. As such, the permanent protection of this heritage is of the highest importance to the international community as a whole.[43]

If designated as World Heritage, Article 4 (a)–(e) requires member states to promote conservation, anticipate threats and in necessary cases 'to take the appropriate legal, scientific, technical, administrative and financial measures necessary for the identification, protection, conservation, presentation and rehabilitation of this heritage'. For sites poorly protected they can be listed as *World Heritage in Danger* triggering further assistance and resources. There are 50 marine places listed in 37 countries including oceanic sites such as the Great Barrier Reef (Australia) and Papahānaumokuākea (Hawaii), and seas including the Wadden Sea (Europe) as well as intertidal, shoreline places such as the Sundarbans (Bangladesh and India). World Heritage listing has proved to be a valuable commodity, drawing considerable global recognition and respect and attracting public interest that has economic tourism benefits. As noted later in the chapter, however, tourists can love natural heritage sites too much and ultimately create new impacts. Furthermore, climate change is impacting many marine areas, and controversy surrounds the use of 'in danger' listing in this context (see text box).

Australia's Great Barrier Reef

This is the largest barrier reef in the world, home to myriad species and utilised by Indigenous peoples for millennia. It also drew early scientific attention from 1770 when Lt Cook navigated the *HMS Endeavour* through the reef, mapped it and collected scientific samples. Later hydrographic surveying of the reef was done from 1800 to 1850. Licensed guano extraction from islands on the reef commenced in 1863. Coral trade began in 1879 with more commercial coral mining from 1900 and later rock phosphate mining from 1918. Pearl and trochus shell, beche-de-mer, dugong and turtle harvesting were other reef-based activities that led to severe depletion by the late 19th and early 20th centuries. In 1920 lime from coral reefs was being applied to alkalise acidic soils for sugarcane production, but by 1960 activities were restricted to reef fishing, tourism and coral collecting industries. The first standalone marine park in Australia was declared around Green Island, which led to increased tourism but activities such as coral collecting were not restricted until 1933.[44] The Great Barrier Reef was placed on the World Heritage List in 1981, noted for its unique natural attributes and immense scientific and environmental benefits. In 2023, the UNESCO World Heritage Committee considered, but stopped short of, listing the Great Barrier Reef as a site that is 'in danger' due to serious threats from pollution and ocean warming.[45]

The Law of the Sea

The *UN Convention on the Law of the Sea* (UNCLOS) defined the maritime zones in the water column (territorial sea, Exclusive Economic Zone and high seas) and seabed (Continental Shelf and the Area). In this sense it divided the ocean both horizontally and vertically. Notably, UNCLOS did not provide a framework, nor any obligations, relating to protected areas. The coastal State was, however, permitted to establish safety zones around artificial islands and installations[46] – such as oil rigs – and although this is based upon safe navigation rather than conservation biodiversity benefits have been identified.[47] Safety zones could also be established 500 metres around scientific research installations.[48] In relation to the territorial sea, the coastal State was permitted to adopt laws for innocent passage with respect to the safety of navigation, regulation of maritime traffic, protection of facilities and installations as well as cables and pipelines.[49] This would, presumably, include designating zones for safe passage and prohibiting access to unsafe areas. The only specific reference to protected areas in the EEZ is found in Article 62, which permitted a coastal State to establish conservation measures in laws relating to 'regulating . . . areas of fishing'.[50] In relation to the high seas, it was not until 2023 when the High Seas Treaty (sometimes known as the BBNJ Agreement) was adopted, that such rules were included.[51] Part III of the Agreement supported the establishment of 'a comprehensive system of area-based management tools, with ecologically representative and well-connected networks of marine protected areas', in areas beyond national jurisdiction, to support conservation and sustainable use of high seas areas.[52] This Agreement thus closed a gap in the international law by providing a mechanism to establish MPAs on the high seas, but as yet none have been declared.

Rio Conference and the Convention on Biological Diversity

In 1992, the UN Conference on Environment and Development (UNCED or the Rio Conference) resulted in the adoption of the Rio Declaration, Agenda 21 and the *Convention on Biological Diversity*. The Rio Declaration and Agenda 21 were not legally binding, but they have been highly influential. The former provided key international environmental law principles (as explained in Chapter 1) including Principle 7 urging States to cooperate to 'conserve, protect and restore the health and integrity of the Earth's ecosystem', although it did not mention area-based measures. Agenda 21 was an action plan for the implementation of sustainable development which encourages coastal States 'to maintain biological diversity and productivity of marine species and habitats' through measures including the 'establishment and management of protected areas'.[53] Although human use was not mentioned in that paragraph, it is clear that the purpose of the protection measures is for the benefit of people and development activities.[54] Furthermore, it provided that

> States should identify marine ecosystems exhibiting high levels of biodiversity and productivity and other critical habitat areas and should provide

necessary limitations on use in these areas, through, inter alia, designation of protected areas. Priority should be accorded, as appropriate, to:

(a) Coral reef ecosystems;
(b) Estuaries;
(c) Temperate and tropical wetlands, including mangroves;
(d) Seagrass beds;
(e) Other spawning and nursery areas.[55]

This both created the impetus to establish protected areas and also a way to prioritise action. The *Convention on Biological Diversity*, also adopted at the Rio Conference, had several legally binding provisions relating to protected areas requiring member States to establish a system of such protected areas where special measures are needed to conserve biodiversity, develop guidelines for their establishment, and promote sound and sustainable management of adjacent areas.[56] These protected areas may be on land or in the water. In a later decision, MPAs were defined as:

> any defined area within or adjacent to the marine environment, together with its overlying waters and associated flora, fauna and historical and cultural features, which has been *reserved by legislation or other effective means*, including custom, with the effect that its marine and/or coastal biodiversity enjoys a higher level of protection than its surroundings.[57] [emphasis added]

The inclusion of 'other effective means', has allowed some traditional and community-based conservation areas to fall within the definition, even where they might not be formally recognised through legislation. Importantly, this could include, for example, the Locally Managed Marine Areas (see text box provided earlier).

The *Convention on Biological Diversity* championed the use of protected area management tools through its programme on *Marine and Coastal Biodiversity*,[58] and by establishing targets focused explicitly on encouraging the designation of more areas (see textbox). In a 2008 decision the Convention Secretariat developed further guidance on designing representative networks of MPAs by identifying five scientific properties: (1) ecologically and biologically significant areas (EBSAs), (2) representativity, (3) connectivity, (4) replicated ecological features and (5) adequate and viable sites. The *Convention on Biological Diversity* EBSAs are special areas of the ocean with scientific criteria that include uniqueness, importance at species' life history stages, significance as habitats for threatened or declining species, vulnerability of the area, productivity, diversity and naturalness.[59] Interestingly, this prioritisation is different to that for marine species where the focus is purely on conservation status – the most threatened or endangered species tend to receive the greatest protection. Most whales, many species of sharks, and all species of turtles, for example, are listed under several treaties as well as receiving domestic legal protection because of their threatened status. So, the most degraded species are given priority rather than those that provide the greatest functional or ecosystem value. Yet the area-based provisions include the protection of the most intact natural, and ecologically or biologically significant, marine areas. Some of the largest MPAs in the world are relatively remote and, although they have received global attention, many are at far less risk from human activity than important (albeit smaller) areas closer to shorelines. These include the Ross Sea in Antarctica, Pitcairn Islands in the Pacific, British Indian Ocean Territory Marine Protected Area (Chagos) in the Indian Ocean, and Papahānaumokuākea in the US Hawaiian Islands.

Area-based global targets and their achievement

TARGETS

Aichi Targets (2010)

Target 11 – By 2020, at least 17 percent of terrestrial and inland water, and 10 percent of coastal and marine areas . . .

Global Biodiversity Targets for Marine Environment (2022)

Target 1 – Ensure that all areas are under participatory, integrated and biodiversity inclusive spatial planning and/or effective management processes addressing land- and sea use change, to bring the loss of areas of high biodiversity importance, including ecosystems of high ecological integrity, close to zero by 2030 . . .

Target 2 – Ensure that by 2030 at least 30 percent of areas of degraded terrestrial, inland water, and marine and coastal ecosystems are under effective restoration . . .

GOALS

SDGs (2015)

SDG 14.5 – By 2020, conserve at least 10 percent of coastal and marine areas . . .

EFFECTIVENESS

Protected Planet World Database on Protected Areas

18,720 MPAs comprising 816% of the ocean

MPA Atlas

2.9% of the ocean is fully or highly protected from fishing impacts

---

Other international law incorporating area-based tools

Other treaties focused on different industries and purposes but also included area-based tools. Under the *International Convention for the Prevention of Pollution from Ships was Adopted in 1973 with Amendments in 1978* (MARPOL 73/78),[60] 'Special Areas' can be established where stricter controls are applied to discharges from ships (of oil, sewage, noxious liquid substances, garbage or air pollution) because the oceanic space has particular oceanographic or ecological characteristics. In some cases an entire sea is listed with respect to multiple threats, such as the Mediterranean Sea regarding oil and garbage.[61] MARPOL also provides for an area to be recognised as a 'Particularly Sensitive Sea Area' (PSSA) based on ecological, scientific or socio-economic criteria. The designation of a PSSA is accompanied by tailored 'associated protective measures' such as ships' routing, speed, discharge or anchoring restrictions, or more broadly operational criteria and prohibited activities.[62] Existing PSSAs include the Great Barrier Reef (Australia), Galapagos Islands (Ecuador) and Papahānaumokuākea (US);[63] several of these areas are subject to a number of other designations and legal protections (including under the World Heritage Convention at the international level, and domestic MPA laws). The Special Areas and PSSAs provide important recognition of the catastrophic damage that can be done by shipping, particularly in enclosed and semi-enclosed seas and sites, and seek to address the risk through maritime restrictions.

Specific regional agreements

The Antarctic Treaty and related agreements collectively known as the Antarctic Treaty System (ATS) is a unique and remarkably effective area-based treaty system that regulates human activities in Antarctica. The Antarctic Treaty, originally signed by 12 nations in 1959, established Antarctica as a place to be used exclusively for peaceful purposes and to guarantee freedom to conduct scientific investigation, a situation that remains today.[64] Subsequent agreements built upon the Antarctic Treaty foundation, including the 1964 *Agreed Measures for the Conservation of Antarctic Fauna and Flora* with the first Antarctic specially protected areas being established under this instrument. In 1975 the international Scientific Committee on Antarctic Research (SCAR) established a scientific program Biological Investigations of Marine Antarctic Systems and Stocks (BIOMASS) to determine how the 'living resources' of the Antarctic marine ecosystem could be managed in a sustainable way. Over the next decade, the concept of the ocean as an ecosystem emerged, where the marine environment was perceived as an interconnected whole and that changes affecting one species could be expected to impact on other species and on the physical environment.

But while the he Antarctic Treaty, had created an international framework for managing human activities on the Antarctic continent – those affecting land, ice and water south of latitude 60° South – it did not provide any protection for the living marine resources of the Southern Ocean north of that latitude.

In the years after World War II, many traditional fishing grounds in the Northern Hemisphere had experienced catastrophic collapse from overfishing. These included the Californian sardine fishery in the 1950s, the Scandinavian herring fishery in the late 1960s, the Peruvian anchovy fishery in the early 1970s, and the northern cod fishery in the Atlantic Ocean in the early 1990s.[65] As with the whaling industry in the early 20th century, commercial fishers began casting their gaze towards the vast waters of the Southern Ocean as the last frontier for large-scale fisheries.

Amidst speculation that the over-exploitation of whales in the Southern Ocean had resulted in an abundance of Antarctic krill, and that krill could provide a valuable new source of protein for humans, the Soviet Union sent a fisheries research vessel into the Southern Ocean in 1964 to assess krill stocks and to determine whether they could be harvested on a commercial basis. A new industry was born, and by 1970, the Soviets were marketing krill butter and krill cheese, as well as a red-coloured krill paste. Before long marine scientists were warning that large-scale krill harvesting was adversely affecting the larger marine mammals that depended on them.[66] By the early 1980s, Antarctic Treaty member states were considering how to respond to the rapid expansion of the Antarctic krill fisheries by the Soviet Union and Ukraine and, to a lesser extent by Japan. Their negotiations culminated in an agreement known as the *Convention on the Conservation of Antarctic Marine Living Resources* (CCAMLR). The Convention extended the reach of international governance under the Antarctic Treaty to include all marine living resources as far north as the Antarctic Convergence, around latitude 55° South, and recognised that predators and prey formed part of an interconnected marine ecosystem. It identified Antarctic krill as the keystone species of the Southern Ocean ecosystem and acknowledged that unregulated krill fishing – or simply a poor breeding season – could have a detrimental impact on all species that depended on it for food, and especially on those with no alternatives.[67] The aim of the Convention was to regulate the harvesting of species in what was regarded as one of the world's last remaining wildernesses. It also provided for the establishment of an international commission which recognised that some nations would continue to exploit the ocean's resources but declared that they should not deplete its 'stocks' or adversely affect other species in the ecosystem. Member states agreed to pay a subscription based on their annual harvest.

The 1991 *Protocol on Environmental Protection to the Antarctic Treaty* provided for the designation of Antarctic Specially Protected Areas (ASPA) and Antarctic Specially Managed Areas (ASMA).[68] CCAMLR has also adopted a General Framework for the establishment of MPAs and created specific protected areas including the Ross Sea region MPA, support for the protection of the values of the Antarctic Specially Managed and Protected Areas.[69] Antarctica has also received protected area protections from the International Maritime Organisation, with Special Areas designated in Antarctic waters under oil, noxious liquid substances and garbage Annexes of MARPOL.[70]

Tourism in MPAs

The rapid expansion of marine protected areas has created an opportunity to develop new livelihoods and non-consumptive industries based on tourism, where once extractive fishing and other industries were widespread. The popularity of seaside recreation gathered momentum in Europe in the 18th century, initially amongst members of the aristocracy who were inspired by its restorative health benefits and depictions of the sea by Romantic artists and writers. By the 19th century, city dwellers were discovering the pleasures of the beach for holiday activities such as beachcombing and sea bathing. The shoreline was also a place for learning about marine natural history, with marine flora and fauna collections and displays of living marine animals in aquaria becoming popular.[71] Recreational uses of the ocean have continued to expand, presenting new challenges for marine and coastal environments. With the development of marine ecotourism and deep sea recreation since the 1980s, for example, visitors are now able to access sensitive offshore breeding and feeding areas, particularly those considered to be important 'sites of fidelity' for charismatic species. Marine-based tourism, for example, offers visitors opportunities to interact directly with marine animals through activities such as whale watching, swimming with sea lions and sharks, snorkelling and diving. The accessibility and affordability of these activities has hastened the growth of enterprises built upon them.

Importantly, no global treaty exists for eco-tourism, although the Convention on Migratory Species and the International Whaling Commission have endorsed some strategies and tools,[72] and best practice legal measures have been distilled and shared amongst nations, often led by NGOs.[73] Sites of fidelity can be protected using protected area management, but industry-based codes of conduct have been developed to prevent negative visitor impacts through participant pressure, feeding and baiting, and vessel impacts.[74] This is an area where international law could play a valuable role in the future particularly by setting minimum enforceable standards, perhaps drawing upon existing documents such as the *Manual of Regulations and Guidelines Relevant to Tourism and Non-Governmental Activities in the Antarctic Treaty area*.[75]

Protecting the unprotected

Some marine areas and ecosystems have been left behind in legal history, with no legal mechanism at all providing for their protection. As noted earlier (see Chapter 7), hydrothermal vents are found in the deep sea mostly located in mid-oceanic, high seas areas.[76] The 2023 High Seas Treaty offers a new opportunity to protect such areas, providing a framework for the designation of areas beyond national jurisdiction – protected areas in the High Seas. Part III of the Agreement provides for proposals for MPAs to be submitted to the secretariat,[77] publicised and assessed,[78] with decisions being made by consensus or by a three-quarter majority of voting representatives at the conference of the parties.[79] This includes 22 indicative criteria for identification of areas set out in Annex I, which include those developed by the *Convention on Biological Diversity* but also others including fragility, sensitivity and vulnerability as well as categories of special importance for species and habitats. This new Agreement therefore develops the law on MPAs and fills an important gap that is important for hydrothermal vents but also other high seas habitats and sites.

Area-based measures work by limiting anthropogenic activities that negatively impact species and ecosystems, giving populations a chance to thrive and/or rebound. In that sense, protected area management works well in controlling human activity as it is relatively easy to understand regulations that limit certain activities in specific places. But there are no fences in the ocean and determining locations with accuracy is not easy – even with GPS – and many marine species are highly mobile. Nevertheless, it is through area-based measures that scientific concepts such as ecosystem-based management can best be applied, provided that the designated area 'matches' that of the ecosystem. The benefits of protected area management include increased spill-over effects into surrounding areas, although where ecosystems or species ranges extend beyond legal or political boundaries, a single marine park may not be possible, given jurisdictional limits. Legal regimes, for example, often separate the water column from the seabed and, in some cases, different depths in the ocean (pelagic and benthic). In other cases, species may range across artificial boundaries between national jurisdictional areas (adjacent territorial seas or EEZs for example) requiring the development of bi- and multilateral transboundary MPAs.[80]

On land, area-based measures have become more sophisticated as our terrestrial developments have expanded and evolved. Rather than a single-use area, multiple-zones are frequently seen in terrestrial parks that provide for activities such as conservation, scientific research, compatible industries (e.g., tourism, bee-keeping), as well as buffer zones. This approach is also evident in marine areas where zoning might include various types of fishing, research, shipping, tourism, and traditional use, as well as highly protected and special management areas. The Great Barrier Reef in Australia was a pioneering example of marine zoning combining conservation and sustainable use, including multiple-use management first introduced in 1981.[81]

Conclusion

Area-based tools to conserve and manage marine species and ecosystems have long been used to restrict human activities and impacts, but the use of these tools in more contemporary times has lagged behind fishing regulations and species conservation. As with the legal history of oceans, seas and shorelines demonstrated in other chapters of this book, there is a strong intersection between government interventions and scientific knowledge. This is most clearly seen in relation to the selection of sites of critical importance, classification of areas and the development of management criteria. Yet, there is also evidence that exploitation continues to trump conservation, with the designation of MPAs that contribute to global goals being in low-value areas or spaces where human pressures are already reduced.

Until recently, it could be argued that there was an uncomfortable mismatch between approaches to species conservation – whereby those with the poorest conservation status are afforded the highest levels of protection – and area-based measures, where greater recognition has been given to those with greater biodiversity/ecological value and intactness. However, the 2023 High Seas Treaty has included a far greater range of characteristics which combine both approaches. As noted earlier, it remains to be seen how effective this approach will be. Another noteworthy development has been the efforts made to address mismatches between national jurisdictions and regime authority areas with species ranges and the extension of ecosystems to create a representative, connected and networked approach. This can be seen through the development of transboundary MPAs[82] and agreements between range States,[83] as well as cooperative arrangements between RFMOs with control and management of different fish stocks and pelagic areas and RSCs focused on environmental health, including benthic (sea floor) areas.[84]

A key focus of international efforts has been to increase the percentage of marine and coastal areas designated as protected areas. Although targets have not been achieved as yet, the percentage of land and sea areas designated for protection has increased dramatically. But often these remain 'paper parks', with limited active management and inadequate effectiveness. Ensuring full implementation of management measures and the monitoring and assessment of effectiveness will be vital for the future. Definitional issues are part of the problem. The IUCN definition has been widely endorsed, leading to the common usage of the term MPA. Nonetheless, the approach has been criticised as focusing too heavily on the purposes for which the MPA was declared rather than protection provided.[85] It is clear that some safety and security zones around infrastructure provide great biodiversity benefits. The Aichi Targets, SDGs and Global Biodiversity Framework have all focused on increasing the number and size of MPAs. Some large MPAs in remote locations, formally designated for conservation, may remain 'paper parks' or be of limited conservation benefit. Suggestions have been made that an alternative approach could involve a regulation-based classification system with a focus on potential impacts of permitted activities and the rules that control and manage them.[86] Here the IUCN, produces its *Green List of Protected and Conserved Areas*,[87] just as it does in the species conservation area through the publication of its *Red List of Threatened Species*.[88] The Green List sites include those meeting the IUCN Green List Standard, demonstrating that the areas respect and engage with local communities, involve planning design that secures the sites values, effective management, successful conservation results for nature and people and a clear contribution to climate change. This approach seeks to establish a benchmark for meeting 21st-century challenges.[89] Achieving these outcomes will involve more than human effort, and it is in this context that technology could be better utilised.

Area-based measures provide further evidence of legal tools being deployed in response to problems as they emerge and focused on elements of the environment that we most directly benefit from. More intrinsic values, where they are recognised by the law, are often suppressed in favour of national, food and economic security concerns. Although cultural values are recognised within the World Heritage Convention, sacred sites have all but disappeared from legal history to the detriment of the peoples and non-human species that depend on them. In any event, increasing the number of protected areas will not prevent the impacts of climate change. Just as mobile species cannot be kept within these areas, existing conservation laws cannot constrain warming and acidifying seas or erosion and extreme weather events along shorelines. In some cases, species can move to more hospitable places, but protected areas that are the subject of legal instruments rely upon geographical definitions that do not allow for boundaries to easily be moved.

Area-based measures alone may not be sufficient to protect species and ecosystems, and more nuanced combinations of species-, area- and activity-based measures may be necessary, given the global crisis in ocean health. International law has frequently included these tools in combination. For example, the Whaling Convention was initially established as an activity-based treaty focusing on whaling, but it also included particular species-focused measures and provided for the designation of whale sanctuaries. UNCLOS also provides rules for activities such as fishing, shipping and marine scientific research, and identifies some particular species (depleted, threatened or endangered, vulnerable, dependent and associated species, rare and fragile ecosystems) and special areas. It is in this context that the adoption of the High Seas Treaty in 2023 is a welcome development, filling a gap in the law and providing a contemporary example of combining activity-, species- and area-based measures. Nevertheless, significant challenges remain to ensure that MPAs, of all descriptions and in all oceanic spaces, are fully implemented and remain fit for purpose in the changing ocean environment.

Notes

1 See Chapters 1 and 2.
2 See, for example, Chapters 4, 5, and 6.
3 There is a confusing array of terminology associated with protected areas, but the International Union for the Conservation for Nature and Natural Resources

(IUCN) – a global NGO – took the lead in 1999, in defining MPAs and classifying them into six management categories, ranging from strict nature reserves to protected areas with sustainable use. In 2008, IUCN provided a definition of MPAs, including that the main purpose of delineating the area must be conservation (although other objectives can also be included), and it is this definition that is widely used today: 'a clearly defined geographical space, recognised, dedicated and managed through legal or other effective means, to achieve the long-term conservation of nature with associated ecosystems services and cultural values': Jon Day et al., *Guidelines for Applying the IUCN Protected Area Management Categories to Marine Protected Areas*, 2nd ed. (Gland: IUCN, 2010), 8.

4 Mark Spalding and Lynne Zeitlin Hale, "Marine Protected Areas: Past, Present And Future – A Global Perspective," in *Big, Bold and Blue: Lessons from Australia's Marine Protected Areas*, ed. James Fitzsimons and Geoff Wescott (Clayton South: CSIRO Publishing, 2016), 9.

5 See "Regional Fisheries Bodies," *FAO*, accessed January 15, 2024, www.fao.org/fishery/en/rfb. Fisheries regulation and the RFMO regimes are examined in detail in Chapter 4.

6 "Regional Seas Programme," *UNEP*, accessed January 15, 2024, www.unep.org/topics/ocean-seas-and-coasts/regional-seas-programme/regional-seas-programme. This programme is examined in detail in Chapter 9.

7 See Jerod A. Merkle et al., "Site Fidelity as a Maladaptive Behavior in the Anthropocene," *Frontiers in Ecology and the Environment* 20, no. 3 (2022): 187–94.

8 Lucien Chauvin, "The Unlikely Treasure Off Peru's Coast," *The Washington Post* (June 21, 2018), www.washingtonpost.com/graphics/2018/world/in-peru-guano-bird-droppings-are-the-new-gold/.

9 See Chapters 4 and 7.

10 Marine pollution law is explored in Chapter 9.

11 In relation to the US guano trade the Guano Islands Act, 1856, permitted the US to claim any unclaimed, uninhabited island with seabird guano on it, with the fertiliser to be sold back to American farmers: Paul F. Johnston, "The Smithsonian and the 19th Century Guano Trade: This Poop Is Crap," *Smithsonian* (May 31, 2017), https://americanhistory.si.edu/blog/smithsonian-and-guano.

12 R. E. Johannes, "Traditional Marine Conservation Methods in Oceania and Their Demise," *Annual Reviews of Ecological Systems* 9 (1978): 349–64, 353; Kurt Johnson, "Cultural Tabu: How an Ancient Ocean Custom Is Saving Fiji's Reefs," *The Guardian* (June 20, 2020), www.theguardian.com/world/2020/jun/20/cultural-tabu-how-an-ancient-ocean-custom-is-saving-fijis-reefs.

13 See also R. E. Johannes, "The Renaissance of Community-based Marine Resource Management in Oceania," *Annual Review of Ecology and Systematics* 33 (2002): 317–40.

14 "Locally Managed Marine Areas Network," *LMMA Network*, accessed February 14, 2024, https://lmmanetwork.org/.

15 Deer preserves and royal game reserves, for example, in Feudal Europe: Curt Meine, "Conservation Movement, Historical," *Encyclopaedia of Biodiversity* 1 (2001): 883–96.

16 One of the earliest publications was John Evelyn's *Sylva* (Royal Society, 1662), and later writers highlighted the risks of deforestation and desertification. Thoreau and others explored the philosophical works on the value of nature and living closely with it.

17 "Yellowstone National Park," *National Park Service*, accessed February 14, 2024, www.nps.gov/yell/index.htm.

18 Interestingly, the Royal National Park included mangroves, seagrasses and a benthic marine habitat within its boundaries: Spalding and Zeitlin Hale, "Marine Protected Areas," 9.

19 Marine parks, like national parks, are geographically defined areas, with particular natural values associated with them, but they are three dimensional and the fluid nature of the saltwater environment, the inability to fence them, and the inherent mobility of species within them differ significantly.

20 R. Kearney, C. D. Buxton, and G. Farebrother, "Australia's No-Take Marine Protected Areas: Appropriate Conservation or Inappropriate Management of Fishing?" *Marine Policy* 36 (2012): 1064.

21 In this chapter, protected area management is used to refer to any area-based measure, and marine protected area (MPA) is used for conservation-focused spaces. Therefore, MPAs are one example of protected area management in action, with others being sanctuary zones, aquatic reserves, maritime safety zones, etc.

22 Day et al., *Guidelines*, 9–10.

23 Almudena Cánovas-Molina and Eduardo García-Frapolli, "Untangling Worldwide Conflicts in Marine Protected Areas: Five Lessons from the Five Continents," *Marine Policy* 121 (2020): 104185.

24 Eleanor Ainge Roy, " 'Quite Odd': Coral and Fish Thrive on Bikini Atoll 70 Years after Nuclear Tests," *The Guardian* (July 15, 2017), www.theguardian.com/world/2017/jul/15/quite-odd-coral-and-fish-thrive-on-bikini-atoll-70-years-after-nuclear-tests.

25 D. Mccauley et al., "Marine Defaunation: Animal Loss in the Global Ocean," *Science* 347, no. 6219 (2015): 1255641, referring to J. S. Davis et al., "Scales of Eden: Conservation and Pristine Devastation on Bikini Atoll," *Environmental Planning D: Society and Space* 25 (2007): 213–35.

26 See Chapter 6.

27 Doug Beare et al., "An Unintended Experiment in Fisheries Science: A Marine Area Protected by War Results in Mexican Waves in Fish Numbers-At-Age," *Naturwissenschaften* 97, no. 9 (2010): 797–808. But other research shows that the war provided only a temporary reprieve and technologies developed during and post-war facilitated greater harvests thereafter: Paul Holm, "World War II and the 'Great Acceleration' of North Atlantic Fisheries," *Global Environment* 10, no. 10 (2012): 66–91.

28 Angelique K. Howard, "The Impacts of Cruises on the Ocean: What Has COVID-19 Changed?" *American Bar Association* (May 2, 2022), www.americanbar.org/groups/environment_energy_resources/publications/mr/20220502-the-impacts-of-cruises-on-the-ocean/.

29 Michael Kriegl et al., "Marine Protected Areas: At the Crossroads of Nature Conservation and Fisheries Management," *Frontiers in Marine Science* 8 (2021). www.frontiersin.org/articles/10.3389/fmars.2021.676264/full.

30 The FAO provides an excellent database for searching the national legislation in any given State, covering thematic areas such as the sea, environment, fisheries, agriculture etc: "FAOLEX Database," *FAO*, accessed February 1, 2024, www.fao.org/faolex/country-profiles/en/.

31 International Convention for the Regulation of Whaling, Article V(1)(c).

32 Convention on the Conservation of Antarctic Seals (1972), Article 3.

33 Article II. See Chapter 7 for further details.

34 Stockholm Declaration Principle 4.

35 Range states are those that exercise jurisdiction of any part of a migratory species range as well as states that have vessels registered to them that take migratory species on the high seas.

36 Convention on the Conservation of Migratory Species of Wild Animals (1979) (Convention on Migratory Species), Article V (5).

37 Convention on Migratory Species Article II.
38 Ramsar Article 1.1
39 Articles 3 and 4.
40 Ramsar Convention Secretariat, "Wise Use of Wetlands: Concepts and Approaches for the Wise Use of Wetlands," in *Ramsar Handbooks for the Wise Use of Wetlands*, 4th ed., vol. 1. (Gland: Ramsar Convention Secretariat, 2010), 6.
41 For an interactive map and database of all Ramsar Sites globally, see "Ramsar Sites Information Service," accessed February 14, 2024, https://rsis.ramsar.org.
42 "Operational Guidelines for the Implementation of the World Heritage Convention," in *UNESCO* (Paris: UNESCO, 2021), accessed February 26, 2024, https://whc.unesco.org/en/guidelines/.
43 Ibid.
44 Ben Daley and Peter Griggs, "Mining the Reefs and Cays: Coral, Guano and Rock Phosphate Extraction in the Great Barrier Reef, Australia, 1844–1940)," *Environment and History* 12, no. 4 (2006): 395–433; and Ben Daley and Peter Griggs " 'Loved to Death': Coral Collecting in the Great Barrier Reef, Australia, 1770–1970," *Environment and History* 14, no. 1 (2008): 89–119.
45 "Australia's Great Barrier Reef Stays Off UNESCO Danger List, Still under 'Serious Threat'," *Reuters* (August 1, 2023), www.reuters.com/business/environment/australias-great-barrier-reef-off-unesco-danger-list-still-under-serious-threat-2023-08-01.
46 UNCLOS Article 60.
47 Sean Van Elden, Jessica J. Meeuwig, and Richard J. Hobbs, "Offshore Platforms as Novel Ecosystems: A Case Study from Australia's Northwest Shelf," *Ecology and Evolution* 12, no. 2 (2022): e8496.
48 UNCLOS Article 260.
49 UNCLOS Article 21.
50 UNCLOS Article 62(4)(c).
51 Agreement under the United Nations Convention on the Law of the Sea on the Conservation and Sustainable Use of Marine Biological Diversity of Areas beyond National Jurisdiction (2023).
52 High Seas Treaty, Article 17.
53 Agenda 21, para. 17.7.
54 Agenda 21, para. 17.3.
55 Agenda 21, 17.86.
56 Convention on Biological Diversity, Article 8.
57 "COP 7 Decision VII/5," *Convention on Biological Diversity*, accessed December 19, 2023, www.cbd.int/decision/cop/?id=7742.
58 "Marine and Coastal Biodiversity," *Convention on Biological Diversity*, accessed March 15, 2024, www.cbd.int/marine/.
59 "Background on the EBSA Process," *CBD Ecologically or Biologically Significant Areas*, accessed December 19, 2023, www.cbd.int/ebsa/about.
60 "Pollution Prevention," *IMO*, accessed November 1, 2023, www.imo.org/en/OurWork/Environment/Pages/Pollution-Prevention.aspx.
61 "Special Areas under MARPOL," *IMO*, accessed February 26, 2024, www.imo.org/en/OurWork/Environment/Pages/Special-Areas-Marpol.aspx
62 "Particularly Sensitive Sea Areas," *IMO*, accessed December 19, 2023, www.imo.org/en/ourwork/environment/pages/pssas.aspx.
63 Ibid.
64 There have been some unsuccessful efforts to allow mining and resource extraction, fishing restrictions remain controversial and the ATS parties remain divided on the

establishment of marine protected areas. Yet overall, the focus on peaceful scientific investigation persists.

65 See Chapter 4 for further discussion of fisheries regulation.

66 Cassandra M. Brooks and David G. Ainley, "Fishing the Bottom of the Earth: the Political Challenges of Ecosystem-Based Management," in *Handbook on the Politics of Antarctica*, ed. Alan D. Hemmings, Klaus Dodds, and Peder Roberts (Cheltenham: Edward Elgar, 2017), 422.

67 Henrik Osterblom and Olof Olsson, "CCAMLR: An Ecosystem Approach to the Southern Ocean in the Anthropocene," in *Handbook on the Politics of Antarctica*, ed. Klaus Dodds, Alan D. Hemmings, and Peder Roberts (Cheltenham: Edward Elgar Publishing, 2017), 408–9.

68 Antarctica has its own database of protected areas: "Antarctic Protected Areas Database," *Secretariat of the Antarctic Treaty*, accessed February 1, 2024, www.ats.aq/devph/en/apa-database.

69 "CCAMLR Conservation Measures," accessed February 26, 2024, https://cm.ccamlr.org/.

70 "Special Areas under MARPOL."

71 Helen Rozwadowski, *Vast Expanses: A History of the Oceans* (London: Reaktion Books, 2018), 113–18.

72 "Whale Shark Interaction Guidelines," *Convention on Migratory Species*, accessed February 26, 2024, www.cms.int/en/publication/whale-shark-interaction-guidelines accessed February 26, 2024; and "Management Strategies and Tools," *International Whaling Commission*, accessed February 26, 2024, https://wwhandbook.iwc.int/en/responsible-management/management-strategies

73 "Shark and Ray Tourism Best Practice," *Ocean Earth Foundation*, accessed February 26, 2024, https://tierramar.com.au/portfolio-view/shark-and-ray-tourism-best-practice/; and "Global Best Practice Guidance for Responsible Whale and Dolphin Watching," *World Cetacean Alliance*, accessed February 26, 2024, https://worldcetaceanalliance.org/wp-content/uploads/2019/07/WCA-Global-Best-Practice-Guidance-Whale-Watch.pdf

74 For example, "Code of Conduct," *Madagascar Whaleshark Project*, accessed February 26, 2024, www.madawhalesharks.org/get-involved/code-of-conduct/

75 "Tourism and Non-Governmental Activities," *Secretariat of the Antarctic Treaty*, accessed February 14, 2024, www.ats.aq/e/tourism.html.

76 "Hydrothermal Vent," *Wikipedia*, accessed February 26, 2024, https://upload.wikimedia.org/wikipedia/commons/thumb/e/ed/Distribution_of_hydrothermal_vent_fields.png/1920px-Distribution_of_hydrothermal_vent_fields.png.

77 High Seas Treaty Article 17.

78 High Seas Treaty Articles 17 and 18.

79 High Seas Treaty Article 19.

80 For example, the Lubombo TFCA is the first marine transfrontier conservation area in Africa, created in 2007 by Mozambique, South Africa and Swaziland, focusing on marine turtle conservation. An example of a multilateral MPA is the Pelagos Sanctuary for Cetaceans in the Ligurian Sea of the Mediterranean involving cooperation among France, Italy and Monaco. A multilateral initiative which falls short of the definition of an MPA is the Coral Triangle Initiative, accessed February 26, 2024, www.coraltriangleinitiative.org/.

81 Jon C. Day, Richard A. Kenchington, John M. Tanzer, and Darren S. Cameron, "Marine Zoning Revisited: How Decades of Zoning the Great Barrier Reef Has Evolved as an Effective Spatial Planning Approach for Marine Ecosystem-based Management," *Aquatic Conservation: Marine and Freshwater Ecosystems* 29, no. S2 (2019): 9–32.

82 Dorothy C. Zbicz, "Marine Transboundary Conservation," *Global Transboundary Conservation Network*, accessed February 1, 2024, www.tbpa.net/page.php?ndx=49.
83 "Agreements," *Convention on Migratory Species*, accessed February 1, 2024, www.cms.int/en/cms-instruments/
84 Collective Arrangement," *OSPAR Commission*, accessed February 1, 2024, www.ospar.org/about/international-cooperation/collective-arrangement.
85 Bárbara Horta e Costa et al., "A Regulation-Based Classification System for Marine Protected Areas (MPAs)," *Marine Policy* 72 (2016): 192–98.
86 Ibid., 197. See also Celia Ojeda-Martinez et al., "A Conceptual Framework for the Integral Management of Marine Protected Areas," *Ocean & Coastal Management* 52 (2009): 89, regarding the need for a conceptual framework to simplify MPA management.
87 "IUCN Green List of Protected and Conserved Areas," *IUCN*, accessed February 23, 2024, https://iucngreenlist.org/.
88 See Chapter 7.
89 "IUCN Green List of Protected and Conserved Areas."

Bibliography

Alaimo, Stacy. "Afterword: Adequate Imaginaries for Anthropocene Seas." In *Blue Legalities: The Life and Laws of the Sea*, edited by Irus Braverman and Elizabeth R. Johnson. Durham: Duke University Press, 2019.

"Australia's Great Barrier Reef Stays Off UNESCO Danger List, Still under 'Serious Threat." *Reuters* (August 1, 2023). www.reuters.com/business/environment/australias-great-barrier-reef-off-unesco-danger-list-still-under-serious-threat-2023-08-01.

Beare Doug et al. "An Unintended Experiment In Fisheries Science: A Marine Area Protected by War Results in Mexican Waves in Fish Numbers-at-Age." *Naturwissenschaften* 97, no. 9 (2010): 797–808.

Brooks, Cassandra M., and David G. Ainley. "Fishing the Bottom of the Earth: the Political Challenges of Ecosystem-Based Management." In *Handbook on the Politics of Antarctica*, edited by Alan D. Hemmings, Klaus Dodds, and Peder Roberts. Cheltenham: Edward Elgar 2017.

Cánovas-Molina, Almudena, and Eduardo García-Frapolli. "Untangling Worldwide Conflicts in Marine Protected Areas: Five Lessons from the Five Continents." *Marine Policy* 121 (2020): 104185.

CBD Ecologically or Biologically Significant Marine Areas. "Background on the EBSA Process." Accessed December 19, 2023. www.cbd.int/ebsa/about.

CCAMLR. "CCAMLR Conservation Measures." Accessed February 26, 2024. https://cm.ccamlr.org/.

Chauvin, Lucien. "The Unlikely Treasure Off Peru's Coast." *The Washington Post* (June 21, 2018). www.washingtonpost.com/graphics/2018/world/in-peru-guano-bird-droppings-are-the-new-gold/.

Convention on Biological Diversity. "COP 7 Decision VII/5." Accessed December 19, 2023. www.cbd.int/decision/cop/?id=7742.

Convention on Biological Diversity. "Marine and Coastal Biodiversity." Accessed March 15, 2024. www.cbd.int/marine/

Convention on Migratory Species. "Agreements." Accessed February 1, 2024. www.cms.int/en/cms-instruments/.

Convention on Migratory Species. "Whale Shark Interaction Guidelines." Accessed February 26, 2024. www.cms.int/en/publication/whale-shark-interaction-guidelines.

Coral Triangle Initiative. Accessed February 26, 2024. www.coraltriangleinitiative.org/.
Daley, Ben, and Peter Griggs. "'Loved to Death': Coral Collecting in the Great Barrier Reef, Australia, 1770–1970." *Environment and History* 14, no. 1 (2008): 89–119.
Daley, Ben, and Peter Griggs. "Mining the Reefs and Cays: Coral, Guano and Rock Phosphate Extraction in the Great Barrier Reef, Australia, 1844–1940." *Environment and History* 12, no. 4 (2006): 395–433.
Davis, J. S. et al. "Scales of Eden: Conservation and Pristine Devastation on Bikini Atoll." *Environmental Planning D: Society and Space* 25 (2007): 213–35.
Day, Jon C. et al. *Guidelines for Applying the IUCN Protected Area Management Categories to Marine Protected Areas*. 2nd ed. Gland: IUCN, 2010.
Day, Jon C., Richard A. Kenchington, John M. Tanzer, and Darren S. Cameron. "Marine Zoning Revisited: How Decades of Zoning the Great Barrier Reef Has Evolved as an Effective Spatial Planning Approach for Marine Ecosystem-based Management." *Aquatic Conservation: Marine and Freshwater Ecosystems* 29, no. S2 (2019): 9–32.
FAO. "FAOLEX Database." Accessed February 1, 2024. www.fao.org/faolex/country-profiles/en/.
FAO. "Regional Fisheries Bodies." Accessed January 15, 2024. www.fao.org/fishery/en/rfb.
Holm, Paul. "World War II and the 'Great Acceleration' of North Atlantic Fisheries." *Global Environment* 10, no. 10 (2012): 66–91.
Horta e Costa, Bárbara et al. "A Regulation-based Classification System for Marine Protected Areas (MPAs)." *Marine Policy* 72 (2016): 192–98.
Howard, Angelique K. "The Impacts of Cruises on the Ocean: What Has COVID-19 Changed?" *American Bar Association* (May 2, 2022). www.americanbar.org/groups/environment_energy_resources/publications/mr/20220502-the-impacts-of-cruises-on-the-ocean/.
IMO. "Particularly Sensitive Sea Areas." Accessed December 19, 2023. www.imo.org/en/ourwork/environment/pages/pssas.aspx.
IMO. "Pollution Prevention." Accessed November 1, 2023. www.imo.org/en/OurWork/Environment/Pages/Pollution-Prevention.aspx.
IMO. "Special Areas under MARPOL." Accessed February 26, 2024. www.imo.org/en/OurWork/Environment/Pages/Special-Areas-Marpol.aspx
International Whaling Commission. "Management Strategies and Tools." Accessed February 26, 2024. https://wwhandbook.iwc.int/en/responsible-management/management-strategies.
IUCN. "IUCN Green List of Protected and Conserved Areas." Accessed February 23, 2024. https://iucngreenlist.org/.
Johannes, R. E. "The Renaissance of Community-based Marine Resource Management in Oceania." *Annual Review of Ecology and Systematics* 33 (2002): 317–40.
Johannes, R. E. "Traditional Marine Conservation Methods in Oceania and Their Demise." *Annual Reviews of Ecological Systems* 9 (1978): 349–64.
Johnson, Kurt. "Cultural Tabu: How an Ancient Ocean Custom Is Saving Fiji's Reefs." *The Guardian* (June 20, 2020). www.theguardian.com/world/2020/jun/20/cultural-tabu-how-an-ancient-ocean-custom-is-saving-fijis-reefs.
Johnson, Magnus. "Oceans Need Protection From Scientists Too." *Nature* 433 (2005): 105.
Johnston, Paul F. "The Smithsonian and the 19th Century Guano Trade: This Poop Is Crap." *Smithsonian* (May 31, 2017). https://americanhistory.si.edu/blog/smithsonian-and-guano.
Kearney, R., C. D. Buxton, and G. Farebrother. "Australia's No-Take Marine Protected Areas: Appropriate Conservation or Inappropriate Management of Fishing?" *Marine Policy* 36 (2012): 1064.

Kriegl, Michael et al. "Marine Protected Areas: At the Crossroads of Nature Conservation and Fisheries Management." *Frontiers in Marine Science* 8 (2021). www.frontiersin.org/articles/10.3389/fmars.2021.676264/full.

LMMA Network. "Locally Managed Marine Areas Network." Accessed February 14, 2024. https://lmmanetwork.org/.

Madagascar Whaleshark Project. "Code of Conduct." Accessed February 26, 2024. www.madawhalesharks.org/get-involved/code-of-conduct/.

Mccauley, D. et al. "Marine Defaunation: Animal Loss in the Global Ocean." *Science* 347, no. 6219 (2015): 1255641.

Meine, Curt. "Conservation Movement, Historical." *Encyclopaedia of Biodiversity* 1 (2001): 883–96.

Merkle, Jerod A. et al. "Site Fidelity as a Maladaptive Behavior in the Anthropocene." *Frontiers in Ecology and the Environment* 20, no. 3 (2022): 187–94.

National Park Service. "Yellowstone National Park." Accessed February 14, 2024. www.nps.gov/yell/index.htm.

Ocean Earth Foundation. "Shark and Ray Tourism Best Practice." Accessed February 26, 2024. https://tierramar.com.au/portfolio-view/shark-and-ray-tourism-best-practice/.

Ojeda-Martinez, Celia et al. "A Conceptual Framework for the Integral Management of Marine Protected Areas." *Ocean & Coastal Management* 52 (2009): 89.

OSPAR Commission. "Collective Arrangement." Accessed February 1, 2024. www.ospar.org/about/international-cooperation/collective-arrangement.

Osterblom, Henrik, and Olof Olsson. "CCAMLR: An Ecosystem Approach to the Southern Ocean in the Anthropocene." In *Handbook on the Politics of Antarctica*, edited by Klaus Dodds, Alan D. Hemmings, and Peder Roberts. Cheltenham: Edward Elgar Publishing, 2017.

Ramsar Convention Secretariat. "Wise Use of Wetlands: Concepts and Approaches for the Wise Use of Wetlands." *Ramsar Handbooks for the Wise Use of Wetlands*, 4th ed., vol. 1. Gland: Ramsar Convention Secretariat 2010.

"Ramsar Sites Information Service." Accessed February 14, 2024. https://rsis.ramsar.org.

Roy, Eleanor Ainge. "'Quite Odd': Coral and Fish Thrive on Bikini Atoll 70 Years after Nuclear Tests." *The Guardian* (July 15, 2017). www.theguardian.com/world/2017/jul/15/quite-odd-coral-and-fish-thrive-on-bikini-atoll-70-years-after-nuclear-tests.

Rozwadowski, Helen. *Vast Expanses: A History of the Ocean*. London: Reaktion Books, 2018.

Secretariat of the Antarctic Treaty. "Antarctic Protected Areas Database." Accessed February 1, 2024. www.ats.aq/devph/en/apa-database.

Secretariat of the Antarctic Treaty. "Tourism and Non-Governmental Activities." Accessed February 14, 2024. www.ats.aq/e/tourism.html.

Spalding, Mark, and Lynne Zeitlin Hale. "Marine Protected Areas: Past, Present and Future – A Global Perspective." In *Big, Bold and Blue: Lessons from Australia's Marine Protected Areas*, edited by James Fitzsimons and Geoff Wescott. Clayton South: CSIRO Publishing, 2016.

UNESCO. *Operational Guidelines for the Implementation of the World Heritage Convention*. Paris: UNESCO, 2021. Accessed February 26, 2024. https://whc.unesco.org/en/guidelines/.

UNEP. "Regional Seas Programme." Accessed January 15, 2024. www.unep.org/topics/ocean-seas-and-coasts/regional-seas-programme/regional-seas-programme.

Van Elden, Sean, Jessica J. Meeuwig, and Richard J. Hobbs. "Offshore Platforms as Novel Ecosystems: A Case Study from Australia's Northwest Shelf." *Ecology and Evolution* 12, no. 2 (2022): e8496.

Wikipedia. "Hydrothermal Vent." Accessed February 26, 2024. https://upload.wikimedia.org/wikipedia/commons/thumb/e/ed/Distribution_of_hydrothermal_vent_fields.png/1920px-Distribution_of_hydrothermal_vent_fields.png.

World Cetacean Alliance. "Global Best Practice Guidance for Responsible Whale and Dolphin Watching." Accessed February 26, 2024. https://worldcetaceanalliance.org/wp-content/uploads/2019/07/WCA-Global-Best-Practice-Guidance-Whale-Watch.pdf.

Zbicz, Dorothy C. "Marine Transboundary Conservation." *Global Transboundary Conservation Network*. Accessed February 1, 2024. www.tbpa.net/page.php?ndx=49.

Part IV

The ocean as repository

9 Waste

Discharge, dumping and debris at sea

Only we humans make waste that nature can't digest.

Charles J Moore, Oceanographer

Overview

Ocean currents, microbes and sea creatures all contribute to purifying water and absorbing and cleansing waste. For millennia, this function has been taken for granted by humans. Middens demonstrate that early coastal communities discarded their fish waste and empty shells on the shorelines and in the shallows to be washed clean by the sea.[1] As human populations grew and developed, the impacts became greater. Plato, for example, refers to water pollution in his *Laws*, and Decrees were enacted as early as 430 BCE in Athens to prevent water pollution.[2] Much later, this awareness extended to the marine environment, demonstrated by, for example, a petition to the Governor of Virginia, who in 1698 requested a ban on the killing of whales within the Chesapeake Bay because the 'pollution caused by rotting remains was poisoning fish and making rivers "noisome and offensive"'.[3] These limited examples demonstrate awareness that human activities could, and did, cause pollution, and that some regulatory measures were taken in response. Yet for far too long it was believed that the oceans' ability to absorb waste was unlimited, just as it was believed that marine resources were infinite.[4]

As nations industrialised, and oceanic activities expanded in scale, so too did the potential risks of pollution events with catastrophic impacts on oceans and coasts. On 18 March 1967, the *SS Torrey Canyon* ran aground on Seven Stones Reef off the coast of England.[5] It was carrying crude oil and the damage to the ship caused the cargo to be spilled into the sea. It was the first major oil tanker disaster to attract global attention, involving the largest vessel to be wrecked and the greatest spillage of oil in history at that time. It remains the UK's worst environmental pollution event and set in motion a chain of events that led to a new international treaty that remains in force today.[6]

DOI: 10.4324/9781003005261-14

This chapter largely focuses on four types of marine pollution: (1) accidental discharges from vessels at sea, (2) the deliberate dumping of waste at sea, (3) rubbish and debris washed from the land into ocean areas, and (4) atmospheric pollution impacts on oceans.[7] Early international treaties focused on highly visible and often catastrophic marine pollution in the first two categories. Our legal responses in these areas have been quite effective, as will be seen later. There is, however, no global legal regime for marine plastic debris, although the international community is currently negotiating a new treaty.[8] Furthermore, responses to climate change (including international legal efforts) have not yet proven to be effective at reducing greenhouse gas (GHGs) emissions. Simultaneously, new pollution threats continue to emerge – such as the impacts of noise and light – as well as knowledge of synergistic and multiplicative effects of individual pollutants. Governments, private industry and civil society all have a role in addressing these problems, involving multiple fields from politics and policy, to economics and commerce, as well as science, technology and engineering. Yet it is clear that law can also play a part moving forward. Before exploring current and future developments, the chapter will outline the evolution of laws and legal regimes that seek to prevent, reduce and control marine pollution.

An early focus on land and the evolution of pollution law

By the Middle Ages the disposal of sewage and rubbish into streets and waterways was causing human diseases, including plagues that devastated populations across much of Europe. Although there is relatively little evidence of early pollution laws focused on marine protection, even then some rules were in place although they focused predominantly on air and inland waterways.[9] Ultimately, pollution from these sources affected oceans both directly, as pollutants flowed to shorelines and into marine areas, and indirectly as oceans absorbed air pollution.

The Industrial Revolution saw the expansion of cities, construction of factories and resulting increase in pollution from the burning of coal, deposits of chemicals, metals and animal by-products into waterways. In the US, for example, the Cuyahoga River caught fire in 1936 (and on several subsequent occasions) as floating debris and oil was ignited, and in 1948 thousands of people became ill (and 20 died) in Pennsylvania due to the severity of the air pollution.[10] Such incidents occurred throughout the industrialised world as the disposal of waste was largely unregulated. Pollution also had a disproportionate impact on colonies. As some scholars have shown, the use of land and oceans as dumping grounds has its origins in colonialism and, despite the introduction of regulations to control pollution, many developing countries that were formerly colonies have continued to be at the receiving end of legally permissible polluting industries and practices.[11]

Early pollution laws were adopted in some of these nations.[12] These were foundational and important developments which involved 'command and control' regulations: setting a specific limit for pollution emissions/discharges (such as parts per million) with penalties for breach of these standards, and also mandating particular pollution control technologies by authorised/permitted polluters (i.e., factories and industries). These regulations provided important backstops but no incentive to do better than the minimum, and they did not account for the cumulative effects of multiple discharges, which had yet to be fully appreciated. It was not until the 1980s that laws combined standards and permits with more sophisticated approaches.

The environmental activism that emerged in the 1960s was a contemporary political movement involving community groups and political parties with the shared objectives of environmental protection, social justice and grassroots democracy.[13] Public environmental campaigns gained momentum in the 1970s and 1980s, with growing public awareness of major environmental catastrophes such as the nuclear accidents at Three Mile Island and Chernobyl in 1986, while seminal publications such as Rachel Carson's *Silent Spring*, published in 1962, highlighted the environmental harm caused by the indiscriminate use of chemicals.[14] Carson observed that the use of agricultural and industrial chemicals was frequently permitted under the law and yet had devastating consequences on people and the environment. What followed was the widespread adoption of basic terrestrial pollution laws in many countries around the world, often modelled on the clean air and water laws in the US.[15] It was also during the 1970s that the first genuine marine pollution laws were adopted and, whilst some of these recognised the risk of land-based marine pollution, it was sea-based sources that garnered greater attention. Nevertheless, pollution from land continued with, for example, ocean outfall at the shoreline (albeit of treated sewage) persisting even until today.[16]

The *UN Convention on the Law of the Sea* (UNCLOS)[17] is a global agreement best known for creating legally binding rules that divide the oceans into maritime zones, settling disagreements between nations that had persisted for centuries (see Chapter 2).[18] Fisheries regulation also features strongly in UNCLOS, but so too do rules that aim to maintain the health of the ocean environment (see Chapter 4). UNCLOS Part XII is focused entirely on protection and preservation, and it contains some quite detailed provisions on pollution. For the first time an overarching global obligation was imposed on all nations, in all their maritime activities, that sought to balance the right to exploit the oceans balanced by a duty to care for the marine environment:

> 'States have the obligation to protect and preserve the marine environment'[19] and 'the sovereign right to exploit their natural resources pursuant to their environmental policies and in accordance with their duty to protect and preserve the marine environment'.[20]

In keeping with most treaties and laws, Part XII is divided into different ocean spaces and causes of marine pollution. In UNCLOS these divisions include pollution from vessels, by dumping, through the atmosphere, from seabed activities and land-based sources,[21] as well as hazards, technologies and alien species.[22] A key feature in Part XII is the focus on global and regional cooperation,[23] and this is unsurprising, given the shared nature of ocean spaces and the fact that by the time UNCLOS was adopted in 1982 two marine pollution treaties (explored further later in the chapter) were already in force. Another interesting inclusion in UNCLOS are requirements for monitoring and environmental assessment reports – both of which were relatively new inclusions in international instruments at the time[24] – and 10 detailed Articles on enforcement with discrete obligations placed on coastal, flag and port States.[25] UNCLOS Part XII remains critically important because it establishes a foundation for national, regional and global action, and includes obligations that apply in all marine areas across the world. Although atmospheric pollution has been a focus at the global level – at least with respect to ozone-depleting substances and climate change – and some seabed measures have developed, land-based marine pollution remains regulated at the national level with incoherent standards across the globe. International law did not develop further in this area, and no treaty emerged on land-based marine pollution. What did emerge was regional laws, facilitated by UNCLOS, the most significant of which are the Regional Seas Programmes.

The *Action Plan for the Human Environment* – an outcome document of the United Nations Conference on the Human Environment (1972) (Stockholm Conference) – called for strengthened controls for marine pollution particularly in enclosed and semi-enclosed seas. The result was UNEP's Regional Seas Programme (RSP), which was established in 1974 and received added impetus by UNCLOS' explicit call for cooperation on a regional level.[26] The RSPs are by definition regionally focused and of the 18 in existence today most focus on seas (e.g., Black, Red, Baltic and Mediterranean Seas). None are ocean wide although several cover parts of the Atlantic and Pacific oceans and others are focused on discrete marine environments (Arctic, Caribbean and East Asian Seas regions).[27] The RSPs are supported by Regional Seas Conventions and Action Plans (RSCAPs), which provide inter-governmental frameworks to address the degradation of the oceans and seas at a regional level. Although many provisions are focused on pollution at sea (e.g., oil spills, hazardous waste) there are some land-based pollution measures (e.g., plastics, wastewater and nutrients).[28] Furthermore, many of the RSCAPs have evolved over time to adopt ecosystem-based approaches and contemporary concepts explored in Chapter 1. Where the majority of international laws are at the oceanic scale, the RSPs provide a welcome focus on seas, and also land-based pollution, which until recently had not drawn global attention.

Vessel-sourced pollution

Shipping has been part of human culture for millennia, as explored in Chapter 5. In the ordinary course of operations, ships emit substances such as oils, gases

Figure 9.1 Oil spill response volunteers cleaning up on a beach in Spain, 2004. (Image courtesy of Stephane M Gruesco.)

and particulates, as well as incidental discharges of garbage and wastewater. In addition, the nature of the products that they carry means that if an accident occurs and those cargoes are lost, then the consequences can be dire. The first oil tanker was built in the late 19th century and in the decades that followed, with the increased demand for motor vehicles, transport of fuel by sea expanded rapidly. So too did accidental pollution events, sometimes due to natural disasters but frequently related to standard operations or human error.

The International Maritime Organisation (IMO) is the United Nations (UN) agency tasked with 'safety and security of shipping and the prevention of marine and atmospheric pollution by ships'.[29] One of the most significant early global agreements adopted under the auspices of the IMO was OILPOL (1954), which set standards for when and where cleaning of tanks could occur, including promoting cleaning facilities and establishing 'prohibited zones' extending 50 nautical miles from land in which discharges must remain below 100 parts per million of oil. It was largely successful but limited in scope and ill-equipped to cope with growing industrialisation and transportation of oil.

The *International Convention for the Prevention of Pollution from Ships*, adopted in 1973 with amendments in 1978 (MARPOL 73/78), provided a more comprehensive regime and it remains in force today.[30] It focuses on incidental

Three shipping disasters change the law

The *Torrey Canyon* struck rocks off the UK coast in 1967. The oil itself caused considerable damage, but so too did the oil spill response. The bombing of the slick, and use of detergents to disperse it, caused devastation, particularly to seabirds. Yet it also led to the first mass environmental volunteering of citizens keen to assist in cleaning birds. It was this disaster that triggered the drafting of a new treaty that became the MARPOL Convention.

The *Amoco Cadiz* ran aground on the coast of France in 1978, rupturing the cargo tank and spilling crude oil into the ocean. The media disseminated pictures of the oil spill, which shocked the nation. Millions of sea creatures were killed, with fisheries, mariculture and tourism all effected. The largest global oil spill occurred just the following year, when the *Atlantic Empress* spilt 287,000 tonnes of oil into the ocean in 1979. This accident further influenced the law, yet a larger spill was to come. In 1989 the *Exxon Valdez* oil supertanker ran aground, spilling oil in the Prince William Sound, Alaska. The remoteness of Prince William Sound hindered government and industry response efforts. Immediate effects include the deaths of hundreds of thousands of animals (salmon, sea otters, seals, orca and seabirds). The *Exxon Valdez* spill remains the second worst pollution event in US waters in terms of volume of oil released (after the 2010 Deepwater Horizon incident). It was followed by the *ABT Summer* spill in 1991 (260,000 tonnes). In 1992 amendments were adopted to MARPOL requiring new ships to be fitted with segregated tanks and double hulls to reduce the risk of oil spills, and older vessels gradually taken out of service. Oil spills significantly reduced following these changes to the law, yet despite large lawsuits the damage to the marine and coastal environments still persists from these major events.

and operational waste from ships and takes a preventative approach. Although this could be seen as proactive, it should be remembered that it was triggered by three major shipping disasters (see textbox). Given that all ships discharge small amounts of oil, exhaust fumes and other substances in their normal operations, standards were needed to ensure these were kept to a minimum. The Convention itself includes a framework of provisions and then a series of Annexes provide different detailed rules for various substances discharged in operations. The first Annex (I) related to oil and the mandatory rules that require strict standards to be met, assisted by naval engineering solutions (double-hulled tankers), specific technologies (oily water separators, oil content meters), facilities (Port reception facilities) and plans (ship oil pollution emergency plans). Subsequent Annexes focused on noxious liquid substances in bulk (II), harmful substances in packaged form (III), sewage (IV), garbage (V) and air pollution (VI).

There is little doubt that MARPOL and its Annexes have been successful in reducing large oil spills, a rare example of environmental law achieving its outcomes. MARPOL and Annex I are well-endorsed by States, covering over 98% of the global merchant fleet and 'have been instrumental in the continuous decline of accidental oil pollution . . . over the last 30 years'.[31] The IMO continues to strengthen the laws to reduce emissions from ships through, for example, a 2011 regulation on energy efficiency for ships, 2018 strategy on reducing GHGs from ships and a new regulation on the sulphur content of fuels in 2020.[32] Nevertheless, Annexes II-VI have attracted less support, and new sources of incidental pollution from vessels continue to emerge. Furthermore, it is apparent that oil continues to be released from vessels in the course of their operations, and sometimes in ways intended to deliberately evade the regulations.[33] Recent events demonstrate that the international community must remain vigilant because accidents, often due to human error, continue to occur. For example, in 2020 1,000 tonnes of oil were spilled into Mauritian coastal waters from a Japanese vessel, impacting on a key marine protected area,[34] and in 2021, toxic chemicals and plastic pellets were lost from a Singaporean registered vessel when it sank off the coast of Sri Lanka.[35] Climate change, involving more extreme weather events, may well result in future shipping incidents.

In the second half of the 20th century another vessel-based risk to the marine environment was recognised – marine invasive species. The transport of non-indigenous marine species is probably a very long-standing phenomenon,[36] but it was not until 1854 that Charles Darwin (as well as other contemporaries) drew attention to the role that ships can play in distributing barnacles that had adhered to their hulls (biofouling) and, at almost the same time, water began to be used in England to balance and stabilise ships (ballast).[37] These have become major transfer mechanisms (vectors) for the introduction of marine invasive species. One of the first acknowledged marine invasions occurred in 1903, when the microscopic Asian diatom (*Biddulphia sinensis*) was transported via ballast water into the North Sea.[38] Perhaps the most well-known incidence of ballast water invasion is the introduction of the zebra mussel (*Dreissena polymopha*) in the Great Lakes in North America in 1988.[39] Although most vessels now have mesh filters to prevent large organisms, eggs, larvae and juveniles, as well as microscopic organisms and pathogens, can still be transported. The global impact of invasive species is estimated to cost 423 billion USD per year, with 75% of the impacts being on land, 14% in freshwater ecosystems and 10% in the marine environment.[40] Again it was the IMO that took action, adopting ballast water guidelines in 1991 and biofouling guidelines in 2011, with a new treaty being adopted in 2004 (coming into force in 2017). The *International Convention for the Control and Management of Ships Ballast Water & Sediments* (*Ballast Water*

Convention) strengthened existing regulations around where and when ballast water can be discharged and introduced mandatory technological requirements to treat ballast water facilities on board vessels and at ports.[41] As the Convention came into force relatively recently and therefore it is yet to be seen how effective it will be.

Biofouling, however, has not been regulated in a similar way to ballast water. Indeed, the binding treaty – *International Convention on the Control of Harmful Anti-Fouling Systems on Ships* – only seeks to prevent marine pollution by regulating anti-fouling chemical substances, applied to inhibit the growth of biological material on hulls.[42] Whether invasive species are better addressed as a species conservation issue or a pollution matter is unclear. It is likely that the problem will need to be tackled from both sides, which again highlights the importance of integration between international institutions and legal regimes. As will be seen later, some other incidental vessel-sourced pollution impacts on marine species – such as light and sound – remain unregulated.

Dumping and deliberate disposal

Beyond incidental and accidental pollution from ships, responses were needed to the deliberate dumping of waste at sea. Low-level disposal of organic material, such as fish waste related to fishing, had been disposed of at sea for centuries, but in the mid-19th century the deliberate disposal of munitions began,[43] and then radioactive waste dumping in 1946.[44] Although some national governments adopted early domestic legislation to outlaw the disposal of waste at sea, global attention was drawn to the issue at the Stockholm Conference, where calls were made for a treaty to address deliberate dumping at sea.[45] The result was the *Convention on the Prevention of Marine Pollution by Dumping of Wastes and Other Matter* (London Convention (1972)), which focused exclusively on deliberate disposal at sea[46] – MARPOL and the London Convention are therefore mutually exclusive. The London Convention (1972) sought to prevent pollution by listing substances which were banned from discharge (Annex I), and those that required a permit for them to be disposed of at sea (Annex II). Annex III sets out the criteria and characteristics relevant to obtaining a permit. This listing mechanism is frequently used in international law (see Chapters 7 and 8 for other examples), and the London Convention Annex I included hazardous chemicals, persistent synthetic materials (including plastics), oils, high-level radio-active and warfare waste. Annex II includes other elements, compounds and chemicals, as well as containers and scrap waste, and some radioactive substances.

In 1996, a Protocol to the London Convention was adopted that had the effect of amending the original Convention by creating a 'reverse list' whereby the deliberate dumping of all wastes was prohibited, with exemptions for certain wastes listed in Annex I.[47] The list is not uncontroversial as it includes dredged material (proposed to be removed in 2020), sewage sludge, fish waste, vessels and platforms, inert and inorganic material and natural organic material. Importantly, the Protocol has been amended in response to new issues as they arise. For example, Annex I was amended in 2006 to add carbon dioxide, thereby providing a basis for ocean-based carbon sequestration.[48] In seeking new solutions to climate change, concerns were raised that marine geo-engineering may have unintended consequences.[49] This led to amendments to the London Protocol in 2008, 2020 and 2013 to provide a regulatory framework and precautionary approach to ocean fertilisation.[50] Potentially, the London Protocol now has a mandate for other marine geoengineering, including marine cloud brightening and reflective microparticles (solar radiation modification), as well as enhancing ocean alkalinity and microalgae cultivation/biomass sequestration (carbon dioxide removal).[51]

The dumping of waste continues to attract global attention. In 2023, despite the endorsement of the UN International Atomic Energy Agency, considerable public and State concern was raised when Japan began releasing treated wastewater from the Fukushima nuclear plant into the Pacific Ocean.[52] A future risk is pollution from waste that was dumped prior to the adoption of the London Convention and Protocol, or 'contained' at coastal sites close to the shoreline: such as radioactive materials, in the Arctic, Atlantic and Pacific Oceans, some of which are now leaking.[53] In addition, stockpiles of chemical weapons were disposed of at sea after World War I, at a time when it was considered safe to do so and well before the *Convention on the Prohibition of the Development, Production, Stockpiling and Use of Chemical Weapons and on their Destruction* (Chemical Weapons Convention) was adopted.[54] Other hazardous waste has also been found, highlighting that this legacy issue cannot be ignored, and the global community will need to respond to prevent future impacts.[55]

Nevertheless, the London Convention and Protocol, together with the IMO, successfully regulated the dumping of wastes that were commonly disposed of at sea in the past and have been instrumental in changing from a 'licence to pollute' to a 'permission by exception' approach. The treaty regime also provides for compliance procedures although the success of these to date, and reporting requirements more generally, is limited.[56] The main challenge facing the regime is attracting States to adopt the Convention and Protocol and thereby agree to be bound by them. To date the London Convention has 100 parties and the London Protocol only 53 parties, limiting their global reach and effectiveness.

Atmospheric pollution and climate change

Perhaps the most pervasive contemporary pollution problem is climate change. As early as 1981 Bardach and Santerre noted that '[t]hus far in history, man's influence on climate has not been noticeable; the next few decades may well present a different picture'.[57] Industrialisation and the use of fossil fuels have led to rapid increases in GHG emissions, including higher concentrations of $CO_{2,}$ creating an atmospheric 'blanket' which blocks heat from escaping, causing long-term shifts in temperature and weather patterns.[58] Oceans absorb up to 25% of global anthropogenic CO_2 emissions and the effects on the marine environment include increasing water temperatures, ocean acidification and sea level rise, and for shorelines more extreme weather events leading to storm surges, inundation and coastal erosion. These changes have far-reaching implications for marine living resources (species and whole ecosystems), processes (ocean currents and weather patterns) and human populations. Beyond direct impacts on species and ecosystems, as well as their habitats, biological processes and life cycles may be disrupted and altered: spawning, for example, is linked to ocean temperature.[59] These impacts are already being felt, and modelling shows that they will continue to escalate.[60]

UNCLOS includes a provision on pollution from the atmosphere requiring States to adopt laws to reduce and control pollution and work through international organisations to establish global and regional rules.[61] Yet it was not until 1992 that the *UN Framework Convention on Climate Change* (UNFCCC) was adopted with the goal of preventing 'dangerous anthropogenic interference with the climate system'.[62] This Framework Convention played a critical role in gathering global data by requiring States to develop and publicise 'national inventories of anthropogenic emissions by sources and removals by sinks of all greenhouse gases'[63] and recognised the importance of oceans.[64] The language of climate change evolved to include mitigation (through reducing GHG emissions and/or enhancing carbon sinks) and adaptation (responses to the impacts of climate change including planned retreat, conserving and restoring natural buffers, etc), both of which are relevant to oceans. One implementing agreement under the UNFCCC was the *Kyoto Protocol*, which included specific emission reduction targets for the period 2008–12.[65] This approach of setting quantified targets with timeframes had first been introduced in response to the hole in the ozone layer,[66] but other treaties at this time left such targets as aspirational rather than legally binding.[67] The *Kyoto Protocol* therefore extended the law by setting emissions targets for GHGs listed in Annex A, for each developed nation in Annex B. These goals were not met and negotiations for a second phase of the Protocol beyond 2012 proved controversial, in large part because no targets were given to developing countries. Although these countries were not responsible for historical emissions, some were by 2012 very large emitters (e.g., China and India).

The negotiations for a new Protocol period failed, and instead the *Paris Agreement* was adopted in 2015.[68] Building on the general aims of the UNFCCC, the focus was on 'pursuing efforts to limit the temperature increase to 1.5°C above pre-industrial levels'.[69] This is critical for ocean health, as above this temperature it is estimated that 90% of coral reefs will be lost, fisheries production will be significantly affected and sea level rise will inundate coastal areas affecting millions of people.[70] The *Paris Agreement* adopted a bottom-up approach, requiring each member State to submit a document setting out National Determined Contributions (NDCs) for climate change mitigation and adaptation (i.e., each State can make its own choices for mitigation and adaptation).[71] These NDCs demonstrate different marine-based mitigation commitments, including reducing emissions (such as through the use of renewable energy from the oceans instead of GHG-emitting fossil fuels) and enhancing ocean sinks (blue carbon, carbon sequestration to absorb GHGs), and adaptation initiatives, including coastal protection (e.g., through nature-based solutions involving marine and coastal flora as well as physical infrastructure).

Most States have ratified the UNFCCC and *Paris Agreement* and without them there is little doubt that the impacts of climate change would be greater. The legal regime, however, has not yet been effective at reducing emissions to levels that will prevent climate change. Although many nations have adopted targets based on 'net zero' by 2030 or 2050, these are not legally binding, and even if all States implemented their pledges made under the *Paris Agreement* through NDCs, global temperatures would still increase.[72] At least one reason for this is that there has not yet been sufficient public pressure forcing States to act, as occurred in response to other environmental catastrophes such as oil spills and the extermination of whales.[73] This highlights an important point: governments and industry respond to a combination of scientific concerns and public pressure.

Evolving pollution risks

The earlier discussion shows that there are clear and effective regimes for vessel-sourced pollution and dumping of waste. The climate change regime is sound and widely supported by member States, but the achievement of its goals requires fundamental shifts in industries, economies and societies that law alone cannot affect. Several current developments demonstrate, though, that there are 'gaps' in existing pollution and environmental protection laws. Seabed mining is one such concern, as operations have commenced in some parts of the world. The mineral resources of the seabed were discovered in the late 19th century, but interest in mining seafloor massive sulphides, ferromanganese crusts and polymetallic nodules did not increase until the 1950s.[74] The impacts of such operations are largely unknown, but the proposed processes involve mechanical extraction of resources, by a remotely operated vehicle, and transportation to a support vessel, risking considerable environmental damage at a time when much is still being learnt about the deep sea.[75] Part XI UNCLOS (1982), together with the Implementing Agreement (1994), created a framework for mining in the 'Area' – the seabed under the high seas. The Area was declared to be the common heritage of humankind, and the benefits of mining are to be shared, with the International Seabed Authority authorising exploration and exploitation. In the intervening decades, no such mining has taken place although dozens of exploration permits have been issued.[76] Critically, the ISA was tasked with developing a Mining Code for exploration and exploitation activities, including appropriate environmental protections (see Chapter 6). The deadline for its adoption – 9 July 2023 – has passed and, although the exploration rules are in place, the exploitation regulations remain in draft creating uncertainty and leading to calls for a moratorium.[77]

Rising demand for minerals and metals has also led to interest in the resources of the seabed within State waters (i.e., on the continental shelves of individual nations), where only the general pollution prevention provisions in Part XII UNCLOS apply. As noted earlier, all States have a general obligation to protect and preserve the marine environment, yet some are approving seabed mining. In Papua New Guinea, for example, the controversial Solara 1 project, which planned to mine hydrothermal vents for minerals, failed and led to the country halting deep-sea mining in 2023.[78] Given the uncertainties, lessons from past activities, and emerging awareness of just how little we know about the deep ocean, it would seem prudent to take a more conservative approach. The precautionary principle,[79] in legal terms, provides the justification for doing so.

There are other areas where the pollution impacts are more obscure or at least are not so well known and settled.[80] Both sound and light pollution affect marine and coastal environments, impacting upon many species. Underwater sounds made by vessels, as well as seismic testing, for example, have been demonstrated to have profound behavioural effects on marine species including the ability of whales, dolphins and other cetaceans to communicate.[81] Other species, such as zooplankton, have also been shown to be negatively impacted.[82] Rather than any pollution treaty exploring this issue, it has been the *Convention on Biological Diversity* (CBD) that has reviewed the impacts and management options.[83] Light pollution in the ocean is caused by vessels, oil rigs and platforms, which in the open ocean can impact on behaviours of some fish and cephalopods[84] and on coasts it can disorient and confuse species at the shoreline such as nesting turtles.[85] Scientists have called for governments to respond, but to date they have failed to protect species from these human impacts.[86] Other risks require further investigation, including, for example, the effects of thermal radiation and electromagnetic field emissions from submarine power cables.[87] Addressing these impacts is likely to require amendment of existing laws as, in the case of ships, maritime law requires certain levels of lighting to prevent collisions at sea[88] although this may conflict with obligations under the law of the sea to protect and preserve the marine environment. This draws sharply into focus an issue that is explored further in Chapter 12: the lack of interaction between the growing number of international law regimes.

The most significant ocean pollution concern to emerge in recent years is marine plastic debris. The Great Pacific Garbage patch was discovered in 1997, alerting the world to the growing marine debris problem.[89] No doubt the global community should have responded to land-based marine pollution much earlier, and UNCLOS Article 207 provided an obligation to do so. Yet it was the images of the oceanic garbage patches, marine megafauna struggling with plastic bags and other waste and, closer to home, beaches and shorelines strewn with plastic debris that led to domestic and international responses.[90] Although some soft law initiatives and regional approaches had been championed by UNEP, including through the Regional Seas Programme,[91] no international standards had been set on the generation, disposal and clean-up of marine debris nor regulations for land-based marine pollution more broadly. This has allowed different nations to adopt varying standards and regulations. The result was that much plastic waste flowed, and continues to flow, into the ocean. While some RSPs had specific measures in place, it was not until 2022 that the global community agreed to commence negotiations for a new marine plastic debris treaty.[92] Of course, not all land-based marine pollution is plastic waste (i.e., nutrient run-off, treated sewerage and chemical waste all remain problematic), and not all plastic waste comes from land-based sources (i.e., ghost nets have a significant impact as they are lost at sea). Nevertheless, any new instrument that emerges from current negotiations for a marine plastic debris treaty (see textbox) may address a persistent problem that presents many risks itself and is also compounded by, and exacerbates, climate change.[93]

Case study: A new plastics treaty

UNEP has taken the lead in global land-based marine pollution measures over many decades, supporting nations and adopting soft law initiatives. On 2 March 2022, the United Nations Environment Assembly adopted an historic resolution, with 175 nations agreeing to develop a legally binding agreement. The negotiations cover sustainable production and consumption, alternatives and circular economy approaches, the design of reusable and recyclable products and materials, environmentally sound waste management, and international cooperation in relation to technology transfer and capacity building. Negotiations commenced in June 2023 and will continue with a zero draft in November, with the intention of adopting a final text by the end of 2024.[94]

Finally, it should not be forgotten that sanctioned use of the ocean to dispose of waste still continues today. A little-known example is the oceanic pole of inaccessibility in the Southern Ocean – the farthest point in the ocean from land – known colloquially as *Point Nemo*.[95] It has been used since 1971 as a site to dispose of decommissioned space objects, as its remote location makes it a safe place to crash land space debris.[96] Given the rapid expansion of space actors and activities, it remains to be seen whether this approach to space debris disposal can continue. The issue of disposal of materials jettisoned during space launches has attracted the attention of the London Convention and Protocol, where it was agreed that a dialogue would be initiated with the UN Committee on the Peaceful Uses of Outer Space (the international body with the mandate for global space regulation).[97] Needless to say, the impacts on the ocean environment are entirely unknown.

Conclusion

This chapter has shown that initially governments were reactive and responded to major pollution events, yet there is also evidence of some proactive approaches, particularly around novel technologies associated with climate change. Prevention and precaution have also featured, as in other areas of law focused on conservation and protection of the environment, with tightening controls for substances such as oil and other chemicals over time. This is also an area where there have been efforts to encourage implementation, compliance and enforcement, from reporting requirements to liability for damage, driven by the polluter pays principle.

Many of the legal instruments explored earlier focus on specific environmental concerns making them easier to implement. For example, obligations to prevent and manage pollution from ships, and to ensure the polluter pays should damage occur, involve a small number of identifiable actors (e.g., flag States, shipowners and operators). Measures are less easily implemented in response to cumulative impacts of relatively low levels of pollution that involve multiple stakeholders (e.g., GHGs emissions or nutrients from agricultural run-off) because setting standards for many small emitters, and holding multiple actors responsible and accountable, is harder to manage. Furthermore, scientific research has revealed that some pollutants work in multiplicative and synergistic ways. Although relatively small discharges of individual substances may be harmless, together they can cause far greater damage. In other cases, it is the indirect impacts of pollution that are only now emerging. For example, damage to the ozone layer is known to affect oceans and, while the direct legal responses have been relatively effective at reducing use of ozone depleting substances such as chlorofluorocarbons (CFCs),[98] warming oceans are projected to emit CFCs back into the atmosphere at a faster rate. Significant gaps have also persisted for substances perceived to be 'inert' or less 'hazardous' such as plastic, light, sound and other energy-related emissions. New sources of pollution continue to emerge, and a more precautionary approach is evident, particularly as regards potential technological solutions to climate change and the changing tide of opinion on deep-sea mining. Nevertheless, lethargy, reactivity and a 'licence to pollute' approach means that considerable pollution risks remain for oceans, seas and shorelines.

Notes

1 In the US, for example, in Maine: "Whaleback Shell Midden," *Maine Department of Agriculture, Conservation & Forestry*, accessed November 1, 2023, www.maine.gov/dacf/parks/discover_history_explore_nature/history/whaleback/index.

shtml#:~:text=Shell%20middens%20(also%20often%20called,ceramic%20pots%2C%20and%20stone%20tools; and in California shell middens were created by the Ohlone people. John R. Gillis, *The Human Shore* (Chicago: University of Chicago Press, 2012), 14. In Australia, huge Aboriginal middens have been found comprising thousands of seashells discarded after local meals, some of which are now protected as cultural heritage: see Chapter 10 in this volume.

2 Teresa Kwiatkowska and Alan Holland, "Dark Is the World to Thee: A Historical Perspective on Environmental Forewarnings," *Environment and History* 16, no. 4 (2010): 455–82. See also Richard C. Trexler, "Measures Against Water Pollution in Fifteenth-Century Florence," *Viator* 5 (1974): 445–68.

3 James Wharton, *The Bounty of the Chesapeake: Fishing in Colonial Virginia* (1957) cited in Callum Roberts, *An Unnatural History of the Sea* (Washington, DC: Island Press, 2007), 47.

4 See Chapters 4 and 7 in this volume.

5 Richard Nelsson, "From the Archive: The Torrey Canyon Oil Spill Disaster of 1967," *The Guardian* (March 18, 2017), www.theguardian.com/environment/from-the-archive-blog/2017/mar/18/torrey-canyon-spill-disaster-1967.

6 "Torrey Canyon: The World's First Major Oil Tanker Disaster," *Safety4Sea* (October 3, 2019), https://safety4sea.com/cm-torrey-canyon-the-worlds-first-major-oil-tanker-disaster/.

7 In this chapter, 'marine pollution' refers to waste affecting oceans, seas and shorelines.

8 Explored further later in the chapter.

9 For example, in the UK in 1273 the use of coal was prohibited in London, and in 1306 a Royal Proclamation was issued prohibiting craftsmen from using soft sea-coal in furnaces: "Air Pollution," accessed November 1, 2023, www.air-quality.org.uk/02.php.

10 "A Brief History of Pollution," *NOAA*, accessed November 1, 2023, https://oceanservice.noaa.gov/education/tutorial_pollution/02history.html

11 For example, Anuradha Varanasi, "How Colonialism Spawned and Continues to Exacerbate the Climate Crisis," *Columbia Climate School: State of the Planet* (September 21, 2022), https://news.climate.columbia.edu/2022/09/21/how-colonialism-spawned-and-continues-to-exacerbate-the-climate-crisis/; Max Liboiron, *Pollution Is Colonialism* (Durham: Duke University Press, 2021).

12 For example, the *Federal Water Pollution Control Act 1948* (US), *Air Pollution Control Act of 1955* (US), the *Clean Air Act 1956* (UK) and *Atmospheric Pollution Prevention Act 1965* (South Africa).

13 "History of the Environmental Movement," *Editors of the Encyclopaedia Britannica*, accessed November 1, 2023, www.britannica.com/topic/environmentalism/History-of-the-environmental-movement.

14 See Chapter 1 of this volume for further discussion.

15 For example, in Japan the *Soot and Smoke Regulation Law* was adopted in 1966; in India the *Water (Prevention and Control of Pollution) Act* was adopted in 1974; and in New Zealand the *Clean Air Act* was adopted in 1972.

16 In Australia, for example, coastal sewage outfall was replaced with deep ocean outfall in 1990 at Sydney's famous Bond Beach: Steve Meacham, "What Lies Beneath the Surf Off Bondi Beach," *Sydney Morning Herald* (November 6, 2015), www.smh.com.au/national/nsw/what-lies-beneath-the-surf-off-bondi-beach-20151106-gksa4a.html. Yet it continued in other parts of the country: "Gunnamatta Priority in Push to End Ocean Outfalls," *The Age* (August 13, 2004), www.theage.com.au/national/gunnamatta-priority-in-push-to-end-ocean-outfalls-20040813-gdyg4i.html. Quite significant discharges of sewage have also been documented in other industrialised nations: 'Why Is Sewage Released into Rivers and the Sea?" *BBC* (October 2, 2023), www.bbc.com/news/explainers-62631320.

17 "The United Nations Convention on the Law of the Sea," *UN Division for Ocean Affairs and the Law of the Sea*, accessed November 1, 2023, www.un.org/depts/los/convention_agreements/convention_historical_perspective.htm.
18 See Chapter 2 in this volume.
19 UNCLOS Article 192.
20 UNCLOS Article 193.
21 UNCLOS Articles 207–12.
22 UNCLOS Articles 195–96.
23 UNCLOS Articles 197–201.
24 UNCLOS Articles 204–6.
25 UNCLOS Articles 213–22.
26 The Regional Seas Programme is considered further in Chapter 8 on area-based conservation.
27 "Regional Seas Programme," *UNEP*, accessed November 1, 2023, www.unep.org/explore-topics/oceans-seas/what-we-do/regional-seas-programme.
28 See, for example, West and Central Africa regions and the Abidjan Convention: "West and Central Africa," *UNEP*, accessed November 1, 2023, www.unep.org/explore-topics/oceans-seas/what-we-do/working-regional-seas/regional-seas-programmes/west-and?_ga=2.53164459.2011298785.1696925765-1833720341.1696925765; and the work of the Commission on the Protection of the Black Sea Against Pollution: "Black Sea," *UNEP*, accessed November 1 2023, www.unep.org/explore-topics/oceans-seas/what-we-do/working-regional-seas/regional-seas-programmes/black-sea?_ga=2.128659855.2011298785.1696925765-1833720341.1696925765.
29 "Introduction to IMO," *IMO*, accessed November 1, 2023, www.imo.org/en/About/Pages/Default.aspx.
30 "Pollution Prevention," *IMO*, accessed November 1, 2023, www.imo.org/en/OurWork/Environment/Pages/Pollution-Prevention.aspx.
31 "MARPOL Annex I – Prevention of Pollution by Oil," *IMO*, accessed November 1, 2023, www.imo.org/en/OurWork/Environment/Pages/OilPollution-Default.aspx. See also "MARPOL at 50 – Our Commitment Goes on: Background Paper," *IMO*, accessed November 1, 2023, https://wwwcdn.imo.org/localresources/en/Documents/World%20Maritime%20Theme%202023%20-%20Background%20paper_EN.pdf.
32 "Climate Action and Clean Air in Shipping," *IMO*, accessed November 1, 2023, www.imo.org/en/OurWork/Environment/Pages/Decarbonization%20and%20Clean%20air%20in%20shipping.aspx.
33 Max Bernhard, Julia Bayer and Nina Werkhäuser, "Cargo Ships Dumping Oil into the Sea Go Unpunished," *Deutsche Welle (DW)* (March 22, 2022), www.dw.com/en/exclusive-cargo-ships-dumping-oil-into-the-sea-go-unpunished/a-61201989.
34 "Japanese Ship Company Behind Oil Spill That Led to Environmental Disaster in Mauritius Caused By 'Human Error'," *ABC News* (December 18, 2020), www.abc.net.au/news/2020-12-19/japan-mauritius-oil-spill-coral-reef-human-error/12999920.
35 Sarah Cahlan et al., "Tons of Toxic Cargo," *Washington Post* (June 15, 2021), https://www.washingtonpost.com/world/interactive/2021/sri-lanka-cargo-ship-fire-pollution/.
36 Carlton suggests such distributions have occurred for at least 2000 years: James T. Carlton, "Molluscan Invasions in Marine and Estuarine Communities," *Malacologia* 41, no. 2 (1999): 439–54.
37 Ian C. Davidson et al., "A History of Ship Specialization and Consequences for Marine Invasions, Management and Policy," *Journal of Applied Ecology* 55 (2018): 1799–811. Ships take on water when free of cargo in order to stabilise the ship and then discharge that water when they take on cargo in a different location. If discharged untreated, species living in the ballast water can be introduced into new

ocean environments with devastating effects. Similarly, species that adhere to ships' hulls in one port can become dislodged in another.

38 Charles Elton later wrote his seminal work, *The Ecology of Invasion by Animals and Plants* (Chicago: University of Chicago Press, 1958).

39 David L. Strayer, "Twenty Years of Zebra Mussels: Lessons from the Mollusk That Made Headlines," *Frontiers in Ecology and the Environment* 7, no. 3 (2009): 135–41.

40 IPBES, *Summary for Policymakers of the Thematic Assessment Report on Invasive Alien Species and Their Control of the Intergovernmental Science-Policy Platform on Biodiversity and Ecosystem Services* (Bonn: IPBES Secretariat, 2023).

41 "Ballast Water Management – The Control of Harmful Invasive Species," *IMO*, accessed November 1, 2023, www.imo.org/en/MediaCentre/HotTopics/Pages/BWM-default.aspx.

42 *International Convention on the Control of Harmful Anti-Fouling Systems on Ships*, IMO, accessed November 1, 2023, www.imo.org/en/About/Conventions/Pages/International-Convention-on-the-Control-of-Harmful-Anti-fouling-Systems-on-Ships-(AFS).aspx. New Zealand was the first country in the world to adopt a biological threshold on biofouling: *Craft Risk Management Standard* (2018) under the *Biosecurity Act 1993* (NZ), accessed November 1, 2023, www.mpi.govt.nz/dmsdocument/11668-Biofouling-on-Vessels-Arriving-to-New-Zealand-Craft-Risk-Management-Standard.

43 Jacek Bełdowski, Matthias Brenner, and Kari K. Lehtonen, "Contaminated by War: A Brief History of Sea-Dumping of Munitions," *Marine Environmental Research* 162 (2020): 105189.

44 Dominique P. Calmet, "Ocean Disposal of Radioactive Waste: Status Report," *IAEA Bulletin* 4 (1989): 47–50.

45 See Chapter 1 this volume.

46 "Convention on the Prevention of Marine Pollution by Dumping of Wastes and Other Matter," *IMO*, accessed November 1, 2023, www.imo.org/en/OurWork/Environment/Pages/London-Convention-Protocol.aspx.

47 Ibid.

48 "The London Protocol and London Convention: How Global Regulation Can Deal Responsibly with Climate Change Mitigation Technologies to Protect the Marine Environment," *IMO*, accessed November 1, 2023, https://wwwcdn.imo.org/localresources/en/OurWork/Environment/Documents/London%20Protocol%20Climate%20Change%20Leaflet%202019%20_FINAL_online%20version.pdf. See also, Karen Scott, "From Ocean Dumping to Marine Geoengineering: The Evolution of the London Regime," in *Research Handbook on International Marine Environmental Law*, ed. Rosemary Rayfuse, Aline Jaeckel, and Natalie Klein (Cheltenham: Edward Elgar, 2023).

49 Phillip Williamson, "Ocean Fertilization for Geoengineering: A Review of Effectiveness, Environmental Impacts and Emerging Governance," *Process Safety and Environmental Protection* 90 (2012): 475–88.

50 An LP/LC resolution (LC-LP.1 (2008)) stated that ocean fertilization activities fall within the purview of the LC/LP and that other than for legitimate scientific research ocean fertilization activities should not be allowed: IMO, "Marine Geoengineering Techniques – Potential Impacts." See also, "High Level Review of a Wide Range of Proposed Marine Geoengineering Techniques," *GESAMP* (March 12, 2019), accessed November 1, 2023, www.gesamp.org/publications/high-level-review-of-a-wide-range-of-proposed-marine-geoengineering-techniques.

51 "Marine Geoengineering Techniques – Potential Impacts," *IMO*, accessed November 1, 2023, www.imo.org/en/MediaCentre/PressBriefings/pages/Marine-geoengineering.aspx.

52 Tessa Wong, "Fukushima: What Are the Concerns over Waste Water Release?" *BBC News* (August 25, 2023), www.bbc.com/news/world-asia-66106162; Sakura Murakami, "Fukushima Wastewater Released into the Ocean, China Bans All Japanese Seafood," *Reuters* (August 25, 2023), www.reuters.com/world/asia-pacific/japan-set-release-fukushima-water-amid-criticism-seafood-import-bans-2023-08-23/.

53 For example, Trevor Nace, "Fears Grow That 'Nuclear Coffin' Is Leaking Waste into the Pacific," *Forbes* (May 27, 2019), www.forbes.com/sites/trevornace/2019/05/27/fears-grow-that-nuclear-coffin-is-leaking-waste-into-the-pacific/?sh=5177cf987073. See also IAEA, *Inventory of Radioactive Material Resulting from Historical Dumping, Accidents and Losses at Sea*, IAEA-TECDOC-1776 (Vienna: IAEA, 2015).

54 Astrida Neimanis, "Held in Suspense: Mustard Gas Legalities in the Gotland Deep," in *Blue Legalities*, ed. Irus Braverman and Elizabeth R. Johnson (Durham: Duke University Press, 2020).

55 "Leaking Barrels Containing DDT Dumped Off California Coast Killing Sea Lions," *CBS News* (April 11, 2021), www.cbsnews.com/sanfrancisco/news/leaking-barrels-containing-ddt-dumped-off-california-coast-killing-sea-lions/;

56 Scott, "From Ocean Dumping to Marine Geoengineering," 261.

57 John E. Bardach and Regina Miranda Santerre, "Climate and the Fish in the Sea," *BioScience* 31, no. 3 (1981): 206–15, 213.

58 Scott C. Doney, D. Shallin Busch, Sarah R. Cooley, and Kristy J. Kroeker, "The Impacts of Ocean Acidification on Marine Ecosystems and Reliant Human Communities," *Annual Review of Environment and Resources* 45, no. 1 (2020): 83–112.

59 Bardach and Santerre, "Climate and the Fish in the Sea," 206.

60 Lauren Fimbres Wood, "Better Climate Models Predict Worse Outcomes for Future Marine Ecosystems in Our Warming Oceans," *Scripps Institute of Oceanography* (November 3, 2021), https://scripps.ucsd.edu/news/better-climate-models-predict-worse-outcomes-future-marine-ecosystems-our-warming-oceans.

61 UNCLOS Article 212.

62 UNFCCC Article 2. For an overview, see Linday Maizland, "Global Climate Agreements: Successes and Failures," *Council on Foreign Relations* (September 15, 2023), www.cfr.org/backgrounder/paris-global-climate-change-agreements.

63 UNFCCC Article 4.

64 "The Ocean," *UN Climate Change*, accessed November 1, 2023, https://unfccc.int/topics/ocean.

65 "What Is the Kyoto Protocol?" *UN Climate Change*, accessed November 1, 2023, https://unfccc.int/kyoto_protocol.

66 See "About Montreal Protocol," *UNEP*, accessed November 1, 2023, www.unep.org/ozonaction/who-we-are/about-montreal-protocol.

67 Such as the CBD and the Aichi Targets: see chapter 7 of this volume.

68 "What Is the Paris Agreement?" *UN Climate Change*, accessed November 1, 2023, https://unfccc.int/process-and-meetings/the-paris-agreement.

69 Paris Agreement Article 2.

70 "Global Warming of 1.5°C," *IPCC*, accessed November 1, 2023, www.ipcc.ch/sr15/.

71 Copies of NDCs are publicly accessible at "NDC Registry," *UN Climate Change*, accessed November 1, 2023, https://unfccc.int/NDCREG.

72 "Climate Action Tracker," accessed November 1, 2023, https://climateactiontracker.org/.

73 David I. Little, Stephen R. J. Sheppard, and David Hulme, "A Perspective on Oil Spills: What We Should Have Learned about Global Warming," *Ocean & Coastal Management* 202 (2021): 105509.

74 Douglas Guilfoyle, "The Oceans," in *International Environmental Law: A Case Study Analysis*, ed. G. Nagtzaam, E. Van Hook and D. Guilfoyle (Abingdon: Routledge, 2020).

75 Kathryn A. Miller et al., "An Overview of Seabed Mining Including the Current State of Development, Environmental Impacts, and Knowledge Gaps," *Frontiers in Marine Science* 4 (2017), https://doi.org/10.3389/fmars.2017.00418.
76 "Exploration Contracts," *ISA*, accessed November 1, 2023, www.isa.org.jm/exploration-contracts/.
77 "The Mining Code," *ISA*, accessed November 1, 2023, www.isa.org.jm/the-mining-code/; Angeli Mehta, "Policy Watch: After Fraught Global Meeting, Future of Deep-Sea Mining Still Hangs in Balance," *Reuters* (August 3, 2023), www.reuters.com/sustainability/policy-watch-after-fraught-global-meeting-future-deep-sea-mining-still-hangs-2023–08–03; and Stefan Labbé, "Watch: Footage Alleges Vancouver Company Leaked Mining Waste into Sea," *Vancouver Is Awesome* (January 20, 2023), www.vancouverisawesome.com/highlights/watch-footage-alleges-vancouver-company-leaked-mining-waste-into-sea-6360066.
78 Ben Doherty, "Collapse of PNG Deep-Sea Mining Venture Sparks Calls for Moratorium," *The Guardian* (September 16, 2019), www.theguardian.com/world/2019/sep/16/collapse-of-png-deep-sea-mining-venture-sparks-calls-for-moratorium.
79 Explored in Chapter 1 of this volume.
80 The effects of sound on marine mammals was first documented in the 1970s: Christine Erbe et al., "Effects of Noise on Marine Mammals," in *Effects of Anthropogenic Noise on Animals*, ed. Hans Slabbekoorn et al. (New York: Springer, 2018).
81 Douglas P. Nowacek et al., "Marine Seismic Surveys and Ocean Noise: Time for Coordinated and Prudent Planning," *Frontiers in Ecology and the Environment* 13, no. 7 (2015): 378–86.
82 Robert D. McCauley et al., "Widely Used Marine Seismic Survey Air Gun Operations Negatively Impact Zooplankton," *Nature Ecology & Evolution* 1 (2017): 0195. But other research has demonstrated little impact on oysters, for example: Miles J. G. Parsons et al., "A Large-Scale Experiment Finds No Consistent Evidence of Change in Mortality or Commercial Productivity in Silverlip Pearl Oysters (Pinctada Maxima) Exposed to a Seismic Source Survey," *Marine Pollution Bulletin* (2023): 115480.
83 Simon Harding and Neil Cousins, *Review of the Impacts of Anthropogenic Underwater Noise on Marine Biodiversity and Approaches to Manage and Mitigate Them.* Technical Series No. 99. (Montreal: Secretariat of the Convention on Biological Diversity, 2022), www.cbd.int/doc/publications/cbd-ts-99-en.pdf. See chapter 7 of this volume for further discussion of the CBD regime.
84 Thomas W. Davies, "The Nature, Extent, and Ecological Implications of Marine Light Pollution," *Frontiers in Ecology and the Environment* 12, no. 6 (2014): 347–55.
85 Ruth L. Kamrowski et al., "Coastal Light Pollution and Marine Turtles: Assessing the Magnitude of the Problem," *Endangered Species Research* 19 (2012): 85–98.
86 Martin Austad et al., "The Effects of Temporally Distinct Light Pollution from Ships on Nocturnal Colony Attendance in a Threatened Seabird," *Journal of Ornithology* 164 (2023): 527–36.
87 Bastien Taormina et al., "A Review of Potential Impacts of Submarine Power Cables on the Marine Environment: Knowledge Gaps, Recommendations and Future Directions," *Renewable and Sustainable Energy Reviews* 96 (2018): 380–91.
88 See Chapter 5 of this volume for a discussion of shipping and maritime law.
89 "From Birth to Ban: A History of the Plastic Shopping Bag," *UNEP*, accessed November 1, 2023, www.unep.org/news-and-stories/story/birth-ban-history-plastic-shopping-bag.
90 Bangladesh was the first nation in the world to ban plastic bags in 2002 – albeit as they were clogging drains rather than impacting on the ocean: "The History of Plastic Bag Bans," *Broadway Industries*, accessed November 1, 2023, https://broadwayind.com/the-history-of-plastic-bag-bans/.

91 See Chapter 8 for a discussion of regional approaches to marine conservation and protection.
92 "Intergovernmental Negotiating Committee on Plastic Pollution," *UNEP*, accessed November 1, 2023, www.unep.org/inc-plastic-pollution.
93 Helen V. Ford et al., "The Fundamental Links Between Climate Change and Marine Plastic Pollution," *Science of The Total Environment* 806, no. 1 (2022): 150392.
94 UNEA, *End Plastic Pollution: Towards an International Legally Binding Instrument*, UNEP/EA.5/Res.14 (March 7, 2022), accessed March 15, 2024, www.un.org/en/climatechange/nations-agree-end-plastic-pollution.
95 The closest nation is the Pitcairn Islands.
96 Over 140 Soyuz spacecraft have been disposed of there, along with the MIR space station.
97 Scott, "From Ocean Dumping to Marine Geoengineering," 260.
98 "Ozone Layer Recovery Is on Track, Helping Avoid Global Warming by 0.5°C," *UNEP* (January 9, 2023), accessed November 1, 2023, www.unep.org/news-and-stories/press-release/ozone-layer-recovery-track-helping-avoid-global-warming-05degc#:~:text=Variations%20in%20the%20size%20of,depth%20since%20the%20year%202000.

Bibliography

"Air Pollution." Accessed November 1, 2023. www.air-quality.org.uk/02.php.

Austad, Martin et al. "The Effects of Temporally Distinct Light Pollution from Ships on Nocturnal Colony Attendance in a Threatened Seabird." *Journal of Ornithology* 164 (2023): 527–36.

Bardach, John E., and Regina Miranda Santerre. "Climate and the Fish in the Sea." *BioScience* 31, no. 3 (1981): 206–15.

Bełdowski, Jacek, Matthias Brenner, and Kari K. Lehtonen. "Contaminated by War: A Brief History of Sea-dumping of Munitions." *Marine Environmental Research* 162 (2020): 105189.

Bernhard, Max, Julia Bayer, and Nina Werkhäuser. "Cargo Ships Dumping Oil into the Sea Go Unpunished." *Deutsche Welle (DW)* (March 22, 2022). www.dw.com/en/exclusive-cargo-ships-dumping-oil-into-the-sea-go-unpunished/a-61201989.

Broadway Industries. "The History of Plastic Bag Bans." Accessed November 1, 2023. https://broadwayind.com/the-history-of-plastic-bag-bans/.

Cahlan, Sarah, and others. "Tons of Toxic Cargo." *Washington Post* (June 15, 2021). www.washingtonpost.com/world/interactive/2021/sri-lanka-cargo-ship-fire-pollution/.

Calmet, Dominique P. "Ocean Disposal of Radioactive Waste: Status Report." *IAEA Bulletin* 4 (1989): 47–50.

Carlton, James T. "Molluscan Invasions in Marine and Estuarine Communities." *Malacologia* 41, no. 2 (1999): 439–54.

"Climate Action Tracker." Accessed November 1, 2023. https://climateactiontracker.org/.

Craft Risk Management Standard (2018) under the *Biosecurity Act 1993* (NZ). Accessed November 1, 2023. www.mpi.govt.nz/dmsdocument/11668-Biofouling-on-Vessels-Arriving-to-New-Zealand-Craft-Risk-Management-Standard.

Davidson, Ian C. et al. "A History of Ship Specialization and Consequences for Marine Invasions, Management and Policy." *Journal of Applied Ecology* 55 (2018): 1799–811.

Davies, Thomas W. "The Nature, Extent, and Ecological Implications of Marine Light Pollution." *Frontiers in Ecology and the Environment* 12, no. 6 (2014): 347–55.

Doherty, Ben. "Collapse of PNG Deep-Sea Mining Venture Sparks Calls For Moratorium." *The Guardian* (September 16, 2019). www.theguardian.com/world/2019/sep/16/collapse-of-png-deep-sea-mining-venture-sparks-calls-for-moratorium.

Doney, Scott C., D. Shallin Busch, Sarah R. Cooley, and Kristy J. Kroeker. "The Impacts of Ocean Acidification on Marine Ecosystems and Reliant Human Communities." *Annual Review of Environment and Resources* 45, no. 1 (2020): 83–112.

Editors of the Encyclopaedia Britannica. "History of the Environmental Movement." Accessed November 1, 2023. www.britannica.com/topic/environmentalism/History-of-the-environmental-movement.

Elton, Charle. *The Ecology of Invasion by Animals and Plants*. Chicago: University of Chicago Press, 1958.

Erbe, Christine et al. "Effects of Noise on Marine Mammals." In *Effects of Anthropogenic Noise on Animals*, ed. Hans Slabbekoorn et al. New York: Springer, 2018.

Fimbres Wood, Lauren. "Better Climate Models Predict Worse Outcomes for Future Marine Ecosystems in Our Warming Oceans." *Scripps Institute of Oceanography* (November 3, 2021). https://scripps.ucsd.edu/news/better-climate-models-predict-worse-outcomes-future-marine-ecosystems-our-warming-oceans.

Ford, Helen V. et al. "The Fundamental Links between Climate Change and Marine Plastic Pollution." *Science of The Total Environment* 806, no. 1 (2022): 150392.

Gillis, John R. *The Human Shore*. Chicago: University of Chicago Press, 2012.

Guilfoyle, Douglas. "The Oceans." In *International Environmental Law: A Case Study Analysis*, ed. G. Nagtzaam, E. Van Hook, and D. Guilfoyle. Abingdon: Routledge, 2020.

"Gunnamatta Priority in Push to End Ocean Outfalls." *The Age* (August 13, 2004). www.theage.com.au/national/gunnamatta-priority-in-push-to-end-ocean-outfalls-20040813-gdyg4i.html.

Harding, Simon, and Neil Cousins. *Review of the Impacts of Anthropogenic Underwater Noise on Marine Biodiversity and Approaches to Manage and Mitigate Them*. Technical Series No. 99. Montreal: Secretariat of the Convention on Biological Diversity, 2022. www.cbd.int/doc/publications/cbd-ts-99-en.pdf.

"High Level Review of a Wide Range of Proposed Marine Geoengineering Techniques." *GESAMP* (March 12, 2019). Accessed November 1, 2023. www.gesamp.org/publications/high-level-review-of-a-wide-range-of-proposed-marine-geoengineering-techniques.

IAEA. *Inventory of Radioactive Material Resulting from Historical Dumping, Accidents and Losses at Sea*. IAEA-TECDOC-1776. Vienna: IAEA, 2015.

IMO. "Ballast Water Management – The Control of Harmful Invasive Species." Accessed November 1, 2023. www.imo.org/en/MediaCentre/HotTopics/Pages/BWM-default.aspx.

IMO. "Climate Action and Clean Air in Shipping." Accessed November 1, 2023. www.imo.org/en/OurWork/Environment/Pages/Decarbonization%20and%20Clean%20air%20in%20shipping.aspx.

IMO. "Convention on the Prevention of Marine Pollution by Dumping of Wastes and Other Matter." Accessed November 1, 2023. www.imo.org/en/OurWork/Environment/Pages/London-Convention-Protocol.aspx.

IMO. "Introduction to IMO." Accessed November 1, 2023. www.imo.org/en/About/Pages/Default.aspx.

IMO. "Marine Geoengineering Techniques – Potential Impacts." Accessed November 1, 2023. www.imo.org/en/MediaCentre/PressBriefings/pages/Marine-geoengineering.aspx.

IMO. "MARPOL Annex I – Prevention of Pollution by Oil." Accessed November 1, 2023. www.imo.org/en/OurWork/Environment/Pages/OilPollution-Default.aspx.

IMO. "MARPOL at 50 – Our Commitment Goes On: Background Paper." Accessed November 1, 2023. https://wwwcdn.imo.org/localresources/en/Documents/World%20Maritime%20Theme%202023%20-%20Background%20paper_EN.pdf.

IMO. "Pollution Prevention." Accessed November 1, 2023. www.imo.org/en/OurWork/Environment/Pages/Pollution-Prevention.aspx.

IMO. "The London Protocol and London Convention: How Global Regulation Can Deal Responsibly with Climate Change Mitigation Technologies to Protect the Marine Environment." Accessed November 1, 2023. https://wwwcdn.imo.org/localresources/en/OurWork/Environment/Documents/London%20Protocol%20Climate%20Change%20Leaflet%202019%20_FINAL_online%20version.pdf.

International Convention on the Control of Harmful Anti-Fouling Systems on Ships. Accessed November 1, 2023. www.imo.org/en/About/Conventions/Pages/International-Convention-on-the-Control-of-Harmful-Anti-fouling-Systems-on-Ships-(AFS).aspx.

IPBES. *Summary for Policymakers of the Thematic Assessment Report on Invasive Alien Species and Their Control of the Intergovernmental Science-Policy Platform on Biodiversity and Ecosystem Services*. Bonn: IPBES Secretariat, 2023.

IPCC. "Global Warming of 1.5oC." Accessed November 1, 2023. www.ipcc.ch/sr15/.

ISA. "Exploration Contracts." Accessed November 1, 2023. www.isa.org.jm/exploration-contracts/.

ISA. "The Mining Code." Accessed November 1, 2023. www.isa.org.jm/the-mining-code/.

Jamieson, Alistair. "50 Years after Torrey Canyon Oil Spill, a Unique Record of Nature's Fightback." *NBC News* (April 2, 2017). www.nbcnews.com/news/world/50-years-after-torrey-canyon-oil-spill-unique-record-nature-n737126.

"Japanese Ship Company Behind Oil Spill That Led to Environmental Disaster in Mauritius Caused by 'Human Error'." *ABC News* (December 18, 2020). www.abc.net.au/news/2020-12-19/japan-mauritius-oil-spill-coral-reef-human-error/12999920.

Kamrowski, Ruth L. et al. "Coastal Light Pollution and Marine Turtles: Assessing the Magnitude of the Problem." *Endangered Species Research* 19 (2012): 85–98.

Kwiatkowska, Teresa, and Alan Holland. "Dark Is the World to Thee: A Historical Perspective on Environmental Forewarnings." *Environment and History* 16, no. 4 (2010): 455–82.

Labbé, Stefan. "Watch: Footage Alleges Vancouver Company Leaked Mining Waste into Sea." *Vancouver Is Awesome* (January 20, 2023). www.vancouverisawesome.com/highlights/watch-footage-alleges-vancouver-company-leaked-mining-waste-into-sea-6360066.

"Leaking Barrels Containing DDT Dumped Off California Coast Killing Sea Lions." *CBS News* (April 11, 2021). www.cbsnews.com/sanfrancisco/news/leaking-barrels-containing-ddt-dumped-off-california-coast-killing-sea-lions/.

Liboiron, Max. *Pollution is Colonialism*. Durham: Duke University Press, 2021.

Little, David I., Stephen R. J. Sheppard, and David Hulme. "A Perspective on Oil Spills: What We Should Have Learned about Global Warming." *Ocean & Coastal Management* 202, (2021): 105509.

Maine Department of Agriculture, Conservation & Forestry. "Whaleback Shell Midden." Accessed November 1, 2023. www.maine.gov/dacf/parks/discover_history_explore_nature/history/whaleback/index.shtml#:~:text=Shell%20middens%20(also%20often%20called,ceramic%20pots%2C%20and%20stone%20tools.

Maizland, Lindsay. "Global Climate Agreements: Successes and Failures." *Council on Foreign Relations* (September 15, 2023). www.cfr.org/backgrounder/paris-global-climate-change-agreements.

McCauley, Robert D. et al. "Widely Used Marine Seismic Survey Air Gun Operations Negatively Impact Zooplankton." *Nature Ecology & Evolution* 1 (2017): 0195.

Meacham, Steve. "What Lies Beneath the Surf Off Bondi Beach." *Sydney Morning Herald* (November 6, 2015). www.smh.com.au/national/nsw/what-lies-beneath-the-surf-off-bondi-beach-20151106-gksa4a.html.

Mehta, Angeli. "Policy Watch: After Fraught Global Meeting, Future of Deep-Sea Mining Still Hangs in Balance." *Reuters* (August 3, 2023). www.reuters.com/sustainability/policy-watch-after-fraught-global-meeting-future-deep-sea-mining-still-hangs-2023-08-03.

Miller Kathryn A. et al. "An Overview of Seabed Mining Including the Current State of Development, Environmental Impacts, and Knowledge Gaps." *Frontiers in Marine Science* 4 (2017). https://doi.org/10.3389/fmars.2017.00418.
Moore, Charles. "Seas of Plastic." *Ted2009* (February 2009). www.ted.com/talks/charles_moore_seas_of_plastic.
Murakami, Sakura. "Fukushima Wastewater Released Into the Ocean, China Bans All Japanese Seafood." *Reuters* (August 25, 2023). www.reuters.com/world/asia-pacific/japan-set-release-fukushima-water-amid-criticism-seafood-import-bans-2023-08-23/.
Nace, Trevor. "Fears Grow That 'Nuclear Coffin' Is Leaking Waste Into The Pacific." *Forbes* (May 27, 2019). www.forbes.com/sites/trevornace/2019/05/27/fears-grow-that-nuclear-coffin-is-leaking-waste-into-the-pacific/?sh=5177cf987073.
Neimanis, Astrida. "Held in Suspense: Mustard Gas Legalities in the Gotland Deep." In *Blue Legalities*, edited by Irus Braverman and Elizabeth R. Johnson. Durham: Duke University Press, 2020.
Nelsson, Richard. "From the Archive: The Torrey Canyon Oil Spill Disaster of 1967." *The Guardian* (March 18, 2017). www.theguardian.com/environment/from-the-archive-blog/2017/mar/18/torrey-canyon-spill-disaster-1967.
NOAA. "A Brief History of Pollution." Accessed November 1, 2023. https://oceanservice.noaa.gov/education/tutorial_pollution/02history.html.
Nowacek, Douglas P. et al. "Marine Seismic Surveys and Ocean Noise: Time for Coordinated and Prudent Planning." *Frontiers in Ecology and the Environment* 13, no. 7 (2015): 378–86.
Parsons, Miles J. G. et al. "A Large-Scale Experiment Finds No Consistent Evidence of Change in Mortality or Commercial Productivity in Silverlip Pearl Oysters (Pinctada Maxima) Exposed to a Seismic Source Survey." *Marine Pollution Bulletin* (2023): 115480.
Scott, Karen. "From Ocean Dumping to Marine Geoengineering: The Evolution of the London Regime." In *Research Handbook on International Marine Environmental Law*, edited by Rosemary Rayfuse, Aline Jaeckel, and Natalie Klein. Cheltenham: Edward Elgar, 2023.
Strayer, David L. "Twenty Years of Zebra Mussels: Lessons from the Mollusk That Made Headlines." *Frontiers in Ecology and the Environment* 7, no. 3 (2009): 135–41.
Taormina, Bastien et al. "A Review of Potential Impacts of Submarine Power Cables on the Marine Environment: Knowledge Gaps, Recommendations and Future Directions." *Renewable and Sustainable Energy Reviews* 96 (2018): 380–91.
"Torrey Canyon: The World's First Major Oil Tanker Disaster." *Safety4Sea* (October 3, 2019). https://safety4sea.com/cm-torrey-canyon-the-worlds-first-major-oil-tanker-disaster/.
Trexler, Richard C. "Measures against Water Pollution in Fifteenth-Century Florence." *Viator* 5 (1974): 445–68.
UN Climate Change. "NDC Registry." Accessed November 1, 2023. https://unfccc.int/NDCREG.
UN Climate Change. "The Ocean." Accessed November 1, 2023. https://unfccc.int/topics/ocean.
UN Climate Change. "What Is the Kyoto Protocol?" Accessed November 1, 2023. https://unfccc.int/kyoto_protocol.
UN Climate Change. "What Is the Paris Agreement?" Accessed November 1, 2023. https://unfccc.int/process-and-meetings/the-paris-agreement.
UN Division for Ocean Affairs and the Law of the Sea. "The United Nations Convention on the Law of the Sea." Accessed November 1, 2023, www.un.org/depts/los/convention_agreements/convention_historical_perspective.htm.
UNEA. "End Plastic Pollution: Towards an International Legally Binding Instrument." Accessed March 15, 2024. www.un.org/en/climatechange/nations-agree-end-plastic-pollution.

UNEP. "About Montreal Protocol." Accessed November 1, 2023. www.unep.org/ozonaction/who-we-are/about-montreal-protocol.

UNEP. "Black Sea." Accessed November 1, 2023. www.unep.org/explore-topics/oceans-seas/what-we-do/working-regional-seas/regional-seas-programmes/black-sea?_ga=2.128659855.2011298785.1696925765-1833720341.1696925765.

UNEP. "From Birth to Ban: A History of the Plastic Shopping Bag." Accessed November 1, 2023. www.unep.org/news-and-stories/story/birth-ban-history-plastic-shopping-bag.

UNEP. "Intergovernmental Negotiating Committee on Plastic Pollution." Accessed November 1, 2023. www.unep.org/inc-plastic-pollution.

UNEP. "Ozone Layer Recovery Is on Track, Helping Avoid Global Warming by 0.5°C." Accessed November 1, 2023. www.unep.org/news-and-stories/press-release/ozone-layer-recovery-track-helping-avoid-global-warming-05degc#:~:text=Variations%20in%20the%20size%20of,depth%20since%20the%20year%202000.

UNEP. "Regional Seas Programme." Accessed November 1, 2023. www.unep.org/explore-topics/oceans-seas/what-we-do/regional-seas-programme.

UNEP. "West and Central Africa." Accessed November 1, 2023. www.unep.org/explore-topics/oceans-seas/what-we-do/working-regional-seas/regional-seas-programmes/west-and?_ga=2.53164459.2011298785.1696925765-1833720341.1696925765.

Varanasi, Anuradha. "How Colonialism Spawned and Continues to Exacerbate the Climate Crisis." *Columbia Climate School: State of the Planet* (September 21, 2022). https://news.climate.columbia.edu/2022/09/21/how-colonialism-spawned-and-continues-to-exacerbate-the-climate-crisis/;

Wharton, James. *The Bounty of the Chesapeake: Fishing in Colonial Virginia* (1957) cited in Callum Roberts, *An Unnatural History of the Sea*. Washington, DC: Island Press, 2007.

"Why Is Sewage Released into Rivers and the Sea?" *BBC* (October 2, 2023). www.bbc.com/news/explainers-62631320.

Williamson, Phillip. "Ocean Fertilization for Geoengineering: A Review of Effectiveness, Environmental Impacts and Emerging Governance." *Process Safety and Environmental Protection* 90 (2012): 475–88.

Wong, Tessa. "Fukushima: What Are the Concerns over Waste Water Release?" *BBC News* (August 25, 2023). www.bbc.com/news/world-asia-66106162.

10 Shipwrecks to sea shanties

Safeguarding maritime cultural heritage

Rolling down to Old Maui, me boys
Rolling down to Old Maui
We're homeward bound from the Arctic Ground
Rolling down to Old Maui
Traditional sea shanty

Overview

Cultural heritage associated with oceans, seas and shorelines is incredibly diverse. Exploration, invasion, fishing and harvesting, piracy, naval warfare, scientific research, recreational sailing and cultural activities are some of the myriad ways that humans have engaged with oceans, seas and shorelines, whether on board vessels, in ports and harbours, or on the open ocean, using tools and technologies ancient and modern, and capturing the experiences in journals, artworks, stories, poems and songs.[1]

The heritage significance of shipwrecks comes immediately to mind. Shipwrecks are invariably a subject of interest to maritime historians and archaeologists as well as treasure hunters, private collectors and members of the public. Some shipwrecks have also attracted legal interventions, such as the case of the *RMS Titanic*, one of the best-known shipwrecks, which was found in 1985 in international waters off the coast of Canada. The discovery, conflict over ownership, and the controversial retrieval, display and sale of some objects from the wreck, triggered US legislation, litigation, and an international agreement, and eventually catalysed a new treaty.[2]

Whilst a shipwreck itself attracts much attention, conserving and managing the story of the vessel involves a combination of the underwater remains, related coastal sites and associated objects, which can enrich and add to the narratives of those on board. The history of a port itself can be told through harbour walls, quays and warehouses, charts and maps, journals, warehouse records and sailing orders. Yet a

DOI: 10.4324/9781003005261-15

complete picture is impossible without the intangible heritage associated with these ships and places, including the stories of the people, their knowledge and practices, songs and other cultural expressions. A cultural history of fishing or exploration, for example, generally includes the history of boats and harbours, vessel designs and the gear on board, navigation equipment, charts and maps, journals, sailing orders and landing records, as well as the stories of the seafarers, the clothes they wore, their expert knowledge and technical language, and their songs and stories.

Indigenous and traditional peoples have long understood the interconnectedness of natural and cultural heritage. In India, for example, sacred groves of trees and rivers hold heritage significance.[3] In Australia, coastal and island Indigenous groups relate to land and sea in a holistic way, although the tendency to manage heritage sites as discrete places diminishes this interconnectedness.[4] Such groups relate to their local estuaries, beaches, bays and marine areas as 'sea country', which is 'integral to the identity of each clan' and where each clan member has a kin relationship to particular marine animals and plants, tides and currents.[5] In many other parts of the world species, marine areas and the ocean itself are valued as integral to a group's cultural heritage.[6]

Frequently, natural and cultural heritage intersect, for example, with key events and people where the physical remains may be minuscule but the cultural significance monumental. Places where people worshipped, major battles took place, people migrated from (whether forcibly or voluntarily), and critical figures lived or died can all have heritage significance. In other cases, the creation of cultural heritage objects relies upon living and non-living resources, such as shells, which were often used as a base for cultural expression including art, with the oldest surviving etchings found on a 540,000-year-old shell.[7] One of the world's earliest pieces of jewellery is made from marine snail shells and is 150,000 years old.[8] Other tangible heritage associated with marine environments includes hunting weapons made from narwhal tusks, musical drums made with stretched shark skins, and all kinds of artworks depicting marine creatures. Many of these objects are preserved as cultural heritage that continues to hold value, not only to the particular communities that created them but to all of humanity.

Laws can establish obligations and frameworks for conserving sites and objects, appropriately safeguarding and transmitting intangible heritage, and presenting and interpreting their cultural significance and associated values. Law, therefore, has a vital role to play in safeguarding maritime cultural heritage of fishing, shipping, piracy, war, construction and accidents at sea – all the topics explored in earlier chapters of this book. Unlike these areas of law, however, heritage laws seek to protect the elements that constitute our natural and cultural heritage from anthropogenic damage, and even from the actions of the ocean itself. Relevantly, as will be seen later, maritime cultural heritage laws are not arranged thematically in ways that draw together natural and cultural, tangible and intangible elements. This chapter explores how maritime cultural heritage is accounted for in law, through an examination of the specific legal regimes that focus on sites, objects and intangible elements, as well as underwater cultural heritage more specifically.

What is heritage?

Heritage is what we have inherited and valued as 'worth preserving and sharing with present and future generations'. It can be both natural and cultural: Natural heritage includes living species and ecosystems, as well as geological and physical formations; and cultural heritage is human made and provides the 'context that makes us human' and adds 'to our sense of belonging and group identity'. Some cultural heritage is tangible including physical and material elements, which can be moveable (e.g., books, artworks, tools, clothing and adornments) or immoveable (such as monuments, buildings, archaeological sites). Other cultural heritage is intangible, such as the narratives and stories, knowledge and practices, and language, songs, dances and other cultural expressions of seafarers, which is just as valuable as it provides meaning and context for tangible elements. Some of the most endangered forms of heritage, and the hardest to protect, are intangible because they only exist through their use, practice or performance and are therefore inherently linked to the 'holders' of such heritage.

Shipwrecks, sunken treasure and the law of finds

Seafaring has always been a risky endeavour and, despite advances in vessel design and navigation technologies, it is likely to remain so. Shipwrecks are perhaps the most visible and celebrated examples of maritime cultural heritage, inspiring divers and often becoming the focus of museum exhibitions, literature, art, stories, songs and popular culture. The earliest intact shipwreck that has been found dates back 2,400 years,[9] and the oldest documented maritime incident several thousand years earlier.[10] These incidents gave rise to rules about the rights of 'finders' of lost or abandoned goods recovered or washed ashore, and the rights of those that offered rescue and 'salvage' services for vessels in peril.[11] What evolved was the law of finds and salvage law (see Chapter 5). Thus, it became important to distinguish between cargo deliberately cast or unintentionally lost overboard, leading to particular words such as flotsam, jetsam, lagan or derelict (see textbox).

Here we are concerned with wrecks, cargo and objects associated with ships lost long ago. Historically, wrecks and lost cargo tended to be found in shallow waters close to shore, where identification and ownership could more easily be determined, or at least the location was squarely within State waters. Early diving bells were constructed in the 17th century and by the 19th century technologies were advanced enough to allow for historical objects to be recovered from Henry

VIII's sunken flagship, *Mary Rose*.[12] During the 20th century, more sophisticated diving apparatus, echo sounding and location gear enabled more wrecks and objects to be located, and later underwater autonomous vessels and equipment that can refloat sunken vessels added to their accessibility. This underwater cultural heritage is enormously rich and has immense potential to inform science, history and archaeology. Shipwrecks can also generate income as an object of tourism and can also become artificial reefs.[13] Yet there are many instances of treasure hunters seeking to recover sunken vessels and objects purely for economic gain. Whilst the protection of underwater cultural heritage is critical, there is a marked difference in legal approach between maritime law and the treatment under heritage law. What may be just reward for recovery of objects under one regime could be considered looting and damage under the other.

As noted earlier, the traditional law of finds gives the first finder of a historic item ownership of it, subject to rights of the true owner. The earliest salvage laws provided a means to reward salvors for the recovery of lost vessels and objects.[14] Although laws have differed over time, at the most basic level salvors were granted compensation for voluntary assistance given, to a vessel or cargo owner, to save their property from marine peril. In some cases, the compensation given was exclusive rights to the vessel and/or cargo. In neither case was protection of items of heritage value assured.[15]

Laws for the protection of wrecks, and objects found within them, came much later. The discovery of a 17th-century Dutch ship in waters off the coast of Western Australia in 1975 triggered the adoption of one of the first pieces of shipwreck legislation in the world – *Maritime Archaeology Act 1973* (WA) – and then the later *Historic Shipwrecks Act 1976* (Cth). This legislation protects wrecks and artefacts by vesting ownership and control in the State and allows for protection zones to be declared around underwater sites. Similar laws were adopted in other States including the *Abandoned Shipwrecks Act 1988* (US) and *Protection of Wrecks Act 1973* (UK) for wrecks discovered in national waters. The only international law that mentioned underwater heritage was the *UN Convention on the Law of the Sea* (UNCLOS), adopted in 1982. It includes only two relevant provisions, the first of which relates to international waters:

> All objects of an archaeological and historical nature found *in the area* shall be preserved or disposed of for the benefit of mankind as a whole, particular regard being paid to the preferential rights of the State or country of origin, or the State of cultural origin, or the State of historical and archaeological origin. [emphasis added][16]

The other Article covers all waters:

> States have the *duty to protect objects of an archaeological and historical nature found at the sea* and shall cooperate for this purpose. . . . Nothing in

Figure 10.1 Engraving of French pirate, François l'Olonnais (nicknamed 'Flail of the Spaniards'), who was active in the Caribbean during the 1660s. (Published in Alexandre Olivier Exquemelin, *De Americaensche Zeerovers* [*The Buccaneers of America*], 1678.) Public domain.

> this article affects the rights of identifiable owners, the law of salvage or other rules of admiralty, or laws and practices with respect to cultural exchanges. . . . This article is without prejudice to other international agreements and rules of international law regarding the protection of objects of an archaeological and historical nature. [emphasis added][17]

Nothing further is said in UNCLOS about underwater heritage within areas of national jurisdiction including the extended continental shelf, perhaps because many States had legislation to protect historical shipwrecks and the United Nations Educational, Scientific and Cultural Organization (UNESCO) had released its *1956 Recommendation on International Principles Applicable to Archaeological Excavation* for underwater sites within national jurisdictions.

The language of lost cargo

Flotsam are goods from a sunken vessel that have floated to the surface of the sea or drifted onto the shoreline. As they were unintentionally cast into the sea, they must be returned to the original owner. *Jetsam* are goods that have been intentionally discarded from a ship or wreckage. These goods do not have to be returned to their rightful owner – as they are deemed abandoned – except in the case where the true owner makes a legal claim for them. *Lagan* are also goods that have been cast overboard and sink, but they have a floating marker so that they can be found again and under maritime law these goods must be returned to the true owner. *Derelict* are goods that have been abandoned with no expectation of being returned. These goods can be kept by the finder.

As noted earlier, the discovery of the wreck of *RMS Titanic* in 1985 exposed gaps in legal regulation (see textbox). Because the vessel had been found in international waters – on the seabed under the high seas – national legislation did not apply and salvage laws differed between various nations, leading to confusion and complexity for finders of historical wrecks. In recognition of the significance of underwater cultural heritage (beyond only shipwrecks), the significant technological developments which enabled vessels to be located and accessed outside national waters, and the increasing threats to such sites, drafting began on a broader international treaty in 1993, ultimately leading to a new international instrument – the *Convention on the Protection of the Underwater Cultural Heritage* (2001).

Some maritime law experts have noted that the Convention was developed in response to threats to underwater cultural heritage arising as a result of advances in deep-water technology, but it did address questions of ownership rights in sunken vessels and cargoes, sovereign immunity in the case of sunken warships, how salvage law should be applied, ethical issues surrounding commercial exploitation, and jurisdictional competence to regulate activities beyond territorial sea limits.[18]

It is now widely accepted that underwater cultural heritage includes more than shipwrecks. Underwater ruins, prehistoric caves and landscapes all constitute a precious archaeological resource of significant cultural importance. Many of these sites are unique since material is often much better preserved underwater than on land due to the lack of oxygen, which facilitates deterioration. A highlight of the *Convention on the Protection of the Underwater Cultural Heritage* (2001) was a broadened scope that included vessels, sites, structures, artefacts, human remains 'together with

RMS *Titanic*

The discovery of the wreck of the *RMS Titanic* was a significant event in maritime heritage law, triggering a series of legal interventions including legislation and litigation. The wreck was discovered by a French-US partnership (French Research Institute for Exploitation of the Sea (IFREMER) and Woods Hole Oceanographic Institute (WHOI)). The expedition returned in 1986 to photograph the wreck but did not remove any objects as the discoverers believed it should remain undisturbed. Although found in international waters, the US passed the *RMS Titanic Maritime Memorial Act 1986* seeking to protect the wreck from physical interference until an international agreement could be reached. Subsequently, the US drafted an international agreement with the UK, Canada and France to operationalise the principles in the 1986 Act. The US and UK signed the agreement, which entered into force in 2019, but not Canada and France.

Simultaneously, a salvage law dispute arose. After the wreck had been discovered by IFRMER and the WHOI, IFREMER returned to the site with a US company (Titanic Ventures – later RMS Titanic Inc.) in 1987 and collected 1800 objects. RMS Titanic Inc. collected further objects in 1993, 1994, 1996 and 1998. The company subsequently sought, and was granted, exclusive salvage rights by a US Court in 1996. RMS Titanic Inc. sought to be declared the finder (rather than the salvor) and owner of the wreck and its objects, but this was rejected in 2004 and 2006, and therefore it remains the salvor-in-possession under US law.

their archaeological and natural context' and prehistoric objects – which can accommodate other forms of underwater cultural heritage, including Indigenous landscapes and artefacts but not necessarily intangible heritage.[19]

The key principles in CPUCH include, first, that underwater cultural heritage means 'all traces of human existence . . . having a cultural, historical or archaeological character that have been . . . under water . . . for at least 100 years'.[20] Second, that preservation in situ is conserved as the first option, emphasising the importance of the historical context and based on the knowledge that in most cases the lack of oxygen will slow deterioration. And, third, that States should, individually or cooperatively, protect underwater cultural heritage for the benefit of humanity.

The Convention stipulates that underwater cultural heritage should not be commercially exploited, nor should it be irretrievably dispersed. However, this does not prevent archaeological research or tourist access. Indeed responsible, non-intrusive access is encouraged, recognising that proper respect for human remains should be observed. The Convention encourages scientific research, training in underwater archaeology and the transfer of technology,[21] cooperation and sharing of information and public education,[22] and generally calls upon States to work together, to preserve underwater heritage.[23] It requires parties to ensure their nationals give notification of their intention to explore in the Exclusive Economic Zone (EEZ) or on the continental shelf of another State and report when a discovery is made.[24] Importantly, it is recognised that in situ preservation is preferred, but where objects are recovered they shall be 'deposited, conserved and managed' to ensure their long-term preservation.[25] The Convention contains agreed measures on the protection of heritage in areas beyond national jurisdiction including that States are required to regulate their nationals and vessels including sanctions and procedures for seizure of underwater cultural heritage where necessary.[26]

Of particular note is the Annex to the Convention, entitled *Rules Concerning Activities Directed at Underwater Cultural Heritage*, which is a best practice guide to project management that drew heavily on the *Charter on the Protection and Management of Underwater Cultural Heritage* drafted by the expert body, the International Council on Monuments and Sites (ICOMOS). This is a novel inclusion in an international treaty. It confirms that activities may be authorised if they make a 'significant contribution to protection or knowledge or enhancement of' but do not 'adversely affect' underwater cultural heritage. Conversely, it sets out that commercial exploitation for profit and the irretrievable dispersal of objects is inconsistent with the Convention. Many of the other rules set out how a project is to be designed, including preliminary evaluation, staff qualifications, methodology and techniques used, environmental and safety policies, a documentation programme and a plan for deposition of objects retrieved.

The Convention is an important step forward in setting international standards for underwater cultural heritage preservation and has stimulated revisions of domestic 'shipwreck' laws to accommodate new forms of underwater heritage.[27] It also contributes to capacity building through the inclusion of the Annex. The Convention facilitates research and, for example, tourism, which can incentivise protection and provide livelihoods. But it neither regulates the ownership of heritage, nor does it change the sovereign rights of states. Therefore, it must be implemented in combination with other laws. As the impacts of climate change include sea level rise, more coastal and shoreline heritage sites are likely to become submerged adding to underwater cultural heritage. Simultaneously, technological developments will expand our ability to explore the deep ocean and uncover vessels and objects lost in the past. Many laws are triggered by date, and this too will mean that new items will continuously be added to heritage lists. All of these matters will ensure that underwater cultural heritage, and its protection, remains an important aspect of international and State laws governing the cultural heritage of our marine and coastal environments.

Maritime sites

As permanent human settlements grew, infrastructure was constructed on the shoreline, including ports, harbours, jetties and quays, lighthouses, coastal towns and cities. The earliest heritage laws were not focused on maritime or underwater sites and objects but rather on key monuments, sites and buildings considered to be of national significance. Following the damage and destruction of multiple historic sites across Europe during World War I the need for international agreements began to garner attention. The *Treaty for the Protection of Artistic and Scientific Institutions and Historical Monuments* (Roerich Pact) (1935) was adopted in the Americas and at the international level, the League of Nations – which preceded the United Nations as an inter-governmental organisation – adopted the *Athens Charter* (1931)[28] and then the *Venice Charter* (1964),[29] which provided a benchmark for the conservation and restoration of monuments and sites.[30] These instruments were, in large part, driven by heritage conservation experts, but the further destruction during World War II triggered the newly formed United Nations to act. The *Hague Convention on the Protection of Cultural Property in the Event of Armed Conflicts* (1954) was the first international agreement to focus purely on heritage. It provides a mechanism to identify critical sites (blue) and move heritage objects to protected repositories, but it makes no specific reference to marine or maritime heritage.

The *Convention for the Protection of World Cultural and Natural Heritage* (World Heritage Convention) is the principal treaty that seeks to protect sites including those in terrestrial and marine areas. Its origins lie in several incidents involving sites threatened by flooding, both of which drew international attention. The peacetime construction of the Aswan High Dam that threatened to destroy 22 temples at Abu Simbel along the Nile Valley triggered the 1959 UNESCO campaign to disassemble the temples and reassemble them on higher ground where they remain today.[31] Subsequent rescue campaigns in other parts of the world led to UNESCO initiating the preparation of a draft convention on cultural heritage.[32] The US and the International Union for Conservation of Nature (IUCN) developed proposals for the combined protection of natural and cultural heritage. These were presented at the UN Conference on the Human Environment in Stockholm in 1972 and led to the adoption of the World Heritage Convention.

The Convention seeks to provide a 'system of collective protection' recognising that the destruction and deterioration of heritage sites, not only through decay but also changing social and economic conditions, is a 'harmful impoverishment of the heritage of all the nations of the world'.[33] The Convention therefore provides for the 'listing' of cultural and natural heritage sites of outstanding universal value on the World Heritage List, with States required to identify, protect, conserve, present and transmit these sites to future generations.[34] World Heritage listing offers opportunities for States to benefit from international assistance

Figure 10.2 Submerged remains of Emperor Claudius' nymphaeum, in the underwater Archaeological Park of Baiae. (Image courtesy of Ruthven, 22 July 2018.)

(financial, technical, research, etc),[35] and where a site becomes at risk it can be listed as 'World Heritage in Danger'.[36] Operational guidelines provide selection criteria for the assessment and evaluation of sites, including that a State must be able to show that a site or object will be well managed and legally protected.[37]

Many notable natural marine areas have World Heritage status, including the Galápagos Islands in Ecuador, the Great Barrier Reef in Australia, Papahānaumokuākea in Hawai'i, and the Sundarbans in India and Bangladesh.[38] For these places, the Convention has assisted in drawing global attention and raising public awareness. These natural sites benefit through the World Heritage Marine Programme[39] and are highlighted in a 2013 publication by the World Heritage Centre – *Marine World Heritage: Safeguarding the Crown Jewels of the Ocean*.[40] Maritime cultural heritage sites do not feature in this report and programme, yet there are a number of relevant coastal sites on the World Heritage List. On the shoreline there are historic ports and harbours such as Qal'at al-Bahrain (the Ancient Harbour and Capital of Dilmun with continuous human use from 2300 BC to the 16th century AD) in Bahrain, the Historic Quarter of the Seaport City of Valparaíso in Chile (the first and most important merchant port between the Atlantic and Pacific Oceans), the first colonial capital in Fiji (Levuka Historical Port Town) and Historic Jeddah on the shore of the Red Sea in Saudi Arabia.[41] Other sites include coastal lighthouses such as the Tower of Hercules in Spain and the Cordouan Lighthouse in France, and places associated with human transportation including the Stone Town of Zanzibar in Tanzania (the marine slave trading port in East Africa and also a place where David Livingstone conducted a campaign to end slavery), Aapravasi Ghat (where indentured labourers first set foot in Mauritius) and the Australian Convict Sites (where British prisoners were transported to in the 18th and 19th centuries).

The combination of natural and cultural heritage in the Convention was strengthened with the broader interpretation of 'combined works of nature and man' to include 'cultural landscapes'. Nevertheless, this does not mean that the World Heritage List is comprehensive. Although a Global Strategy was adopted to ensure the World Heritage List is representative and balanced,[42] 27 member States remain without any listings. Thus, the List remains skewed with France, Italy and Spain having 59, 52 and 50 sites, respectively. Although Mexico has 35 and India 42 sites, 34 States have only one listed site.[43] Undoubtedly, the World Heritage Convention has drawn attention to globally significant sites around the world and helped to raise awareness of them. Yet the nomination process is lengthy and costly, involving the drafting of detailed documentation that necessitates expert involvement, which presents a barrier to listing. Tourism, in particular, can provide an incentive for listing as States generate income from presenting World Heritage listed places. In this way, the Convention provides a pathway to economic sustainability whilst showcasing cultural diversity. Tourism can, however, be a two-edged sword and have unwelcome physical and social impacts even as it delivers economic benefits.[44]

Further gaps exist in the World Heritage List. For example, since the Convention relies on State sovereignty, places beyond national jurisdiction cannot be nominated. Historical sites in Antarctica and wrecks in waters beyond the Exclusive Economic Zones (EEZs) (such as the RMS *Titanic*) cannot be listed. In addition, as World Heritage listing only binds member States, the activities of non-State actors – such as terrorists – are beyond its reach. Cultural heritage has been the subject of terrorist attacks in Afghanistan, Iraq, Syria and Mali demonstrating the impotence of UNESCO in such a situation.[45] Although terrorism has not impacted on marine World Heritage sites as yet, it is a future possibility. Furthermore, World Heritage listing does not ensure protection beyond traditional threats, such as the impacts of climate change. Sea level rise, acidification and extreme weather events all pose risks to coastal maritime heritage sites, and UNESCO has identified that 70% of the 50 natural marine World Heritage sites are under threat with two-thirds of them unprepared to deal with these impacts.[46]

Despite efforts by UNESCO to gather knowledge and share best practice, there may be little that can be done to save some sites.[47]

Collections from the conquered and colonised

Over many centuries spoils of war were collected following naval battles and include, for example, vessels and the objects on board.[48] From the 16th century onwards maritime explorers were 'gifted' or 'appropriated' objects from Indigenous peoples, such as the whalebone mallet collected by Captain James Cook on a voyage to New Zealand.[49] Colonisers continued to acquire culturally significant objects from peoples whose lands were occupied as empires expanded. In the 18th century, wider interest in collecting cultural objects, including antiquities obtained by archaeologists through excavations, evolved.[50] This led to the development of antiquities markets, involving both public and private collectors and legal and illicit transactions. It was during the 19th century that legal efforts were made to protect national collections and prevent illegal removal and export of cultural heritage objects. Greece, Italy and France, for example, adopted legislation in the 19th century to protect cultural heritage more generally, while some of the first museum laws were developed in Egypt and Turkey, and many States rich in cultural heritage objects also sought to regulate collecting of antiquities by dealers and archaeologists in an effort to prevent theft, illicit export and losses.[51]

Early international efforts were made by the League of Nations to address the illicit export and facilitate the return of stolen objects, with draft conventions in the 1930s. While the Hague Convention of 1954 addressed wartime theft, it was not until 1970 that an international treaty was adopted relating to peacetime trade. The UNESCO *Convention on the Means of Prohibiting and Preventing the Illicit Import, Export and Transfer of Ownership of* Cultural Property (1970) seeks to balance the interchange of cultural property for scientific, cultural and educational purposes and the prevention of 'theft, clandestine excavation and illicit export'. A framework for authorisation of import, export or transfer of ownership of cultural property declares such movements illicit unless conducted in accordance with its articles.[52] It provides for preventative measures, restitution provisions and an international cooperative framework requiring States to address causes of trafficking, stop current practices and help make reparations.[53] Significantly, the Convention provides for the recovery and return of cultural property illicitly exported, after the date the Convention came into force, provided compensation is paid to any 'innocent purchaser'.[54] Although the Convention provides for the payment of compensation, it does not resolve the critical issue of the ownership of cultural property that has been transferred to a third party.

The later UNIDROIT *Convention on Stolen or Illegally Exported Cultural Objects* (1995) complements the UNESCO Convention. It seeks to harmonise the laws of the different States in relation to the return of cultural property that was stolen or illegally exported. This was a key concern with the earlier UNESCO Convention – private law issues such as time limitations and misuse of good faith defences are different in each State creating significant hurdles for repatriation across national borders.[55] The Convention is an unusual piece of international law as it permits private entities to bring proceedings in foreign courts to enforce the provisions – in other words, it extends beyond nations themselves. Its scope is wider than the UNESCO Convention as it draws specific attention to the loss of significance by an object's removal from a site and the importance of the intact, entire object.[56] Most importantly, it provides that the 'possessor of a cultural object that has been stolen shall return it' even if there is a buyer in good faith, and allows a member State to request a court of another party to order the return.[57] Compensation is only payable if the possessor can show s/he did not know or ought reasonably to have known it was stolen, such as a certificate of authenticity or provenance.[58]

The UNESCO and UNIDROIT Conventions are important public international laws, but they do not apply retrospectively. Many public collections of cultural heritage remain controversial, particularly where objects were 'acquired' through war or during foreign occupation. On independence many former colonies have sought the return of such objects – if not on legal grounds, then moral ones. Human remains taken from traditional peoples in all continents of the world are perhaps the most controversial. Several objects of cultural property associated with oceans, seas and shorelines have been recovered and have led to controversial claims of ownership, although proving ownership remains a challenge in these cases and often involves protracted negotiations and sometimes litigation. In 2015, for example, the Spanish Galleon *San José* was discovered in waters off the coast of Cartagena, Colombia.[59] It had been sunk by the British Navy with a cargo of 200 tonnes of gold and silver coins, precious stones and ceramics belonging to the Viceroy of Peru, with an estimated value of 17 billion USD.[60] Colombia, in whose waters the wreck was found, has claimed ownership, as has Spain as the ship was a Spanish vessel. Relevantly, much of the cargo is likely to have been stolen from Latin American countries that may also have rights to the cargo.

Despite the wealth of laws in this area – both domestic and international – cultural heritage continues to be stolen and artworks such as Rembrandt's *The Storm on the Sea of Galilee* and Van Gogh's *View of the Sea at Scheveningen* remain missing.[61] Such thefts capture public attention, such as the maps taken from public collections by Edward Forbes Smiley III in the US in 2006,[62] made famous by the book *The Map Thief*.[63] It appears that cultural heritage objects associated with oceans, seas and shorelines continue to hold fascination.

From the tangible to the intangible

Whilst monumental sites and historically significant material cultural objects garnered early legal attention, some elements of maritime heritage were not so fortunate. The protection of intangible heritage such as narratives associated with sacred oceanic sites and totem marine species, sea shanties and customary songs of seafarers, traditional navigational and marine ecological knowledge, and artisanal skills associated with boat building, sailing and fishing was not a focus until recently.

Globalisation and technology, including the internet, have allowed international markets to develop for mass-produced goods that are accessible in all corners of the world. The result has been the loss of both artisanal skills and markets for handmade objects as well as reduced interest in traditional arts, crafts, practices and traditions. Some cultural heritage exists only because it continues to be practised and evolves with changes in society. Forms of cultural expression such as language, song, dance, artisanal skills and traditional knowledge cannot be reduced purely to tangible objects such as sound and video recordings, manuals and guides. Its continued use goes hand in hand with objects involved in practising that form of cultural heritage and the distinctive expression and diversity of the societies that value it. This is what is meant by intangible cultural heritage. Although UNESCO first began to specifically focus on intangible cultural heritage in 1971, it was not until 1989 that it adopted the *Recommendation on the Safeguarding of Traditional Culture and Folklore*. This was followed by the *Universal Declaration on Cultural Diversity* (2001) and the Istanbul Declaration (2002). In addition, the *Proclamation of the Masterpieces of the Oral and Intangible Heritage of Humanity*, which commenced in 2001, sought to raise awareness of intangible cultural heritage by drawing public attention to key elements from around the globe. It was with this background that the *Convention for the Safeguarding of Intangible Cultural Heritage* (CSICH) was adopted in 2003 and came into force in 2006.[64]

The CSICH encourages States to identify and protect intangible heritage within their jurisdictions and safeguard it in ways which maintain its functional relevance. 'Intangible heritage' is defined in the context of five domains: oral traditions and expressions, including language; performing arts; social practices, rituals and festive events; knowledge and practices concerning nature and the universe; and traditional craftsmanship.[65] 'Safeguarding' focuses on ensuring the viability of the intangible cultural heritage, its transmission and, where necessary, revitalisation. The obligations of States parties include the identification of intangible heritage within their territories (with the full participation of all stakeholders) and the preparation of inventories. Thereafter States must develop a national policy, designating a relevant authority, fostering research and adopting legal, technical, financial and administrative measures.[66] The Convention also provides guidance on the ways to facilitate protection, including education, awareness raising and capacity building and the full participation, consent and involvement of communities.[67] Other State obligations include periodic reporting matched by international assistance and cooperation as well as specific measures such as the establishment of a *Fund for the Safeguarding of the Intangible Cultural*

Heritage, a *Representative List of the Intangible Cultural Heritage of Humanity*, and a *List of Intangible Cultural Heritage in Need of Urgent Safeguarding* to ensure the visibility of, and raise awareness about, intangible heritage.

The UNESCO site lists many intangible items listed from sea shanties, to tales from the sea, traditional net making and fishing practices such as, for example, shrimp fishing on horseback in Belgium, customary boat building and sailing in Iran, a traditional maritime organisation in Montenegro, and ceremonies commemorating lives lost at sea in China and Malaysia.[68] The safeguarding of these 'treasures' will be incredibly difficult, particularly for those that must continue to practise them if they are to persist. Knowledge must be held by people; songs and music must be performed; fishing, aquaculture and traditional sailing techniques must be practised; and merely listing them will not safeguard them. Maintaining the context, lifestyle and environment for this intangible heritage will be critical. The international focus on intangible cultural heritage has continued with the adoption of the *Convention on the Protection and Promotion of the Diversity of Cultural Expressions*.[69] This Treaty again indicates international concern to protect cultural diversity from the processes of globalisation.

Conclusion

From protecting sacred sites to finding treasure, conserving shipwrecks, sunken cities and Aboriginal middens to safeguarding the intangible element valued and created by coastal peoples and seafarers through time, there are myriad examples of cultural heritage associated with oceans, seas and shorelines. This human heritage has significance for people and communities from the local to the global. Tangible manifestations of our past have always had monetary value and so have needed protection from treasure hunters and looters and other people that seek to benefit from them. Objects associated with key historical vessels and maritime explorers, such as the *Vasa*,[70] the rudder from *HMS Bounty*,[71] Columbus' admiral's desk,[72] Cook's sextant,[73] and objects from King Kamehameha II's sunken yacht,[74] have been placed in national archives and public or private museum collections alongside objects collected by maritime explorers in their voyages.[75] Everyday objects – clothing, simple tools, basic skills – have received less attention and for a long time they did not need protection as they continued to be widely used and practised.

Nevertheless, processes such as globalisation and modernisation have threatened traditional practices, ways of life and elements of intangible cultural diversity that require differing legal responses if they are to be safeguarded. Simultaneously, many combined tangible and intangible cultural heritage elements depend upon more than the human ocean. For example, traditional fishing nets and boats, connected stories and shanties, and the language of fishing depends on fish stocks remaining healthy that allow for the fishing practices to continue. More recently, environmental pressures, including climate change, bring new threats that are much harder for law to address. Lawmakers have had to grapple with rule-making to conserve the tangible and more intangible manifestations of human interactions with oceans, seas and shorelines.

As heritage law has evolved, it has taken novel legal approaches in responding to conservation concerns. For example, the World Heritage Convention combined natural and cultural heritage in one instrument for the very first time, and this has enabled recognition of places that share both values, benefitting Indigenous and traditional peoples in particular. Nevertheless, most other law continues to separate the two despite the inherent linkages.[76] The UNIDROIT Convention extends into the commercial law sphere and thereby creates obligations for actors other than States, including private sector art dealers. The CPUCH also engages with disciplines beyond law to include experts in the field of underwater archaeology, as other heritage law has also drawn heavily on experts. CPUCH has broadened the definition of heritage beyond shipwrecks to include underwater cultural landscapes, Aboriginal middens and sites of significance, as well as acknowledging the importance of practising cultural heritage and its living nature.

The possibility that a single object can transition from being commercial cargo, to pollution, to cultural heritage is curious in itself – although this should not be surprising, given similar artificial and changing classifications such as those for animals.[77] The laws dealing with these objects range across the law of the sea, maritime and salvage law, marine pollution law, and underwater and intangible cultural heritage law. As with other areas of law associated with oceans, seas and shorelines, vertical divisions are made. For example, the water column – and what is floating on it and descending through it – is separated from the sunken objects on the seafloor. Horizontal fragmentation is also reflected in situations where lost cargo that floats on the high seas and into territorial waters is transformed as it touches the shoreline, and in cases where shipwrecks are found in the Area, the continental shelf and barely submerged closer to shore. Interestingly, many of the maritime incidents triggering both salvage and heritage conservation are close to shore. Clearly, the shallow water is a physical factor, but there is – as is commonly the case – a utilitarian aspect as well, with the need to maintain freedom and safety of navigation by ensuring unimpeded waterways, ports and shipping channels. The ways in which we have sought to manage items lost at sea and to protect manifestations of ocean history is, therefore, a microcosm of the philosophies, values and beliefs we have adopted in relation to oceans, seas and shorelines. Simultaneously, it serves to highlight the challenges that remain. Even within the area of heritage law divisions exist with lawmakers categorising heritage and providing separate, albeit similar, regimes for immovable, movable, intangible and underwater cultural heritage. Arguably these divisions, and the artificial boundaries they rely upon, is a further demonstration of the anthropocentric construction of the ocean and how we should treat it.

Human interaction with oceans, seas and shorelines has led to a wide array of culturally valued objects and sites, as well as a diversity of language, legends, laws, and cultural expressions. Despite popular conceptions of cultural heritage, these objects and sites do not have to be old to have significance. Indeed, in many cases, they continue to acquire deeper significance over time as human societies evolve.

Notes

1 Kristen Ounanian et al., "Conceptualizing Coastal and Maritime Cultural Heritage Through Communities of Meaning and Participation," *Ocean and Coastal Management* 212 (2021): 105806.

2 See case study later in the chapter for further details about the legal interventions associated with *RMS Titanic.*

3 Madhave Gadgil, "Sacred Groves: An Ancient Tradition of Nature Conservation," *Scientific American* (December 1, 2018), www.scientificamerican.com/article/sacred-groves-an-ancient-tradition-of-nature-conservation/.

4 Indigenous Working Group Workshop participant cited in: National Oceans Office, *Sea Country: An Indigenous Perspective: The South-East Regional Marine Plan Assessment Reports* (Hobart: National Oceans Office, 2002), 1.

5 Phil Rist et al., "Indigenous Protected Areas in Sea Country: Indigenous-driven Collaborative Marine Protected Areas in Australia," *Aquatic Conservation Marine and Freshwater Ecosystems* 29, no. 2 (2019): 138–51; Dermot Smyth and Miya Isherwood, "Protecting Sea Country: Indigenous Peoples and Marine Protected Areas in Australia," accessed March 15, 2024, www.dermotsmyth.com.au/wp-content/uploads/2019/01/Protecting-Sea-Country.pdf.

6 Native American peoples in the Caribbean have a worldview that 'focuses strongly on the ocean realm': David R. Watters, "Maritime Trade in the Prehistoric Eastern Caribbean," in *Indigenous Peoples of the Caribbean*, ed. Samuel M. Wilson (Miami: University Press of Florida, 1997). In most Pacific Islands, there are cultural values associated with the ocean. In Palau, for example, the *Shark Haven Act 2009* specifically notes that 'Palau's economic and cultural fate is inextricably tied to the ocean'. See also Bas Verschuuren et al., eds., *Sacred Natural Sites: Conserving Nature and Culture* (Abingdon: Earthscan, 2010).

7 "Old Master: 540,000-Year-Old Shell Has Oldest Ever 'Art'," *NBC News* (December 4, 2014), www.nbcnews.com/science/science-news/old-master-540-000-year-old-shell-has-oldest-ever-n261171.

8 Sarah Cascone, "Archaeologists Just Discovered the World's Oldest Jewelry: This Set of 150,000-Year-Old Snail-Shell Beads in Morocco," *Artnet* (November 19, 2012), https://news.artnet.com/art-world/worlds-oldest-jewelry-morocco-2037635.

9 Tasos Kokkinidis, "2400-Year-Old Greek Ship is the Oldest Wreck Yet Discovered," *Greek Reporter* (November 13, 2023), https://greekreporter.com/2022/06/28/2400-year-greek-ship-black-sea.

10 "Oldest Shipwreck," *Guinness World Records*, accessed January 15, 2024, www.guinnessworldrecords.com/world-records/oldest-shipwreck.

11 Safety of life at sea and salvage law are explored in Chapter 4 as part of shipping, maritime and Admiralty law. See Chapter 9 for further discussion of salvage in the context of pollution.

12 Craig Forrest, *International Law and the Protection of Cultural Heritage* (Abingdon: Routledge, 2010), 290.

13 See Chapter 6 for further discussion of how infrastructure can become an artificial reef that provides considerable benefit to marine species.
14 Forrest, *International Law and the Protection of Cultural Heritage*, 289. See chapter 5 for a discussion of salvage laws.
15 Salvage laws differ between jurisdictions, and at the global level the *International Convention on Salvage* 1989 applies.
16 UNCLOS Article 149.
17 UNCLOS Article 303.
18 Sarah Dromgoole, *Underwater Cultural Heritage and International Law* (Cambridge: Cambridge University Press, 2013).
19 CPUCH Article 1. Note that pipelines, cables and similar installations are excluded. For consideration of this infrastructure see Chapter 6.
20 CPUCH Article 1.
21 CPUCH Article 21.
22 CPUCH Articles 19 and 20.
23 CPUCH Article 6.
24 CPUCH Article 9.
25 CPUCH Article 2.
26 CPUCH Articles 17 and 18.
27 For example, one of the older domestic shipwreck laws was the *Historic Shipwrecks Act 1976* (Cth), which was recently reviewed and replaced with the broader *Underwater Cultural Heritage Act 2018* (Cth).
28 "The Athens Charter for the Restoration of Historic Monuments (1931)," *ICOMOS*, accessed January 15, 2024, www.icomos.org/en/167-the-athens-charter-for-the-restoration-of-historic-monuments.
29 "The Venice Charter," *ICOMOS*, accessed January 15, 2024, www.icomos.org/en/participer/179-articles-en-francais/ressources/charters-and-standards/157-thevenice-charter.
30 Neither Charter made specific reference to maritime heritage, and it was not until 2001 that the informal *European Charter for the Conservation and Restoration of Traditional Ships in Operation* (*Barcelona Charter*) focused specifically on active sailing vessels: Juan-Luis Alegret and Eliseu Carbonell, "Maritime Heritage Conservation," in *Routledge Handbook of Ocean Resources and Management*, ed. Hance D. Smith et al. (Abingdon: Taylor & Francis, 2015).
31 "Abu Simbel: The Campaign That Revolutionized the International Approach to Safeguarding Heritage," *UNESCO*, accessed January 15, 2024, https://en.unesco.org/70years/abu_simbel_safeguarding_heritage.
32 "World Heritage Convention," *UNESCO*, accessed January 15, 2024, https://whc.unesco.org/en/convention/.
33 World Heritage Convention, Preamble.
34 World Heritage Convention, Article 4.
35 World Heritage Convention, Articles 19–26.
36 World Heritage Convention, Article 11.
37 UNESCO, *The Operational Guidelines for the Implementation of the World Heritage Convention* (WHC.23/01, September 24, 2023), accessed January 15, 2024, https://whc.unesco.org/en/guidelines/.
38 UNESCO, "World Heritage List," accessed January 15, 2024, https://whc.unesco.org/en/list/.
39 UNESCO, "World Heritage Marine Programme," accessed January 15, 2024, https://whc.unesco.org/en/marine-programme/.

40 UNESCO, *Marine World Heritage: Safeguarding the Crown Jewels of the Ocean* (Paris: UNESCO World Heritage Centre, 2013), accessed April 30, 2024, https://unesdoc.unesco.org/ark:/48223/pf0000220049/PDF/220049eng.pdf.multi.
41 See UNESCO, "World Heritage List."
42 UNESCO, "Global Strategy," accessed January 15, 2024, https://whc.unesco.org/en/globalstrategy/.
43 Although Mexico has 35 sites and India 42.
44 See for example the impacts on natural marine sites outlined in Fanny Douvere, *World Heritage Marine Sites, Managing Effectively the World's Most Iconic Marine Protected Areas* (Paris: UNESCO, 2015), https://unesdoc.unesco.org/ark:/48223/pf0000235316.
45 Irina Bokova, *UNESCO's Response to the Rise of Violent Extremism: A Decade of Building International Momentum in the Struggle to Protect Cultural Heritage*, Occasional Papers in Cultural Heritage Policy no. 5 (Los Angeles: Getty Publications, 2021).
46 UNESCO, "Marine World Heritage in a Changing Climate," accessed January 15, 2024, https://whc.unesco.org/en/climate-change-marine/.
47 UNESCO, "Ocean Science Roadmap for UNESCO Marine World Heritage," accessed January 15, 2024, https://unesdoc.unesco.org/ark:/48223/pf0000379847.locale=en.
48 See Chapter 3 for a discussion of ships taken under the law of 'prize'.
49 National Museums Liverpool, "Objects from the Voyages of Captain James Cook," accessed January 15, 2024, www.liverpoolmuseums.org.uk/stories/objects-voyages-of-captain-james-cook.
50 Forrest, *International Law and the Protection of Cultural Heritage*, 132.
51 Thomas W. Neumann, "Heritage Legislation, the Introduction of: Disciplining Through Law," in *Encyclopedia of Global Archaeology*, ed. C. Smith (New York: Springer, 2014).
52 Article 3.
53 Article 2.
54 UNESCO Article 7.
55 L. V. Prott, "The UNIDROIT Convention on Stolen or Illegally Exported Cultural Objects – Ten Years on," *Uniform Law Review* 14, no. 1–2 (2009): 215–37.
56 Unidroit Convention, Article 5.
57 Unidroit Convention, Articles 3 and 5.
58 Unidroit Convention, Article 6.
59 Alia Shoaib, "18th-Century Spanish Shipwreck Has $17 Billion Worth of Coins and Gems Aboard," *Science Alert* (June 18, 2022), www.sciencealert.com/18th-century-spanish-shipwreck-has-17-billion-worth-of-gold-coins-jewels.
60 J. R. A., "The Battle for Colombia's Sunken Treasure," *The Economist* (August8,2018),www.economist.com/the-economist-explains/2018/08/08/the-battle-for-colombias-sunken-treasure.
61 Lindsay Moroney, "Unsolved Art Heists: The Missing Paintings of Vincent van Gogh," *Artnet* (November 22, 2013), https://news.artnet.com/market/unsolved-art-heists-the-missing-paintings-of-vincent-van-gogh-35614.
62 "Stolen Treasures: The Case of the Missing Maps," *FBI* (September 28, 2006), https://archives.fbi.gov/archives/news/stories/2006/september/maps092806.
63 Michael Blanding, *The Map Thief: The Gripping Story of an Esteemed Rare-Map Dealer Who Made Millions Stealing Priceless Maps* (Sheridan: Gotham, 2014).
64 UNESCO, "Text of the Convention for the Safeguarding of the Intangible Cultural Heritage," accessed January 15, 2024, https://ich.unesco.org/en/convention.
65 CSICH Article 2.

66 CSICH Article 13.
67 CSICH Articles 14 and 15.
68 See UNESCO, "Safeguarding Our Living Heritage," accessed January 15, 2024, https://ich.unesco.org/en/dive&display=biome#tabs; UNESCO, "Browse the Lists of Intangible Cultural Heritage and the Register of Good Safeguarding Practices," accessed January 15, 2024, https://ich.unesco.org/en/lists. See also, UNESCO, "8 June: Join the Living Heritage Entity in Celebrating World Oceans Day!" (June 4, 2021), https://ich.unesco.org/en/news/8-june-join-the-living-heritage-entity-in-celebrating-world-oceans-day-13311.
69 UNESCO, "Convention on the Protection and Promotion of the Diversity of Cultural Expressions," accessed January 15, 2024, www.unesco.org/en/legal-affairs/convention-protection-and-promotion-diversity-cultural-expressions.
70 The world's oldest surviving 17th-century warship, at the Vasa Museum, Sweden: Peta Stamper, "Vasa Museum," *History HIT* (July 15, 2021), www.historyhit.com/locations/vasa-museum/
71 On display at the Fiji Museum: "Fiji Museum," accessed January 15, 2024, http://virtual.fijimuseum.org.fj/template.php?id=2000-492a&next=2000-493&cat=56.
72 At the Boal Museum and Columbus Chapel, US: Stephanie Kalina-Metzger, "Discovering Boalsburg: A Trove of Columbus Artifacts Can Be found in Perhaps the Least Likely Place in the New World," *The Burg* (September 29, 2017), https://theburgnews.com/home-front/discovering-boalsburg-a-trove-of-columbus-artifacts-can-be-found-in-perhaps-the-least-likely-place-in-the-new-world.
73 At the National Maritime Museum, UK: "National Maritime Museum," *Royal Museums Greenwich*, accessed January 15, 2024, www.rmg.co.uk/national-maritime-museum.
74 At the Kauaʻi Museum: "Kauaʻi Museum," accessed January 15, 2024, www.kauaimuseum.org/.
75 Such as the Cook-Forster Collection (Georg-August University of Göttingen, Germany) of artefacts collected during Pacific voyages from 1768 to 80: "Cook's Pacific Encounters: Cook-Forster Collection Online," *National Museum Australia*, accessed January 15, 2024, www.nma.gov.au/explore/features/cook_forster.
76 For example, shipwrecks often become artificial reefs attracting and concentrating myriad species and sometimes whole ecosystems of benefit to conservation and fisheries: Natali Pearson, "The Multispecies Shipwreck," *International Journal of Heritage Studies* 30(6) (2023): 673–86, https://doi.org/10.1080/13527258.2023.2284719. See also Helen Pickering and David Whitmarsh, "Artificial Reefs and Fisheries Exploitation Are View of the 'Attraction versus Production' Debate, the Influence of Design and Its Significance for Policy," *Fisheries Research* 31 (1997): 39–59. See chapter 6 for further discussion.
77 See Chapter 7, where it is noted that the same animal can be classified as domestic, feral, wild, invasive, etc.

Bibliography

Alegret, Juan-Luis, and Eliseu Carbonell. "Maritime Heritage Conservation." In *Routledge Handbook of Ocean Resources and Management*, edited by Hance D. Smith et al. Abingdon: Taylor & Francis, 2015.

Blanding, Michael. *The Map Thief: The Gripping Story of an Esteemed Rare-Map Dealer Who Made Millions Stealing Priceless Maps*. Sheridan: Gotham, 2014.

Bokova, Irina. *UNESCO's Response to the Rise of Violent Extremism: A Decade of Building International Momentum in the Struggle to Protect Cultural Heritage*. Occasional Papers in Cultural Heritage Policy No. 5. Los Angeles: Getty Publications, 2021.

Cascone, Sarah. "Archaeologists Just Discovered the World's Oldest Jewelry: This Set of 150,000-Year-Old Snail-Shell Beads in Morocco." *Artnet* (Nov 19, 2012). https://news.artnet.com/art-world/worlds-oldest-jewelry-morocco-2037635.

Douvere, Fanny. *World Heritage Marine Sites, Managing Effectively the World's Most Iconic Marine Protected Areas*. Paris: UNESCO, 2015. https://unesdoc.unesco.org/ark:/48223/pf0000235316.

Dromgoole, Sarah. *Underwater Cultural Heritage and International Law*. Cambridge: Cambridge University Press, 2013.

"Fiji Museum." Accessed January 15, 2024. http://virtual.fijimuseum.org.fj/template.php?id=2000-492a&next=2000-493&cat=56.

Forrest, Craig. *International Law and the Protection of Cultural Heritage*. Abingdon: Routledge, 2010.

Gadgil, Madhave. "Sacred Groves: An Ancient Tradition of Nature Conservation" *Scientific American* (December 1, 2018). www.scientificamerican.com/article/sacred-groves-an-ancient-tradition-of-nature-conservation/.

Guinness World Records. "Oldest Shipwreck." Accessed January 15, 2024. www.guinnessworldrecords.com/world-records/oldest-shipwreck.

ICOMOS. "The Athens Charter for the Restoration of Historic Monuments (1931)." Accessed January 15, 2024. www.icomos.org/en/167-the-athens-charter-for-the-restoration-of-historic-monuments.

ICOMOS. "The Venice Charter." Accessed January 15, 2024. www.icomos.org/en/participer/179-articles-en-francais/ressources/charters-and-standards/157-thevenice-charter.

J. R. A. 'The Battle for Colombia's Sunken Treasure." *The Economist* (August 8, 2018). www.economist.com/the-economist-explains/2018/08/08/the-battle-for-colombias-sunken-treasure.

Kalina-Metzger, Stephanie. "Discovering Boalsburg: A Trove of Columbus Artifacts Can Be Found in Perhaps the Least Likely Place in the New World." *The Burg* (September 29, 2017). https://theburgnews.com/home-front/discovering-boalsburg-a-trove-of-columbus-artifacts-can-be-found-in-perhaps-the-least-likely-place-in-the-new-world.

"Kaua'i Museum." Accessed January 15, 2024. www.kauaimuseum.org/.

Kokkinidis, Tasos. "2400-Year-Old Greek Ship Is the Oldest Wreck Yet Discovered." *Greek Reporter* (November 13, 2023). https://greekreporter.com/2022/06/28/2400-year-greek-ship-black-sea.

Moroney, Lindsay. "Unsolved Art Heists: The Missing Paintings of Vincent van Gogh." *Artnet* (November 22, 2013). https://news.artnet.com/market/unsolved-art-heists-the-missing-paintings-of-vincent-van-gogh-35614

National Museum Australia. "Cook's Pacific Encounters: Cook-Forster Collection Online." Accessed January 15, 2024. www.nma.gov.au/explore/features/cook_forster.

National Museums Liverpool. "Objects from the Voyages of Captain James Cook." Accessed January 15, 2024. www.liverpoolmuseums.org.uk/stories/objects-voyages-of-captain-james-cook.

National Oceans Office. *Sea Country: An Indigenous Perspective: The South-East Regional Marine Plan Assessment Reports*. Hobart: National Oceans Office, 2002.

Neumann, Thomas W. "Heritage Legislation, the Introduction of: Disciplining Through Law." In *Encyclopedia of Global Archaeology*, edited by C. Smith. New York: Springer, 2014.

"Old Master: 540,000-Year-Old Shell Has Oldest Ever 'Art'." *NBC News* (December 4, 2014). www.nbcnews.com/science/science-news/old-master-540-000-year-old-shell-has-oldest-ever-n261171.

Ounanian, Kristen et al. "Conceptualizing Coastal and Maritime Cultural Heritage Through Communities of Meaning and Participation." *Ocean and Coastal Management* 212 (2021): 105806.

Pearson, Natali. "The Multispecies Shipwreck." *International Journal of Heritage Studies* (2023). https://doi.org/10.1080/13527258.2023.2284719.

Pickering, Helen, and David Whitmarsh. "Artificial Reefs and Fisheries Exploitation Are View of the 'Attraction Versus Production' Debate, the Influence of Design and Its Significance for Policy." *Fisheries Research* 31 (1997): 39–59.

Prott, L. V. "The UNIDROIT Convention on Stolen or Illegally Exported Cultural Objects – Ten Years On." *Uniform Law Review* 14, no. 1–2 (2009): 215–37.

Rist, Phil et al. "Indigenous Protected Areas in Sea Country: Indigenous-driven Collaborative Marine Protected Areas in Australia." *Aquatic Conservation Marine and Freshwater Ecosystems* 29, no. 2 (2019): 138–51.

Royal Museums Greenwich. "National Maritime Museum." Accessed January 15, 2024. www.rmg.co.uk/national-maritime-museum.

Shoaib, Alia. "18th-Century Spanish Shipwreck Has $17 Billion Worth of Coins And Gems Aboard." *Science Alert* (June 18, 2022). www.sciencealert.com/18th-century-spanish-shipwreck-has-17-billion-worth-of-gold-coins-jewels.

Smyth, Dermot, and Miya Isherwood. "Protecting Sea Country: Indigenous Peoples and Marine Protected Areas in Australia." Accessed March 15, 2024. www.dermotsmyth.com.au/wp-content/uploads/2019/01/Protecting-Sea-Country.pdf.

Stamper, Peta. "Vasa Museum." *History HIT* (July 15, 2021). www.historyhit.com/locations/vasa-museum/.

"Stolen Treasures: The Case of the Missing Maps." *FBI* (September 28, 2006). https://archives.fbi.gov/archives/news/stories/2006/september/maps092806.

UNESCO. "8 June: Join the Living Heritage Entity in Celebrating World Oceans Day!" (June 4, 2021). https://ich.unesco.org/en/news/8-june-join-the-living-heritage-entity-in-celebrating-world-oceans-day-13311.

UNESCO. "Abu Simbel: The Campaign That Revolutionized the International Approach to Safeguarding Heritage." Accessed January 15, 2024. https://en.unesco.org/70years/abu_simbel_safeguarding_heritage.

UNESCO. "Browse the Lists of Intangible Cultural Heritage and the Register of Good Safeguarding Practices." Accessed January 15, 2024. https://ich.unesco.org/en/lists.

UNESCO. "Convention on the Protection and Promotion of the Diversity of Cultural Expressions." Accessed January 15, 2024. www.unesco.org/en/legal-affairs/convention-protection-and-promotion-diversity-cultural-expressions.

UNESCO. "Global Strategy." Accessed January 15, 2024. https://whc.unesco.org/en/globalstrategy/.

UNESCO. "Marine World Heritage in a Changing Climate." Accessed January 15, 2024. https://whc.unesco.org/en/climate-change-marine/.

UNESCO. *Marine World Heritage: Safeguarding the Crown Jewels of the Ocean*. Paris: UNESCO World Heritage Centre, 2013. Accessed April 30, 2024. https://unesdoc.unesco.org/ark:/48223/pf0000220049/PDF/220049eng.pdf.multi.

UNESCO. "Ocean Science Roadmap for UNESCO Marine World Heritage." Accessed January 15, 2024. https://unesdoc.unesco.org/ark:/48223/pf0000379847.locale=en.

UNESCO. "Safeguarding Our Living Heritage." Accessed January 15, 2024. https://ich.unesco.org/en/dive&display=biome#tabs.

UNESCO. "Text of the Convention for the Safeguarding of the Intangible Cultural Heritage." Accessed January 15, 2024. https://ich.unesco.org/en/convention.

UNESCO. *The Operational Guidelines for the Implementation of the World Heritage Convention* (WHC.23/01, September 24, 2023). Accessed January 15, 2024. https://whc.unesco.org/en/guidelines/.

UNESCO. "World Heritage Convention." Accessed January 15, 2024, https://whc.unesco.org/en/convention/

UNESCO. "World Heritage List." Accessed January 15, 2024. https://whc.unesco.org/en/list/.

UNESCO. "World Heritage Marine Programme." Accessed January 15, 2024. https://whc.unesco.org/en/marine-programme/.

Verschuuren, Bas et al., eds. *Sacred Natural Sites: Conserving Nature and Culture*. Abingdon: Earthscan, 2010.

Watters, David R. "Maritime Trade in the Prehistoric Eastern Caribbean." In *Indigenous Peoples of the Caribbean*, edited by Samuel M. Wilson. Miami: University Press of Florida, 1997.

11 Ways of knowing

Ocean knowledge, research and data

Knowledge of the oceans is more than a matter of curiosity. Our very survival may hinge upon it.

US President John F. Kennedy Jr., 1961[1]

Overview

Knowledge – the array of facts, information and skills acquired through experience or education – shapes our ways of thinking about the ocean and informs how we use and manage it.[2] Over the course of human history, different groups have built their own bodies of knowledge about oceans, seas and shorelines. In turn, this knowledge has informed the creation of culturally distinctive rules and practices that reflect a group's particular beliefs, values and interactions with their ocean environment. This is as true for oceanographers and maritime lawyers as it is for village chiefs and traditional knowledge-holders.

As we have noted in earlier chapters, western scientific knowledge and its application for practical purposes has been the predominant force in shaping international and domestic laws that seek to regulate human uses and activities in the ocean environment, reflecting the powerful influence of a worldview that has, for the most part, applied that knowledge to prioritise economic and social benefits over environmental stewardship. As will be seen later, the only global framework for marine scientific research is found within the *UN Convention on the Law of the Sea* (UNCLOS). However, despite attempts to embrace a more ecocentric approach, the law of the sea – as Susan Reid has observed – is 'still caught in the undertow of Western imaginaries of mastery' that have justified the 'voracious extractivism' of the ocean for human benefit.[3] 'It is an imaginary underpinned by cornerstone neoliberal values: cheap nature converted for capitalism's gain. Through its discursive practices, UNCLOS opens the seabed for business'.[4] Indeed, the legal regimes that directly regulate human activities – such as fishing and shipping – are necessarily anthropocentric and make little attempt to incorporate consideration of the ocean's intrinsic needs.

DOI: 10.4324/9781003005261-16

The principles and rules that have evolved in western and industrialised societies to govern human uses of oceans, seas and shorelines and their resources can be found in the law of the sea, marine environmental law, maritime (shipping) law and fisheries regulation. They comprise a mixture of traditional rules for using ocean space and new legal concepts devised in response to emerging scientific and technical knowledge in marine and coastal environments.[5] This centrality of science is as prominent today as it was in the 20th century, with the UN Decade of Ocean Science for Sustainable Development (2021–2030) declaring its primary focus as 'the science we need for the ocean we want'.[6] Nevertheless, scientific advances and new technological developments have always been a double-edged sword. On the one hand, they have greatly enhanced knowledge of marine environments, producing an ever-increasing array of gear and equipment, revolutionising the collection of data, and delivering significant material benefits to human societies. However, they have also exposed the marine environment to destructive exploitation and damage from emissions, waste and turbidity.[7]

International lawmakers have been grappling with this paradox since at least the 1972 Stockholm Declaration, which acknowledged that new scientific discoveries and technological advances were creating environmental problems, even as they offered the means to identify, avoid and control them.[8] At the conclusion of negotiations for UNCLOS in 1982, Jens Evensen of Norway noted how modern international law continued to be shaped by the 'industrial and military technological revolution' that offered great gains for humanity while also having the potential to harm the marine environment through 'the rampant consumption of the world's dwindling stock of non-renewable resources'.[9] The forces of science and technology continue to influence ocean governance today, and lawmakers confront ever more complex challenges in ensuring that international and domestic laws governing the ocean environment are fit for purpose.[10]

This chapter focuses on knowledge and information about oceans and everything within them. We examine how different types of knowledge have shaped the international legal framework for oceans, seas and shorelines and, conversely, how law has been used as a tool to control the production of marine scientific research but less so its use.

Different knowledge systems

Traditional knowledge

Humans have been building knowledge about life in the ocean since the earliest peoples lived with and explored its vast surfaces, edges and depths; established intimate cultural relationships with local environments; and harvested its resources. In the process, they have developed traditional knowledge and practices that, in many places, have been handed down to successive generations. Traditional knowledge has been defined as:

> Knowledge, innovations and practices of indigenous and local communities around the world. Developed from experience gained over the centuries and adapted to the local culture and environment, traditional knowledge is transmitted orally from generation to generation. It tends to be collectively owned and takes the form of stories, songs, folklore, proverbs, cultural values, beliefs, rituals, community laws, local language and agricultural practices, including the development of plant species and animal breeds. Traditional knowledge is mainly of a practical nature, particularly in such fields as agriculture, fisheries, health, horticulture, forestry and environmental management in general.[11]

Amongst many coastal and island societies – including Indigenous and tribal communities – traditional knowledge is unique to their particular place and culture and continues to inform local practices that reflect a world view emphasising an ethical relationship between humans and other life forms based on reciprocity and respect. This form of local knowledge draws on the lessons and experiences of ancestors, and is reflected in laws and forms of governance that have evolved into specific rules, duties and obligations about how the society should care for its ocean environment.[12] This cultural and ecological knowledge is diverse and includes information about places, seasons and appropriate methods for harvesting marine and coastal resources, managing saltwater areas, traditional sea trade or travel routes, making observations about changes in the abundance and distribution of particular species over time, protecting cultural sites associated with the knowledge and practices of past generations, and recognising the interconnectedness of people, marine life and the oceanic realm.

Some legal experts argue that traditional knowledge can enrich scientific knowledge of marine species and provide an alternative approach to marine governance.[13] Some traditional knowledge and local practices, for example, can be used to respond to environmental cues in similar ways to adaptive management, and have attracted renewed interest in contemporary environmental conservation contexts.[14] This contribution of traditional knowledge to environmental health and stewardship is now widely recognised in western scientific practices, and has increasingly been reflected in international and domestic law. The 1989 *Convention Concerning Indigenous and Tribal Peoples in Independent Countries*,[15] for example, acknowledged the link between environmental protection, traditional marine activities and the maintenance of culture, as well as the importance of education programmes that incorporate traditional knowledge, technologies and value systems.[16] The *Convention on Biological Diversity* (CBD) required States to respect, preserve and maintain traditional knowledge, innovations and practices, promote its application, and ensure its benefits are fairly shared,[17] and there have been some successes in implementing its provisions. In 1987, for example, scientists on an expedition in India discovered Kani tribal people eating the fruit of a sacred plant – *Arogyapaacha* (*Trichopus zeylanicus*) – to boost their energy. Scientific analysis by India's Tropical Botanic Gardens and Research Institute (TBGRI) revealed 12 active compounds in the plant's leaves with medicinal properties, including increasing stamina, reducing stress and controlling tumours. The TBGRI used the plant to develop a drug called 'Jeevani', drawing worldwide attention and multiple commercial patent applications for drugs based on the plant's properties. However, the TBGRI subsequently decided to enter into a controversial equitable benefit-sharing arrangement with the Kani tribe, in accordance with the CBD, and established a trust fund to share the commercial benefits with Kani tribal members whose traditional medicinal knowledge enabled the development of the drug.[18]

The 2010 *Nagoya Protocol on Access to Genetic Resources and the Equitable Sharing of Benefits Arising from Their Utilization to the Convention on Biological Diversity* provided more detail and clarity on how benefit sharing could be achieved.[19] It expanded obligations in the CBD and specified that prior informed consent must be obtained from Indigenous peoples before accessing traditional knowledge associated with genetic resources (Article 7) and that benefits are equitably shared (on mutually agreed terms) arising from the use of that knowledge (Article 5).[20] The 2023 High Seas Treaty (Article 10) subsequently recognised traditional rights and knowledge of Indigenous peoples and local communities in relation to marine genetic resources in areas beyond national jurisdiction and the need for the fair and equitable sharing of benefits.[21] Furthermore, traditional knowledge and the scientific input of Indigenous peoples, alongside best available science, is referred to as a basis for proposals for high seas marine protected areas (Article 19), emergency measures in the case of human-caused or natural disasters (Article 24), environmental impact assessments (Article 31), and capacity building and technology transfer (Articles 43 and 44). This recent Agreement is perhaps evidence of growing respect for traditional knowledge and the rights of Indigenous custodians.[22]

Western scientific knowledge

Western scientific knowledge and traditional knowledge share similarities in that both involve observations and the collection of information or data. However, they also differ in several important ways. As noted earlier, traditional knowledge is place-specific, while western scientific knowledge relies on universal rules. Traditional knowledge tends to be subjective and qualitative, while western scientific knowledge relies on objectivity and quantitative methods. Finally, traditional knowledge is concerned with the relationships between humans and their environment while western science tends to isolate particular phenomena from their surroundings in order to study them.[23] Compared with traditional knowledge, modern western scientific understanding of the marine environment is relatively recent, rooted in the natural philosophies of ancient civilisations in Egypt, Mesopotamia, western and eastern Europe and subsequently transformed during the Scientific Revolution of the 16th and 17th centuries as European empires embarked on long-distance voyages to explore the oceanic realm beyond established maritime trading routes.[24] Individual naturalists who secured a passage aboard these voyages of exploration published their observations and developed theories about the oceanic realms they encountered, as well as visual representations of ocean tides, currents, magnetism, atmosphere and depths that informed ocean maps and navigational charts.[25] The English pirate, explorer and naturalist William Dampier, for example, was involved in three circumnavigations in the late 17th and early 18th centuries, establishing a reputation for his knowledge of navigation, winds and ocean currents. His books documenting his travels and observations became hugely popular and influenced the work of later maritime naturalist-explorers, including Alexander von Humboldt, Joseph Banks and James Cook.[26] Other European maritime nations supported voyages in different parts of the world that had similar impacts. In the 18th century, Spanish naturalists Pehr Löfling and Félix De Azara undertook studies in Latin America, for example, and early Dutch naturalists published on the natural environment of the Indian Ocean region and southeast Asia.[27]

By the mid-19th century, marine scientific research was evolving into a series of specialised areas of study, including geology, biology, physics, botany, zoology and meteorology, and scientists accompanying imperial voyages of exploration gathered large amounts of data. For maritime powers such as Britain and the US, sponsoring the scientific study of the ocean helped to consolidate their economic and political influence across vast oceanic realms. By forging an alliance between the scientific study of the ocean and their geopolitical and commercial ambitions, they transformed the chaotic and unknowable ocean into an ordered space that could be used to expand their global influence.[28] The most notable of these early scientific voyages was that of the British *Challenger* expedition (1872–76). During its four-year circumnavigation, the scientists aboard amassed data about the physical and chemical properties of the deep ocean and laid the foundations for the modern science of oceanography.[29]

By this time, the commercial imperatives of maritime trade had become a driving force for the development of government-sponsored scientific research and institutions focused on building knowledge of the ocean environment and marine species.[30] The production of hydrographic charts to guide maritime navigation, for example, went hand in hand with the dramatic expansion of the shipping and whaling industries in the late 19th and early 20th centuries. Hydrographic surveys were considered part of the freedom of navigation in the high seas because of their importance for safe navigation by ships. By mapping the ocean's physical and chemical features and gathering data about its life forms, scientists also profoundly shaped the way that western societies, and laws, came to envision the marine environment. This knowledge, acquired through research and exploration, was largely seen as a resource to be utilised for development and economic gain, with limited awareness of the importance of ocean processes for human and planetary health. As Reidy and Rozwadowski have observed, the industrialised maritime nations were able to claim de facto control over, large areas of ocean space by insisting on the principle of the freedom of the seas and the dominance of western scientific knowledge:

> Because use of the ocean in that period was suffused with the doctrine of the freedom of the seas, the ocean was constructed as a space amenable to control by any nation that could master its surface and use its resources effectively.[31]

Figure 11.1 Engraving of scientists and crew on board *HMS Challenger* in 1872–76 examining marine specimens dragged up by the *Challenger*'s nets. (Published in *The Sea: Its Stirring Story of Adventure, Peril & Heroism*, Vol. 1, 1887, page 8; British Library.)

Similarly, this principle enabled unrestricted marine scientific research and exploration on the high seas. Little regard was paid to local knowledge acquired by coastal communities over successive generations, nor to the needs of the oceanic realm itself and the life within it.

Marine scientific research

Early marine scientific research was catalysed by growing awareness of problems such as overfishing. Basic scientific studies regarding commercial fisheries in the North and Baltic Seas, for example, were triggered by the Kiel Commission, established by the Prussian Government in 1870, and in 1902 similar concerns led to the creation of the International Council for the Exploration of the Sea (ICES).[32] Since the beginnings of modern ocean science in the late 19th century, marine scientific research has evolved into a broad field encompassing data collection and analysis in oceanography, chemistry, biology, ecology, geology, geophysics, hydrography and fisheries science, deploying technologies ranging from traditional in-person observation and simple techniques such as dredging, sediment coring and echo sounding traverses, to sophisticated practices using remotely operated vehicles, satellites and artificial intelligence to explore previously inaccessible areas of the marine environment or to more accurately track species and ocean processes.

Some areas of the ocean are far better understood than others, and building on basic scientific knowledge, long-term and sustained observation programs have been established to document changes over time. Such research plays a crucial role in monitoring and mitigating the environmental impacts of human activities on oceans, seas and shorelines, as well as underpinning many maritime activities including shipping, fishing, offshore energy production, and security and defence. However, whilst the development of marine scientific research has been nothing short of revolutionary in human understanding of oceans, seas and shorelines, marine scientists are keenly aware of how little is known about the abyssal ocean, often described as the least understood geographical and geomorphological areas on Earth.[33] Estimates suggest that over 90% of ocean species are not yet classified and 80% of the ocean remains unexplored.[34] Such research is regarded as important, not just for documenting marine resources but also to assist coastal States in addressing the impacts of climate change and pollution on the marine environment.

Marine scientific research in international law

Conducting marine scientific research

Prior to World War II, the marine sciences were largely unregulated and undertaken in accordance with customary international laws developed over time.[35] Rapid advances in new technologies after World War II provided the impetus for the development of oceanography and the marine sciences, creating new opportunities for further basic research as well as long-term scientific monitoring and data collection in marine environments. State-sponsored marine research programs followed, particularly focusing on research activities related to offshore marine resources and military security. In response to increasing concerns about expanding opportunities for the exploration and exploitation of marine resources, the international legal community began to develop specific provisions to govern marine scientific research activities.[36] The first regulatory regime was introduced in the 1958 *Geneva Convention on the Continental Shelf*, and it sought to give coastal States discretion to limit research conducted into natural resources on their continental shelf.[37] The 1958 Conventions did not address the question of marine scientific research in the high seas, so States were free to conduct their research activities without constraint.

The regulation of marine scientific research subsequently proved to be one of the most difficult issues to resolve during negotiations for the UNCLOS. In 1970, amidst Cold War geopolitical tensions, the *UN Declaration of Principles Governing the Seabed and the Ocean Floor, and the Subsoil Thereof, Beyond the Limits of National Jurisdiction* sought to promote the importance of State cooperation in scientific research for peaceful purposes through the development of international programs and the dissemination of information emerging from marine scientific research. The Seabed Committee expanded on this legal framework in its work for the Third UN Conference on the Law of the Sea (conducted between 1973 and 1992), recommending the transfer of technology and scientific research in Exclusive Economic Zones. However, tensions emerged during negotiations, between those States with advanced research programs opposing limitations on their freedom to conduct research, and coastal States – many of which were newly independent and still developing – which sought to control research activities within areas of national jurisdiction. States with major research programs argued that, by controlling such research, developing States would not be able to reap the benefits of improved knowledge in such fields as weather forecasting and the study of ocean currents. Coastal States, on the other hand, argued their right to protect their marine resources in a regulated marine science research regime.[38]

States were unable to agree on a definition for marine scientific research reflecting differences over whether the regulation of marine scientific research should relate to 'pure' or 'fundamental' research purposes (to increase humankind's knowledge of the marine environment), or to 'applied' research (for the subsequent exploitation of marine resources), or both.[39] Ultimately, the parties failed to reach a consensus on a formal definition and agreed instead to describe the principles.[40] These included the right of all States to conduct marine scientific research subject to the rights of other States, to facilitate its development, and to conduct it exclusively for peaceful purposes for mutual benefit using appropriate scientific methods and respecting the sovereignty and jurisdiction of other States.[41] Importantly, UNCLOS provided that coastal States have the right to regulate and authorise marine scientific research in their territorial seas, exclusive economic zones and continental shelves.

As the European Commissioner, Joe Borg, noted in 2005, marine scientific research provided the basis for policymaking in most regions. In the case of fisheries, for example, marine scientific research played a key role in providing States with scientific advice on the state of fish stocks and the total annual catch in the different fisheries. He noted that there is a legal obligation that the decision-making process shall be 'based on sound scientific advice. . . . Without scientific advice our common policy could not work'.[42] In this sense, the regime under UNCLOS supports similar fisheries research to the very early programs in the late 19th century. Yet the effectiveness of the regulatory regime for marine scientific research has been tested over the years. In the 1990s, for example, Japan attempted to circumvent restrictions on commercial harvesting of the critically endangered migratory southern bluefin tuna by describing it as an 'experimental fishing program' in accordance with marine scientific research principles. It led to New Zealand and Australia imposing a port ban on the fishing vessels involved and initiating proceedings at the International Tribunal for the Law of the Sea in Hamburg.[43]

The UNCLOS provisions on marine scientific research sought to achieve a balance between the rights of coastal States and the rights of other States to conduct research, but not how it may be done nor for what purpose. Whilst, it is generally accepted that marine scientific research means any form of scientific investigation concerned with the marine environment, questions have been raised about whether the marine scientific research provisions in UNCLOS can be applied to new and emerging technologies, methods and practices.[44] The UN Division of Ocean Affairs and the Law of the Sea Office (DOALOS) has twice provided guidelines on marine scientific research and declined to provide a definition, highlighting only that exploration, survey activities, monitoring, prospecting and exploitation are dealt with in other parts of UNCLOS and are similarly undefined.[45] Scholars have pointed to the need for UNCLOS to be interpreted as a living document that can flex to meet changing circumstances, and that it should not be constrained by the historical compromises at the time of its negotiation.[46] Nevertheless, the nature of activities such as remote sensing and sustained ocean observing, for example, makes the consent and advanced notice process set out in UNCLOS practically challenging, leading to calls for updated DOALOS guidelines or specific procedures to be developed.[47]

Global Ocean Observing System (GOOS)

In 1991, the Intergovernmental Oceanographic Commission of UNESCO created the Global Ocean Observing System (GOOS) to facilitate scientific monitoring and collection of data about the health of the ocean's biological, physical and biogeochemical health. GOOS was established as part of international efforts to improve global climate change forecasts and manage marine resources to mitigate the effects of natural disasters.[48] By undertaking long-term in-situ observations of the ocean environment above and below the surface at global scales, scientists were seeking to 'ground truth' the data received remotely via satellites. Under the CBD, GOOS is used to coordinate the various autonomous ocean observation systems that collect physical and geological data for a range of purposes (such as tsunami warning systems), as well as biogeochemical and biological samples and data from areas beyond national jurisdiction (such as microorganisms sampled for DNA sequence analysis). The main purpose of the data is to identify what needs protection and whether measures such as Marine Protected Areas are effective in preventing environmental damage. Significantly, data already collected suggests that only 7% of the ocean's surface is monitored in a sustained manner, while marine life and ecosystems in the deep ocean (below 200 metres) are scarcely monitored at all.[49]

Who has the right to undertake marine scientific research?

The matter of who has the right to undertake marine scientific research was specifically addressed in UNCLOS (Part XIII, Section 3), based on the maritime zones and boundaries recognised under international law. Coastal States, for example, have the exclusive right to regulate and conduct marine scientific research in their territorial sea, EEZ and continental shelf, and to allow projects by other States or scientific organizations providing it is for peaceful purposes and designed to increase scientific knowledge of the marine environment for the benefit of humanity. However, coastal States can withhold their consent for marine scientific research projects for certain reasons, including instances where the projects are related to exploration and exploitation of their natural resources. In return, those engaged in marine scientific research are required to share the results of the research with the coastal State. Meanwhile, UNCLOS provides for all States and international organisations, irrespective of geographical location, to undertake marine scientific research in areas beyond national jurisdiction. As some observers noted, the provisions for marine scientific research in the Convention have tended to benefit developed countries but not developing States without the necessary scientific capability or access to scientific knowledge. Indeed, the equitable sharing of knowledge, information and data in marine scientific research has been a contested area during negotiations for international treaties.

UNCLOS (Article 266) provided for States to actively promote the development of marine scientific and technological capacity of other States, particularly developing land-locked and geographically disadvantaged States, and the transfer of marine technology on an equitable basis for the benefit of all.[50] In addition to sharing the benefits of marine scientific research, technology transfer is also seen as critical in enhancing international environmental regimes and an incentive for developing nations to adopt them. However, the question of whether wealthy States with advanced marine research technologies are obliged to transfer that knowledge to developing States remains a sticking point in international law. As Jessica Lehman has argued, 'knowledge, technology, and geopolitics are woven together in how questions of ocean governance are framed and, potentially, answered'.[51]

In 2020, the IOC Global Ocean Science Report noted that 'the technical capacity of ocean science remains unequally distributed among countries and regions', a point reiterated in the UN Sustainable Development Goal 14.a.[52] Member States of UNCLOS sought to address these and other challenges during negotiations for the High Seas Treaty (also known as the BBNJ Agreement), adopted in 2023. Historically, developed States had the technology and capacity to explore the deep ocean for new resources and argued that the freedom of the seas principle should apply. The obligation to share scientific knowledge and technologies was a major point of debate in the negotiations, but this obligation became a key principle of the Treaty (Article 5) wherein all parties are obliged to recognise the freedom of marine scientific research and 'the principle of equity, and the fair and equitable sharing of benefits' arising from activities with respect to marine genetic resources and related digital sequence information.[53]

Best available scientific evidence

At the 42nd meeting of the CCAMLR Commission in 2023, Russia proposed that a clear and transparent scientific and legal definition for 'best available scientific evidence' was needed. The proposal argued that three proposed new MPAs in the Southern Ocean were not based on the best available evidence. However, the majority of CCAMLR members rejected Russia's proposal as being contrary to established international practice, wherein the scientific information informing the proposed MPAs was peer reviewed and evaluated to ensure scientific integrity. Whilst the motives for Russia's position were unclear, the proposal was seen by some as a political manoeuvre to undermine CCAMLR's consensus decision-making process, and part of a 'worrying trend' to block conservation measures using 'spurious science'.[54]

Significantly, the Treaty expressly aimed to regulate the exploitation of resources such as microorganisms, bacteria, algae, corals and other living resources, imposing controls on the use of marine genetic resources by requiring fair and equitable access and the sharing of benefits with developing States without the technical or financial capabilities to collect such resources. In particular, the BBNJ provides that activities involving 'material of marine plant, animal, microbial or other origin containing functional units of heredity of actual or potential value', as used in genetics and microbiology research as well as products used in medicine, cosmetics, food supplements and industrial processes, 'are in the interest of all states and for the benefit of all humanity [and must take] into particular consideration the interests and needs of developing states' (Article 11).

Using marine scientific research

Concerns were raised during the negotiations for UNCLOS about the scope of marine scientific research, preventing agreement on a formal definition. This debate also highlighted a 'regulatory paradox', wherein the scientific knowledge that could play a key role in identifying environmental threats and developing effective environmental protection measures, could be inhibited by regulatory measures to protect the marine environment in the process of conducting that research.[55] In order to address this problem, UNCLOS explicitly recognised the close relationship between 'the study, protection and preservation of the marine environment', and promoted the cooperation between States during scientific research to identify and monitor the associated environmental risks.[56] UNCLOS also acknowledged that marine research is necessary for the exploitation of marine resources, and required States to use the 'best scientific evidence available' when establishing conservation and management policies.[57] Similarly, the later UN Fish Stocks Agreement (1995) reiterated that conservation and management measures for fish stocks should be based on the same principle.[58]

UNCLOS (1982) did not specifically include bioprospecting as a form of marine scientific research, reflecting a lack of consensus on the meaning of 'pure' and 'applied' research.[59] When parties to the UN agreed to the *Convention on Biological Diversity* in 1992 to address the alarming acceleration of biodiversity loss, they recognised that scientific research was required to further knowledge of marine ecosystems and species but did not distinguish between 'pure' research for scientific knowledge purposes and 'applied' research for commercial gain.[60] The scientific expert advisory body to the convention subsequently noted the problem of distinguishing between research, exploration and exploitation in relation to marine genetic resources:

> While marine scientific research is primarily undertaken with a view to furthering knowledge of the evolutionary relationship between various organisms or of the adaptive mechanisms allowing organisms to thrive in an extreme environment with unique characteristics, some prospective activities are run to discover commercially useful information and resources for subsequent industrial, chemical, agricultural or medical purposes. However,

> what may have been, in the first place, an expedition with scientific purposes, where intent of economic gain was absent, may result in the genetic resources being transferred to industry for biotechnological applications.[61]

Meanwhile, technological advances increasingly enabled scientists to undertake marine scientific research in more extreme marine environments beyond State jurisdiction, and companies with the technical capacity began exploring these potentially lucrative areas, with a view to patenting the genetic material recovered.

Some States have sought to clarify the legal issues arising from increasing commercial interest in biotechnology. In 2003, for example, the UK invited proposals for a study of the complex legal, moral and environmental issues relating to marine biotechnology, noting that the international law of the sea had not kept pace with the commercialisation of biotechnology research. In response to these concerns, member States negotiated the *Nagoya Protocol* as a supplementary agreement to the *Convention on Biological Diversity*. As discussed earlier, the aim was to provide a transparent legal framework for fair and equitable sharing of benefits arising out of the utilisation of marine genetic resources, recognising that biodiversity provides value to all humans and to those States with sovereign rights over their genetic resources and traditional knowledge. Importantly, the CBD also addressed the right of coastal States to own and utilise marine genetic resources within their jurisdiction (in accordance with UNCLOS). As in UNCLOS negotiations, the problem of equitable sharing of the benefits of marine resources was regarded as a key issue, with some critics arguing that marine bioprospecting required advanced technology and knowledge, thereby favouring wealthy States. In addition, corporations were potentially able to profit from marine genetic resources and associated traditional knowledge while excluding Indigenous coastal communities.

Under UNCLOS, coastal States are permitted to control research activities in marine areas within their jurisdiction, but research undertaken beyond national jurisdiction is the responsibility of the flag State of the ship being used to conduct the research at sea. Whilst such research activities may yield crucial information for conserving and managing the marine environment, they may also have unintended harmful consequences to marine ecosystems and species. Indeed, using the ocean as a laboratory raises scientific, environmental, legal and policy questions and highlights the need for internationally agreed guidelines that ensure such activities are environmentally responsible.[62]

Advanced marine technologies are also facilitating the development of new and more efficient extractive practices, some of which have the potential to inflict catastrophic damage on sensitive marine environments. The technological capacity to explore previously inaccessible areas of the ocean environment, for example, means that scientists have been able to identify new microorganisms that possess unique biochemical responses to extreme conditions such as high pressure, darkness, lack of oxygen, extreme heat (300°C) in hydrothermal vents, and sub-zero temperatures below sea ice. The unique properties of these microorganisms are seen as a potential source of enzymes that could be used in industrial processes involving extreme physical and chemical conditions. This treasure trove of newly discovered organisms with genetic properties has the potential to be processed for a range of applications such as new pharmaceutical drugs, cosmetics and 'environmentally friendly' chemicals for use in agriculture, aquaculture and fisheries. As the marine biologist Helen Scales has noted, the deep ocean is a 'weird chemistry cupboard' with the potential to yield many new benefits, not just to wealthy nations and corporations but to the whole of humanity.[63] The attention being drawn to marine genetic resources of the high seas is reminiscent of the interest in mining polymetallic nodules on the seabed in the 1960s and 1970s, and subsequent discussions about its merits during negotiations for UNCLOS.[64]

Whose knowledge counts?

One of the issues for the international legal regime for ocean governance relates to the question of who provides scientific research and advice to inform policy making. From its creation in 1945, the United Nations determined that international ocean governance organisations should be supported by scientific bodies. In 1969, the United Nations established the Joint Group of Experts on the Scientific Aspects of Marine Environmental Protection (GESAMP) to provide 'authoritative, independent, interdisciplinary scientific advice to organisations and governments to support the protection and sustainable use of the marine environment'.[65] GESAMP continues to provide advice to ten UN organisations with responsibilities for the marine environment on matters of common interest, for consistency, and to avoid duplication.[66]

During negotiations for the Convention on Biological Diversity in the 1980s, it was agreed that the new treaty required an expert group to provide scientific, technical and technological advice on measures to be undertaken to protect biological diversity. Parties to the Convention also created the Clearing-House Mechanism to promote 'scientific and technical cooperation, knowledge sharing and information exchange'.[67] Indeed most environmental treaties have scientific advisory committees.[68] Other scientific bodies advising international fisheries organisations include the Scientific Committee (SCAR), which advises the Commission of Antarctic Marine Living Resources (CCAMLR) and the Scientific Committee of the South East Atlantic Fisheries Organization (SEAFO), both of which provide scientific advice for conservation and management measures.[69]

However, while the biophysical sciences have played, and continue to play, a key role in advising international ocean governance, there has been a growing awareness amongst policymakers of the importance of recognising the social-ecological dimensions. This has seemingly assumed greater importance as remote sensing technologies render the ocean as an object of scientific study, detached from human affairs.[70] As noted earlier, there have been calls for greater recognition of traditional knowledge in marine scientific research.[71] In 2019, for example, Indigenous delegates to the Global Ocean Observing System (GOOS)[72] issued the *Aha Honua*, a declaration calling on the international ocean observing community to 'establish meaningful partnerships with indigenous communities, organizations, and Nations to learn and respect each other's ways of knowing'.[73] In the social sciences more broadly, fisheries have tended to dominate marine research, although marine scientists are increasingly recognising the importance of understanding how humans interact with the ocean more broadly, such as how coastal communities relate to marine protected areas.[74] The importance of expanding scientific collaborations was recognised in UNCLOS (Article 242) and in the UN High Seas Treaty, but challenges remain in trying to integrate the natural and social sciences in ocean governance – a task identified in the UN Decade of Ocean Science for Sustainable Development (2021–2030). Priorities for strengthening 'ocean knowledge-based solutions', for example, include areas such as developing ocean literacy and community resilience to ocean hazards.[75]

Technological developments

Underwater remote/uncrewed technologies

The development of increasingly advanced technologies has provided greater scope for ocean research and monitoring as well as more efficient practices. As discussed in Chapter 3, Automatic Identification Systems (AIS) were initially employed in the ocean environment to track vessels at sea and monitor their safe passage in potentially dangerous stretches of water. Since the 1990s, AIS have been increasingly used to detect illegal, unreported and unregulated fishing (see Chapter 4) and breaches of international law regarding discharges at sea under the 1983 International Convention for the Prevention of Pollution from Ships (MARPOL) (see Chapter 7). Vessel Monitoring Systems (VMS), a form of AIS used to monitor the location and movement of commercial fishing vessels, have become a crucial tool for State fisheries management authorities to detect illegal activities in their EEZ.[76] However, while some States require the use of VMS on foreign-flagged vessels licensed to fish in their EEZs, international law does not mandate their use.[77] It is clear that providing a more consistent legal approach to the use of AIS and VMS could enhance marine protection and conservation.

The development of uncrewed vehicles such as autonomous surface ships and remotely operated underwater vessels has also revolutionised ocean research. However, autonomous oceanic surface vehicles include merchant and military ships, as well as research vessels, and can create significant problems for regulators who must first decide whether they are ships for the purposes of the law of the sea. The International Maritime Organization, in particular, is faced with the challenge of keeping pace with rapid developments in the commercial use of autonomous vessels to ensure that the regulatory framework provides for the safety of lives, cargo and ships.[78]

The application of these new technologies can also be greatly beneficial. For marine scientific research, some surface vehicles are utilised in long-term monitoring projects and stay at sea for extended periods, capturing vast amounts of hydrographic and oceanographic data.[79] The advent of remotely operated underwater vessels (often known as 'ROVs' or 'AUVs') in the 1950s has, over time, had a significant impact on scientific understanding of the ocean environment.[80] Whilst these technologies can assist with oceanic activities such as physically dangerous tasks, salvage operations and oil and gas exploration and operations, they can also conduct millions of observations and in doing so provide critical scientific information that improves our basic understanding of the ocean, explore changes in the marine environment and more sustainably pursue blue economy activities. Whilst they may be uncontroversial where the use of these vessels is clear and unequivocal and the collected data publicly shared, they have, however, raised maritime security concerns where their purpose has been questioned.[81] This highlights the limitations of the UNCLOS regime for marine scientific research such as the problem of having multiple sub-fields of law (law of the sea, maritime security law, shipping law etc) regulating one type of technology according to the purpose for which it is being used.

Sharing the benefits? New technologies and the law of the sea

With rapid advances in marine technologies used for exploring, mapping, monitoring, protecting, collecting data and extracting resources in the marine environment, concerns about equity have become central to the United Nations Agenda 2020 sustainable development goals. The 1982 UNCLOS (Part XIV) provides a legal framework for regulating the use of marine technology and sharing knowledge, information and data with developing States. Nevertheless, 'technology transfer' has proved difficult.[82] In 2023, UN member States reached agreement on the Biodiversity Beyond National Jurisdiction (BBNJ) to tackle environmental degradation, fight climate change and prevent biodiversity loss. Crucially, marine technology transfer and capacity building formed one of the four pillars of the BBNJ, aimed at helping developing States to engage in marine scientific research and technological innovation through a clearinghouse mechanism designed as an open access platform for information sharing.[83]

Other remote sensing and satellite technology and data

Satellite technologies also greatly enhance the capacity to monitor the marine environment and to sample and gather ocean data remotely, yielding information about previously unknown and inaccessible areas such as deep-sea vents and the water column beneath sea ice. Satellite remote sensing falls under international space law, rather than law of the sea or marine environmental law, guided by a set of internationally agreed principles. These provide rights for sensing nations and for the sensed States and, while they do not address oceans in particular, they require that activities should be for the benefit of all nations.[84]

As noted earlier, state-of-the-art ships and uncrewed submersibles are used to gather data, samples and images, locate deepwater fish habitats, map seabed topography, and trace natural seafloor 'seeps' from gases in the water column. Researchers also experiment with the marine environment to obtain data and test hypotheses as to how it responds to such interventions.[85] For example, scientists release low-frequency acoustic signals that can be detected up to 18,000 kilometres from their source to investigate whether global ocean temperatures are increasing. In this way, these new technologies are assisting to build fundamental knowledge about the ocean.

Figure 11.2 Members of the Unmanned Underwater Vehicle detachment, Commander, Task Group (CTG) 56.1, guide a UUV as it is lowered into the water. (Image courtesy of U.S. Navy by Mass Communication Specialist 1st Class Peter Lewis/Released, ID 130605-N-AZ907-046, 5 June 2013.)

In recent years the UNESCO Intergovernmental Oceanographic Commission has collaborated with an international network of expert volunteer taxonomic specialists to undertake a program called Ocean Census, a global alliance aiming to 'accelerate the discovery and protection of ocean life'. It involves a partnership between the United Nations World Register of Marine Species (WoRMS) and a private global consortium led by The Nippon Foundation (formerly the Japan Shipbuilding Industry Foundation) and Nekton in 2023. In this 21st-century version of the 19th-century *Challenger* expedition, Ocean Census involves scientists from across the world exploring biodiversity hotspots to discover new life in the ocean depths, while networks of taxonomists use the aggregated data to create a complete picture of the species discovered. Importantly, this open-sourced data is freely available to everyone for non-commercial use, accessed via a network of data centres coordinated by the Ocean Census Biodiversity System. Under the Nagoya Protocol, all new data discovered in territorial waters are owned by the host nation while under UNCLOS all species, specimens and data from international waters are part of the collective commons and open access for the common benefit of humankind.[86]

Marine Genetic Resources

The study and use of marine genetic resources is a relatively recent activity. Humans have long known that certain organisms contain properties that are useful for making or preserving food such as bread and dairy products. The term 'biotechnology', first coined in 1919, refers to this process of making products and processes to benefit human health and welfare, using raw materials derived from living organisms. Under the 2023 High Seas Treaty (Article 1), marine genetic resources (MGR) include 'any material of marine plant, animal, microbial or other origin containing functional units of heredity of actual or potential value'. Compared with those found on land, marine genetic resources have been more challenging to identify and extract. Research programs such as the Census of Marine Life and Marine Microbial Biodiversity, Bioinformatics and Biotechnology have served helped to stimulate scientific and commercial interest in the potential of MGR, and some have already become important for industries such as pharmaceuticals, cosmetics, aquaculture and biomedicine.[87] The regulatory framework adopted in the High Seas Treaty (2023) is being implemented. Its effectiveness has yet to be tested.

The proliferation of ocean data has also encouraged governments to collaborate with the private sector. One of the fundamental aims of UNCLOS was to advance scientific research for the whole ocean and facilitate the international exchange of data, and there are now many examples of new partnerships between governments, private industry and non-governmental organisations and institutions addressing the growing demands for ocean information and relieving the pressure on public funding for marine scientific research.

Private and not-for-profit research organisations are also increasingly involved in collecting their own ocean data. However, gaps remain in the regulatory regime for ocean data collection and use, raising questions about who owns the data collected privately and how it is managed under international law.[88] UNCLOS, for example, does not address the intellectual property rights of data with the potential for commercial exploitation since such rights are generally regulated by private agreement rather than international law. Article 241 of the Convention states that marine scientific research ‘shall not constitute the legal basis for any claim to any part of the marine environment or its resources’, but some observers have argued that intellectual property rights arising from bioprospecting might constitute such a claim.[89] There are other areas of concern regarding the legal status of private data collection. The use of satellite data as evidence of a violation of public international law, for example, highlights problems in relation to privacy, liability and the reliability of the data, particularly in cases where the data has been collected by private entities.[90]

Conclusion

Developments in marine scientific research and technology since UNCLOS was negotiated in the 1970s have profoundly changed the ways in which research is undertaken in the marine environment. Whilst enabling humans to investigate areas previously unknown or inaccessible, these developments have also created significant challenges for the international community in managing and regulating new and emerging practices and technologies in marine scientific research, exposing heightened tensions and blurred boundaries between pure and applied research. Law and science are similarly concerned with rules and order based on knowledge, but they use knowledge to serve different purposes: law is based on stability and predictability and describes how society should function, while western science aims to understand how the world actually functions.[91] These differences underpin some of the challenges for international law in regulating the development of new research technologies and increased exposure of marine environments to human intervention.

Many aspects of international law predate the application of advanced marine technologies, raising questions about whether the legal framework is adequate to regulate them. Tensions also remain between the need to promote crucial research while protecting and preserving the marine environment from potentially damaging impacts. The Arctic Ocean, for example, is undergoing rapid change as climate change and increased human activity impact on the region’s sea ice and marine environment, driving the development of new satellite remote-sensing and in-situ monitoring technologies to investigate this remote, dynamic and sensitive region. However, UNCLOS obligations intended to protect and preserve the marine environment may be serving to inhibit this urgent research.[92]

A major issue for international law has been the question of who controls marine scientific research and data, who has access to the marine technology capable of undertaking research, monitoring and enforcement in the marine environment, and who benefits from it. Negotiations for the High Seas Treaty signed in 2023 exposed lingering tensions over obligations to transfer technology and equitably share the benefits. Many industrialised States were opposed to these requirements in UNCLOS, and it appears that similar concerns may hinder the implementation of the High Seas Treaty. Nevertheless, bioprospecting is expected to expand in the coming decades. In 2023, for example, the global marine biotechnology market was growing rapidly in value and is estimated to reach $7.69 billion by 2027.[93] As with all technological interventions in natural ecosystems, exploiting these new forms of 'blue biotechnology' is likely to bring considerable environmental risk and require a new regulatory framework, particularly where harvesting is to be undertaken on a large scale.

Efforts to regulate marine scientific research have resulted in a legal framework that broadly recognises the fundamental right of all States to conduct marine research, subject to rights and duties of other States, for the benefit of all humankind for peaceful purposes with appropriate scientific methods. Nevertheless, whilst much work has been done to define marine scientific research, the lack of a legal definition, combined with the rapid development of science and technology in the marine environment, has created legal uncertainties, particularly in relation to who is legally entitled to undertake marine scientific research and what activities are subject to the marine scientific research regime.[94] This has been further complicated by the fact that what constitutes best practice in marine scientific research has not remained static, particularly when 'objective' scientific knowledge about marine characteristics and processes has subsequently been shown to be wrong. Even so, scientific practices will continue to evolve in response to new technologies, insights and understandings of the marine environment, and lawmakers will persist in relying upon the integrity of marine scientific research as the epistemic basis for marine environmental protection.[95]

Notes

1 President John F. Kennedy Jr., "Letter to the President of the Senate on Increasing the National Effort in Oceanography," *The American Presidency Project* (March29,1961),www.presidency.ucsb.edu/documents/letter-the-president-the-senate-increasing-the-national-effort-oceanography.

2 Kira Gee, "The Ocean Perspective," in *Maritime Spatial Planning*, ed. J Zaucha and K Gee (Cham: Springer International Publishing, 2019), 24.

3 Susan Reid, "Ocean Justice: Reckoning with Material Vulnerability," *Cultural Politics* 19, no. 1 (March 2023): 108 and 110.

4 Susan Reid, "Solwara 1 and the Sessile Ones," in *Blue Legalities: The Life and Laws of the Sea*, ed. Irus Braverman and Elizabeth R. Johnson (Durham: Duke University Press, 2020), 27.
5 Jin-Hyun Paik, "Disputes Involving Scientific and Technical Matters and the International Tribunal for the Law of the Sea," in *New Knowledge and Changing Circumstances in the Law of the Sea*, ed. Tomas Heidar (Leiden: Brill Nijhoff, 2020), 15.
6 UNESCO, "United Nations Decade of Ocean Science for Sustainable Development (2021–2030)," www.unesco.org/en/decades/ocean-decade#:~:text=The%20United%20Nations%20has%20proclaimed,support%20countries%20in%20creating%20improved. For an overview of all the UN Decades see "International Decades," *United Nations*, accessed May 7, 2024, www.un.org/en/observances/international-decades.
7 Peter J. Cook and Chris Carleton, "Introduction," in *Continental Shelf Limits: The Scientific and Legal Interface*, ed. Peter J. Cook and Chris Carleton (Oxford: Oxford University Press, 2000), 3, cited in Hilde J. Woker, Rozemarijn J. Roland Holst, and Harriet Harden-Davies, "New Technology and the Protection of the Marine Environment," in *Research Handbook on International Marine Environmental Law*, 2nd ed., ed. R. Rayfuse, A. Jaeckel, and N. Klein (Cheltenham, Glos: Edward Elgar, 2023), chapter 18; and Anna-Maria Hubert, "The New Paradox in Marine Scientific Research: Regulating the Potential Environmental Impacts of Conducting Ocean Science," *Ocean Development & International Law* 42 (2011): 329–30.
8 *Declaration on the Human Environment (Stockholm Declaration)*, adopted by the UN Conference on the Human Environment, Stockholm (June 16, 1972), Principle 18.
9 Jens Evensen, "The Effect of the Law of the Sea Conference Upon the Process of the Formation of International Law: Rapprochement Between Competing Points of View," in *The Developing Order of the Oceans*, Proceedings of the 18th Annual Conference of the Law of the Sea Institute, ed. Robert B. Krueger and Stefan A. Riesenfeld (Honolulu: Law of the Sea Institute, University of Hawaii, 1984), 25–26.
10 See, for example, House of Lords, *UNCLOS: The Law of the Sea in the 21st Century* (London: HL Paper 159, 2022), accessed March 15, 2024, https://committees.parliament.uk/publications/9005/documents/159002/default/
11 Secretariat of the Convention on Biological Diversity, Article 8(j): Traditional Knowledge and the Convention on Biological Diversity, 2007.
12 Meg Parsons and Lara Taylor, "Why Indigenous Knowledge Should Be an Essential Part of How We Govern the World's Oceans," *The Conversation* (June 8, 2021), https://theconversation.com/why-indigenous-knowledge-should-be-an-essential-part-of-how-we-govern-the-worlds-oceans-161649.
13 See for example Steven M. Alexander, Jennifer F. Provencher, Dominique A. Henri et al., "Bridging Indigenous and Science-Based Knowledge in Coastal And Marine Research, Monitoring, and Management in Canada," *Environmental Evidence* 8, no. 36 (2019), https://doi.org/10.1186/s13750-019-0181-3.
14 See, for example, R. E. Johannes, "The Renaissance of Community-Based Marine Resource Management in Oceania," *Annual Review of Ecology and Systematics* 33 (2002): 317–40; and Fikret Berkes, Johan Colding and Carl Folke, "Rediscovery of Traditional Ecological Knowledge as Adaptive Management," *Ecological Applications* 10, no. 5 (2000): 1251–62.
15 *ILO No. 169 – Indigenous and Tribal Peoples Convention, 1989 (No. 169)*, accessed March 15, 2024, www.ilo.org/dyn/normlex/en/f?p=NORMLEXPUB:12100:0::NO:12100:P12100_INSTRUMENT_ID:312314:NO.
16 "What the Convention Says about Traditional Knowledge, Innovations and Practices," *CBD*, accessed March 15, 2024, www.cbd.int/traditional/what.shtml.

17 This was the first time that such a treaty sought to provide justice for peoples whose knowledge and practices had been appropriated over centuries as a springboard for many lucrative pharmaceutical and other products developed in industrialised nations. CBD Articles 8(j), 10(c), 15.5, 17.2 and 18.4. J. Amiott, "Investigating the Convention on Biological Diversity's Protections for Traditional Knowledge," *Journal of Environmental and Sustainability Law* 11, no. 1 (2003): 2–37.

18 Anil K. Gupta, *WIPO-UNEP Study on the Role of Intellectual Property Rights in the Sharing of Benefits Arising from the Use of Biological Resources and Associated Traditional Knowledge* (Ahmedabad: World Intellectual Property Organization and the United Nations Environment Programme, 2004), 103–21; and World Intellectual Property Organization, *Intellectual Property and Genetic Resources, Traditional Knowledge and Traditional Cultural Expressions* (Geneva: World Intellectual Property Organization, 2020).

19 *Nagoya Protocol on Access to Genetic Resources and the Fair and Equitable Sharing of Benefits Arising from Their Utilization (ABS) to the Convention on Biological Diversity* (2010), accessed March 15, 2024, www.cbd.int/abs/.

20 M. Buck and C. Hamilton, "The Nagoya Protocol on Access to Genetic Resources and the Fair and Equitable Sharing of Benefits Arising from their Utilization to the Convention on Biological Diversity," *Review of European Community and International Environmental Law* 20, no. 1 (2011): 47–61.

21 *Agreement under the United Nations Convention on the Law of the Sea on the Conservation and Sustainable Use of Marine Biological Diversity of Areas Beyond National Jurisdiction* (2023), accessed March 15, 2024, https://treaties.un.org/doc/Treaties/2023/06/20230620%2004-28%20PM/Ch_XXI_10.pdf.

22 See H. L. Marrie, *Emerging Trends in the Generation, Transmission and Protection of Traditional Knowledge*. Presentation to the 18th Session of the UN Permanent Forum on Indigenous Issues (New York: United Nations, 2019), www.un.org/development/desa/indigenouspeoples/wp-content/uploads/sites/19/2019/04/TK-Emerging-trends-in-the-generation-transmission-and-protection-of-TK-final-paper.pdf.

23 See for example Fulvio Mazzocchi, "Western Science and Traditional Knowledge: Despite Their Variations, Different Forms of Knowledge Can Learn from Each Other," *EMBO Reports* 7, no. 5 (May 2006): 463–66.

24 See for example David C. Lindberg, *The Beginnings of Western Science*, 2nd ed. (Chicago: University of Chicago Press, 2007), 1–20.

25 Early naturalists included Carl Linnaeus and Georges Cuvier in the 18th century, and the 19th-century British naturalists Charles Darwin and Edward Forbes. Knowledge about the marine environment also came from seafarers whose experiences aboard ships brought them into close contact with the ocean's biophysical features.

26 William Dampier's *Discourse of Winds, Breezes, Storm Tides and Currents* (circa 1700) was one of the earliest publications to describe ocean currents. See Alex George, "William Dampier as a Natural Historian," *The Great Circle* 37, no. 1 (2015): 36–52.

27 Manuel Ruiz Rejón, "Félix De Azara, and Pehr Löfling, the First Naturalists in a Great Frontier," *Bioscience* (December 29, 2021), www.bbvaopenmind.com/en/science/bioscience/felix-de-azara-pehr-loefling-naturalist/; and Theodore W. Pietsch, ed., *Cuvier's History of the Natural Sciences* (Paris: Publications Scientifiques due Muséum, 2015), https://books.openedition.org/mnhn/2761.

28 Helen M. Rozwadowski, "Introduction," in Michael S. Reidy and Helen M. Rozwadowski, "The Spaces in between: Science, Ocean, Empire," *Isis* 105, no. 2 (June 2014): 336.

29 The voyage covered 68,890 nautical miles and discovered over 4,000 previously unknown marine species. The results were published in the *Report of the Scientific Results of the Exploring Voyage of H.M.S. Challenger during the Years 1873–76* (Edinburgh: Neill, 1880–1895).
30 Reidy and Rozwadowski, "The Spaces in Between," 343.
31 Ibid., 350.
32 Bruno Pinto, "Historical Connections between Early Marine Science Research and Dissemination: The Case Study of Aquarium Vasco Da Gama (Portugal) from Late 19th Century to Mid-20th Century," *ICES Journal of Marine Science* 74(6) (2017): 1522–30, https://doi/org/10.1093/icesjms/fsx029.
33 Gaps include a complete inventory of marine biodiversity, habitat maps and information for small-scale fisheries, and knowledge about the deep-sea. Emmanuella Doussis, "Marine Scientific Research: Taking Stock and Looking Ahead," in *The Future of the Law of the Sea: Bridging Gaps Between National, Individual and Common Interests*, ed. Gemma Andreone (Rome: Springer, 2017), 88. [87–103]
34 "How Many Species Live in the Ocean?" *NOAA*, accessed March 15, 2024, https://oceanservice.noaa.gov/facts/ocean-species.html.
35 United Nations, *Marine Scientific Research, A Revised Guide to the Implementation of the Relevant Provisions of the United Nations Convention on the Law of the Sea*, Division for Ocean Affairs and the Law of the Sea (New York: United Nations, 2010), 1.
36 Hubert, "The New Paradox," 330.
37 1958 Geneva Convention on the Continental Shelf, Article 5.
38 UN, *Marine Scientific Research*, 3.
39 For an excellent summary of the history, see DOALOS, *Marine Scientific Research: A Revised Guide to the Implementation of the Relevant Provisions of the United Nations Convention on the Law of the Sea* (New York: United Nations, 2010), accessed February 13, 2024, www.un.org/depts/los/doalos_publications/publicationstexts/msr_guide%202010_final.pdf.
40 These have been expanded upon the DOALOS marine scientific research guidelines: ibid.
41 UNCLOS Part XIII, Articles 238–40.
42 Joe Borg, "The Role of Marine Research in a Maritime Policy for the Union," Statement at the Conference *25 Years Alfred-Wegener Institute for Polar and Sea Research*, Speech 05/450, cited in Tim Daniel, "Marine Scientific Research under UNCLOS: A Vital Global Resource?" *International Hydrographic Review* 7, no. 2 (August 2006): 14.
43 The Tribunal granted an injunction and, while it was later lifted, led to Japan's abandonment of the program. See Daniel, "Marine Scientific Research under UNCLOS," 14.
44 Abraham Joseph, "Marine Scientific Research in UNCLOS: A Critical Overview," *AALCO Journal of International Law* 9 (2020): 1–2; and Hilde Woker, Bernhard Schartmuller, Knut Ola Dolven, and Katalin Blix, "The Law of the Sea and Current Practices of Marine Scientific Research in the Arctic," *Marine Policy* 115 (May 2020), https://doi.org/10.1016/j.marpol.2020.103850.
45 In 1991 and a revised guide in 2010: DOALOS, *Marine Scientific Research: A Revised Guide*, para. 14.
46 Luciana Fernandes Coelho, "Marine Scientific Research and Small Island Developing States in the Twenty-First Century: Appraising the United Nations Convention on the Law of the Sea," *The International Journal of Marine and Coastal Law* 37 (2022): 493–528.

47 "IOC Circular Letter No 2938," *UNESCO IOC* (March 15, 2023), https://unesdoc.unesco.org/ark:/48223/pf0000384772.
48 "The Global Ocean Observing System," accessed May 7, 2024, www.goosocean.org.
49 GOOS coordinates observations through 13 ocean observing networks, 15 regional alliances and 76 national focal points. Data is shared via the GOOS BioEco Portal, the Ocean Biodiversity Information System (OBIS), and the Deep Ocean Observing Strategy (DOOS). See "With the 'High Seas Treaty' on Biodiversity Signed, What Do We Need to Do Next?" *UNESCO News* (October 26 2023), www.unesco.org/en/articles/high-seas-treaty-biodiversity-signed-what-do-we-need-do-next.
50 "Technology transfer" is a term used to describe how skills, knowledge and intellectual property rights are moved between people or organisations. It has evolved as a key legal concept in recognition of the fact that innovation and the commercialisation of new technologies underpin economic development and prosperity.
51 Jessica Lehman, "The Technopolitics of Ocean Sensing," in *Blue Legalities: The Life and Laws of the Sea*, ed. Irus Braverman and Elizabeth R. Johnson (Durham: Duke University Press, 2020), 166.
52 Kirsten Isensee, ed., *Global Ocean Science Report 2020: Charting Capacity for Ocean Sustainability* (Paris: UNESCO Intergovernmental Oceanographic Commission, 2020), 25.
53 Chuxiao Yu, "Implications of the UNCLOS Marine Scientific Research Regime for the Current Negotiations on Access and Benefit Sharing of Marine Genetic Resources in Areas Beyond National Jurisdiction," *Ocean Development & International Law* 51, no. 1 (2020), https://doi.org/10.1080/00908320.2019.1677018/.
54 *Report of the Forty-Second Meeting of the Commission*, CCAMLR-42 (Hobart, October 31, 2023): 19–21, https://meetings.ccamlr.org/system/files/meeting-reports/CCAMLR-42%20preliminary%20report.pdf; and Lynda Goldsworthy, "Consensus Decision-Making in CCAMLR: Achilles' Heel or Fundamental to Its Success?" *International Environmental Agreements: Politics, Law and Economics* 22 (2022): 411–37, https://doi.org/10.1007/s10784-021-09561-4.
55 Hubert, "The New Paradox," 331.
56 Preamble to UNCLOS.
57 UNCLOS Articles 61 and 119.
58 *Agreement for the Implementation of the Provisions of the UN Convention on the Law of the Sea of 10 December 1982 Relating to the Conservation and Management of Straddling Fish Stocks and Highly Migratory Fish Stocks*, Articles 5, 6, 10 and 15.
59 United Nations, *The Law of the Sea: Marine Scientific Research – A Revised Guide to the Implementation of the Relevant Provisions of the United Nations Convention on the Law Of The Sea* (New York: UN Division for Ocean Affairs and the Law of the Sea, 2010), 4. Some participants argued that "pure" research did not aim directly at industrial exploitation but was designed to obtain knowledge of the ocean's natural processes and phenomena necessary for navigation and other uses of the ocean and airspace above it.
60 The 1992 Convention on Biological Diversity (CBD). The CBD refers to research for "conservation and sustainable use of biological diversity" (Article 12).
61 Subsidiary Body on Scientific, Technical and Technological Advice, *Study of the Relationship between the Convention on Biological Diversity and the United Nations Convention on the Law of the Sea with regard to the Conservation and Sustainable Use of Genetic Resources on the Deep Seabed*, UNEP/CBD/SBSTTA/8/INF/3/Rev.1 (February 22, 2003), para. 101. 'Biotechnology' refers to the use of biological knowledge to solve problems and make useful products, particularly for therapeutic purposes.

62 Philomène A. Verlaan, "Experimental Activities That Intentionally Perturb the Marine Environment: Implications for the Marine Environmental Protection and Marine Scientific Research Provisions of the 1982 United Nations Convention on the Law of the Sea," *Marine Policy* 31, no. 2 (March 2007): 210–6.
63 Helen Scales cited in Bryony Cottam, "An Ocean of Opportunity," *Geographical* (September 21, 2023), https://geographical.co.uk/wildlife/helen-scales-on-the-blue-economy/.
64 Despite several international ventures to extract manganese, nickel, copper and cobalt ores from the seabed in the 1970s, the commercial value of polymetallic nodules was not realised at that time although recent demand for these metals has revived commercial interest. See for example James R. Hein, Kira Mizell, Andrea Koschinsky, and Tracey A. Conrad, "Deep-Ocean Mineral Deposits as a Source of Critical Metals for High- and Green-Technology Applications: Comparison with Land-based Resources," *Ore Geology Reviews* 51 (June 2013): 1–14.
65 "Joint Group of Experts on the Scientific Aspects of Marine Environmental Protection," *GESAMP*, accessed January 9, 2024, www.gesamp.org/. GESAMP currently involves 17 experts from a range of disciplines coordinating studies and assessments undertaken by working groups.
66 GESAMP's UN organisation sponsors include UNEP, IMO, FAO and the ISA. The IMO itself has its Marine Environment Protection Committee: "Structure of IMO," *IMO*, accessed February 26, 2024, www.imo.org/en/about/pages/structure.aspx.
67 "Clearing-House Mechanism," *Convention on Biological Diversity*, accessed January 9, 2024, www.cbd.int/chm/.
68 See for example CITES Animals and Plants Committee and CMS Scientific Council. IUCN provides advice to other bodies such as the World Heritage Convention
69 The FAO has its Committee on Fisheries with a mandate to conduct periodical reviews of fishery and aquaculture problems: "COFI – Committee on Fisheries," *COFI*, accessed February 26, 2024, www.fao.org/policy-support/mechanisms/mechanisms-details
70 Emma McKinley, Rachel Kelly, Mary Mackay et al., "Development and Expansion in the Marine Sciences: Insights from the Global Community," *iScience* 25, no. 8 (August 19, 2022), https://doi.org/10.1016/j.isci.2022.104735.
71 Marrie, *Emerging Trends in the Generation, Transmission and Protection of Traditional Knowledge.*
72 GOOS is led by UNESCO-IOC and since 1991 has provided essential information to support marine health, including providing observing tools and technologies, information systems, scientific analysis and forecasts for the global community: GOOS, www.goosocean.org/
73 Indigenous Delegates at OceanObs'19, "Aha Honua Coastal Indigenous Peoples' Declaration at OceanObs'19," (2019), accessed May 7, 2024, www.oceanobs19.net/wp-content/uploads/2019/09/Indigenous-Ocean-Obs19-Declaration_8.5x15_Final.pdf.
74 Mary Jane Proulx, Lydia Ross, Christina Macdonald, Shayla Fitzsimmons, and Michael Smit, "Indigenous Traditional Knowledge and Ocean Observing: A Review of Successful Partnerships," *Frontiers in Marine Science* 8 (2021), https://doi.org/10.3389/fmars.2021.703938. Narissa Bax et al., "Ocean Resource Use: Building the Coastal Blue Economy," *Reviews in Fish Biology and Fisheries* 32, no. 1 (2022): 189–207.
75 UNESCO, "A New Wave of Transformative Decade Actions Boosts the Ocean Decade Global Movement on the Road to 2030" (June 8, 2023), https://oceandecade.org/news/a-new-wave-of-transformative-decade-actions-boosts-the-ocean-decade-global-movement-on-the-road-to-2030/.

76 A not-for-profit organisation called Global Fishing Watch has used publicly available satellite tracking data and State-sponsored vessel monitoring systems to develop the 'first open-access online platform for the visualization and analysis of vessel-based human activity at sea'. See Global Fishing Watch, https://globalfishingwatch.org-/?gclid=Cj0KCQiAv8SsBhC7ARIsALIkVT07xLzZagN5VKXHFJy6R9QIh5RBs61UK9QWA3Ivak2TnKXnMQWaHg8aAoPwEALw_wcB. Woker et al., "New Technology and the Protection of the Marine Environment."

77 UNCLOS provides the legal basis for coastal States to manage living marine resources within their EEZs. See Erik Jaap Molennaar and Martin Tsamenyi, "Satellite-based Vessel Monitoring Systems: International Legal Aspects and Developments in State Practice," *Food and Agriculture Organization Legal Papers Online* 7 (April 2000), www.fao.org/3/bb040e/bb040e.pdf.

78 "Autonomous Shipping," *IMO*, accessed February 13, 2024, www.imo.org/en/MediaCentre/HotTopics/Pages/Autonomous-shipping.aspx.

79 See, for example, "Autonomous Surface Vehicles," *National Oceanography Centre*, accessed February 13, 2024, https://noc.ac.uk/facilities/marine-autonomous-robotic-systems/asv.

80 Peter I. Macreadie et al., "Eyes in the Sea: Unlocking the Mysteries of the Ocean Using Industrial, Remotely Operated Vehicles (ROVs)," *Science of The Total Environment* 634 (2018): 1077–91.

81 Terri Moon Cronk, "Chinese Seize U.S. Navy Underwater Drone in South China Sea," *US Department of Defense* (December 16, 2016), www.defense.gov/News/News-Stories/Article/Article/1032823/chinese-seize-us-navy-underwater-drone-in-south-china-sea/.

82 UNESCO IOC, First Meeting of the Advisory Body of Experts on the Law of the Sea: Transfer of Marine Technology (Paris, June 11–13, 2001), IOC/ABE-LOSI/8, https://unesdoc.unesco.org/ark:/48223/pf0000122697; and UNESCO IOC, *Ocean Science Report 2020: Charting Capacity for Ocean Sustainability* (Paris: UNESCO, 2020), https://unesdoc.unesco.org/ark:/48223/pf0000375147.

83 Harriet Harden-Davies, "Marine Technology Transfer: Towards a Capacity-Building Toolkit for Marine Biodiversity beyond National Jurisdiction," in *Marine Biodiversity of Areas Beyond National Jurisdiction*, ed. Myron H. Nordquist and Ronan Long, *Centre for Oceans Law and Policy* 24 (2021): 231–38; and European Commission, "Ocean Biodiversity: Global Agreement on Protection and Sustainable Use of Resources and Biodiversity in High Seas," *EU Press Release* (March 4, 2023), https://ec.europa.eu/commission/presscorner/detail/en/ip_23_1382.

84 "Principles Relating to Remote Sensing of the Earth from Outer Space," *UNGA Resolution 41/65*, www.unoosa.org/oosa/en/ourwork/spacelaw/principles/remote-sensing-principles.html.

85 Woker et al., "New Technology and the Protection of the Marine Environment."

86 Ocean Census, accessed May 7, 2024, https://oceancensus.org/. United Nations SDGs, *World Register of Marine Species (WoRMS)*, accessed May 7, 2024, https://sdgs.un.org/partnerships/world-register-marine-species-worms#:~:text=The%20aim%20of%20a%20World,organisms%2C%20including%20information%20on%20synonymy.

87 Saurabh Bahatia, "History, Scope and Development of Biotechnology," *Introduction to Pharmaceutical Biotechnology* 1 (May 2018): 1–61.

88 For examples of challenges in managing ocean data, see Amy Trice, Chris Robbins, Nidhisha Philip, and Matt Rumsey, *Challenges and Opportunities for Ocean Data to Advance Conservation and Management* (Washington, DC: Ocean Conservancy, 2021), 3.

89 Daniel, "Marine Scientific Research under UNCLOS," 16.
90 Woker et al., "New Technology and the Protection of the Marine Environment."
91 Hilde Woker, "Interactions between Law and Science Within the Law of the Sea: A Systems Theory Perspective," in *The Law of the Sea: Normative Context and Interactions with Other Legal Regimes*, ed. Nele Matz-Lück, Øystein Jensen, and Elise Johansen (Abingdon: Routledge, 2022), 16–18.
92 Woker et al., "The Law of the Sea and Current Practices of Marine Scientific Research in the Arctic," 8.
93 "Global Marine Biotechnology Market Forecasted to Grow by 2027," *ISAAA Inc* (August 30, 2023), www.isaaa.org/kc/cropbiotechupdate/article/default.asp?ID=20387.
94 Doussis, "Marine Scientific Research," 98–99.
95 Patricio Bernal and Alan Simcock, "Marine Scientific Research," in *The First Global Integrated Marine Assessment: World Ocean Assessment 1*, ed. L. Inniss and A. Simcock (New York: United Nations, 2016), 1–18.

Bibliography

Agreement under the United Nations Convention on the Law of the Sea on the Conservation and Sustainable Use of Marine Biological Diversity of Areas Beyond National Jurisdiction (2023). Accessed March 15, 2024. https://treaties.un.org/doc/Treaties/2023/06/20230620%2004-28%20PM/Ch_XXI_10.pdf.

Alexander, Steven M., Jennifer F. Provencher, Dominique A. Henri et al. "Bridging Indigenous and Science-Based Knowledge in Coastal and Marine Research, Monitoring, and Management in Canada." *Environmental Evidence* 8, no. 36 (2019). https://doi.org/10.1186/s13750-019-0181-3.

Amiott, J. "Investigating the Convention on Biological Diversity's Protections for Traditional Knowledge." *Journal of Environmental and Sustainability Law* 11, no. 1 (2003): 2–37.

Bahatia, Saurabh. "History, Scope and Development of Biotechnology." *Introduction to Pharmaceutical Biotechnology* 1 (May 2018): 1–61.

Bax, Narissa et al. "Ocean Resource Use: Building the Coastal Blue Economy." *Reviews in Fish Biology and Fisheries* 32, no. 1 (2022): 189–207.

Berkes, Fikret, Johan Colding, and Carl Folke. "Rediscovery of Traditional Ecological Knowledge as Adaptive Management." *Ecological Applications* 10, no. 5 (2000): 1251–62.

Bernal, Patricio, and Alan Simcock. "Marine Scientific Research." In *The First Global Integrated Marine Assessment: World Ocean Assessment 1*, edited by L. Inniss and A. Simcock. New York: United Nations, 2016.

Buck, M., and C. Hamilton. "The Nagoya Protocol on Access to Genetic Resources and the Fair and Equitable Sharing of Benefits Arising from Their Utilization to the Convention on Biological Diversity." *Review of European Community and International Environmental Law* 20, no. 1 (2011): 47–61.

CBD. "What the Convention Says about Traditional Knowledge, Innovations and Practices." Accessed March 15, 2024. www.cbd.int/traditional/what.shtml.

COFI. "COFI – Committee on Fisheries." Accessed February 26, 2024. www.fao.org/policy-support/mechanisms/mechanisms-details.

Convention on Biological Diversity. "Clearing-House Mechanism." Accessed January 9, 2024. www.cbd.int/chm/.

Cook, Peter J., and Chris Carleton. "Introduction." In *Continental Shelf Limits: The Scientific and Legal Interface*, edited by Peter J. Cook and Chris Carleton. Oxford: Oxford University Press, 2000.

Cottam, Bryony. "An Ocean of Opportunity." *Geographical* (September 21, 2023). https://geographical.co.uk/wildlife/helen-scales-on-the-blue-economy/.

Cronk, Terri Moon. "Chinese Seize U.S. Navy Underwater Drone in South China Sea." *US Department of Defense* (December 16, 2016). www.defense.gov/News/News-Stories/Article/Article/1032823/chinese-seize-us-navy-underwater-drone-in-south-china-sea/.

Daniel, Tim. "Marine Scientific Research Under UNCLOS: A Vital Global Resource?" *International Hydrographic Review* 7, no. 2 (August 2006): 14.

DOALOS. *Marine Scientific Research: A Revised Guide to the Implementation of the Relevant Provisions of the United Nations Convention on the Law of the Sea*. New York: United Nations, 2010. Accessed February 13, 2024. www.un.org/depts/los/doalos_publications/publicationstexts/msr_guide%202010_final.pdf.

Doussis, Emmanuella. "Marine Scientific Research: Taking Stock and Looking Ahead." In *The Future of the Law of the Sea: Bridging Gaps Between National, Individual and Common Interests*, edited by Gemma Andreone. Rome: Springer, 2017.

European Commission. "Ocean Biodiversity: Global Agreement on Protection and Sustainable Use of Resources and Biodiversity in High Seas." *EU Press Release* (March 4, 2023). https://ec.europa.eu/commission/presscorner/detail/en/ip_23_1382.

Evensen, Jens. "The Effect of the Law of the Sea Conference Upon the Process of the Formation of International Law: Rapprochement Between Competing Points of View." In *The Developing Order of the Oceans*, Proceedings of the 18th Annual Conference of the Law of the Sea Institute, edited by Robert B. Krueger and Stefan A. Riesenfel. Honolulu: Law of the Sea Institute, University of Hawaii, 1984.

Fernandes Coelho, Luciana. "Marine Scientific Research and Small Island Developing States in the Twenty-First Century: Appraising the United Nations Convention on the Law of the Sea." *The International Journal of Marine and Coastal Law* 37 (2022): 493–528.

Gee, Kira. "The Ocean Perspective." In *Maritime Spatial Planning*, edited by J. Zaucha and K. Gee. Cham: Springer International Publishing, 2019.

George, Alex. "William Dampier as a Natural Historian." *The Great Circle* 37, no. 1 (2015): 36–52.

GESAMP. "Joint Group of Experts on the Scientific Aspects of Marine Environmental Protection." Accessed January 9, 2024. www.gesamp.org/.

"Global Fishing Watch." Accessed March 15, 2024. https://globalfishingwatch.org/.

"Global Marine Biotechnology Market Forecasted to Grow by 2027." *ISAAA Inc* (August 30, 2023). www.isaaa.org/kc/cropbiotechupdate/article/default.asp?ID=20387.

Goldsworthy, Lynda. "Consensus Decision-Making in CCAMLR: Achilles' Heel or Fundamental to Its Success?" *International Environmental Agreements: Politics, Law and Economics* 22 (2022): 411–37.

Gupta, Anil K. *WIPO-UNEP Study on the Role of Intellectual Property Rights in the Sharing of Benefits Arising from the Use of Biological Resources and Associated Traditional Knowledge*. Ahmedabad: World Intellectual Property Organization and the United Nations Environment Programme, 2004.

Harden-Davies, Harriet. "Marine Technology Transfer: Towards A Capacity-Building Toolkit for Marine Biodiversity beyond National Jurisdiction." In *Marine Biodiversity of Areas Beyond National Jurisdiction*, edited by Myron H. Nordquist and Ronan Long, *Centre for Oceans Law and Policy* 24 (2021): 231–38.

Hein, James R., Kira Mizell, Andrea Koschinsky, and Tracey A. Conrad. "Deep-Ocean Mineral Deposits as a Source of Critical Metals for High- and Green-Technology Applications: Comparison with Land-based Resources." *Ore Geology Reviews* 51 (June 2013): 1–14.

House of Lords. *UNCLOS: The Law of the Sea in the 21st Century*. London: HL Paper 159, 2022. Accessed March 15, 2024. https://committees.parliament.uk/publications/9005/documents/159002/default/.

Hubert, Anna-Maria. "The New Paradox in Marine Scientific Research: Regulating the Potential Environmental Impacts of Conducting Ocean Science." *Ocean Development & International Law* 42 (2011): 329–30.

ILO Convention No. 169 Concerning Indigenous and Tribal Peoples in Independent Countries. Accessed March 15, 2024. www.ilo.org/dyn/normlex/en/f?p=NORMLEXPUB:12100:0::NO:12100:P12100_INSTRUMENT_ID:312314:NO.

IMO. "Autonomous Shipping." Accessed February 13, 2024. www.imo.org/en/MediaCentre/HotTopics/Pages/Autonomous-shipping.aspx.

IMO. "Structure of IMO." Accessed February 26, 2024. www.imo.org/en/about/pages/structure.aspx.

Indigenous Delegates at OceanObs'19. "Aha Honua Coastal Indigenous Peoples' Declaration at OceanObs'19." Accessed March 15, 2024. www.oceanobs19.net/wp-content/uploads/2019/09/Indigenous-Ocean-Obs19-Declaration_8.5x15_Final.pdf.

Isensee, Kirsten, ed. *Global Ocean Science Report 2020: Charting Capacity for Ocean Sustainability*. Paris: UNESCO Intergovernmental Oceanographic Commission, 2020.

Johannes, R. E. "The Renaissance of Community-Based Marine Resource Management in Oceania." *Annual Review of Ecology and Systematics* 33 (2002): 317–40.

Joseph, Abraham. "Marine Scientific Research in UNCLOS: A Critical Overview." *AALCO Journal of International Law* 9 (2020): 1–2.

Kennedy Jr., President John F. "Letter to the President of the Senate on Increasing the National Effort in Oceanography." *The American Presidency Project* (March 29 1961). www.presidency.ucsb.edu/documents/letter-the-president-the-senate-increasing-the-national-effort-oceanography.

Lehman, Jessica. "The Technopolitics of Ocean Sensing." In *Blue Legalities: The Life and Laws of the Sea*, edited by Irus Braverman and Elizabeth R. Johnson. Durham: Duke University Press, 2020.

Lindberg, David C. *The Beginnings of Western Science*. 2nd ed. Chicago: University of Chicago Press, 2007.

Macreadie, Peter I. et al. "Eyes in the Sea: Unlocking the Mysteries of the Ocean Using Industrial, Remotely Operated Vehicles (ROVs)." *Science of The Total Environment* 634 (2018): 1077–91.

Marrie, H. L. "Emerging Trends in the Generation, Transmission and Protection of Traditional Knowledge." In *Presentation to the 18th Session of the UN Permanent Forum on Indigenous Issues*. New York: United Nations, 2019. www.un.org/development/desa/indigenouspeoples/wp-content/uploads/sites/19/2019/04/TK-Emerging-trends-in-the-generation-transmission-and-protection-of-TK-final-paper.pdf.

Mazzocchi, Fulvio. "Western Science and Traditional Knowledge: Despite Their Variations, Different Forms of Knowledge Can Learn from Each Other." *EMBO Reports* 7, no. 5 (May 2006): 463–66.

McKinley, Emma, Rachel Kelly, Mary Mackay et al. "Development and Expansion in the Marine Sciences: Insights from the Global Community." *iScience* 25, no. 8 (19 August 2022). https://doi.org/10.1016/j.isci.2022.104735.

Molennaar, Erik Jaap, and Martin Tsamenyi. "Satellite-based Vessel Monitoring Systems: International Legal Aspects and Developments in State Practice." *Food and Agriculture Organization Legal Papers Online* 7 (April 2000). www.fao.org/3/bb040e/bb040e.pdf.

Nagoya Protocol on Access to Genetic Resources and the Fair and Equitable Sharing of Benefits Arising from Their Utilization (ABS) to the Convention on Biological Diversity (2010). Accessed March 15, 2024. www.cbd.int/abs/.

National Oceanography Centre. "Autonomous Surface Vehicles." Accessed February 13, 2024, https://noc.ac.uk/facilities/marine-autonomous-robotic-systems/asv.

NOAA. "How Many Species Live in the Ocean?" Accessed March 15, 2024. https://oceanservice.noaa.gov/facts/ocean-species.html.

"Oceans Census." Accessed May 7, 2024. https://oceancensus.org/.

Paik, Jin-Hyun. "Disputes Involving Scientific and Technical Matters and the International Tribunal for the Law of the Sea." In *New Knowledge and Changing Circumstances in the Law of the Sea*, edited by Tomas Heidar. Leiden: Brill Nijhoff, 2020.

Parsons, Meg, and Lara Taylor. "Why Indigenous Knowledge Should Be an Essential Part of How We Govern the World's Oceans." *The Conversation* (June 8, 2021). https://theconversation.com/why-indigenous-knowledge-should-be-an-essential-part-of-how-we-govern-the-worlds-oceans-161649.

Pietsch, Theodore W., ed. *Cuvier's History of the Natural Sciences*. Paris: Publications Scientifiques due Muséum, 2015. https://books.openedition.org/mnhn/2761.

Pinto, Bruno. "Historical Connections Between Early Marine Science Research and Dissemination: The Case Study of Aquarium Vasco Da Gama (Portugal) from Late 19th Century to Mid-20th Century." *ICES Journal of Marine Science* 74(6) (2017): 1522–30. https://doi.org/10.1093/icesjms/fsx029.

"Principles Relating to Remote Sensing of the Earth from Outer Space." *UNGA Resolution* 41/65. www.unoosa.org/oosa/en/ourwork/spacelaw/principles/remote-sensing-principles.html.

Proulx, Mary Jane, Lydia Ross, Christina Macdonald, Shayla Fitzsimmons, and Michael Smit. "Indigenous Traditional Knowledge and Ocean Observing: A Review of Successful Partnerships." *Frontiers in Marine Science* 8 (2021). https://doi.org/10.3389/fmars.2021.703938.

Reid, Susan. "Ocean Justice: Reckoning with Material Vulnerability." *Cultural Politics* 19, no. 1 (March 2023): 108, 110.

Reid, Susan. "Solwara 1 and the Sessile Ones." In *Blue Legalities: The Life and Laws of the Sea*, edited by Irus Braverman, and Elizabeth R. Johnson. Durham: Duke University Press, 2020.

Rejón, Manuel Ruiz. "Félix De Azara and Pehr Löfling, the First Naturalists in a Great Frontier." *Bioscience* (December 29, 2021). www.bbvaopenmind.com/en/science/bioscience/felix-de-azara-pehr-loefling-naturalist/.

Report of the Forty-Second Meeting of the Commission, CCAMLR-42 (Hobart, October 31, 2023). Accessed May 7, 2024. https://meetings.ccamlr.org/system/files/meeting-reports/CCAMLR-42%20preliminary%20report.pdf.

Report of the Scientific Results of the Exploring Voyage of H.M.S. Challenger during the Years 1873–76. Edinburgh: Neill, 1880–1895.

Rozwadowski, Helen M. "Introduction." In Michael S. Reidy and Helen M. Rozwadowski. "The Spaces in Between: Science, Ocean, Empire." *Isis* 105, no. 2 (June 2014): 336.

Subsidiary Body on Scientific, Technical and Technological Advice. *Study of the Relationship between the Convention on Biological Diversity and the United Nations Convention on the Law of the Sea with Regard to the Conservation and Sustainable Use of Genetic Resources on the Deep Seabed*. UNEP/CBD/SBSTTA/8/INF/3/Rev.1 (February 22, 2003).

"The Global Ocean Observing System." Accessed May 7, 2024. https://goosocean.org/.

Trice, Amy, Chris Robbins, Nidhisha Philip, and Matt Rumsey. *Challenges and Opportunities for Ocean Data to Advance Conservation and Management*. Washington, DC: Ocean Conservancy, 2021.

UNESCO. "A New Wave of Transformative Decade Actions Boosts the Ocean Decade Global Movement on the Road to 2030." (June 8, 2023). https://oceandecade.org/news/a-new-wave-of-transformative-decade-actions-boosts-the-ocean-decade-global-movement-on-the-road-to-2030/.

UNESCO. "United Nations Decade of Ocean Science for Sustainable Development (2021–2030)." Accessed March 15, 2024. www.unesco.org/en/decades/ocean-decade#:~:text=The%20United%20Nations%20has%20proclaimed,support%20countries%20in%20creating%20improved.

UNESCO IOC. *First Meeting of the Advisory Body of Experts on the Law of the Sea: Transfer of Marine Technology*. Paris, Jun 11–13, 2001, IOC/ABE-LOSI/8. https://unesdoc.unesco.org/ark:/48223/pf0000122697.

UNESCO IOC. "IOC Circular Letter No 2938." (March 15, 2023). https://unesdoc.unesco.org/ark:/48223/pf0000384772.

UNESCO IOC. *Ocean Science Report 2020: Charting Capacity for Ocean Sustainability*. Paris: UNESCO, 2020. https://unesdoc.unesco.org/ark:/48223/pf0000375147.

United Nations. "International Decades." Accessed May 7, 2024. www.un.org/en/observances/international-decades.

United Nations. *Marine Scientific Research, a Revised Guide to the Implementation of the Relevant Provisions of the United Nations Convention on the Law of the Sea*, Division for Ocean Affairs and the Law of the Sea. New York: United Nations, 2010.

United Nations. *The Law of the Sea: Marine Scientific Research – A Revised Guide to the Implementation of the Relevant Provisions of the United Nations Convention on the Law of the Sea*. New York: UN Division for Ocean Affairs and the Law of the Sea, 2010.

United Nations SDGs. "World Register of Marine Species (WoRMS)." Accessed May 7, 2024. https://sdgs.un.org/partnerships/world-register-marine-species-worms#:~:text=The%20aim%20of%20a%20World,organisms%2C%20including%20information%20on%20synonymy.

Verlaan, Philomène A. "Experimental Activities That Intentionally Perturb the Marine Environment: Implications for the Marine Environmental Protection and Marine Scientific Research Provisions of the 1982 United Nations Convention on the Law of the Sea." *Marine Policy* 31, no. 2 (March 2007): 210–16.

"With the 'High Seas Treaty' on Biodiversity Signed, What Do We Need to Do Next?" *UNESCO News* (October 26, 2023). www.unesco.org/en/articles/high-seas-treaty-biodiversity-signed-what-do-we-need-do-next.

Woker, Hilde. "Interactions between Law and Science Within the Law of the Sea: A Systems Theory Perspective." In *The Law of the Sea: Normative Context and Interactions with Other Legal Regimes*, edited by Nele Matz-Lück, Øystein Jensen, and Elise Johansen. Abingdon: Routledge, 2022.

Woker, Hilde, Bernhard Schartmuller, Knut Ola Dolven, and Katalin Blix. "The Law of the Sea and Current Practices of Marine Scientific Research in the Arctic." *Marine Policy* 115 (May 2020). https://doi.org/10.1016/j.marpol.2020.103850.

Woker, Hilde J., Rozemarijn J. Roland Holst, and Harriet Harden-Davies. "New Technology and the Protection of the Marine Environment." In *Research Handbook on International Marine Environmental Law*, 2nd ed., edited by R. Rayfuse, A. Jaeckel, and N. Klein. Cheltenham, Glos: Edward Elgar, 2023.

World Intellectual Property Organization. *Intellectual Property and Genetic Resources, Traditional Knowledge and Traditional Cultural Expressions*. Geneva: World Intellectual Property Organization, 2020.

Yu, Chuxiao. "Implications of the UNCLOS Marine Scientific Research Regime for the Current Negotiations on Access and Benefit Sharing of Marine Genetic Resources in Areas Beyond National Jurisdiction." *Ocean Development & International Law* 51, no. 1 (2020). https://doi.org/10.1080/00908320.2019.1677018/.

Part V

The ocean as future

12 Anthropocene ocean

Turning the tide of ocean governance

The ocean is the blue heart of the planet — we should take care of our heart. It's what makes life possible for us.

Dr Sylvia Earle, Mission Blue

Overview

Humans have always depended on the planet's oceanic realm and developed rules and customs to control how it is used. In establishing an international law of the sea, European empires sought to colonise the oceans, control maritime trade routes and maintain productivity by claiming sovereignty over coastal seas and shorelines. In the process, they embedded the principles of freedom of and sovereignty over the seas into an international legal regime ripe for control and exploitation.[1] The development of a modern legal regime for oceans, seas and shorelines has been built on these early laws. It codified customary international law by establishing defined maritime zones and formalised the rights and duties of States in using and conserving the ocean environment and its resources (see Chapter 2). It regulated shipping and trade on the world's oceans and seas, including navigation, salvage, collisions, and the safety of seafarers and cargo (see Chapters 1, 5). Violence and conflict at sea also have ancient origins, with unwritten maritime rules, codes and customs evolving over centuries into maritime piracy law and the laws of war (see Chapter 3). Global fisheries regulations were developed to control and manage extraction of living marine resources (see Chapter 4). International marine environmental law emerged relatively recently in response to the growing public awareness of threats to the marine environment from pollution, mining and land-based activities (see Chapters 6, 7, 8, 9, 11), and a related but separate legal field developed to conserve tangible and intangible heritage sites, objects and stories associated with the marine environment (see Chapter 10).

During the 20th century, western scientific knowledge and technologies came to dominate the development of the law of the sea, with lawmakers relying on

DOI: 10.4324/9781003005261-18

geographic measurement and delimitation data, marine biological, ecological and technological knowledge, and oceanographic information (see Chapter 11).[2] The result is a complex legal landscape designed for legal convenience, based on a piecemeal regulatory framework that has divided the seas vertically (the shoreline, seabed and water column), horizontally (by geographical area) and spatially (by depth). As lucrative commercial opportunities for deep seabed minerals and marine genetic resources beckon, the international legal regime designed to protect and conserve oceans has prioritised the conservation of selected areas and ecosystems while permitting extractive activities in others, and protected certain valued or charismatic marine species while licensing the harvesting of others. In all cases, the needs of the ocean and its inhabitants have been rendered subordinate to human needs.

At the same time the Anthropocene – a term used to signify the impact of human activity on the planet – has manifested as a climate crisis involving, amongst other things, ocean warming and acidification, marine pollution and loss of marine biodiversity, creating tipping points from which there can be no return.[3] While legal regimes may have had some success in regulating human activities in ocean environments – most notably in laws promoting maritime safety and security – they have proven to be largely ineffectual in preventing the environmental catastrophes unfolding in the world's oceans. 'The Anthropocene', as Louis J Kotzé and others have recently argued, 'requires of us to rethink global governance challenges and effective responses with a holistic understanding of the earth system as a single intertwined social-ecological system'.[4] In this chapter, we assess key strengths and weaknesses in the current legal regimes for oceans, seas and shorelines, and consider the opportunities that emerge by transitioning to a more holistic approach to ocean law and governance.

An extractive imaginary

On the surface of it, international ocean laws may be considered 'fit for purpose' since they aim to address many of the more damaging impacts of human activities. The *International Convention for the Prevention of Pollution from Ships* (MARPOL),[5] for example, aims 'to achieve the complete elimination of intentional pollution of the marine environment by oil and other harmful substances and the minimization of accidental discharge of such substances',[6] while the *Convention on Biological Diversity* includes 'the conservation of biological diversity, the sustainable use of its components and the fair and equitable sharing of the benefits arising out of the utilization of genetic resources'.[7] However, many of the treaties explored in this book are a product of their time. The *International Convention for the Regulation of Whaling*, for example, aimed 'to provide for the proper conservation of whale stocks and thus make possible the orderly development of the whaling industry',[8] while the *UN Convention on the Law of the Sea* (UNCLOS) focused on

> a legal order for the seas and oceans which . . . will promote the peaceful uses of the seas and oceans, the equitable and efficient utilization of their resources, the conservation of their living resources, and the study, protection and preservation of the marine environment.[9]

In doing so, UNCLOS effectively locked in an 'extractive imaginary'[10] and, as a result, extractive industries such as industrial-scale fishing and exploratory seabed mining activities are now pursued in the face of demonstrable unsustainability. Indeed, laws created under UNCLOS such as those regulating marine scientific research and total allowable catches remain unchanged, even as the member States of the UN agree that they are difficult to implement.

The political imperative

The most significant challenge for international lawmakers is to ensure that laws and treaties are implemented effectively.[11] Under the *Vienna Convention on the Law of Treaties*, for example, the first step in implementing international laws is gaining States' written agreement to a treaty via signature and ratification. International treaties may set international standards and obligations, but these are invariably actioned through domestic law and policy, which requires the political support of a State. Global standards only work effectively if all nations are bound by them, and the political will to adopt a treaty will depend upon the national benefits outweighing the costs of doing so – something which is not always obvious from the treaty wording. Various efforts have been made to encourage States to become parties to key global treaties. An example of efforts to address this challenge is the Marine Environment Protection of the South-East Asian Seas (MEPSEAS) initiative, which focuses on encouraging States in the region to join the International Maritime Organisation (IMO) marine environment protection conventions.[12]

Providing model legislation can encourage States to ratify a convention by providing guidance and examples on what to include in domestic statutes. For example, model frameworks have encouraged States in the Pacific region to implement the Ballast Water Convention.[13] There are, however, three critical elements necessary for effective implementation at the domestic level: political support, resourcing (financial and technical as well as legal), and public support from State institutions, individuals, community groups and private industry. These matters are not isolated, although they may all be driven by political imperatives. If there is public support for new law, for example, then governments are likely to find the political will for implementation, including budgets to resource practical measures such as raising public awareness of environmental problems and solutions. In turn, the domestic legislation must be developed with the public's participation and legal measures should encourage compliance. In many cases, full-scale enforcement is likely to be prohibitively expensive so, if a law is to work effectively, governments and citizens must be willing to comply with it.

The development of international laws and treaties is often a lengthy process, with negotiators having to navigate complex geo-political, economic and cultural issues. In 2004, for example, the UN established a group to explore the conservation of marine biodiversity beyond national jurisdiction, but it would take 20 years and five negotiating rounds for member States to agree to adopt the *Implementing agreement under the United Nations Convention on the Law of the Sea on the conservation and sustainable use of marine biological diversity of areas beyond national jurisdiction* (High Seas Treaty). This treaty was designed as a mechanism for creating marine protected areas, regulating the harvest of marine genetic resources (of which scientists still know relatively little), ensuring that environmental impact assessments inform decisions, and building capacity to benefit the high seas.[14] The decision to commence negotiations for a new international legally binding instrument on plastic pollution under the auspices of UNEP has included a commitment to a much shorter two-year timeline.[15] Nevertheless, a considerable period has elapsed since Edward Carpenter first discovered small pieces of plastic floating in remote parts of the Atlantic Ocean in 1971, and Charles Moore identified the Great Pacific Garbage Patch in 1996.[16] Furthermore, while Article 207 UNCLOS calls upon States to develop laws to address land-based marine pollution, no global treaty has been agreed at the time of writing.[17]

Interconnected ocean

The land-ocean binary and fragmentation of marine and coastal law has resulted in serious challenges for ocean governance, compounded by the sectorisation and specialisation of laws, and the conflicting aims of economic, extractive and conservation treaty regimes. As discussed in Chapter 1, the doctrine of freedom of the seas and the binary separation of land and sea has fundamentally shaped laws governing oceans, seas and shorelines. These principles were enshrined in UNCLOS, and arguably facilitated over-exploitation, although the treaty also required States to protect and preserve the marine environment and to conserve and manage living resources. However, these fundamental legal principles impede attempts to introduce a more holistic approach to ocean governance, in part since the jurisdictional boundaries and division of species, area and activity-based laws are misaligned with the fluid, interconnected nature of marine ecosystems. Ecosystem-based management and integrated coastal zone management, as outlined in Chapter 1, have gone some way towards redressing this fragmentation of ocean space, while marine spatial planning and concepts such as sustainable development and the blue economy seek to reflect the three-dimensional nature of the ocean and to integrate sectors and industries to provide holistic approaches. However, whilst these initiatives are important, they have been applied in a piecemeal fashion and do not provide a coherent, foundational raison d'être for ocean law and governance. As some legal scholars have noted, international treaty-based law has evolved to meet the complexities of the rule of law[18] and does not address the dynamic, self-organising nature of the Earth system, nor offer a coordinated legal solution to the interconnectedness of the marine environment and the challenges it faces.[19]

Blue growth

The central aim of international fisheries law is to manage the exploitation of marine living resources, although lawmakers have included provision for equal access to marine resources whilst ensuring that catches are sustainable. In addition, unifying concepts such as sustainable development and, in the commercial context, environmental, social and corporate governance, aim to balance environmental concerns with socio-cultural and economic development, and these concepts have resulted in fisheries regulation embracing some conservation approaches. For example many Regional Fishery Management Organisations, initially focused purely on regulating harvests, now also embed conservation management measures.[20] Similarly, environmental law now includes utilisation measures. The 1992 *Convention on Biological Diversity*, for example, sought to balance conservation and utilisation, and aimed to build respect for and use of traditional knowledge and customary practices of Indigenous and local communities by embedding the concept of stewardship or custodianship in arrangements concerned with biodiversity conservation, management and sustainable use. Article 8(j) provided that:

> Subject to national legislation, respect, preserve and maintain knowledge, innovations and practices of indigenous and local communities embodying traditional lifestyles relevant for the conservation and sustainable use of biological diversity and promote their wider application with the approval and involvement. of the holders of such knowledge, innovations and practices and encourage the equitable sharing of the benefits arising from the utilization of such knowledge innovations and practices.[21]

Nevertheless, this provision is subject to national legislation, which may present a barrier to the adoption of new legal approaches. Furthermore, the 'blue economy' concept is based on the belief that market mechanisms can address the often-competing objectives of economic growth based on ocean activities, improved environmental outcomes and enhanced human well-being.[22] The idea of the blue economy is highly attractive for coastal States because it provides the opportunity to sustainably develop economies and reduce poverty whilst also protecting marine ecosystems and safeguarding ocean health. Shipping and transport, fisheries and aquaculture, seabed mining, energy from the oceans, and tourism are all areas that have been identified for 'blue growth'.[23] However, the blue economy is also premised on the belief that oceans can absorb further sectoral growth and development without providing holistic solutions that respect the interconnectedness of ocean processes, marine species and ecosystems.

The socio-ecological dimensions

Historically, international law has been the domain of States and domestic law-making the role of government. Other actors such as corporations, associations and groups, civil society, Indigenous peoples, minorities and individuals have rarely been involved, even though they are key stakeholders and must adhere to the law. Nevertheless, lawmakers have been motivated to respond when the abuse of marine environments or species has fuelled public outrage. Simultaneously, acceptance of laws by private industry and civil society is crucial for compliance, which arguably requires heightened public engagement and recognition by governments that they have a role to play as ocean stewards. The UN Ocean Decade has embraced this idea, albeit focusing on advancing scientific knowledge of the ocean.

Just as western science has become the dominant knowledge system for the marine environment, so too have western legal systems overshadowed approaches to marine and coastal governance, even in some post-colonial and non-western contexts. This has been driven by international law, which is dominated by industrialised nations. Initiatives such as Third World Approaches to International Law (TWAIL) seek to address power imbalances and overcome the more oppressive aspects of international law. Specific legal mechanisms have also been embraced that account for the differing contributions made by, and responsibilities of, developing nations for environmental degradation, including in oceans, seas and shorelines.[24] There have also been some attempts in recent years to integrate traditional knowledge within international law. However, ocean environmental laws have often suppressed and, in some cases displaced, other forms of knowledge and stewardship of marine and coastal species, systems and processes. In homogenising our legal approaches, lawmakers have missed the opportunity to embrace the wisdom of these other ways of knowing, including those that recognise the intrinsic rights of the ocean environment and marine species.

Theories of ocean governance

The concept of ocean governance includes formal (governmental) and informal (private industry and civil society) actors, institutions, laws, rules and codes of conduct, instruments and processes, all of which will be needed to address global concerns facing oceans, seas and shorelines.

Given that States and governments are not the only stakeholders affected by marine and coastal challenges, it is appropriate that other actors – such as private industry and civil society – are engaged in solutions. This is more so the case when issues of ethics and compliance are considered on which legal effectiveness depends. The governance concept has led to the development of a number of theories which are already evident in governance discourse, and which could be translated from theory into practice as we seek more effective ways to manage human-ocean interactions. For example, good governance has been articulated as a set of principles including efficiency and effectiveness, accountability and transparency widely endorsed at the global level and by governments worldwide. In that sense, adopting a way forward aligned with good governance principles is the lowest-hanging fruit. Concepts such as multi-layered or multi-tiered governance are already evident in marine and coastal law and address vertical fragmentation from international law to national legislation and local laws. Nexus governance seeks to overcome some of the horizontal sectorisation and again is not a controversial concept. Similarly, collaborative governance, which respects all views and peoples including minorities and other ways of knowing and doing, aligns with concepts of justice and TWAIL and although harder to achieve are not controversial. Yet each of these approaches to governance are themselves siloed.

Towards a new ocean imaginary

Unifying ocean laws

A fundamental principle of law is that it must be precise and capable of being understood and interpreted by all people.[25] Lawmakers have sought, for example, to clearly distinguish between marine and coastal components and to create laws for marine places, activities and objects. However, these divisions and classifications have sometimes created perverse outcomes. In the process of delineating oceanic boundaries, for example, laws override or dissolve the dynamic and complex nature of this fluid environment for pragmatic purposes. The result is that land is treated as separate from water and water from ice, while maritime zones and jurisdictions depend upon agreed political boundaries and measurements of depth and distances from the shoreline. In maritime law, naval, merchant, fishing and cruise ships are regulated under different laws, as are the industries to which they relate, while an object on board a vessel, on the seabed, floating in the water column offshore, or lapping at the shoreline is treated differently under separate laws. Some species are given multiple legal designations – fish can be declared native and endemic, introduced, invasive or alien – and those that are harvested in one place may be protected in another. If kept in an aquarium, they are treated differently again. Underpinning these legal complexities is the belief that nature is property, a premise that can no longer be countenanced as the sole basis for making laws relating to human uses of the ocean.

The fragmentation of laws relating to oceans, seas and shorelines is demonstrated by the number of distinct categories of legal sub-fields explored in this book – law of the sea, maritime law, marine environmental law, and underwater cultural heritage law. Similar fragmentation is also evident at the domestic level in State laws and governance arrangements. Fragmentation is a problem if it reduces effectiveness of law and hampers the achievement of outcomes. We have highlighted multiple examples where the separation of sectors and jurisdictional boundaries have translated into legal frameworks which conflict and can work against marine and coastal health, or at the least reduce their effectiveness. Laws in the EEZ of one nation, for example, are invariably different from those in an adjacent maritime zone, oblivious to the fact that species migrate between these areas and tides and current transport water, energy, nutrients and pollutants. Surface activities inevitably have impacts at greater depths. Targeted fishing of a few species influences the balance of ecosystems, offshore oil and gas operations can have positive and negative effects on species and marine areas, and legal regimes for climate change inherently relate to the atmosphere but the impacts are just as significant in the marine environment. Sustainable development provides valuable foundational elements that can serve as decision-making tools, incorporating principles of conservation, polluter pays, the precautionary approach, and integration, which would help to address this fragmentation. The principle of integration has featured in environmental law for almost 50 years, but in practice it has been difficult to achieve.

Recognising the rights of the ocean

Fundamentally, law is a tool developed by humans to regulate human behaviour and to ensure that human needs are met.[26] Marine environmental laws, for example, are predicated on human needs.[27] Provisions to ensure that humans have access to a ‘healthy environment’ or an ‘environment of quality’ are included in over 75% of the world’s national constitutions,[28] and the global community has recognised such rights through the UN General Assembly and UN Human Rights Council Resolutions.[29] Scholars working in the field of the rights of nature have suggested that granting such rights offers a radical solution to the biodiversity crisis, and a means by which to achieve ocean justice.[30] This approach recognises the intrinsic values of the ocean and its non-human inhabitants, and grants them legal rights to support their needs.

In 1982, 111 countries adopted the *United Nations World Charter for Nature*, declaring rights (and human responsibilities) for all living things.[31] In 2010 the United Nations released the *Experts’ Summary Report on Harmony with*

Universal Declaration of Ocean Rights

In 2023, an alliance campaigning for the rights of nature presented a proposal to the UN General Assembly for the development of a Universal Declaration of Ocean Rights by 2030. It aims to recognise that the ocean has inherent rights and intrinsic value, and that these rights – to have representation and a voice in international and domestic law – should be recognised in a consistent and coherent way through common standards and principles in ocean governance.[38] This proposal is one part of a wider rights-of-nature movement advocating for an ecocentric value system by granting legal rights and protections to non-human entities, such as animals, trees, rivers, and to specific ecosystems such as Antarctica.[39] In each case the aim is to recognise an aspect of the natural world as an autonomous entity, essentially granting legal personhood rights to the natural world. In 2012 a group of scientists and ethicists argued that dolphins and whales should be recognised as non-human persons and granted a legally enforceable right to life under international law, based on evidence that they possess intelligence, self-awareness and complex behaviour, properties no longer considered unique to humans.[40]

Nature – Theme: Earth Jurisprudence, noting the 'fundamental legal rights of ecosystems and species to exist, thrive and regenerate'.[32] As discussed in Chapter 7, some States have also recognised the rights of nature in domestic environmental laws, responding to increasing public pressure to address environmental degradation and a growing awareness that human and environmental health are inextricably linked.[33] Ecuador, for example, adopted the constitutional rights of nature in 2008 while Bolivia recognised Mother Earth as a 'dynamic living system comprising an indivisible community of all living systems and living organisms, interrelated, interdependent and complementary, which share a common destiny'.[34] Rights have been granted to certain rivers including the Rio Altrato in Colombia and Whanganui in New Zealand, while in 2017 the High Court of Uttarakhand in India declared:

> [T]he [g]laciers, including Gangotri & Yamunotri, rivers, streams, rivulets, lakes, air, meadows, dates, jungles, forests, wetlands, grasslands, springs and waterfalls, legal entity/legal person/juridical person/moral person/artificial person having the status of a legal person, with all corresponding rights . . . of a living person, in order to preserve and conserve them.[35]

To date, no non-human marine species has been given such rights, although there have been court proceedings in which proponents argued that some animals should have the same legal rights as people. In 2016, for example, an Argentinian court granted a habeas corpus lawsuit filed on behalf of a chimpanzee called Cecilia, declaring her to be a non-human legal person, while the Supreme Court of Colombia ordered the release of an Andean Bear, finding it a 'sentient being'.[36] However, in similar cases in the US and other countries, the argument that chimpanzees have cognitive abilities similar to humans and should have non-human legal rights was defeated. While the legal rights of the ocean are not yet widely recognised, the ethical principles underpinning them are finding their way into law. As Harden-Davies et al have noted, precedents already exist for a rights of nature approach in ocean governance that recognise the inherent importance of ecosystems, the role of the State as ocean custodians or stewards, and the importance of local participatory decision-making.[37]

A shared ocean ethic

Most of the laws discussed in this book are regulatory in nature. They provide rules around what is permitted and what is prohibited, and create systems for decision-making such as listing of species, declaration of marine parks, licensing of activities such as fishing and mining, and set standards for ship design. As noted in Chapter 11, tension exists between an ethical approach to law-making that values non-human species and ecosystems 'simply because they exist', and the utilitarian approach designed to maintain the benefits derived from the ocean.[41] Human engagement with the oceanic realm is increasingly compressed into the idea of the ocean providing humans with goods and services. However, it is also clear that nature as property is a failed philosophy, despite some attempts to embrace sustainability measures in international and domestic laws.

Nevertheless, law has a role to play in shaping the conditions for more holistic, ocean-centred thinking. Using law as a framework, one approach is to utilise market-based mechanisms, taxes and financial incentives to bring about the changes needed. Market-based regulations, such as emission trading schemes in the maritime transport sector, have become key tools in climate change mitigation policies, although some observers consider that these have been ineffective, particularly at a global level.[42] Another approach is to promote the concept of ocean literacy at a local and regional level. Indeed, the success of the UN's Sustainable Development Goals largely depends on local initiatives that support sustainable ocean use. In 2021, for example, the Brazilian city of Santos became the first jurisdiction to introduce an ocean literacy law as part of a public policy for school education. In announcing the new law, the Mayor of Santos talked about how local communities can do their part in transforming society by implementing an 'oceanic culture' in schools and promoting local knowledge, sustainable practices, and science-based decision-making.[43]

While ocean literacy may not in itself foster ocean-centred thinking at a global level, some studies suggest that ethical values and reciprocity, when shared by groups of people, are powerful drivers of social change.[44] Indeed, embedding the concept of a shared 'ocean ethic' in legal frameworks may become a critical tool for lawmakers in addressing the current trajectory of marine species extinction, degraded ecosystems, and reduced resources and services for human benefit, paradoxically restoring the principles and practices of marine stewardship that underpin traditional Indigenous relationships with the sea.[45] The notion of environmental stewardship has emerged in recent years as a powerful way of promoting positive interactions between humans and their environments in conservation and management policies and practices, particularly at the local level. Fisheries management, for example, is increasingly focused on the role of small-scale fishers in stewarding local resources, such as Chile's Territorial Use Rights Fisheries program.[46] An almost forgotten principle of international environmental law – subsidiarity – could be an anchor for such approaches, as it requires decision-making to be taken at the lowest appropriate governance level.

Ocean-centred governance

There is little doubt that, while legal approaches have evolved, they are generally too slow, reactive, and incremental to provide an effective response to the current climate, pollution, overharvesting, and biodiversity crises affecting the world's oceans. It is clear that swift and transformative change is needed, and it is here that an earth system law approach offers some light at the end of the tunnel.[47] Earth system governance is informed by earth system science. This approach recognises that current institutions, frameworks and approaches are unable to bring about 'societal change at the level and speed needed to mitigate and adapt to earth system transformation'[48] and 'respond to interconnected multiscalar "super wicked"' planetary challenges.[49] It also recognises that boundaries between 'humans and non-humans', 'flows of energy, materials and information', and 'planetary risks' are becoming blurred and that the earth is a 'single intertwined social-ecological system'.[50] Significantly, it questions 'how normative systems, such as those embedded in law, could embrace an earth system perspective'.[51]

Some of the most compelling solutions to the multiple crises of the Anthropocene have emerged from the Earth System Governance Project.[52] Kotzé and others have summarised the concept of 'earth system law' as aiming to 'make law more sensitive to and reflective of the functioning of the earth system as a social-ecological system'.[53] One element of this approach involves adopting a unifying, global '*Grundnorm*' such as 'planetary integrity' that would operate as a principle underpinning all specific instruments.[54] In this way an earth system law paradigm 'makes it possible to appreciate more fully the complexity of planetary earth system transformations and the multiple multiscalar challenges these create'.[55] Although the concept of ecological integrity is not new, the planetary lens of earth system law is novel[56] and attractive. Importantly, it has the potential to address a number of the challenges explored earlier and throughout this book: the slow, reactive, incrementalist approach to law-making; the dominance of western, industrialised States to the exclusion of others; the absence of more-than-human perspectives; and the fragmentation of legal frameworks across ocean spaces, maritime jurisdictions and marine sectors. Approaches to regime interaction and collaborative arrangements between treaty secretariats could, in part, address these complexities, but it would not provide a holistic solution along the lines envisaged by Kotzé and others. Climate change – a planetary systems crisis – is driving many ocean challenges. An earth system approach might therefore provide a means by which oceans governance, maritime law and marine environmental law can integrate and work with other areas of law such as criminal, investment and corporate law.

Earth system law is a nascent concept, but it has already attracted the attention of law of the sea and oceans governance scholars. Stephens, for example, supports 'the adoption of global ocean governance goals informed by the "Planetary Boundaries" framework' to 'move beyond an extractive imaginary and help address regime coordination challenges'.[57] As discussed in Chapter 11, some scholars are advocating for a 'new Ocean ethos' and 'Ocean-centered governance'.[58] Such an approach is similarly founded on systems thinking. It recognises 'the Ocean as a living entity, advancing law, policy, and institutional action that centers the needs of the Ocean in decision-making', and promoting a 'greater respect for all living things on Earth by recognizing that nonhumans have inherent rights and value'.[59] This approach could help to overcome diversity/incrementalism and provide some coherence, as well as aid integration, by cutting across the legal and scientific siloes that separate the human and non-human elements of the ocean environment.

Antarctica and the Southern Ocean – a case study in integrated ocean governance

The legal regime for the Antarctic region offers valuable lessons for addressing the legal challenges of ocean governance. In 1959, little more than a decade after World War II, a group of 12 nations active in Antarctic science managed to establish a single legal regime for this remote and inhospitable polar region. The Antarctic Treaty and its related agreements (known collectively as the Antarctic Treaty System) initially aimed at demilitarising the region and prohibiting nuclear proliferation, setting aside disputes over territorial sovereignty and promoting international scientific cooperation.[60]

By the 1970s, the Treaty parties were debating how best to conserve the region's fauna and flora, and initially agreed on measures to protect the land and ice shelves (but not the surrounding high seas) and a separate agreement to conserve the region's seals (*Convention for the Conservation of Antarctic Seals*) in 1972.[61] International attention turned to the region's other 'living resources' (mainly krill and finfish) and non-living resources (especially hard minerals and hydrocarbons). By then, commercial whaling had become uneconomic, with many of the region's populations of large whales decimated from nearly a century of industrial harvesting, while the markets for whale products were shrinking with the introduction of alternative materials. In addition, public anti-whaling sentiment was on the rise with reports that industrialised whaling had pushed some whale species to the edge of extinction. In 1982 the International Whaling Commission, empowered under the *International Convention for the Regulation of Whaling*, agreed to 'pause' commercial whaling of all species for the 1985/1986 season.[62] Some States had already banned commercial whaling and the international community, albeit with some outliers, followed suit.[63] Also in 1982, the *Convention on the Conservation of Antarctic Marine Living Resources* came into force as part of the Antarctic Treaty System in response to the impact of krill harvesting on Southern Ocean marine life dependent on krill for food. It was one of the first ocean treaties to embed the precautionary ecosystem approach, putting the marine ecosystem ahead of financial concerns.

At the same time, Treaty members were engaged in negotiations for a convention to facilitate the development of a mining regime in Antarctica and, in 1988, the *Convention on the Regulation of Antarctic Mineral Resource Activities* (CRAMRA) was open for signature.[64] In the following year, the Australian and French governments announced that they would not ratify CRAMRA, and instead advocated for a World Park or Wilderness Reserve in Antarctica. New Zealand followed suit in 1990.[65] Within a decade, what had begun as a legal arrangement to regulate mining in an environmentally sensitive region ended with an entirely new legal regime in the form of the *Madrid Protocol on Environmental Protection to the Antarctic Treaty*, an international agreement that prohibited any activity relating to mineral resources for at least 50 years.[66]

Conclusion

The crisis facing the world's oceans is socio-ecological in nature and planetary in scale. The question is whether western legal frameworks are capable of responding to these urgent planetary challenges. Our planet's oceanic realm is essential to human health, well-being and survival – an essential source of food and materials, a highway between continents and islands, a scientific laboratory, a source of inspiration and knowledge, a cultural repository and a spiritual entity. As this book shows, the relationship between humans and oceans has evolved over time, resulting in a plethora of laws designed to ensure that the ocean continues to meet human needs.[67] Nevertheless, law is never static, and it can be reshaped or reimagined entirely. Some attempts have been made, for example, to introduce a holistic, transboundary and rights-based approach to ocean governance, although these are not yet at scales to be fully effective. However, new ideas have emerged in recent years that offer some glimmer of hope, including the idea of granting rights to the ocean in order to give it legal standing, and the concept of Earth system law as a way of transforming the philosophical premise of the current legal regime without changing its normative function. The former is, arguably, easier to envisage (given that legal rights have already been granted to some rivers and forests). The latter idea offers a particularly exciting way forward, although it requires perhaps the greatest conceptual leap. As Kotzé et al have argued, an Earth system law paradigm offers a 'reimagination of law' and a 'plan of action' that could lead to 'transformational solutions'.[68] If law is to play a more meaningful role in securing the health of oceans, then it must become more holistic, inclusive and effective.

Fundamentally, law is a regulatory tool constructed by people, yet the laws that human land-dwellers have designed are arguably ill-equipped to protect the vast, dynamic, life-giving oceanic realm in the Anthropocene. The dominant legal system that has evolved over many centuries is as complex and multi-dimensional as the ocean itself but, as this book shows, it is failing to mitigate the multiple physical, ecological and social crises affecting the health of our planetary ocean. It may be that we are witnessing the 'quiet crossing of ocean tipping points',[69] as law flounders in the shallows encumbered by indecision, ongoing negotiation and lack of political will to take action. This book has explored some of the key challenges we face if we are to restore the health and integrity of our oceans, seas and shorelines. Ultimately, we argue that we must fundamentally reimagine our relationship with the powerful forces of Earth's oceanic realm and the planetary system as a whole.

Notes

1 Elizabeth R. Johnson and Irus Braverman, "Introduction," in *Blue Legalities: The Life and Laws of the Sea*, ed. Irus Braverman and Elizabeth R. Johnson (Durham: Duke University Press, 2020), 13.

2 Jin-Hyun Paik, "Disputes Involving Scientific and Technical Matters and the International Tribunal for the Law of the Sea," in *New Knowledge and Changing Circumstances in the Law of the Sea*, ed. Tomas Heidar (Leiden: Brill Nijhoff, 2020), 15.

3 The Anthropocene concept was adopted by Stoermer and Crutzen in 2000 to describe a new geological epoch in which human activities have become a significant

geological force. Paul J. Crutzen and Eugene F. Stoermer, "The 'Anthropocene'," *International Geosphere-Biosphere Programme Newsletter* 41 (2000): 17–18; Paul J. Crutzen, "The 'Anthropocene'," in *Earth System Science in the Anthropocene: Emerging Issues and Problems*, ed. Eckart Ehlers and Thomas Krafft (New York: Springer, 2006); and Louis J. Kotzé, "Earth System Law for the Anthropocene," *Sustainability* 11 (2019): 6796.

4 Louis J. Kotzé et al., "Earth System Law: Exploring New Frontiers in Legal Science," *Earth System Governance* 11, no. 100126 (2002): 1; and Louis J. Kotzé and Rakhyun E. Kim, "Earth System Law: The Juridical Dimensions of Earth System Governance," *Earth System Governance* 1, no. 100003 (2019): 1.

5 For all of the International Maritime Organisation (IMO) treaties see "List of IMO Conventions," *IMO*, accessed March 1, 2024, www.imo.org/en/about/Conventions/Pages/ListOfConventions.aspx.

6 MARPOL Preamble.

7 *Convention on Biological Diversity* Article 1. The Convention Secretariat maintains its own website: "Convention on Biological Diversity," accessed March 1, 2024, www.cbd.int/.

8 *International Convention for the Regulation of Whaling* Preamble. For the full text see "IWC Key Documents," *International Whaling Commission*, accessed March 1, 2024, https://iwc.int/commission/convention.

9 Preamble to the United Nations Convention on the Law of the Sea. It should be noted that UNCLOS also committed 'to the realization of a just and equitable international economic order' and the 'economic and social advancement of all peoples of the world'. For the full text see "United Nations Convention on the Law of the Sea," *United Nations*, accessed March 1, 2024, www.un.org/depts/los/convention_agreements/texts/unclos/closindx.htm.

10 Surabhi Ranganathan, "Decolonization and International Law: Putting the Ocean on the Map," *Journal of the History of International Law* 23 (2021): 161–83.

11 Atul Setalvad, "Paper Laws," *Economic and Political Weekly* 23, no. 29 (1988): 1467–70.

12 "MEPSEAS: Marine Environment Protection of the South-East Asian Seas," *United Nations SDGs*, accessed May 7, 2024, https://sdgs.un.org/partnerships/mepseas-marine-environment-protection-south-east-asian-seas.

13 "Model Shipping (Ballast Water Management) Regulations," *Pacific Environment Data Portal*, accessed February 27, 2024, https://pacific-data.sprep.org/dataset/model-shipping-ballast-water-management-regulations.

14 The official text of the treaty can be found at UN Treaty Collection website: https://treaties.un.org/Pages/ViewDetails.aspx?src=TREATY&mtdsg_no=XXI-10&chapter=21&clang=_en.

15 "Intergovernmental Negotiating Committee on Plastic Pollution," *UNEP*, accessed February 27, 2024, www.unep.org/inc-plastic-pollution. Negotiations continue and it has yet to be seen whether the goal of agreeing upon a final text by the end of 2024 is achieved.

16 For a full history, see Chelsea M. Rochman, "The Story of Plastic Pollution: From the Distant Ocean Gyres to the Global Policy Stage," *Oceanography* 33, no. 3 (2020): 60–70, https://doi.org/10.5670/oceanog.2020.308.

17 "Intergovernmental Negotiating Committee on Plastic Pollution"; Earth Law Center, *Advancing Ocean Justice in the Global Plastics Treaty* (New York: Earth Law Center, 2024), www.earthlawcenter.org/ocean-plastic?eType=EmailBlastContent&eId=f2d9804b-49c1-4286-9871-b543d833973a. Negotiations continue and it has yet to be seen whether the goal of agreeing upon a final text by the end of 2024 is achieved.

18 The rule of law ensures that all people and organisations are bound by the same law, whether they are citizens, corporations, governments or lawmakers. In essence it means that no one is above the law. See also Chapter 1.
19 See for example Louis J. Kotzé, "Earth System Law for the Anthropocene: Rethinking Environmental Law Alongside the Earth System Metaphor," *Transnational Legal Theory* 11, nos. 1/2 (2020): 75–104, https://doi.org/10.1080/20414005.2020.1776556. Rakhyun E. Kim and H. van Asselt, "Global Governance: Problem Shifting in the Anthropocene and the Limits of International Law," in *Research Handbook on International Law and Natural Resources*, ed. E. Morgera and K. Kuloveski (Cheltenham: Edward Elgar, 2016), 473–95. Jutta Brunnee, "The Rule of International (Environmental) Law and Complex Problems," *The International Rule of Law: Rise or Decline?* ed. Heike Krieger, Georg Nolte, and Andreas Zimmermann (Oxford: Oxford Academic, online ed., 2019), https://doi.org/10.1093/oso/9780198843603.003.0014.
20 See, for example, "Conservation and Management Measures and Resolutions," *Western Central Pacific Fisheries Commission*, accessed February 27, 2024 https://cmm.wcpfc.int/.
21 United Nations, "Convention on Biological Diversity" (1992), https://treaties.un.org/pages/ViewDetails.aspx?src=TREATY&mtdsg_no=XXVII-8&chapter=27.
22 Michelle Voyer et al., "Maritime Security and the Blue Economy: Intersections and Interdependencies in the Indian Ocean," *Journal of the Indian Ocean Region* 14, no. 1 (2018): 28, 29.
23 Lyndon E. Llewellyn and others, "A Roadmap to a Sustainable Indian Ocean Blue Economy," *Journal of the Indian Ocean Region* 12, no. 1 (2016): 52, 52–66.
24 One of the most relevant principles is 'common but differentiated responsibilities': see *Rio Declaration*, principle 7.
25 Philip E. Steinberg, Berit Kristoffersen, and Kristen L. Shake, "Edges and Flows: Exploring Legal Materialities and Biophysical Politics of Sea Ice," in *Blue Legalities: The Life and Laws of the Sea*, ed. Irus Braverman, and Elizabeth R. Johnson (Durham: Duke University Press, 2020), 100.
26 See for example Principle 1 of the *Rio Declaration* "Human beings are at the centre of concerns for sustainable development. They are entitled to a healthy and productive life in harmony with nature".
27 The Preamble to the *Convention on Biological Diversity* notes that "ultimately, the conservation and sustainable use of biological diversity will strengthen friendly relations among States and contribute to peace for humankind".
28 "Constitute Project," accessed February 27, 2024, www.constituteproject.org/.
29 See Human Rights Council, *Resolution 48/12*, UN Doc. A/HRC/RES/48/12 (October 18, 2021) recognising environmental rights.
30 Harriet Harden-Davies, Fran Humphries, Michelle Maloney, Glen Wright, Kristina Gjerde, and Marjo Vierros, "Rights of Nature: Perspectives for Global Ocean Stewardship," *Marine Policy* 122, no. 104059 (2020): 1–11.
31 G.A. Res. 37/7, *World Charter on Nature* (October 28, 1982) cited in Oliver A Houck, "Noah's Second Voyage," *Tulane Environmental Law Journal* 31, no. 1 (Winter 2017): 7.
32 *Experts' Summary Rep. on Harmony with Nature – Theme: Earth Jurisprudence*, U.N. Doc M l 1/266 (August 1, 2016) cited in Oliver A Houck, "Noah's Second Voyage," *Tulane Environmental Law Journal* 31, no. 1 (Winter 2017): 7.
33 Harden-Davies et al., "Rights of Nature," 10.
34 Ibid., 2 (Table 1).
35 *Lalit Miglani v. State of Uttarkhand*, Writ Petition (PIL) No. 140 of 2015, 64 (India) cited in Houck, "Noah's Second Voyage," 3.

36 Houck, "Noah's Second Voyage," 3. *Habeas corpus* is a writ brought before a court to determine whether a person in custody has been unlawfully detained. In this case the proceeding was brought on behalf of an ape.
37 Harden-Davies et al., "Rights of Nature," 8.
38 The principles of ocean rights were developed with a diverse group of experts, including policy, business, law, Indigenous peoples and scientists. Earth Law Center, "Towards a University Declaration of Ocean Rights (UDOR)," accessed February 11, 2024, https://earthlawcenter.squarespace.com/s/UDOR_Concept-Note-1.pdf.
39 Earth Law Center, "Universal Declaration of River Rights," accessed February 11, 2024, www.earthlawcenter.org/river-rights; and Antarctic Rights, "A Voice for Antarctica," accessed February 11, 2024, https://antarcticrights.org/.
40 Ian Sample, "Whales and Dolphins 'Should Have Legal Rights'," *The Guardian* (February 21, 2012), www.theguardian.com/world/2012/feb/21/whales-dolphins-legal-rights. Also see "Orcas, Dolphins, and Whales: Non-Human Persons and Animal Rights," *Bill of Health*, Harvard Law School (March 27, 2018), https://blog.petrieflom.law.harvard.edu/2018/03/27/orcas-dolphins-and-whales-non-human-persons-and-animal-rights/; and Linda Nowlan, "Why the Southern Resident Killer Whales Should Have the Same Rights as People," *The Conversation* (April 26, 2019), https://theconversation.com/why-the-southern-resident-killer-whales-should-have-the-same-rights-as-people-115287.
41 Peter Auster, Rod Fujita, Stephen Robert Kellertm et al., "Developing an Ocean Ethic: Science, Utility, Aesthetics, Self-Interest, and Different Ways of Knowing," *Conservation Biology* 23, no. 1 (2009): 233–35.
42 Jason Monios, "The Moral Limits of Market-Based Mechanisms: An Application to the International Maritime Sector," *Journal of Business Ethics* 108 (2003): 283–99.
43 "Ocean Literacy Law Is Signed in Santos, Brazil," *UNESCO News* (November 19, 2021), updated April 20, 2023, www.unesco.org/en/articles/ocean-literacy-law-signed-santos-brazil.
44 Susanne Stoll-Kleemann, "Feasible Options for Behaviour Change toward More Effective Ocean Literacy: A Systematic Review," *Frontiers in Marine Science* 6, no. 273 (May 28, 2019), www.frontiersin.org/articles/10.3389/fmars.2019.00273/full.
45 Mia Strand, Nina Rivers, and Bernadette Snow, "Reimagining Ocean Stewardship: Arts-Based Methods to 'Hear' and 'See' Indigenous and Local Knowledge in Ocean Management," *Marine Conservation and Sustainability* 9 (2022), https://doi.org/10.3389/fmars.2022.886632.
46 Nathan J. Bennett, Tara S. Whitty, Elena Finkbeiner, Jeremy Pittman, Hannah Bassett, Stefan Gelcich, and Edward H. Allison, "Environmental Stewardship: A Conceptual Review and Analytical Framework," *Environmental Management* 61 (2018): 597–614.
47 Biermann et al. argue that 'swift and transformative structural change in global governance is needed'. Frank Biermann et al., "Transforming Governance and Institutions for Global Sustainability: Key Insights from the Earth System Governance Project," *Current Opinions in Environmental Sustainability* 4 (2012): 57.
48 Biermann et al., "Transforming Governance," 51–60.
49 Louis J. Kotzé and Rakhyun E. Kim, "Towards Planetary Nexus Governance in the Anthropocene: An Earth System Law Perspective," *Global Policy* 13 (2022): 86–97. See also Kotzé, "Earth System Law for the Anthropocene."
50 Kotzé et al., "Earth System Law: Exploring New Frontiers in Legal Science."
51 Ibid.
52 The Earth System Governance Project is a research initiative under the auspices of the *International Human Dimensions Programme on Global Environmental Change*

(IHDP) sponsored by the *International Council for Science, International Social Science Council* and the *United Nations University: Earth System Governance*, www.earthsystemgovernance.org/.
53 Kotzé et al., "Earth System Law: Exploring New Frontiers in Legal Science," 2.
54 Ibid.
55 Kotzé and Kim, "Earth System Law: Exploring New Frontiers in Legal Science," 88.
56 Peter Bridgewater, Rakhyun E. Kim, and Klaus Bosselmann, "Ecological Integrity: A Relevant Concept for International Environmental Law in the Anthropocene?" *Yearbook of International Environmental Law* 25, no. 1 (2015): 61–78.
57 Tim Stephens, "Global Ocean Governance in the Anthropocene: From Extractive Imaginaries to Planetary Boundaries?" *Global Policy* 13 Supp (2022): 76–85.
58 Michelle Bender, Rachel Bustamante, and Kelsey Leonard, "Living in Relationship with the Ocean to Transform Governance in the UN Ocean Decade," *PLoS Biology* 20, no. 1 (2022): e3001828.
59 Ibid.
60 The Treaty remains in force indefinitely. By 2024, there were 56 State signatories representing two-thirds of the world's population. "The Antarctic Treaty 50 Years on," *Australian Antarctic Magazine* 20 (2011).
61 *Convention for the Conservation of Antarctic Seals* 1972.
62 ICW, "Commercial Whaling," https://iwc.int/management-and-conservation/whaling/commercial. See also Malgosia Fitzmaurice, "International Convention for the Regulation of Whaling," *Audio-visual Library of International Law*, accessed March 15, 2024, https://legal.un.org/avl/ha/icrw/icrw.html.
63 The moratorium on whaling continues to this day, and the global whale watching industry has grown exponentially and is now estimated to be worth more than USD 2 billion. Some States have continued to engage in small-scale whaling, although the moratorium remains in place for ocean areas beyond national jurisdiction. In 2010, the International Whaling Commission considered a proposal to allow commercial whaling in the Southern Ocean under certain conditions in order to bring Japan's 'scientific whaling' under the IWC's jurisdiction. Japan subsequently withdrew from the IWC and its Southern Ocean whaling operations to focus on commercial whaling in its Exclusive Economic Zone. See Sarah Clarke, "Greenpeace Makes Waves over Whaling Plan," *ABC News* (February 23, 2010), www.abc.net.au/news/2010-02-23/greenpeace-makes-waves-over-whaling-plan/340926. Daniel Hurst, "Japanese Whaling Is Down but Not Out," *The Interpreter* (April 3, 2020), www.lowyinstitute.org/the-interpreter/japanese-whaling-down-not-out; International Whaling Commission, "The Benefits and Impacts of Whale Watching," accessed March 15, 2024, https://wwhandbook.iwc.int/en/responsible-management/benefits-and-impacts-of-whale-watching#:~:text=The%20benefits%20of%20whale%20watching,people%20in%2020092%2C3.
64 Antarctic Treaty, "Report of the Eleventh Consultative Meeting" (1981), https://documents.ats.aq/ATCM11/fr/ATCM11_fr001_e.pdf. "Convention on the Regulation of Antarctic Mineral Resource Activities," https://documents.ats.aq/recatt/att311_e.pdf.
65 Australia's refusal to ratify CRAMRA constituted a veto.
66 Secretariat of the Antarctic Treaty, "The Protocol on Environmental Protection to the Antarctic Treaty," www.ats.aq/e/protocol.html.
67 Reg A. Watson and A. Tidd, "Mapping Nearly a Century and a Half of Global Marine Fishing: 1869–2015," *Marine Policy* 93 (2018): 171–77, 176.
68 Kotzé et al., "Earth System Law: Exploring New Frontiers in Legal Science," 6–7.
69 Christoph Heinze, Thorsten Blenckner, Helena Martins, Dagmara Rusiecka, Ralph Döscher, Marion Gehlen, Nicolas Gruber, Elisabeth Holland, Øystein Hov, Fortunat

Joos, John Brian Robin Matthews, Rolf Rødven, and Simon Wilson, "The Quiet Crossing of Ocean Tipping Points," *Proceedings of the National Academy of Science USA* 118, no. 9 (March 2, 2021), https://doi.org/10.1073/pnas.2008478118.

Bibliography

Antarctic Rights. "A Voice for Antarctica." Accessed February 11, 2024. https://antarcticrights.org/.

Antarctic Treaty. "Report of the Eleventh Consultative Meeting." (1981). Accessed March 15, 2024. https://documents.ats.aq/ATCM11/fr/ATCM11_fr001_e.pdf.

Auster, Peter et al. "Developing an Ocean Ethic: Science, Utility, Aesthetics, Self-Interest, and Different Ways of Knowing." *Conservation Biology* 23, no. 1 (2009): 233–35.

Bender, Michelle, Rachel Bustamante, and Kelsey Leonard. "Living in Relationship with the Ocean to Transform Governance in the UN Ocean Decade." *PLoS Biology* 20, no. 1 (2022): e3001828.

Bennett, Nathan J., Tara S. Whitty, Elena Finkbeiner, Jeremy Pittman, Hannah Bassett, Stefan Gelcich, and Edward H. Allison. "Environmental Stewardship: A Conceptual Review and Analytical Framework." *Environmental Management* 61 (2018): 597–614. https://link.springer.com/article/10.1007/s00267-017-0993-2.

Biermann, Frank et al. "Transforming Governance and Institutions for Global Sustainability: Key Insights from the Earth System Governance Project." *Current Opinions in Environmental Sustainability* 4 (2012): 57.

Bridgewater, Peter, Rakhyun E. Kim, and Klaus Bosselmann. "Ecological Integrity: A Relevant Concept for International Environmental Law in the Anthropocene?" *Yearbook of International Environmental Law* 25, no. 1 (2015): 61–78.

Brunnee, Jutta. "The Rule of International (Environmental) Law and Complex Problems." In *The International Rule of Law: Rise or Decline?* edited by Heike Krieger, Georg Nolte, and Andreas Zimmermann. Oxford, Oxford Academic, online ed, 2019. https://doi.org/10.1093/oso/9780198843603.003.0014.

Clarke, Sarah. "Greenpeace Makes Waves over Whaling Plan." *ABC News* (February 23, 2010). www.abc.net.au/news/2010-02-23/greenpeace-makes-waves-over-whaling-plan/340926.

"Constitute Project." Accessed February 27, 2024. www.constituteproject.org/.

"Convention on Biological Diversity." Accessed March 1, 2024. www.cbd.int/.

"Convention on the Regulation of Antarctic Mineral Resource Activities." Accessed March 15, 2024. https://documents.ats.aq/recatt/att311_e.pdf.

Crutzen, Paul J. "The 'Anthropocene'." In *Earth System Science in the Anthropocene: Emerging Issues and Problems*, edited by Eckart Ehlers and Thomas Krafft. New York: Springer, 2006.

Crutzen, Paul J., and Eugene F. Stoermer. "The 'Anthropocene'." *International Geosphere-Biosphere Programme Newsletter* 41 (2000): 17–18.

Earth Law Center. *Advancing Ocean Justice in the Global Plastics Treaty*. New York: Earth Law Center, 2024. www.earthlawcenter.org/ocean-plastic?eType=EmailBlastContent&eId=f2d9804b-49c1-4286-9871-b543d833973a.

Earth Law Center. "Towards a University Declaration of Ocean Rights (UDOR)." Accessed 11 February 2024. https://earthlawcenter.squarespace.com/s/UDOR_Concept-Note-1.pdf.

Earth Law Center. "Universal Declaration of River Rights." Accessed 11 February 2024. www.earthlawcenter.org/river-rights.

"Earth System Governance Project." Accessed March 15, 2024. www.earthsystemgovernance.org/.

Fitzmaurice, Malgosia. *International Convention for the Regulation of Whaling*. Audio-visual Library of International Law. Accessed March 15, 2024. https://legal.un.org/avl/ha/icrw/icrw.html.
Harden-Davies, Harriet, Fran Humphries, Michelle Maloney, Glen Wright, Kristina Gjerde, and Marjo Vierros. "Rights of Nature: Perspectives for Global Ocean Stewardship." *Marine Policy* 122, no. 104059 (2020): 1–11.
Heinze, Christoph et al. "The Quiet Crossing of Ocean Tipping Points." *Proceedings of the National Academy of Science USA* 118, no. 9 (2 March 2021). https://doi.org/10.1073/pnas.2008478118.
Houck, Oliver A. "Noah's Second Voyage." *Tulane Environmental Law Journal* 31, no. 1 (Winter 2017): 7.
Human Rights Council, *Resolution 48/12*, UN Doc. A/HRC/RES/48/12 (October 18, 2021).
Hurst, Daniel. "Japanese Whaling Is Down but Not Out." *The Interpreter* (April 3, 2020). www.lowyinstitute.org/the-interpreter/japanese-whaling-down-not-out.
IMO. "List of IMO Conventions." Accessed March 1, 2024. www.imo.org/en/about/Conventions/Pages/ListOfConventions.aspx.
International Whaling Commission. "Commercial Whaling." Accessed March 15, 2024. https://iwc.int/management-and-conservation/whaling/commercial.
International Whaling Commission. "IWC Key Documents." Accessed March 1, 2024. https://iwc.int/commission/convention.
International Whaling Commission. "The Benefits and Impacts of Whale Watching." Accessed March 15, 2024. https://wwhandbook.iwc.int/en/responsible-management/benefits-and-impacts-of-whale-watching#:~:text=The%20benefits%20of%20whale%20watching,people%20in%2020092%2C3.
Johnson, Elizabeth R., and Irus Braverman. "Introduction." In *Blue Legalities: The Life and Laws of the Sea*, edited by Irus Braverman and Elizabeth R. Johnson. Durham: Duke University Press, 2020.
Kim, Rakhyun E., and H. van Asselt. "Global Governance: Problem Shifting in the Anthropocene and the Limits of International Law." In *Research Handbook on International Law and Natural Resources*, edited by E. Morgera and K. Kuloveski. Cheltenham: Edward Elgar, 2016.
Kotzé, Louis J. "Earth System Law for the Anthropocene." *Sustainability* 11 (2019): 6796.
Kotzé, Louis J. "Earth System Law for the Anthropocene: Rethinking Environmental Law Alongside the Earth System Metaphor." *Transnational Legal Theory* 11, nos. 1/2 (2020): 75–104.
Kotzé, Louis J., and Rakhyun E. Kim. "Earth System Law: The Juridical Dimensions of Earth System Governance." *Earth System Governance* 1, no. 100003 (2019): 1.
Kotzé Louis J., and Rakhyun E. Kim. "Towards Planetary Nexus Governance in the Anthropocene: An Earth System Law Perspective." *Global Policy* 13 (2022): 86–97.
Kotzé, Louis J. et al. "Earth System Law: Exploring New Frontiers in Legal Science." *Earth System Governance* 11, no. 100126 (2002): 1.
Llewellyn, Lyndon E. et al. "A Roadmap to a Sustainable Indian Ocean Blue Economy." *Journal of the Indian Ocean Region* 12, no. 1 (2016): 52.
Monios, Jason. "The Moral Limits of Market-Based Mechanisms: An Application to the International Maritime Sector." *Journal of Business Ethics* 108 (2003): 283–99.
Nowlan, Linda. "Why the Southern Resident Killer Whales Should Have the Same Rights as People." *The Conversation* (April 26, 2019). https://theconversation.com/why-the-southern-resident-killer-whales-should-have-the-same-rights-as-people-115287.
"Ocean Literacy Law Is Signed in Santos, Brazil." *UNESCO News* (November 19, 2021). www.unesco.org/en/articles/ocean-literacy-law-signed-santos-brazil, updated April 20, 2023.

"Orcas, Dolphins, and Whales: Non-Human Persons and Animal Rights." *Bill of Health*, Harvard Law School (March 27, 2018). https://blog.petrieflom.law.harvard.edu/2018/03/27/orcas-dolphins-and-whales-non-human-persons-and-animal-rights/.

Pacific Environment Data Portal. "Model Shipping (Ballast Water Management) Regulations." Accessed February 27, 2024. https://pacific-data.sprep.org/dataset/model-shipping-ballast-water-management-regulations.

Paik, Jin-Hyun. "Disputes Involving Scientific and Technical Matters and the International Tribunal for the Law of the Sea." In *New Knowledge and Changing Circumstances in the Law of the Sea*, edited by Tomas Heidar. Leiden: Brill Nijhoff, 2020.

Ranganathan, Surabhi. "Decolonization and International Law: Putting the Ocean on the Map." *Journal of the History of International Law* 23 (2021): 161–83.

Rochman, Chelsea M. "The Story of Plastic Pollution: From the Distant Ocean Gyres to the Global Policy Stage." *Oceanography* 33, no. 3 (2020): 60–70.

Sample, Ian. "Whales and Dolphins 'Should Have Legal Rights'." *The Guardian* (February 21, 2012). www.theguardian.com/world/2012/feb/21/whales-dolphins-legal-rights.

Secretariat of the Antarctic Treaty. "The Protocol on Environmental Protection to the Antarctic Treaty." Accessed March 15, 2024. www.ats.aq/e/protocol.html.

Setalvad, Atul. "Paper Laws." *Economic and Political Weekly* 23, no. 29 (1988): 1467–70.

Steinberg, Philip E., Berit Kristoffersen, and Kristen L. Shake. "Edges and Flows: Exploring Legal Materialities and Biophysical Politics of Sea Ice." In *Blue Legalities: The Life and Laws of the Sea*, edited by Irus Braverman and Elizabeth R. Johnson. Durham: Duke University Press, 2020.

Stephens, Tim. "Global Ocean Governance in the Anthropocene: From Extractive Imaginaries to Planetary Boundaries?" *Global Policy* 13 Supp (2022): 76–85.

Stoll-Kleemann, Susanne. "Feasible Options for Behaviour Change Toward More Effective Ocean Literacy: A Systematic Review." *Frontiers in Marine Science* 6, no. 273 (2019). www.frontiersin.org/articles/10.3389/fmars.2019.00273/full.

Strand, Mia, Nina Rivers, and Bernadette Snow. "Reimagining Ocean Stewardship: Arts-Based Methods to 'Hear' and 'See' Indigenous and Local Knowledge in Ocean Management." *Marine Conservation and Sustainability* 9 (2022): https://doi.org/10.3389/fmars.2022.886632.

"The Antarctic Treaty 50 Years on." *Australian Antarctic Magazine* 20 (2011). www.antarctica.gov.au/magazine/issue-20-2011/policy/the-antarctic-treaty-50-years-on/.

UNEP. "Intergovernmental Negotiating Committee on Plastic Pollution." Accessed February 27, 2024. www.unep.org/inc-plastic-pollution.

United Nations. "Convention on Biological Diversity." (1992). Accessed March 15, 2024. https://treaties.un.org/pages/ViewDetails.aspx?src=TREATY&mtdsg_no=XXVII-8&chapter=27.

United Nations. "United Nations Convention on the Law of the Sea." Accessed March 1, 2024. www.un.org/depts/los/convention_agreements/texts/unclos/closindx.htm.

United Nations SDGs. "MEPSEAS: Marine Environment Protection of the South-East Asian Seas." Accessed May 7, 2024. https://sdgs.un.org/partnerships/mepseas-marine-environment-protection-south-east-asian-seas.

Voyer, Michelle et al. "Maritime Security and the Blue Economy: Intersections and Interdependencies in the Indian Ocean." *Journal of the Indian Ocean Region* 14, no. 1 (2018): 28.

Watson, Reg A., and Tidd, A. "Mapping Nearly a Century and a Half of Global Marine Fishing: 1869–2015." *Marine Policy* 93 (2018): 171.

Western Central Pacific Fisheries Commission. "Conservation and Management Measures and Resolutions." Accessed February 27, 2024. https://cmm.wcpfc.int/.

Index

Antarctic 33, 89, 93, 100–1, 130, 173, 198, 204–7, 255, 281, 310, 312–3
Anthropocene 9, 301–3, 314
aquaculture 88, 93–4, 100, 259, 281, 285, 305
Aquaculture Stewardship Council 95, 100
Arctic 5–6, 8, 31, 94, 149–50, 173, 195, 224, 229, 245
Areas beyond national jurisdiction 202, 207, 271, 277, 304
armed conflict 63, 66, 68, 253

biodiversity 9, 26, 29, 153, 169, 177–8, 182, 193–4, 202–4, 209, 279–80, 283, 285, 302, 304–5, 311
biomimicry 183
bioprospecting 279–80, 287
bottom trawling 92
boundary 41–3, 45–8, 50, 52–4, 156, 208–9, 314

Carson, Rachel 28, 43, 144, 169, 223
catch limit 90, 95, 175, 176
climate change 2, 9, 17, 26, 40, 43–4, 101, 173, 178–9, 201, 210, 222, 224, 227, 229–31, 234, 252, 255, 259, 274, 277, 283, 286, 308, 310, 312
compliance 26–7, 33, 89, 96–9, 130, 174, 177, 198, 229, 234, 304, 306–7; *see also* enforcement
crime 34, 60–1, 64, 69–72, 99, 174
culture 1–3, 20, 61, 87, 144, 224, 247, 258, 270, 310
customary international law 20, 26, 53, 61, 64, 66–7, 274
customary law 1, 8, 18–20, 68, 84, 117, 126, 170–1, 195

debris, marine 232–3
dispute 5, 18, 19, 25, 26, 33, 42, 46, 48, 51, 66, 116, 117–9, 131, 156–7, 175, 251, 312–3

ecolabelling 100
ecosystem services 177, 200
ecotourism 180, 207
enforcement 25–6, 33, 64–5, 71, 88, 98–9, 125, 129, 174, 181, 198, 224, 287, 304
environmental impact assessment 29, 182, 304
ethics 102, 170, 181–2, 250, 270, 307, 309–11
Exclusive Economic Zones (EEZs) 26, 28, 48–9, 51, 53, 83, 88–91, 98, 130, 154, 156, 176, 202, 208, 252, 255, 275, 277, 282, 308
extinction 9, 17, 27, 94, 95, 169, 171, 175, 177, 178, 182, 199, 311, 313

fisheries 7, 22–3, 27–8, 31, 34, 44, 47, 51, 71, 84–5, 87–102, 130, 154, 176, 194, 196–8, 206, 223, 226, 230, 269, 274, 276, 281–2, 301, 305, 311
Food and Agriculture Organization (FAO) 27, 71, 87, 89–92, 96–8, 100, 194
freedom of the seas 6, 9, 18, 22–3, 25–6, 31, 34, 41, 46, 53, 88, 98, 151, 273, 278, 304

geoengineering 229
greenhouse gas (GHG) emissions 129, 178–9, 222, 227, 229–31, 234

hazardous waste 27, 115, 224, 228–9, 234
human rights 26, 31, 32, 97, 125–6, 308

illegal, unreported and unregulated fishing (IUU) 89, 91, 96–7, 99–101, 130, 282
implementation 26, 30, 33, 97, 123–4, 149, 153, 174, 200, 202, 209, 234, 287, 303
Indigenous peoples 3, 8, 44, 94, 173, 177, 201, 271, 306
International Law Commission 47
International Maritime Organization (IMO) 27, 66, 71, 115, 119–21, 126, 129–31, 149, 154, 157, 206, 225, 227, 229, 283, 303
International Tribunal for the Law of the Sea 276

justice 8–9, 20, 28, 34, 52, 54, 94, 102, 127, 174, 181–2, 223, 307–8

mariculture 85, 93–4, 102, 226
marine park 193, 196, 197, 200, 201–2, 208, 310
Marine Stewardship Council 100
maritime transport 63, 310; *see also* shipping
maritime zones 6, 18, 26, 27, 33, 40–1, 47–8, 50–4, 88, 175–6, 202, 223, 277, 301, 307
megafauna 94, 100, 182, 200, 232
Migration 41, 51, 69–70, 173
Millennium Development Goals 30
mining 144, 146, 150–3, 157, 180, 201, 231–2, 234, 281, 301, 303, 305, 310, 313

non-governmental organisations (NGOs) 31–2, 97, 100, 171, 174, 180, 196, 199, 207, 286

observer 31, 98, 286, 310
oceanography 145, 147, 205, 251, 268, 272, 274, 275, 276, 283, 285, 302
oil 3, 28, 52–3, 115, 121, 131, 144, 146–54, 156–7, 193, 195, 197, 202, 205, 221–2, 224–7, 231–2, 234, 283, 302, 308
overharvesting 17, 94, 311

piracy 9, 27, 60–72, 116, 118, 122, 125, 131, 245, 246, 301; *see also* biopiracy
political will 303, 314
polluter pays principle 234, 398
plastic 27, 222, 224, 227, 228, 232–4, 304
precaution 29, 100, 229, 234, 308, 313
prevention 131, 149–50, 154, 205, 225, 228, 232, 256, 282, 302
prior informed consent 271

radioactive 228–9
refugee 125–6
regional fishery management organisations (RFMOs) 88–93, 96–102, 194, 209, 305
renewable energy 148, 150, 231
reporting 93, 96, 99, 174, 200, 229, 234, 258
responsibility 20, 21, 28, 89, 126, 131, 280
Rio Conference 30, 202–3
Rio Declaration on Environment and Development 29, 30, 176, 202

sharks 84, 100, 174, 175, 180, 182, 203, 207, 246
shipping 18, 27, 30, 48, 63, 65, 115–131, 146, 149, 156, 157, 169, 179, 193, 195, 197, 205, 208, 210, 224–7, 246, 260, 268, 269, 272, 274, 283, 301, 305; *see also* maritime transport
social impact 255
sovereignty 4, 6, 21, 23, 46, 49, 52–3, 89, 126, 155, 255, 275, 301, 312
stewardship 21, 40, 102, 170, 181, 193, 268, 270, 305–6, 311
Stockholm Declaration on the Human Environment 28–9, 32, 269
sustainable development 7, 29–31, 176, 202, 203, 269, 282, 304–5
Sustainable Development Goals (SDGs) 30, 97, 176, 205, 209, 283

technology 6, 63, 68, 96–7, 123, 129–30, 144, 146, 150, 152, 179, 181, 210, 222,

233, 250, 252, 258, 269, 271, 275, 277–8, 280, 283–7
total allowable catch 90–1, 96, 303
traditional knowledge 17–8, 21, 170, 258, 268, 269–71, 280, 282, 305, 306

UN Environment Programme (UNEP) 28, 194
UN Office on Drugs and Crime (UNODC) 70, 99

whales 8, 28, 94, 100, 174, 176, 180, 194, 203, 206, 221, 231, 232, 310, 313
wildlife 28, 31, 88, 147, 170–1, 174, 176, 183, 199
World Charter for Nature 308
World Trade Organization 91, 99–100

Kolibri 360 GmbH
Ferdinand-Jühlke-Straße 7
99095 Erfurt, Deutschland
produktsicherheit@kolibri360.de